PEOPLE TO KNOW IN BLACK HISTORY & BEYOND

Recognizing the Heroes and Sheroes Who Make the Grade (Vol. 2)

PEOPLE TO KNOW IN BLACK HISTORY & BEYOND

Recognizing the Heroes and Sheroes
Who Make the Grade (Vol. 2)

Written and Compiled by
Doctor Bob Lee

Edited by
Yvonne Rose

BOB LEE ENTERPRISES
New York City

PEOPLE TO KNOW IN BLACK HISTORY & BEYOND (VOL. 2)
Published by Bob Lee Enterprises
Make the Grade Foundation
244 Madison Avenue, #500
New York, NY 10016
Makethegrade4u@gmail.com
www.MaketheGradeFoundation.Org

Bob Lee, Publisher & Editorial Director
Yvonne Rose, Editor
QualityPress.info, Production Coordinator

ALL RIGHTS RESERVED No part of this book may be reproduced or transmitted in any form or by any means – electronic or mechanical, including photocopying, recording or by any information storage and retrieved system without written permission from the authors, except for the inclusion of brief quotations in a review. Make the Grade Foundation books are available at special discounts for bulk purchases, sales promotions, fund raising or educational purposes.

Copyright © 2020 by Bob Lee
Paperback ISBN #: 978-0-9970948-5-5
Hardcover ISBN #: 978-0-9970948-4-8
Ebook ISBN #: 978-0-9970948-6-2
Library of Congress Control Number: 2020920499

DEDICATION

I dedicate *People to Know in Black History & Beyond,* first and foremost to Mom, who passed away on March 30, 2020 during the Covid-19 Pandemic. My Mother, Anna Lee, who was 90-years-old lived a fruitful live as the Mother of seven children; the Grandmother of eleven; the Great Grandmother of twenty-two and the Great Great Grandmother of four. She always knew that I would be a leader, a teacher and a role model to all in the community. Mom, I love you and miss you.

In addition, I dedicate *People to Know in Black History & Beyond* to the Heroes and Sheroes of the World who have devoted their lives to building a better future for our community with Positivity, Purpose and Progression, along with others who continue to Make the Grade.

In particular, to the new Heroes and Sheroes who are frontline workers in the fight against COVID-19. I pray for the health and safety of nurses, doctors, medical staff, grocery store workers, police, firefighters, paramedics, and all essential workers during this global pandemic…and beyond. And to the Frontline workers risking their lives and sometimes losing their lives to help us go on living our lives.

I pray for the families of those Heroes and Sheroes, who were affected by the loss of time and the loss of lives by those they held near and dear to them while they fought a great fight.

CONTENTS

DEDICATION i
PREFACE vii
INTRODUCTION 1
PART ONE: NOTABLE PEOPLE WHO MAKE THE GRADE 3
  CHAPTER ONE – THE PARENT
  Featuring World Renowned Parents 7
  Kobe and Vanessa Bryant 9
  Stephen and Ayesha Curry 20
  George Edward Foreman 31
  Boris Kodjoe and Nicole Ari Parker 37
  Ciara Princess Harris and Russell Wilson 44
  CHAPTER TWO – THE TEACHER
  Featuring Educators that Influenced the Nation 60
  Edward Alexander Bouche 66
  Maria Tecla Artemisia Montessori 69
  Kelly Miller 72
  Henry Louis "Skip" Gates Jr. 77
  Michael McFarland 82
  CHAPTER THREE – THE STUDENT
  Featuring Students that Made a Difference 85
  Jesse Ernest Wilkins Jr. 87
  Diane Nash 91
  The Greensboro Four 98
  Moziah Bridges 101

CHAPTER FOUR - THE COMMUNITY
Featuring Civil Rights Leaders and Activists 18TH – 19TH Century. 104

Elizabeth Freeman 106

Thaddeus Stevens 110

Lucretia Mott 118

Charles Lenox Remond 123

Henry Highland Garnet 128

Laura Cornelius Kellogg 133

Anna Eleanor Roosevelt 138

María Rebecca Latigo de Hernández 148

Civil Rights Leaders and Activists 20TH Century 151

Harriette Vyda Simms and Harry Tyson Moore 153

Marvel Jackson Cooke 158

Willa Beatrice Brown 161

Amelia Isadora Platts 166

Lou Hamer Townsend 172

Martin Luther King Jr. 180

Ruth Bader Ginsburg 190

John Robert Lewis 200

Kamala Devi Harris 211

CHAPTER FIVE – SPIRITUALITY
Featuring Religious Leaders 223

Richard Allen 224

John J. Jasper 229

Ida B. Robinson 234

Frederick K.C. Price 237

Archbishop Wilton D. Gregory 240

Capers C. Funnye Jr 244

Alphonso R. Bernard, Sr. 249

Bernice Albertine King 253

CHAPTER SIX – HEALTH & SCIENCE
Featuring Medical Professionals and Scientists 261

Rebecca Lee Crumpler 263

William Augustus Hinton 268

Bessie Virginia Blount 272

James Edward Bowman Jr. 276

Neil deGrasse Tyson 279

CHAPTER SEVEN - FINANCIAL LITERACY
Featuring Business Moguls 284

Robert Louis Johnson 286

Catherine Liggins Hughes 289

Debra L. Lee, Esq. 293

Aliko Dangote 297

Michael Jeffrey Jordan 301

Jeffrey Preston Bezos (Jorgensen) 307

PART TWO: MORE NOTABLE PEOPLE WHO HAVE DONE EXTRAORDINARY THINGS TO MAKE THE GRADE 311

More Educators Who Make the Grade… 315

More Civil Rights Leaders and Activists Who Make the Grade… .. 323

More Religious Leaders Who Make the Grade… 356

More Business Moguls Who Make the Grade… 360

Inventors and Scientists Who Make The Grade… 369

Athletes Who Make the Grade… 378

Actors And Actresses Who Make the Grade… 406

Professional Dancers Who Make the Grade 425

Singers and Musicians Who Make the Grade 438

Authors Who Make the Grade 450
Publishers Who Make the Grade 457
Politicians, Lawyers and Other Leaders Who Make the Grade 462
Military Notables Who Make the Grade 485
Media and Public Relations Experts Who Make the Grade 493
Featuring WBLS-Radio Personalities 493
ABOUT THE AUTHOR DOCTOR BOB LEE 511
IN CONCLUSION 515
REFERENCES 516
INDEX 517
NOTES 520

PREFACE

Black Studies can be traced back as far back as the Atlanta University Conferences held from 1898 to 1914. This early formulation was under the auspices of W.E.B. DuBois in marking the inauguration of the first scientific study of the conditions of Black people that covered important aspects of life (e.g., health homes, the question of organization, economic development, higher education, voting).

William Edward Burghardt Du Bois was an American sociologist, socialist, historian, civil rights activist, Pan-Africanist, author, writer and editor. Born in Great Barrington, Massachusetts, Du Bois grew up in a relatively tolerant and integrated community, and after completing graduate work at the University of Berlin and Harvard, where he was the first African American to earn a doctorate, he became a professor of history, sociology and economics at Atlanta University. Du Bois was one of the founders of the National Association for the Advancement of Colored People (NAACP) in 1909.

As the second African American to earn a doctorate from Harvard, Carter G. Woodson became one of the first scholars of African American history. During his time spent at Harvard, Woodson also became known for writing the contributions of Black Americans into the national spotlight.

Woodson was born in 1875 to former slaves. He was unable to attend school for much of his childhood because he had to help his parents financially. He ended up entering high school at the age of

20, completed his studies, and received his diploma two years later. After high school, Woodson taught in West Virginia before earning his undergraduate degree at Berea College. He received a master's degree from the University of Chicago in 1908, and a Doctor of History from Harvard in 1912.

By 1915, Carter G. Woodson who is frequently touted as the "Father of Black History, had founded the Association for the Study of Negro Life and History (ASNLH) in marking a brave new era for Black curriculum. The group was founded to promote historical research, publish books on Black life and history, promote the study of Black history through clubs and schools and, in a noble effort, to foster harmony between the races by interpreting one history to the other. It was during this period that the Historically Black Colleges and Universities (HCBUs) began to respond to scholarly activities in history and social science.

The Black Power movement of the late 1960s helped to redefine African American identity and establish a new racial consciousness. As influential as this period was in the study and enhancement of the African Diaspora, this movement spawned the academic discipline known as Black Studies on our college and university campuses. While there are more than 100 Black Studies degree programs nationwide, it can be confirmed that the beginning of this curriculum evolved from a student strike at San Francisco State University in 1968. Young people there forced the establishment of the Division of Ethnic Studies and departments of Black, Asian, Chicano and Native studies.

INTRODUCTION

People to Know in Black History & Beyond not only presents the accomplishments of hundreds of Heroes and Sheroes but it offers you, the reader, a glimpse of the subject's background and family structure as it relates to the social and economic pressures that existed during their lifetime. Knowledge is power and by learning about the accomplishments of so many people who were not born privileged, perhaps it will, among other things, help to eradicate many racial stereotypes. It is important that we adults teach the children to understand from whence we came by devoting some time to the study of the history, culture, sociology, religion, and politics of black people in the United States as well as the people of African origin worldwide.

In actuality, 90% of the people featured in this book are descendants of slaves who were brought forcibly to the United States more than four centuries ago. it not only features African slave descendants but also descendants from many other countries of the African diaspora.

Intensive academic efforts to reconstruct African American history began in the late 19th century and is discussed by. W. E. B. Du Bois in *The Suppression of the African Slave Trade to the United States of America*. Mr. Du Bois estimates that, from 1807 to 1862, not less than a quarter of a million of Africans were brought to the United States in defiance of law and humanity.

People to Know in Black History & Beyond begins its journey in the 18th Century with Community Activists who put their lives on the line for their families, communities and country and brings you right up to present day 21st Century Heroes & Sheroes.

The 66 featured Men and women have made great contributions to society primarily through education, activism, health & science, parental leadership, religion and economics not only in America but throughout the World. In addition, ***People to Know in Black History & Beyond*** highlights 150 of the country's trendsetters in arts and communications, as well as renowned scientists, athletes and authors.

There are so many people of all nationalities who have sacrificed and aspired to greatness, whose shoulders we stand on. They are special people doing special things …people that may have been overlooked, particularly because they were minorities… people who have masterminded things that benefit *all* the people of the world…beyond Black History. By understanding their mission and following their example, you may become inspired enough to build your legacy and become an example for future generations to follow.

So, whether you are researching Black History or whether you just want to learn more about the building of America, we hope this book will help you appreciate those people who were determined to win at all costs.

PART ONE

NOTABLE PEOPLE WHO MAKE THE GRADE

Part One of **PEOPLE TO KNOW IN BLACK HISTORY & BEYOND** incorporates those Heroes and Sheroes who have exhibited strong leadership qualities as **Parents, Teachers, Students, Community Activists,** or in the field of **Spirituality, Health & Science** and **Financial Literacy**.

PEOPLE TO KNOW IN BLACK HISTORY & BEYOND

There's more to life than basketball. The most important thing is your family and taking care of each other and loving each other, no matter what.
— **Stephen Curry**

CHAPTER ONE – THE PARENT
FEATURING WORLD RENOWNED PARENTS

According to the Merriam-Webster dictionary, a parent is a person who brings up and cares for another. However, being a parent does not necessarily mean that you biologically passed your genetics to a child. A parent can take on different forms, such as stepparent, grandparent, legal guardian, or a combination.

Being a parent is a major responsibility. You are in charge of raising an individual to the point of adulthood with the goal of turning him or her into a valuable member of the community. This undertaking requires care, love, understanding and the ability to keep the children on the right path. If done right, it is one of the hardest things you will do, but it also will be one of the most rewarding.

The parents included in this chapter are positive role models for their children and for many of the children in their communities and throughout the world. They are all celebrities who exemplify the characteristics necessary to shelter and guide their children to become responsible adults. Spirituality is a common denominator present within their households and communication is key. All of the featured parents, by their own admission, "put family first."

KOBE AND VANESSA BRYANT

Kobe and Vanessa Bryant got married in 2001, and the couple went on to welcome four beautiful little girls into their world. Kobe was a devoted family man. In the days after the tragic helicopter crash, fans and athletes remembered not only Kobe's incredible legacy as a basketball player but also his reputation as a loving family man who was devoted to his wife, Vanessa, and their daughters.

Natalia, now 17, was born in 2003, and she became a big sister when Gianna arrived in 2006. A decade later, Kobe, the Philadelphia native and Vanessa, 37, welcomed Bianka, now 3. In January 2019, the pair announced that they were expecting baby No. 4. "Vanessa and I are beyond excited to announce that we are expecting another #mambacita to go along with Natalia, Gianna and Bianka. New Year, New Baby! Baby Mamba on the Way 2019."

The couple met when Vanessa was a senior in high school. Her classmates were stunned when she caught the eye of then-20-year-old Los Angeles Lakers star, Kobe Bryant.

Though many know the Black Mamba as one of the greatest players of all time, not as many know the woman who was by his side since the first years of his career. However, the Bryants weathered drama on and off the court while growing their family and cementing themselves as one of the most well-known couples in basketball.

Vanessa Urbieta Cornejo Laine was born on May 5, 1982. Her parents were protective and didn't let her date much.

Vanessa was born in Huntington Beach, California. The second child of Sofia Laine, Vanessa is of Mexican, and Irish, English, German descent. When Vanessa was three years old her parents divorced and she and her older sister, Sophie were raised by their single mother until a few years later when her mother married businessman Stephen Laine. Vanessa's last name was legally changed to Laine in 2000 when she took her stepdad's last name, even though he never adopted her.

After she got married she changed her name to Vanessa Marie Bryant. In 2002, her mother divorced Stephen Laine and the family lived in Anaheim and Temecula before moving to West Garden Grove. Vanessa attended St. Boniface Parochial School in 1996 and was a member of the varsity cheerleading squad before transferring to Marina High School using her ex-stepfather's dad's home address.

During the summer before her senior year of high school in 1999, Vanessa was spotted at a concert and asked to appear in a music video alongside rappers Snoop Dogg and Tha Eastsidaz for their song "G'd Up"; she wore a metallic bikini for her debut as a music-video model. Shortly after the shoot, the 17-year-old was called to appear in another music video. That's when she met 20-year-old Los Angeles Laker Kobe Bryant.

Kobe asked Vanessa for her number on November 28, 1999, and the pair went to Disneyland on their first date, with bodyguards trailing them at the park. Vanessa soon became widely known as Kobe's other half, and their relationship caused a stir while she was attending her senior year at Marina High School in Huntington Beach, California. She brought pictures of Kobe to school, and her classmates would all be extremely excited. Vanessa would let them look at the pictures, but they couldn't touch them. Kobe would send roses to the school office and pick up Vanessa from class in his Mercedes. Vanessa graduated with honors in 2000.

Vanessa became a fixture at Kobe's side in appearances, at games and on red carpets before he proposed at her 18th birthday party, just six months after they met. In April 2001, less than two years after they first met, the couple got married at St. Edward the Confessor Catholic Church in Southern California's Dana Point. The ceremony was intimate and had only 12 attendants, Neither Kobe's parents nor his sisters went to the wedding because they disapproved of him getting married so young and to someone who was not African American.

As Kobe's star continued to rise, Vanessa was by his side. The couple thrilled fans when they announced in September 2002 that they were expecting a daughter. The couple's first child, Natalia Diamante Bryant, was born on January 19, 2003. Natasha's middle name was an acknowledgement of Vanessa's love of diamonds. Three years after the birth of their first child, Gianna Bryant was born on May 1, 2006. Kobe stated, "The arrival of our daughter early this morning is an incredible blessing for me and my family. We are all full of beautiful emotions after what has been such an incredible day."

As Kobe continued to dominate the court, the couple turned to philanthropic efforts to give back to Los Angeles. In 2007, the couple expanded their philanthropic reach when they established the Vivo Foundation, which would later become known as the Kobe and Vanessa Bryant Foundation. The organization's mission statement says it is dedicated to helping children and families in need with financial and educational resources and "encouraging young people to stay active through sports."

The Bryants would later double their efforts in 2011 by founding a charitable organization that sought to fight homelessness and support homeless for youth in Los Angeles. In addition to their groups, the Bryants supported various other charities, including Stand Up to Cancer and the Make-A-Wish Foundation.

Vanessa and the couple's daughters were a fixture in the audience at Kobe's games. Sitting courtside was one of the many perks the family had access to when Kobe was the highest-paid player in the NBA.

In 2016, Kobe and Vanessa welcomed their third daughter, Bianka Bryant, shortly before the basketball star announced his retirement. Three years later, the couple welcomed their fourth daughter in 2019, Capri Kobe Bryant.

Vanessa and her daughters were a focal point of Kobe's growing image as a family man as the retired player focused on working with charities and women's sports. The former Lakers player tried to foster a love of sports in his daughters, and Gianna said she wanted to carry on her father's basketball legacy. The new chapter of Kobe's career expanded on the family's existing efforts to encourage young athletes, and the father of four initially pulled away from basketball but became more involved in it as his daughter Gianna showed a flourishing interest in the sport. Vanessa stated that *the 13-year-old Gianna could have become "the best player in the WNBA."* Kobe coached his daughter's team, the Mambas, and established the Mamba Sports Academy, which hosts a wide variety of athletes for holistic training, practices, and tournaments alongside NBA and WNBA players.

Kobe Bean Bryant (August 23, 1978 - January 26, 2020) won five NBA championships and the 2008 MVP Award with the Los Angeles Lakers. Although later seasons were marred by injuries, he surpassed Michael Jordan for third place on the NBA all-time scoring list in December 2014 and retired in 2016 after scoring 60 points in his final game. On January 26, 2020, Kobe Bryant was in a helicopter crash that killed him his 13-year-old daughter, Gigi, and seven others.

Kobe Bryant was born in Philadelphia, Pennsylvania the youngest of three children and the only son of former NBA player Joe Bryant and Pamela Cox Bryant. He was also the maternal nephew of NBA player John "Chubby" Cox. His parents named him after the famous beef of Kobe, Japan, which they saw on a restaurant menu. His middle name, Bean, was derived from his father's nickname "Jellybean." Kobe's family was Catholic and he had always practiced his faith.

Kobe started playing basketball when he was aged three, and the Lakers were his favorite team when he was growing up. In 1984, after ending his NBA career, the elder Bryant took the family to Italy, where he played in the Italian League. Kobe was six years old at the time. After two years, they moved first to Reggio Calabria, then to Pistoia and Reggio Emilia. Kobe became accustomed to his new lifestyle and learned to speak fluent Italian. He was especially fond of Reggio Emilia, which he considered a loving place and where some of his best childhood memories were made. Kobe began to play basketball seriously while living in Reggio Emilia. Kobe's grandfather would mail videos of NBA games for Bryant to study. Another source of inspiration was animated European films about sports, from which he learned more about basketball. He also learned to play soccer and his favorite soccer team was A.C. Milan. Growing up in Italy alongside two athletic older sisters, Shaya and Sharia, Kobe became an avid player of both basketball and soccer. During summers, Kobe would come back to the United States to play in a basketball summer league.

When Kobe was thirteen, he and his family moved back to Philadelphia, where he enrolled in eighth grade at Bala Cywynd Middle School. Kobe earned national recognition as the top high-school basketball player in the country during a spectacular high school career at Lower Merion High School in Ardmore, located in the Philadelphia suburb of Lower Merion. He played on the varsity basketball team as a freshman. Kobe Bryant became the first freshman in decades to start for Lower Merion's varsity team, but the team finished with a 4–20 record. The following three years, the Aces compiled a 77–13 record, with Kobe playing all five positions. During his junior year, he averaged 31.1 points, 10.4 rebounds, 5.2 assists, 3.8 blocks and 2.3 steals and was named Pennsylvania Player of the Year while also earning a fourth-team *Parade* All-American nomination, attracting attention from college recruiters in the process. Duke, Michigan, North Carolina and Villanova were at the top of his list. However, after high schooler Kevin Garnett went in the first round of the 1995 NBA draft; Kobe also began contemplating going directly to the pros.

At Adidas ABCD Camp, Bryant earned the 1995 senior MVP award while playing alongside future NBA teammate Lamar Odom. While in high school, then 76ers coach John Lucas invited Kobe to work out and scrimmage with the team, where he played one-on-one with Jerry Stackhouse. In his senior year of high school, Bryant led the Aces to their first state championship in 53 years. During the run, he averaged 30.8 points, 12 rebounds, 6.5 assists, 4 steals, and 3.8 blocked shots in leading the Aces to a 31–3 record. Bryant ended his high school career as Southeastern Pennsylvania's all-time leading scorer at 2,883 points, surpassing both Wilt Chamberlain and Lionel Simmons.

Kobe Bryant received several awards for his outstanding performance during his senior year at Lower Merion. These included being named Naismith High School Player of the Year, Gatorade Men's National Basketball Player of the Year, a McDonald's All-American, a first-team *Parade* All-American and a *USA Today* All-USA First Team player. Ultimately, the 17-year-old Kobe Bryant made the decision to go directly into the NBA, becoming only the sixth player in NBA history to do so. Kobe 's news was met with a lot of publicity at a time when prep-to-pro NBA players were not very common (Garnett being the only exception in 20 years). His basketball skills and SAT score of 1080 would have ensured admission to any college he chose, but he did not officially visit any campuses.

Upon graduation, he declared for the 1996 NBA draft and was selected by the Charlotte Hornets with the 13th overall pick; the Hornets then traded him to the Lakers. As a rookie, Bryant earned himself a reputation as a high-flyer and a fan favorite by winning the 1997 Slam Dunk Contest, and he was named an All-Star by his second season. In his second season with the Lakers, Kobe Bryant was voted a starter for the 1998 All-Star Game, becoming the youngest All-Star in NBA history at 19. The shooting guard then teamed up with superstar center Shaquille O'Neal to win three consecutive NBA championships and was voted first-team all-NBA from 2002-2004. He also inked multi-year endorsement deals with Adidas, Sprite and other top sponsors.

After the Lakers lost the 2004 NBA Finals, O'Neal was traded and Bryant became the cornerstone of the Lakers. Although the Lakers struggled after O'Neal left in 2004, Bryant performed brilliantly. He scored 81 points, the second-highest single-game mark in NBA history,

He led the NBA in scoring during the 2005–06 and 2006–07 seasons. In 2006, he scored a career-high 81 points against the Toronto Raptors; the second most points scored in a single game in league history, behind Wilt Chamberlain's 100-point game in 1962.

In 2008, Kobe Bryant was named Most Valuable Player and carried his team to the NBA Finals, where they lost to the Boston Celtics. In the 2009 NBA Finals, the Lakers beat the Orlando Magic to win the championship. Shortly afterward, Kobe was part of the memorial service to honor friend and music superstar Michael Jackson. The following year, the Lakers won their second straight title by defeating the Celtics.

At 34 years and 104 days of age, Kobe Bryant became the youngest player in league history to reach 30,000 career points. He became the all-time leading scorer in Lakers franchise history on February 1, 2010, surpassing Jerry West. Kobe was also the first guard in NBA history to play at least 20 seasons. His 18 All-Star designations are the second most all time, while it is the record for most consecutive appearances as a starter. Kobe Bryant's four All-Star MVP Awards are tied with Bob Pettit for the most in NBA history. He gave himself the nickname "Black Mamba" in the mid-2000s, and the epithet became widely adopted by the general public.

Kobe Bryant led the team to two consecutive championships in 2009 and 2010, and was named NBA Finals MVP on both occasions. He played on both the 2008 and 2012 U.S. Olympic teams, winning consecutive gold medals with teammates Kevin Durant, LeBron James and Carmelo Anthony, among several other top players. In 2012, Bryant was honored as one of the 35 Greatest McDonald's All-Americans.

Kobe continued to be among the top players in the league through 2013, when he suffered a torn Achilles tendon at age 34. Kobe worked hard to return to the court before fracturing his knee just six games into the 2013-2014 season. The veteran All-Star surpassed Michael Jordan for third all-time on the NBA scoring list in December 2014, but his season ended due to injury for the third straight year when he sustained a torn rotator cuff in January 2015.

Although Bryant returned in time for the start of the 2015-2016 NBA season, he personally struggled alongside his young Lakers teammates. In November 2015, he announced that he would retire at the end of the season. "This season is all I have left to give," he wrote on The Players' Tribune website. "My heart can take the pounding. My mind can handle the grind, but my body knows it's time to say goodbye."

The announcement drew a strong reaction, particularly from NBA Commissioner Adam Silver. "With 17 NBA All-Star selections, an NBA MVP, five NBA championships with the Lakers, two Olympic gold medals and a relentless work ethic, Kobe Bryant is one of the greatest players in the history of our game," Silver said in a statement. "Whether competing in the finals or hoisting jump shots after midnight in an empty gym, Kobe has an unconditional love for the game."

On April 13, 2016, Bryant dazzled a sold-out crowd at the Staples Center and fans everywhere in the last game of his career, scoring 60 points and leading the Lakers to a win against the Utah Jazz. It was Bryant's sixth 60-point game of his career.

An all-star lineup of Laker icons also paid tribute to Bryant, including O'Neal, Phil Jackson, Pau Gasol, Derek Fisher, Lamar Odom and Magic Johnson. "We are here to celebrate greatness for 20 years," Johnson said. "Excellence for 20 years. Kobe Bryant has never cheated the game, never cheated us as the fans. He has played through injury; he has played hurt. And we have five championship banners to show for it."

Kobe Bryant announced his retirement from the Lakers with a poem on The Players' Tribune website, titled "Dear Basketball." The athletic great soon sought the best in other fields to turn his poem into a short film, including Disney animator Glen Keane and composer John Williams. The result was a beautifully rendered five-minute, 20-second film, which debuted at the 2017 Tribeca Film Festival. In 2018, Kobe Bryant won the Academy Award for Best Animated Short Film for his 2017 film *Dear Basketball*.

Among their philanthropic endeavors, the Bryants partnered with the non-profit After-School All-Stars as part of the Kobe & Vanessa Bryant Family Foundation. Kobe also ran an annual summer camp called the Kobe Basketball Academy.

Kobe Bryant won five NBA titles with the Los Angeles Lakers while establishing himself as one of the game's all-time greats. on January 26, 2020 Kobe Bean Bryant at age 41, along with his 13-year-old daughter Gianna died tragically in a helicopter crash in Calabasas. Vanessa and Kobe Bryant were married for 19 years before Kobe's sudden death.

During her husband's and daughter's memorial service Vanessa, spoke about her "soulmate" Kobe, describing him as a doting dad and devoted husband who went above and beyond the basketball legend the public admired. "He was my sweet husband and the beautiful father of our children," Vanessa said. "He was mine. He was my everything. Kobe loved me more than I could ever put into words. We balanced each other out. I have no idea how I deserved a man that loved and wanted me more than Kobe. God knew they couldn't be on this Earth without each other. He had to bring them home to have them together. Babe, you take care of our Gigi. I got Nani, BB, and Coco. We are still the best team."

STEPHEN AND AYESHA CURRY

Stephen and Ayesha Curry are parents to two beautiful daughters, Ryan and Riley, and one handsome son, Canon. Stephen Curry may dominate on a basketball court, but at home he and his wife, Ayesha, play man-to-man defense to keep up with their three active children. Stephen Curry isn't a superhero, but he plays one on TV. The Golden State Warriors point guard's marksmanship has earned him wide acclaim as the best basketball player on the planet. Yet, when he's not busy winning league MVP awards or NBA championships, he is the loving husband of Ayesha and doting dad of three children.

Steph and Ayesha tied the knot on July 30, 2011. Just before the newlyweds celebrated their first anniversary Ayesha gave birth to their first child, a daughter named Riley, on July 19, 2012. Ayesha described her as a "borderline honeymoon baby."

In January, the couple announced in an Instagram post that they were expecting their second child. Steph wrote, "Didn't think it was possible but My #WCW just got even sexier! Baby #2 on the way. Been blessed beyond belief already and I praise Him daily! God is great!" The doting dad continued to gush when Ryan Carson Curry made her debut on July 12, 2015.

Three years later, the Curry family revealed in a February Instagram post that their family would grow to five. Ayesha Curry gave birth to the couple's first son, Canon W. Jack Curry, on July 2, 2018. *All three of the Curry children were born in July, three years apart.*

The Currys agree that parenthood is a full-time job in itself. They feel that the amount of stuff you get done in a day is insane. They wonder what they were doing with their time before they had children. It's an event just to get all of them out of the house at once. *When they get in the car and have brought everything they need, and everybody has socks on, it's like a dream come true.*

Ayesha Disa Curry, born March 23, 1989 is the daughter of John and Carol (Chin) Alexander and has four siblings: Maria, Janiece, Jaz and Chad. Her mother is of Afro-Jamaican and Chinese-Jamaican descent while her father is of mixed African-American and Polish descent. She was born and raised in Toronto. At age 12, Ayesha acted as the love interest in the music video for "Too Young for Love" by Suga Prince (now known as Sevn Thomas).

When Ayesha was 14, her family moved to Charlotte, North Carolina. She first gained an interest in cooking at a young age. With her mother operating a salon in the basement of their home, Ayesha would watch as her babysitter cooked Trinidadian curry and roti and brought it down to customers.

After graduating from Weddington High School, Ayesha moved to Los Angeles to become an actress, appearing in mostly bit parts. She was in a film short *Underground Street Flippers* (2009), The TV movie *Dan's Detour of Life* (2008), was Girl #1 in the direct to DVD movie *Love for Sale* (2008). Ayesha also had guest roles in several television shows and movies.

Ayesha and Stephen met in a church youth group in Charlotte when they were 15 and 14 years old. It wasn't until years later when Ayesha was pursuing her acting career in Hollywood and Stephen was visiting for an awards show, that the two started dating. Ayesha soon moved back to Charlotte, close to where Stephen was playing college basketball at Davidson College. As of 2016, they resided in Walnut Creek, California. In July 2019, Steph Curry paid $31 million for a home in Atherton, California

Steph's family had moved back to Charlotte, North Carolina in 2002 after his father Dell retired from the NBA. That's when Steph Curry would meet Ayesha Alexander, a fellow member of the youth group at the Central Church of God. Ayesha wasn't allowed to date in high school but found another way to convey her interest — a mutual love of candy, specifically Maynards Fuzzy Peach. The Toronto native would share the treats from her home country with Steph. That's how she would flirt with him, in a way. She would find him after church, barely say two words, and walk away. He would look at her like 'God, she's so lame.' He clearly liked it… It definitely left an impression.

Ayesha graduated from high school early and at 17-years-old moved to Los Angeles to pursue an acting career. By then Steph had started to make a name for himself in the basketball world, having just led his Davidson Wildcats to the NCAA tournament's Elite Eight. When he got an opportunity to attend a basketball camp in L.A. he decided to look up Ayesha on Facebook for a reunion.

She declined but left the door open for a meeting if he was ever in the area again. The following week, while in town again for the ESPY awards, he tried his luck. This time she agreed and the two spent their first date drinking chai tea lattes and hitting up Hollywood tourist spots like the Walk of Fame and Kodak Theatre.

Ayesha moved back to Charlotte and the pair officially started dating. A year later, Steph declared for the NBA draft and was selected seventh overall by the Golden State Warriors. Despite moving out to Oakland without his love, the two remained closely connected.

Two years into their relationship, Steph decided to take things to the next level. The couple stopped at his parents' house after his sister's volleyball match, supposedly to pick up a board game. Instead, he surprised Ayesha with a sweet and sentimental proposal in the driveway.

Steph and Ayesha tied the knot in the same church where they met in 2002, nine years before.

After their marriage Ayesha started a food blog, despite not having any professional chef training. Her culinary career started in 2014, when she prepared her first meal as a YouTube instructional cooking demonstration on her channel *Little Lights of Mine,* which sells its own brand of extra virgin olive oil, from which 10% of all proceeds are donated to the charity No Kid Hungry. Ayesha Curry is also the author of several videos on her channel.

In May 2016 Steph Curry paid homage to his wife as he received the first unanimous MVP award in NBA history. "None of this is possible without you," he said. "You've given me the opportunity to go out here and work as hard as I do, spend the hours I need to do at the gym, during practice, in games, on the road – all the while holding down the house and doing the little things that keep our family going."

That same year, Ayesha Curry collaborated with chef Michael Mina in The Mina Test Kitchen of International Smoke, a Bay Area pop-up restaurant, and released her cookbook "The Seasoned Life."

On September 20, 2017, Ayesha Curry was named as a spokesperson for CoverGirl, becoming the first spokesperson for the brand who is not an actress or singer.

In 2019 The Mina/Curry International Smoke restaurant opened another location at One Paseo in Carmel Valley, San Diego.

On Mother's Day 2019, Stephen Curry revealed a special edition of his "Under Armour" signature Curry 3Zero's dedicated to the real "Chef Curry," Ayesha. The colorway matched her recently published cookbook. In 2013 Steph had signed with the footwear and apparel company through 2024. His signature Under Armour shoe is one of the top selling basketball shoes in the world.

Wardell Stephen "Steph" Curry II was born March 14, 1988 in Akron, Ohio. Stephen is the son of Sonya Adams Curry, a former volleyball player and a current school administrator and Dell Curry, former NBA player with the Cleveland Cavaliers. Like Steph, his younger brother, Seth, is also an NBA player, and his younger sister, Sydel, played volleyball at Elon University.

The Curry siblings grew up in Charlotte, North Carolina, where their father spent most of his NBA career with the Charlotte Hornets. Dell often took Steph and Seth to his games, where they would shoot with the Hornets during warm-ups.

The family briefly relocated to Toronto, where Dell finished out his career as a member of the Raptors. During this time, Steph played for the Queensway Christian College boys' basketball team, leading them to an undefeated season. He was also a member of Toronto 5-0, a club team that plays across Ontario, pitting him against future fellow NBA players Cory Joseph and Kelly Olynyk. Steph Curry led the team to a 33-4 record, en route to winning the provincial championship.

Following Dell's retirement, the family moved back to Charlotte and Steph enrolled at Charlotte Christian School, where he was named all-conference, all-state, and led his team to three conference titles and three state playoff appearances. Because of his father's storied career at Virginia Tech, Steph wanted to play college basketball for the Hokies, but was only offered a walk-on spot due in part to his slender 160-pound frame.

Steph Curry grew up immersed in basketball as the son of 16-year NBA veteran sharpshooter Dell Curry. Steph learned the intricacies of the game from his father. However, his keen shooting and high "basketball IQ" were not enough to persuade college coaches to overlook his wiry frame and unremarkable 6-foot height. Steph did not receive scholarship offers from major college basketball programs; so he ultimately chose to attend Davidson College, which had aggressively recruited him since the tenth grade.

Davidson (North Carolina) College, had an enrollment of fewer than 2,000 students. Stephen Curry quickly made his mark, however, averaging 21.5 points per game as a freshman to lead all first-year players in the country. As a team member for the Davidson Wildcats, Steph was twice named Southern Conference Player of the Year and set the all-time scoring record for both Davidson and the Southern Conference.

During his sophomore season in 2007-2008, Steph again led the Southern Conference in scoring, averaging 25.5 points per game while adding 4.7 rebounds per game and 2.8 assists per game. He led the Wildcats to a 26–6 regular season record, and a 20–0 conference record.

Steph Curry became a national sensation when he led 10th-seeded Davidson on an improbable run to the Elite Eight of the National Collegiate Athletic Association men's top-division basketball championship tournament in a performance that featured what would soon be recognized as his signature shot: a three-pointer from well outside the line. As a result of Curry's exceptional play, Davidson earned its third straight NCAA Tournament bid. Steph also set the single-season NCAA record for three-pointers made.

His junior season average of 28.6 points per game led the country, and he was named a consensus first-team All-American. He was then selected by the Golden State Warriors of the National Basketball Association (NBA) with the seventh overall pick in the 2009 NBA Draft. Steph Curry finished his rookie season with 166 three-pointers, which were the most ever by a rookie in NBA history.

Steph made an immediate impact with the Warriors, becoming the team's starting point guard and averaging 17.5 points per game in his first season. A series of ankle sprains led to Steph's playing just

26 games in the 2011–12 season, and he underwent off-season ligament surgery. He then signed a modest four-year $44 million contract extension that allowed Golden State to surround its budding star with other talented players.

A six-time NBA All-Star, Curry has been named the NBA Most Valuable Player (MVP) twice and won three NBA championships with the Warriors. Many players and analysts have called him the greatest shooter in NBA history. He is credited with revolutionizing the game of basketball by inspiring teams to regularly utilize the three-point shot.

During the 2012–13 season, Curry set the NBA record for three-pointers made in a regular season, with 272 and earned his first All-Star selection.

In 2014–15 Steph was named the league's Most Valuable Player (MVP). In the following postseason, he propelled the Warriors to the franchise's first title in 40 years over the Cleveland Cavaliers. The following season, he became the first player in NBA history to be elected MVP by a unanimous vote and to lead the league in scoring while shooting above 50–40–90.

He surpassed his record in 2015 with 286, and again in 2016 with 402. Steph Curry is currently third in all-time made three-pointers in NBA history, and alongside teammate Klay Thompson, the pair have earned the nickname of the Splash Brothers; in 2013–14, they set the record for combined three-pointers in an NBA season with 484, a record they broke the following season (525). Again in the 2015–16 season (678), the Warriors broke the record for the most wins in an NBA season en route to reaching the 2016 NBA Finals, which they lost to the Cleveland Cavaliers.

On July 1, 2017, Steph Curry agreed to a five-year, $201 million extension with the Warriors, becoming the first NBA player to sign a supermax contract worth over $200 million. He officially signed the contract on July 25.

On December 1, 2017 he scored 23 points and passed Jason Kidd for eighth place on the "career three-pointers made" list in a 133–112 win over the Orlando Magic. On December 4, in a 125–115 win over the New Orleans Pelicans, Steph Curry hit five three-pointers to become the fastest NBA player to achieve the milestone of 2,000 career three-pointers, achieving that mark in just 597 games, 227 less than the previous fastest player to achieve that mark, Ray Allen. In that same game, Steph injured his right ankle and subsequently missed 11 games, returning to action on December 30 and scoring 38 points with a season-high 10 3-pointers in a 141–128 win over the Memphis Grizzlies. Steph shot 13 for 17 and 10 of 13 from deep in 26 minutes for his ninth 30-point game of the season. It also marked his ninth career game with 10 or more 3s, the most by any player in NBA history.

On January 6, 2018 in a 121–105 win over the Los Angeles Clippers, Steph Curry scored 45 points in three quarters. On January 25th, he scored 25 points in a 126–113 win over the Minnesota Timberwolves. Steph became the fifth player in Warriors history to score 14,000 points, ending the game with 14,023 and joining Wilt Chamberlain (17,783), Rick Barry (16,447), Paul Arizin (16,266) and Chris Mullin (16,235) on the franchise list. On January 27, he scored 49 points—with 13 of those over the final 1:42—and hit eight 3-pointers, lifting the Warriors past the Boston Celtics 109–105.

Steph Curry helped the Warriors return to the NBA Finals in 2017, 2018 and 2019, winning back-to-back titles in 2017 and 2018. As of January 2019, Steph Curry ranks third in NBA history in career three-point field goal percentage and holds four of the top five seasons in terms of total three-pointers made. He is also the fastest player in league history to make 2,000 career three-pointers.

Steph is considered by many to be the greatest shooter in NBA history. He is credited with revolutionizing the game of basketball by inspiring basketball teams, from high school to the NBA, to regularly utilize the three-point shot. Analysts have referred to him as "the Michael Jordan of the three-point era," stating that he did for the three-point shot what Jordan did for the dunk.

A seemingly perfect marriage like Ayesha and Steph Curry's doesn't happen without putting in lots of work. The biggest thing is they have great role models. Both of their parents are still married and have been married for 30-plus years, and the one thing that their parents all shared with the couple—some through learning it the hard way, some through just making sure that they do it—is just making sure that they put each other first, even before the children, as tough as that sounds. So, like their parents, Ayesha and Steph have put their relationship ahead of any other commitments – including their children.

Stephen and Ayesha Curry are devoted Christians who have been outspoken about their Christian faith. Steph spoke about his faith during his MVP speech by saying, "People should know who I represent and why I am who I am, and that's because of my Lord and Savior." He also said the reason that he pounds his chest and points up is that he has a "heart for God" and as a reminder that he plays for God.

Ayesha Curry speaks of her faith, saying: "It's the foundation for everything that I do, really. ... With my relationship with my husband, it's what it's founded on." When Steph decided to play basketball, Ayesha had the same conversation with him that he had with her. 'Whatever you do, do it well, but do it for God. I think that's what has kept us grounded. When I started my blog called 'Little Lights of Mine,' my whole goal was to do the things I wanted to do, but all while being a light for Him."

In 2012, Steph Curry started donating three insecticide-treated mosquito nets for every three-pointer he made to the United Nations Foundation's Nothing But Nets campaign to combat malaria. He was first introduced to the malaria cause by Davidson teammate Bryant Barr when they were both in school. Steph visited the White House in 2015 and delivered a five-minute speech to dignitaries as part of President Barack Obama's launch of his President's Malaria Initiative strategy for 2015–2020.

Also in 2015, after winning the MVP award following his impressive season, Steph donated his prize vehicle—a 2016 Kia Sorento—to the East Oakland Youth Development Center, a local non-profit organization located in the backyard of Oracle Arena.

In October 2018, Steph Curry signed on as executive producer of the film *Breakthrough*, released in April 2019. Steph was also executive producer of the film *Emanuel*, released in select theaters on June 17, 2019. The film focuses on the responses of family members of victims of the 2015 Charleston church shooting.

Founded in September 2019 by three-time NBA champion and two-time MVP Stephen Curry and entrepreneur, host and *The New York Times* bestselling author Ayesha Curry, Eat. Learn. Play. Foundation seeks to unleash the potential of every child and pave the way for amazing kids and bright futures. Ayesha and Steph Curry are passionate about giving back to the community and they have teamed up to do just that with their new foundation, while teaching their children about life's values.

GEORGE EDWARD FOREMAN

George Edward Foreman (January 10, 1949) remains the oldest world heavyweight champion in history, and the second oldest in any weight class after Bernard Hopkins (at light heavyweight). He retired in 1997 at the age of 48, with a final record of 76 wins (68 knockouts) and 5 losses.

George Foreman was born in the town of Marshall Texas. He was raised by his mother, Nancy Foreman, and his stepfather J.D. Foreman who his mother married after he was born. George's biological father was Leroy Moorehead. George had a brother, Roy Foreman.

He's a two-time heavyweight boxing champion; But George Foreman will be the first to tell you the most important title he's ever held is "Dad." George realizes how swiftly and hopes his kids don't make the same mistakes that he did through his many decades from being a teenager up to a grandfather.

George's children are the one thing he's most proud of, in his heart. Some of them have gone on to stand the test, to get a college education, and that's the hardest thing in the world to achieve; but most of all they're good parents, and that's what is so important to him. George feels that when you're raising children, you've got to understand that you should put certain things first. Time is number one, embracing is number two, and never allowing them out of your life, that's number three. Don't ever let them think that they're going to someday be out of your life. You've got to understand that each child is different, and you've got to treat them differently.

George has had to stop what he was doing professionally a lot of times and say, "No, I just can't do it, my child is graduating from school." He knew that he had to be there for them, even if it meant sitting out on the field watching them perform when it was freezing; and when he could be making $100,000 at some special appearance. George's decisions would be made so his children would know that they were number one in his life.

George Foreman has been married to Mary Joan Martelly since 1985. He had four previous marriages: to Adrienne Calhoun from 1971 to 1974, Cynthia Lewis from 1977 to 1979, Sharon Goodson from 1981 to 1982, and Andrea Skeete from 1982 to 1985.

George Foreman has 12 children: five sons and seven daughters. His five sons are George Jr., George III ("Monk"), George IV ("Big Wheel"), George V ("Red"), and George VI ("Little Joey"). On his website, Foreman explains, "I named all my sons George Edward Foreman so they would always have something in common. I say to them, 'If one of us goes up, then we all go up together, and if one goes down, we all go down together!' He also tells people, "If you're going to get hit as many times as I've been hit by Mohammad Ali,

Joe Frazier, Ken Norton, Evander Holyfield - you're not going to remember many names.

George III, as with his father, has pursued a career in boxing and entrepreneurship. George IV appeared on the second season of *American Grit*, where he placed seventh.

The two daughters from his marriage are Natalia and Leola. His three daughters from a separate relationship are Michi; Freeda, who had a 5-1 record as a pro boxer, retired in 2001, and died in 2019 at age 42. He adopted a daughter, Isabella Brandie Lilja (Foreman), in 2009, and another, Courtney Isaac (Foreman), in 2012. Isabella Foreman lives in Sweden, where she has blogged since 2010 under the name of BellaNeutella.

An impoverished youth, Foreman often bullied younger children and didn't like getting up early for school. He became a mugger and brawler on the hard streets of Houston's Fifth Ward by age 15.

Luckily, he was saved by the Lyndon B. Johnson Job Corps, a program developed to help disadvantaged kids by teaching them vocational job skills. Foreman traveled to California which is where he met Doc Broaddus, who was a Job Corps counselor and a boxing coach. It was Broaddus who encouraged Foreman to become a boxer.

Once he began to train at the gym, Foreman rapidly established an impressive amateur record. The culmination of his amateur boxing career came at the 1968 Summer Olympics in Mexico City, where he won a gold medal in only his 25th amateur fight. He got extra attention when he brandished an American flag after his win. In 1969, Foreman turned professional and within two years, he was ranked the No. 1 challenger by the WBA and WBC. By 1972, Foreman had a perfect 37-0 record which included 35 knockouts.

Foreman won the world heavyweight title with a second-round knockout of then-undefeated Joe Frazier in 1973. He got his shot at the world heavyweight championship when he fought Joe Frazier on January 22, 1973, in Kingston, Jamaica. Frazier was the favorite going into the bout, but Foreman knocked him down six times enroute to a second-round knockout. An unprecedented TV audience watched Foreman become the champ because the fight was HBO Boxing's first-ever broadcast.

After becoming the champion, Foreman successfully defended his title twice. He beat Puerto Rican heavyweight champion Jose Roman in only 50 seconds, which at the time was the shortest heavyweight championship match ever. Foreman also beat Ken Norton, who had just beaten Muhammad Ali, in a mere two rounds. Winning those two fights then set up one of the most famous fights in history: "The Rumble in the Jungle" between Foreman and Muhammad Ali in 1974.

After not fighting in 1975, Foreman returned to boxing and won five consecutive fights, all by knockout. Then in Puerto Rico on March 17, 1977, Foreman lost in a decision to Jimmy Young. It was in his dressing room after the fight that Foreman had a religious experience, what he referred to as an epiphany, that changed his life forever. Unable to secure another title opportunity, Foreman decided to retire after his loss to Jimmy Young.

Foreman gave up boxing, and became a born-again Christian, devoting his life to God, charity and his family. He was ordained a minister in 1978 and began preaching in his hometown of Houston, Texas. In 1980, Foreman founded The Church of the Lord Jesus Christ. In 1984, he founded the George Foreman Youth and Community Center, a non-denominational place for kids who needed direction like he once did.

However, by the mid-1980s, Foreman was running out of money and people around him were advising him to close the Youth and Community Center. Foreman saw how much the Center was helping people, so he was determined to do what was necessary to keep it open. So, in 1987, after not fighting for almost 10 years to the day, Foreman returned to the ring.

While there was no shortage of detractors, Foreman proved them all wrong when he kept piling up win after win. In fact, Foreman had won 24 consecutive fights during his comeback, including 22 by knockout. Now at age 42, Foreman's success and popularity earned him a chance at the title against unbeaten Evander Holyfield. The fight went the full 12 rounds and while Holyfield won in a decision, Foreman gained a great deal of credibility.

After more than a year out of the ring, On Nov. 5, 1994, Foreman took on the new champ, Michael Moorer, and knocked him out in the 10th round. With the victory, at the age of 45, Foreman became the oldest fighter ever to win the heavyweight crown, as well as the boxer with the most time between one world championship and the next. Foreman gave away his titles in 1995, after defending them against Axel Schultz and refusing a rematch.

Foreman has been inducted into the World Boxing Hall of Fame and International Boxing Hall of Fame. The International Boxing Research Organization rates Foreman as the eighth greatest heavyweight of all time. In 2002, he was named one of the 25 greatest fighters of the past 80 years by *The Ring* magazine. *The Ring* ranked him as the ninth greatest puncher of all time. He was a ringside analyst for HBO's boxing coverage for twelve years until 2004.

Outside boxing, Foreman is a successful entrepreneur and known for his promotion of the George Foreman Grill, which has sold more than 100 million units worldwide. In 1999, he sold the naming rights to the grill for $138 million.

George Foreman is a retired American boxer and highly successful entrepreneur who has a net worth of $300 million. Foreman tends to his ministry at The Church of the Lord Jesus Christ where he preaches four times a week. He also loves spending free time with his family on his 40-acre estate in Marshall, Texas.

BORIS KODJOE AND NICOLE ARI PARKER

Nicole Ari Parker and Boris Kodjoe met and fell in love on the set of Showtime's "Soul Food." When Boris walked into their first rehearsal, Nicole thought of him as the really hot guy that got to play her boyfriend in the first couple of episodes. The couple got married on May 21, 2005.

Before she met Boris, Nicole detailed the conversation she had with God and the work she had to put in to prepare her for what she asked for. Some of the work included self-reflection, self-care (physically and mentally) and forgiveness.

Nicole and Boris are one of Hollywood's most buzzed-about couples who get asked that whole secret-to-their-marriage-success question often. She chalks their lasting love up to the little things. And making out, of course. She's also concluded that being happy with yourself affects pretty much everything else, stating, "I think as I mature, because we're going on 14 years married, I know that I'm going to have to bring my own happiness to the dinner table. It's so much better when something wonderful happened to me that day that I bring it home. Even if it's something small or finding the tea that we both love, like I found it in a weird little market or something. I have to fill myself up and bring that into the home. I would say your own happiness, sex and talking, are the keys to making marriage work."

Nicole Ari Parker and Boris Kodjoe are the proud parents of two children - Sophie Tei Naaki Lee (born March 2005) and Nicolas Neruda Kodjoe (born October 2006). Nicole became pregnant with Nicolas when Sophie was just 10 months old. So, the children are only 19 months apart. Nicole was completely overwhelmed, so they hired Rosie who was supposed to be a short-term nanny to help out with both babies.

One of the lessons that Rosie taught them was the importance of embracing the good, bad, and ugly of child development. The young parents learned from their nanny that crying is essential at every age. One day both kids were in a state of crying their eyes out. Rosie could see that Nicole was clueless about what to do and she had started crying too. Rosie just looked at Nicole as she calmly picked up Nicolas in one arm and took the hand of Sophie with the other and told Nicole, "Don't worry Nikki, it's no big deal. They are babies, babies cry. This is the time for crying." Those words have stayed with Nicole and Boris ever since.

Nicole and Boris' first-born, Sophie, was born with spina bifida, which is a birth defect that happens when a baby's backbone (spine) does not form normally. As a result, the spinal cord and the nerves that branch out of it may be damaged. As almost-newlyweds, Nicole and Boris were thrust into an accelerated fast track, not only on how to be married, but with a child that needed extreme handling with care. Sophie accelerated that process, because Nicole used to cry all the time — she never thought she would be needing to use a catheter that looked like something from the Stone Ages on her infant daughter. It was from those moments that Nicole realized she had to emotionally step up. There was a time when Sophie looked at her and asked her why she was crying. She was literally looking at Nicole's face for validation and she had to protect her during those years by being strong.

Now, more than a decade later, Sophie and brother Nicolas are progressively learning how to do things on their own. They're teenagers now ... and needless to say, they rarely cry anymore. As parents, Nicole and Boris sometimes miss the children needing them to wipe their little faces, but their supposed "short-term" nanny, Rosie, is still an important part of all of their lives.

Not only does Nicole encourage the kids to open up to them about their questions, but Nicole keeps it real with them as well, whether she's encouraging Sophie to zip her sweatshirt up a little higher or speaking to Nico about racism. Nicole recalled when Nico was playing water guns outside with his friends, two little blonde girls [when he was 10]. She suddenly realized what could have happened if a cop came around the corner and saw her kid sporting a curly afro, with a gun in his hand, at the beach. Because of the potential danger to their child, Nicole and Boris had to tell Nico that they would have to take the gun away from him.... Issues like that have been a challenge to Nicole and Boris, as parents.

Nicole Ari Parker was born on October 7, 1970 in Baltimore, Maryland. She is the only child of Donald, a dentist, and Susan, a health care entrepreneur. Her parents are both African American. Nicole married Boris Kodjoe in Gundelfingen, Germany. On her wedding license document in German her name is written Nicole Ari Ofuatye-Kodjoe (born Parker).

Nicole Ari Parker was a student of Tony Greco (Phillip Seymour Hoffman's acting teacher). She also studied at Stonestreet Studios, the independent film studio in NYC, the advanced conservatory for screen acting, directing, and producing for NYU Tisch School of the Arts Drama.

Nicole's résumé speaks for itself. Nicole Ari Parker, graduate of NYU's Tisch School of the Arts, is an actress, model and producer. Her filmography boasts over 50 credits. She made her screen debut with a leading role in the critically acclaimed independent film *The Incredibly True Adventure of Two Girls in Love* (1995) and went on to appear in *Boogie Nights* (1997), directed by Paul Thomas Anderson.

Nicole has starred in a number of movies, including *Blue Streak* (1999), *Remember the Titans* (2000), *Brown Sugar* (2002), *Welcome Home Roscoe Jenkins* (2008), *Black Dynamite* (2009), and *Almost Christmas* (2016). On television, Parker played the leading role of attorney Teri Joseph in the Showtime drama series *Soul Food* (2000-04), for which she received five NAACP Image Awards for Outstanding Actress in a Drama Series nominations. She also starred in the short-lived UPN romantic comedy *Second Time Around* (2004-05) and the ABC drama *Time After Time* (2017). In 2017, she joined the cast of Fox's prime-time soap opera *Empire* playing Giselle Barker.

Recently, she's added a new title to her growing list of accomplishments: business owner. Parker is living proof that following a dream — even an unexpected one — is possible. She recently launched the performance headband company Gymwrap.

Boris Frederic Cecil Tay-Natey Ofuatey-Kodjoe, better known as **Boris Kodjoe**, was born March 8, 1973. Kodjoe was born in Vienna, Austria, the son of Ursula, a German psychologist of partially Jewish descent, and Eric Kodjoe, a Ghanaian physician who is of the Ga-Adangbe people[. His namesake is the Russian poet and writer Boris Pasternak. Kodjoe's matrilineal

great-grandmother was Jewish and was murdered in the Holocaust; his maternal grandmother survived the war in hiding. Kodjoe's parents divorced when he was six years old. He grew up in the vicinity of Freiburg im Breisgau. Kodjoe is fluent in German, English, and French, and speaks some Spanish. He has a brother named Patrick and two sisters named Nadja and Lara.

Kodjoe attended Virginia Commonwealth University on a tennis scholarship, and graduated with a bachelor's degree in marketing in 1996. A four-year letterman on the Rams' men's tennis team, he is currently ninth in school history with 75 career singles wins. Tied for third in doubles victories with 66, he was paired with Jonas Elmblad on 37 of them, also third all-time. His brother Patrick Kodjoe played for VCU's basketball team. A back injury ended Boris' tennis aspirations, but he was quickly signed as a model and soon after, entered acting. In 1995, he was featured in TLC's music video for "Red Light Special."

Named one of the "50 Most Beautiful People in the World" by *People* magazine in 2002, Kodjoe is perhaps best known as one of the seven regular cast members from the Showtime drama

Soul Food, which aired from 2000 to 2004. He appeared in the 2002 film *Brown Sugar* and starred in the short-lived sitcom *Second Time Around* with his *Soul Food* co-star Nicole Ari Parker, whom he eventually married on May 21, 2005, in Gundelfingen, Germany. Kodjoe and his Nicole are members of Cascade United Methodist Church in Atlanta, Georgia. The family resides in Los Angeles, California.

Kodjoe played the role of David Taylor, the wayward son of Pastor Fred Taylor, in the October 2005 film *The Gospel*. He performed in a play called *Whatever She Wants*, starring Vivica A. Fox, and made an appearance on the fifth season of *Nip/Tuck*. He was also in the 2009 science fiction film *Surrogates*. Kodjoe appeared as Luther in the film *Resident Evil: Afterlife* and he also appeared on *Franklin & Bash* in 2010.

In 2013, Kodjoe began starring in the BET comedy parody series *Real Husbands of Hollywood*. In 2014 he was cast as regular on the ABC primetime soap opera *Members Only* created by Susannah Grant. In 2015, Kodjoe began a recurring guest-star role in Fox's *The Last Man on Earth* television series.

In July 2018, Kodjoe landed a recurring role in second season of the *Grey's Anatomy* spin-off series, *Station 19*. In October, he was promoted to a series regular after his appearance in the season premiere as the new fire captain, Robert Sullivan. Nicole and Boris competed against one another on a February 2019 episode of *Lip Sync Battle*. Kodjoe also portrayed O.J. Simpson in the film Nicole and O.J., which was released in March 2019.

Nicole Ari Parker is madly in love with her husband, Boris Kodjoe. She spoke about the moment she met the man of her dreams on the set of "Soul Food." She says, "When Boris walked into the first rehearsal, I thought of him as the really hot guy that got to play my boyfriend in the first couple of episodes." The couple connected and found it easy to talk to each other and laugh and be comfortable… and then she married him.

Nicole and Boris go out on dates; work out together and make sure they look good for each other. In addition, the Kodjoes are extremely excited and motivated to be a voice for those unheard, and to provide education about prevention and a possible cure for the birth defect, spina bifida.

They founded Sophie's Voice Foundation in honor of their daughter. By dedicating themselves to a healthy lifestyle they found ways to address not only their daughter's mental, physical and medical needs but also the needs of their entire family. Nicole and Boris have committed their resources and celebrity to educating multicultural communities worldwide on the importance of families working together to build healthy lifestyles one day at a time.

CIARA PRINCESS HARRIS AND RUSSELL WILSON

Seattle Seahawks quarterback **Russell Carrington Wilson** and singer, songwriter, dancer, and model **Ciara Princess Harris,** co-own the Seattle Sounders Soccer Team. Talk of their relationship kicked off when Ciara and Russell had attended an April 2015 White House State Dinner in honor of Japanese Prime Minister Shinzo Abe and his wife, Akie Abe.

"I told somebody that's the girl I want to be with before I even met her," Wilson said during a July 2015 interview with The Rock Church in San Diego. "Before I met her, I was like, 'I'm probably going to end up with Ciara.'" It was also during this interview that Wilson revealed that he and Ciara, both devout Christians, had taken a vow of celibacy until they were married in 2016.

The power couple had begun dating in early 2015 and during a vacation in the Seychelles in March 2016, the pair became engaged after Russell proposed with a 16-carat ring. They publicly announced their engagement on March 11, 2016. They had a short, four-month engagement and on July 6, 2016, they tied the knot at Peckforton Castle in Cheshire, England in front of 100 family members and friends, including bridesmaids La Anthony, Kelly Rowland, and Serena Williams.

Three months after their nuptials, Ciara announced via Instagram that she was pregnant with the pair's first child, writing, "On this special Birthday I received an abundance of love from friends and family… and I'm excited to finally share one of the Greatest Gifts of All that God could give."

On April 29, 2017, they welcomed their daughter, Sienna Princess Wilson. "More than anything, when you have your own family and it continues to grow, it's a special thing," Wilson told the *Seattle Post-Intelligencer* in 2017. "I'm truly grateful every day to get to come home and it puts a smile on my face every time."

Together, Ciara and Russell have one child. Russell takes great pride in being a father and is quite open about his love for his family on social media. In January 2020, Ciara announced they were expecting again. This will be the couple's second child together, and Ciara's third. Ciara also has a son, Future Zahir, born on May 19, 2014, from her previous relationship with rapper, Future. Ciara and Future had been engaged in October 2013 but ended the engagement in August 2014.

Because of her songwriting successes, Ciara's love life has made headlines for years; lately, it's because of how joyous it seems. When she appeared on *The View* to discuss her album, *Beauty Marks*, and to release the music video for the single of the same name, her love interest was obvious. There was beautiful imagery of her wedding to Seattle Seahawks' quarterback Russell Wilson, and of the birth of their 2-year-old daughter, Sienna Princess.

During that same appearance on *The View*, she got emotional when talking about her relationship with her husband, who had just surprised his mom with a new home for Mother's Day. "God is good," Ciara said through tears, following a taped message from Russell, their daughter Sienna, and Ciara's son Future, 4. "When you allow yourself to be vulnerable, you become your strongest," she said, adding, "When I met the love of my life it was not only loving me, it was to love my son."

Naturally, Ciara has since spoken about how Russell has organically taken to fatherhood. "He's been such an incredible father since day one," she told *E! News* in 2018. "He's so loving and very patient. He also likes to have fun—he's very spontaneous and we just have a good time as a family."

Ciara Princess Harris was born in Austin, Texas, on October 25, 1985, the only child of Jackie and Carlton Clay Harris. An army brat, she grew up in Germany, New York, Utah, California, Arizona, and Nevada. She was named after the Revlon fragrance "Ciara" which was introduced in 1973 and is still sold today. During her teens, Ciara and her family settled in Atlanta, Georgia.

In her mid-teens, Ciara formed the all-girl group, Hearsay, with two of her friends. The group recorded demos, but as time went on, they began to have differences and eventually parted ways. Despite this setback, Ciara was still determined to reach her goal and signed a publishing deal as a songwriter.

Her first writing credit was on Blu Cantrell's debut album, *So Blu* for the song "10,000 Times." She also wrote the song "Got Me Waiting" for R&B singer Fantasia Barrino's debut album, *Free*

Yourself. It was when she was writing songs that she met music producer, Jazze Pha, whom she called her "music soulmate." In 2002, the two recorded four demos, "1, 2 Step", "Thug Style," "Pick Up the Phone," and "Lookin' at You". With Jazze Pha's help, Ciara signed a record deal with LaFace Records.

In 2004, Ciara released her debut studio album *Goodies*, which spawned four singles: "Goodies", "1, 2 Step", "Oh" and "And I". "Goodies" topped the *Billboard* Hot 100 chart. The album was certified triple platinum by the Recording Industry Association of America (RIAA), and garnered four nominations at the 48th Annual Grammy Awards. Ciara was also featured on Missy Elliott's "Lose Control" and Bow Wow's "Like You", both of which reached number three on the *Billboard* Hot 100. In 2006, Ciara released her second studio album, *Ciara: The Evolution*, which spawned the hit singles "Get Up", "Promise", "Like a Boy" and "Can't Leave 'em Alone". The album reached number one in the U.S. and was certified platinum.

Ciara's third studio album, *Fantasy Ride* (2009) was less successful than her first two albums. However, it produced the international top-ten single "Love Sex Magic", featuring Justin Timberlake, which received a Grammy Award nomination for Best Pop Collaboration with Vocals. The following year, Ciara released her fourth studio album *Basic Instinct*, which included the R&B top-five single "Ride", but was met with low sales, continuing a downward trend in her commercial performance. Ciara signed a new record deal with Epic Records in 2011. In 2013, she released her fifth studio album, *Ciara*, which spawned the R&B top-ten single "Body Party". Her sixth album, *Jackie* (2015), included the singles "I Bet" and "Dance like We're Making Love".

In 2006, Ciara made her film debut in *All You've Got*, and later appeared in the films *Mama, I Want to Sing!* (2012) and *That's My Boy* (2012). In 2013, she had a recurring role in the US TV series, *The Game*. In 2016, Ciara signed a signed a modeling contract with IMG. That year, she became a Global Brand Ambassador for the cosmetics giant Revlon.

Since making her musical debut in 2004, Ciara has attained eight *Billboard* Hot 100 top-ten singles. She has also received many awards, including three BET Awards, three MTV Video Music Awards, three MOBO Awards, and one Grammy Award. As of 2015, Ciara has sold over 23 million records worldwide.

At the 48th Annual Grammy Awards, Ciara received four nominations for Best New Artist, Best Rap/Sung Collaboration for "1, 2 Step", Best Rap Song for Missy Elliott's single "Lose Control", and won her last nomination, Best Short Form Music Video for "Lose Control".

On December 5, 2006, Ciara released her second studio album, *Ciara: The Evolution*. According to the singer, the title of the album is "about so much more than just my personal growth – it's about the evolution of music, the evolution of dance, the evolution of fashion." The source of the album's creativity, such as the sound and edge, come from Ciara in general. *Ciara: The Evolution* became Ciara's first number one album on the U.S. *Billboard* 200 and second on the Top R&B/Hip-Hop Albums charts with sales of more than 338,000 becoming her highest first week of sales to date. The album went on to be certified platinum by the RIAA in the United States, within only five weeks of its release, and has sold 1.3 million copies, according to Nielsen SoundScan. It sold over two million copies worldwide.

In October 2008, Ciara was honored as *Billboard*'s "Woman of the Year", because of her success as a recording artist and leadership in embracing the changing music business.

In July 2009, Ciara headlined the *Jay-Z & Ciara Live* tour with Jay-Z. In February 2010, Ciara along with Pitbull were featured on the remix to Ludacris' hit single "How Low". The following month, Ciara made a cameo appearance in the music video of Usher's single, "Lil' Freak".

Ciara released her fourth studio album, *Basic Instinct*, on December 14, 2010. The lead single, "Ride", which features Ludacris, was released on April 26, 2010. It peaked at number forty-two on the U.S. *Billboard* Hot 100, number three on the U.S. Hot R&B/Hip-Hop Songs chart, becoming her twelfth top ten hit on the chart, and number seventy-five on the UK Singles Chart. The accompanying music video won the award for "Best Dance Performance" at the 2010 Soul Train Music Awards. In November 2010, Ciara performed at the Summerbeatz tour alongside Flo Rida, Jay Sean, Akon, Travie McCoy and Ja Rule. In the summer of 2011, Ciara was a part of the Malibu Rum Tour. She performed in seven shows across the US.

In May 2011, Ciara was removed from the Jive Records website roster. On July 12, 2011, it was reported that she had reunited with L.A. Reid by signing with his record label Epic Records, and was confirmed in September 2011.

Aside from music in 2012, Ciara also starred in two movies during this time. She starred in the straight-to-DVD film, *Mama, I Want to Sing!*. She played Amara Winter, a preacher's daughter who was discovered by a well-established musician. She appeared as Brie in the 2012 comedy film, *That's My Boy*. Ciara made an appearance as herself playing Lauren London's best friend on the Season 6 premiere of BET's *The Game* which aired on March 26, 2013, she continued to be a recurring cast member throughout the season.

In late January 2014, Ciara premiered a live version of a song entitled "Anytime" at the Degree Women Grammys Celebration in Los Angeles, on February 2, 2014, Ciara premiered the studio version produced Boi-1da and Katalyst featuring her then-boyfriend and rapper Future. After her engagement to Future, Ciara revealed to *W* in April 2014 that her sixth studio album would be predominantly inspired by her then-fiancé. Ciara gave birth to her first child in May 2014. After claims of Future's infidelity during their relationship had surfaced, it was reported that the couple's engagement had been called off. Following their very public break-up, Ciara's album release was further postponed to 2015, and during this time the singer "quietly" recorded new music, while concentrating on motherhood.

"I Bet", the lead single from her upcoming album *Jackie*, was released on January 26, 2015. In May 2015, Ciara embarked on her first headlining tour in six years. The month-long Jackie Tour kicked off on May 3, 2015 in Chicago and included stops in New York, Boston, New Orleans, Dallas, and Los Angeles. The first round of US dates wrapped May 31 in San Francisco. Ciara's sixth album, *Jackie*, was released on May 1, 2015. It includes the singles "I Bet" and "Dance like We're Making Love". The album debuted at number 17 on the *Billboard* 200 with 25,000 equivalent album units (19,900 in sales) and has the lowest first-week sales amongst her first six albums.

Ciara is currently working on a seventh studio album and has stated that the album will feature her undertaking a new musical direction. On January 27, 2017, it was announced that Ciara had signed a deal with Warner Bros. Records. On July 17, 2018, Ciara released her new single and its accompanying music video, "Level Up". The song is the first single from her upcoming seventh studio album. Ciara announced her seventh studio album, *Beauty Marks*, released on May 10, 2019. In addition to "Level Up", the album has spawned the singles "Freak Me", "Dose", "Greatest Love" and "Thinkin Bout You". Ciara performed "Thinkin Bout You" at the 2019 *Billboard* Music Awards.

In 2019, Ciara judged alongside David Dobrik and Debbie Gibson in a new musical competition on Nickelodeon titled *America's Most Musical Family*.

Ciara is known for her often "breathy soprano" vocals. With the release of her debut single "Goodies", Ciara was referred to as the Princess of Crunk&B. Her third album, *Fantasy Ride*, saw the singer showcasing a new pop and dance direction. Ciara's music is generally contemporary R&B, but it also incorporates other genres including hip hop, crunk, dance-pop, electropop and funk. Critics have described her singles "Goodies", "1, 2 Step", "Get Up", and "Go Girl" as club bangers.

Ciara's debut album featured production from Jazze Pha who discovered her. Critics compared the album to late singer Aaliyah and said it had qualities of Destiny's Child. On her second album, Ciara worked with one of her debut album collaborators Lil Jon on "That's Right", sampling Pretty Tony's "Fix It in the Mix". She has also taken to sampling songs from other artists such as: Lyn Collins's "Think (About It)" and Rob Base's "It Takes Two" on "Make It Last Forever", Jive Rhythm Trax's 80's electro cut "122 BPM" on "C.R.U.S.H" and also Harold Melvin & the Blue Notes' "If You Don't Know Me by Now", sampling the chorus of the song onto "Never Ever".

Ciara stated, "Whenever someone asks me who inspires me to do what I do, I always say Michael Jackson. That's it for me. He's everything to me. He's going to be remembered in so many ways for me. I feel it's important for me to continue to let my generation know how important he was to music." Ciara also cites Whitney Huston, Aaliyah, TLC, SWV,

Monica and Salt-N-Pepa, as influences. Her second studio album *Ciara: The Evolution* (2006) was influenced by Michael Jackson, Prince, and pop singer Madonna. During the recording of her fifth self-titled album *Ciara* (2013), she was inspired by Al Green and Missy Elliott.

Ciara became the face of Jay-Z's Rocawear clothing line and spokesperson for the women campaign entitled "I Will Not Lose", which debuted in the summer of 2007. In the October issue of *Vibe Magazine*, she appeared, apparently nude, on the magazine cover but claimed *Vibe* had airbrushed her clothes off. She told *MTV News* that she was hurt by the photos and was quite shocked when she finally got her hands on the month's issue. She later confirmed that she was in fact clothed. In September 2008, Ciara contributed to the song "Just Stand Up!" with fifteen other female artists, who shared the stage to perform the song live on September 5, 2008 during the "Stand Up to Cancer" television special. The proceeds from the single were given to the fundraiser. The television special helped raise $100 million for cancer research.

In 2009, Ciara became the face of Dosomething.org's "Do Something 101" campaign to raise school supplies for those in need at the start of the school year. She filmed a public service announcement to endorse the campaign.

In 2009, Ciara signed a multimillion-dollar deal with the modeling agency Wilhelmina Models. After signing the deal, she has been in many magazine spreads. In addition to that, she also has her eyes set on beginning a new clothing line. In June 2008, she was in talks with the department store Steve & Barry's to create an affordable clothing line, but it never happened. On November 9, 2009, it was announced that Ciara would be modeling in the German edition of *Vogue*. During that time, it was also announced that Ciara would be the new face of a major multimedia ad campaign for Verizon's smartphone the LG Chocolate Touch. Ciara filmed a commercial for the campaign, which features her dancing to her 2009 single, "Work" In March 2010, it was officially confirmed and announced that Ciara was the spokesperson in the new ad campaign for Adidas Originals. A commercial for the campaign was released the same month, featuring numerous other celebrities.

On May 12, 2016, it was announced that Ciara signed a modeling contract with IMG. Later that year, she became a Global Brand Ambassador for the cosmetics giant Revlon.

Russell Carrington Wilson was born November 29, 1988 at The Christ Hospital in Cincinnati, and grew up in Richmond, Virginia, the son of Harrison Benjamin Wilson III, a lawyer, and Tammy (Turner) Wilson, a legal nurse consultant. He has an older brother, Harrison IV, and a younger sister, Anna. Wilson started playing football with his father and brother at the age of four and played his first organized game for the Tuckahoe Tomahawks youth football team in sixth grade.

Wilson's great-great-grandfather was a slave to a Confederate colonel and was freed after the American Civil War. Wilson's paternal grandfather, Harrison B. Wilson Jr., was a former president of Norfolk State University who played football and basketball at

Kentucky State University, and his paternal grandmother, Anna W. Wilson, was on the faculty at Jackson State University. Wilson's maternal grandfather was noted painter A. B. Jackson.

Wilson's father played football and baseball at Dartmouth and was a wide receiver for the San Diego Chargers preseason squad in 1980. Wilson's brother, Harry, played football and baseball at the University of Richmond, and his sister Anna plays basketball for Stanford. Wilson's father died on June 9, 2010 at age 55 due to complications from diabetes.

Wilson attended Collegiate School, a preparatory school in Richmond, Virginia. As a junior in 2005, he threw for 3,287 passing yards and 40 passing touchdowns and rushed for 634 rushing yards and 15 rushing touchdowns. He was named an all-district, all-region, and all-state player. Wilson was twice named the *Richmond Times-Dispatch* Player of the Year.

As a senior, he threw for 3,009 passing yards, 34 passing touchdowns, and seven interceptions. In addition, he rushed for 1,132 yards and 18 touchdowns. That year, he was named an all-conference and all-state player as well as conference player of the year. He was featured in *Sports Illustrated* magazine for his performance in the state championship game win. Wilson also served as his senior class president.

During his time in high school, Wilson attended the Manning Passing Academy, a summer football clinic run by multiple NFL MVP winner Peyton Manning. Due to this encounter, Manning recognized Wilson many years later when the latter had flown to Denver to discuss the prospect of getting drafted by the Denver Broncos, where Manning had recently signed.

In addition to playing football, Wilson was also a member of the Collegiate School basketball and baseball teams. Wilson committed to North Carolina State University on July 23, 2006. He also received a football scholarship offer from Duke University.

Wilson redshirted during the 2007 season at NC State. In 2008, Wilson initially split time at quarterback with senior Daniel Evans and junior Harrison Beck. However, Evans and Beck saw no regular season action after Week 2 and Week 5, respectively. Thereafter, Wilson led the team to a 4–3 record in the regular season which NC State finished out on a four-game winning streak. During a win over East Carolina, Wilson threw for 201 yards and three touchdowns. He threw for two touchdowns in each of the last six games in the regular season.

In the 2008 PapaJohns.com Bowl against Rutgers, Wilson threw for 186 yards and a touchdown and rushed for 46 yards before halftime. Late in the first half, he scrambled to the Rutgers' four-yard line, where he was tackled and suffered a knee sprain. With Wilson sitting out the remainder of the game, his replacements threw a combined total of three interceptions with NC State eventually losing, 23–29. Over the course of the season, he completed 150 of 275 attempts for 1,955 yards and 17 touchdowns with just one interception. He also recorded 116 carries for 394 yards and four touchdowns. The Atlantic Coast Conference (ACC) named him the first-team All-ACC quarterback. It was the first time in the conference's history that a freshman quarterback was named to the first team.

Prior to the 2009 season, Wilson was named as the quarterback on the pre-season all-ACC football team on July 12. On September 19, Wilson broke Andre Woodson's all-time NCAA record of 325 consecutive pass attempts without an interception against Gardner–

Webb. The 379-pass streak ended in a game against Wake Forest on October 3. Wilson held the record until November 10, 2012, when it was broken by Louisiana Tech quarterback Colby Cameron. Wilson was named honorable mention All-ACC in 2009.

Wilson led the 2010 Wolfpack to a 9–4 season that included a 23–7 win over West Virginia in the 2010 Champs Sports Bowl. He led the ACC in passing yards per game (274.1) and total offensive yards per game (307.5). He was named second-team All-ACC and runner-up for ACC Football Player of the Year. In May 2010, Wilson graduated from NC State in three years with a BA in communication and took graduate-level business courses in the fall semester during the 2010 football season.

In January 2011, Wilson announced that he would report to spring training with the Colorado Rockies organization. NC State head coach Tom O'Brien expressed reservations with Wilson's decision, saying "Russell and I have had very open conversations about his responsibilities respective to baseball and football. While I am certainly respectful of Russell's dedication to baseball these last several years, within those discussions I also communicated to him the importance of his time commitment to NC State football."

O'Brien and his staff reached out to NFL coaches and general managers on Wilson's behalf, but he failed to receive an invitation to the 2011 NFL Scouting Combine.

On April 29, 2011, O'Brien announced that Wilson had been granted a release from his football scholarship with one year of eligibility remaining.

On June 27, 2011, Wisconsin head coach Bret Bielema announced that Wilson had committed to Wisconsin for the 2011 season. In the season opener against UNLV, Wilson passed for 255 yards and two passing touchdowns in a 51–17 victory. He also rushed for 62 yards, including a 46-yard touchdown run. At the end of the regular season, Wilson was named first team All-Big Ten by both the coaches and media. He also won the Griese-Brees Big Ten Quarterback of the Year award.

In the inaugural Big Ten Championship Game on December 3, Wilson threw for three touchdowns and led the Badgers to a 42–39 win over the Michigan State Spartans. Wilson was named the game's Grange-Griffin MVP. In December 2011, Wilson was named a third team All-American by Yahoo! Sports, and he finished ninth in the voting for the Heisman Trophy with 52 points.

He played college football for the University of Wisconsin during the 2011 season, in which he set the single-season FBS record for passing efficiency (191.8) and led the team to a Big Ten title and the 2012 Rose Bowl appearance. Wilson initially played football and baseball for North Carolina State University from 2008 to 2010 before transferring to Wisconsin. He played minor league baseball for the Tri-City Dust Devils in 2010 and the Asheville Tourists in 2011 as a second baseman, and as of 2019 his professional baseball rights are held by the Trenton Thunder, a Double-A affiliate of the New York Yankees. He was selected by the Seahawks with the 12th pick in the third round (75th overall) of the 2012 NFL Draft. After beating out Matt Flynn for the starting job during training camp, Wilson ended up having a successful debut season, tying Peyton Manning's then record for most passing touchdowns by a rookie (26) and was named the Pepsi NFL Rookie of the Year.

Wilson has been named to seven Pro Bowls and has started in two Super Bowls, winning Super Bowl XLVIII. He holds the record for most wins by an NFL quarterback through seven seasons (75) and is one of two quarterbacks in NFL history with a career passer rating over 100. On April 15, 2019, Wilson signed a four-year, $140 million contract extension to remain with the Seahawks through the 2023 season, making him the highest paid player in the NFL.

2019 proved to be a year for the couple. Shortly after Russell Wilson inked a new contract with the Seattle Seahawks Ciara wrote in an Instagram caption to celebrate the news. "I watch you put everything on the line every Sunday in pure amazement," "Your dedication, consistency, and commitment to the game never wavers. You're always the first person in, and the last person out. You're 1 of 1. The hardest working man I know! Giving God All the praise."

Shortly after, the couple announced the formation of Why Not You Productions, a new company that will focus on the creation of scripted and unscripted projects for film, television and digital, with the intention of "inspiring and aspiring narratives and human interest stories," per the announcement.

"While we work in different fields in our day-to-day, we are excited to come together to collaborate and create stories that we hope will touch people's lives," Wilson and Ciara said in a joint statement to *The Hollywood Reporter*. "We are both storytellers at heart and we want to be able to share stories that uplift people and inspire others to create positive change. That's ultimately what we want this company to represent."

Through the storm, it seems Ciara found her way to the sunshine. "You know my husband's pretty awesome and you know it's been an incredible journey," Ciara told *Access Hollywood* at the 2019 Billboard Music Awards in May. "Time goes by so fast and we've been having the time of our lives. We call it organized chaos because obviously with him doing football and me doing music, the worlds are both moving fast and kinda like in two different directions, but sometimes parallel at the same time."

In August 2019, Ciara and her husband Russell Wilson became part of the ownership group of Seattle Sounders FC in Major League Soccer.

> *Culture and education have no bounds or limits; now man is in a phase In which he must decide for himself how far he can proceed in the culture that belongs to the whole of humanity.*
> *- Maria Montessori*

CHAPTER TWO – THE TEACHER
FEATURING EDUCATORS THAT INFLUENCED THE NATION

Education is a powerful agent of change; it improves health and livelihoods, contributes to social stability and drives long-term economic growth. In addition, education can open the door to a whole new world of opportunities and put you on the path to success. The men and women featured in this chapter are all teachers. Several of them are children of former slaves, who were taught to read at a time when books were hard to come by. Their parents raised them to value the meaning of a good education…sometimes in a one-room schoolhouse, which they walked to, several miles from home.

However, education is not only gaining book knowledge, it can also teach you practicality. Education doesn't mean that you should just go to school and college daily and take exams; it is meant for gathering knowledge and relating that knowledge to your lives. It is also meant to instill in you desire and determination, which are keys to your success

Many of the educators featured here were most likely told as children that "an education will give you the knowledge and tools you need to feel confident in the workplace and it can prepare you to handle any situation that might come your way." Whether you're pursuing an education in healthcare, business, information technology, or the trades, the expertise you gain can also be applied to everyday situations.

An education can greatly improve your quality of life and exposes you to new people and experiences which can have a positive impact on your life. Above all, a good educator must have passion for the subject matter he or she is teaching and for the students who put their trust in their teacher.

Education is irrespective of caste, creed and gender, by gaining knowledge people can stand out as equal with all the other persons from different caste and creed. It is a platform to prove the equity by defeating all barriers.

A good education will protect a person both financially and also help them to live their life on their feet. It helps to break through the social evils like racism and poverty line. It is the perfect platform to cultivate a person as a leader with the necessary human emotions and values. A good education can offer the best platform for women to prove they are equal to men in society; therefore, it is essential that women should be equally educated along with men. We salute the eight teachers featured on this chapter who have made the grade as esteemed heroes and sheroes.

HALLIE QUINN BROWN

Hallie Quinn Brown (March 10, 1849 – September 16, 1949) was an African-American educator, writer and activist, born in Pittsburgh, Pennsylvania. She was one of six children. Her parents, Frances Jane Scroggins and Thomas Arthur Brown, were freed slaves.

When she was fifteen years old, Hallie, her parents and siblings migrated to a farm near Chatham, Canada. Hallie's father was an incredibly bright man, known as "Mr. Brown, the walking encyclopedia". Her mother was also well-educated, a counselor to the students at Wilberforce school. Her brother, Jeremiah, became a politician in Ohio.

In 1868, Hallie began a course of study in Wilberforce University, Ohio, from which she graduated in 1873 with the degree of Bachelor of Science.

Realizing that a great field of labor lay in the South, Brown, with true missionary' spirit, left her pleasant home and friends to devote herself to the noble work she had chosen. She started her career by teaching at a country school on a plantation in South Carolina, where she endured the rough life as best she could and taught a large number of children from neighboring plantations. She also taught a class of aged people, who were then able to read the Bible. She next took charge of a school on Sonora Plantation, in Mississippi. Her plantation school had no windows, but it was well ventilated, and the rain beat in fiercely. Not being successful in getting the authorities to fix the building, she secured the willing service of two of her larger students. She mounted one mule, and the two boys another, and thus they rode to the gin mill. They got cotton seed, returned, mixed it with earth, which formed a plastic mortar, and with her own hands she pasted up the holes.

Her fame as instructor spread, and her services were secured as teacher at Yazoo City. On account of the unsettled state of affairs in 1874-5, she was compelled to return North. Thus, the South lost one of its most valuable missionaries. Brown then taught in Dayton, Ohio, for four years. Owing to ill health, she gave up teaching. After taking a course in elocution, she was persuaded to travel for her alma mater, Wilberforce, and started on a lecturing tour, concluding at Hampton Normal School in Virginia (now Hampton University), where she was particularly welcomed.

In 1886, she graduated from Chautauqua, and in 1887 received the degree of Master of Science from her alma mater, Wilberforce, being the first woman to do so. *Hallie Brown was also dean of Allen University in Columbia, South Carolina, from 1885 to 1887.* Though elected as instructor in elocution and literature at Wilberforce University, she declined the offer in order to accept a position at Tuskegee Institute. She was principal of Tuskegee Institute in

Alabama during 1892–93 under Booker T. Washington. She became a professor at Wilberforce in 1893, and was a frequent lecturer on African American issues and the temperance movement, speaking at the international Woman's Christian Temperance Union conference in London in 1895 and representing the United States at the International Congress of Women in London in 1899.

In 1893, Brown presented a paper at the World's Congress of Representative Women in Chicago along with four more African American women who were presented at the conference: Anna Julia Cooper, Fannie Barrier Williams, Fanny Jackson Coppin, and Sarah Jane Woodson Early.

Brown was a founder of the Colored Woman's League of Washington, D.C., which in 1894 merged into the National Association of Colored Women. She was president of the Ohio State Federation of Colored Women's Clubs from 1905 until 1912, and of the National Association of Colored Women from 1920 until 1924. She spoke at the Republican National Convention in 1924 and later directed campaign work among African-American women for President Calvin Coolidge. Brown was inducted as an honorary member of Delta Sigma Theta.

For several years Hattie Brown traveled with "The Wilberforce Grand Concert Company", an organization for the benefit of Wilberforce College. She read before hundreds of audiences, and tens of thousands of people. She possessed a magnetic voice, seeming to have perfect control of the muscles of the throat, and could vary her voice successfully. As a public reader, Brown enthused her audiences. In her humorous selections, she often caused "wave after wave" of laughter; and she often moved her audience to tears. She was a prominent member of the A. M. E.

Church; also, a member of the "King's Daughters," "Human Rights League," and the "Isabella Association."

Brown died on September 16, 1949, in Wilberforce, Ohio, and is buried at Massies Creek Cemetery in Cedarville, Ohio.

EDWARD ALEXANDER BOUCHET

Edward Alexander Bouchet (September 15, 1852 – October 28, 1918) was a physicist and educator. By completing. his dissertation in physics at Yale in 1876, Bouchet became the first African-American to earn a Ph.D. from any American university.

Edward was born at home in New Haven, Connecticut, to parents William and Susan (Cooley) Bouchet. His father William, a former slave, worked as a servant and later as a porter at Yale University. He also acted as a deacon at the Temple Street Church in New Haven.

The youngest of four children, Edward was enrolled in the Artisan Street Colored School with only one teacher, who nurtured his academic abilities. At that time, there were only three schools in New Haven open to black children. Edward attended the New Haven High School from 1866 to 1868 and then Hopkins School from 1868 to 1870, where he was named valedictorian (after graduating first in his class).

That fall, Edward entered Yale College (later renamed Yale University) in pursuit of a bachelor's degree—a remarkable endeavor for the time, as there were few opportunities for African Americans seeking higher education. Edward Bouchet ranked sixth in his class on graduation from Yale. On the basis of his academic record Edward was elected to the Phi Beta Kappa Society. In 1874; he had become one of the first African Americans to graduate from Yale College. After graduating, Edward stayed on for two more years and completed his Ph.D. in physics. He was among the first 20 Americans (of any race) to receive a Ph.D. in physics; only a handful of other people had earned that same degree in the country's history.

Despite his impressive achievement, Bouchet could not land a college professorship due to his race. He moved to Philadelphia in 1876 and took a position at the Philadelphia's Institute for Colored Youth (now Cheyney University of Pennsylvania), where he taught physics and chemistry for the next 26 years; but then the school changed its direction in 1902 to focus on offering vocational training. So, he resigned at the height of the W. E. B. Du Bois-Booker T. Washington controversy over the need for an industrial vs. collegiate education for blacks.

Edward Bouchet spent the next 14 years holding a variety of jobs around the country. First, he worked for Sumner High School in St. Louis, Missouri; and between 1905 and 1908, he was director of academics at St. Paul's Normal and Industrial School in Lawrenceville, Virginia (presently, St. Paul's College). He was then principal and teacher at Lincoln High School in Gallipolis, Ohio from 1908 to 1913. He joined the faculty of Bishop College in Marshall, Texas in 1913. Illness finally forced him to retire in 1916 and he moved back to New Haven. Edward Bouchet died there, in his childhood home, in 1918, at age of 66. He had never married and had no children.

Since his passing, Bouchet has received numerous honors. Yale University installed a tombstone to remember him in 1998, and the school's Graduate School of Arts and Sciences established the Edward Alexander Bouchet Graduate Honor Society in his name. Yale also gives out the Bouchet Leadership Award to academics who help advance diversity in higher education.

MARIA TECLA ARTEMISIA MONTESSORI

Maria Tecla Artemisia Montessori (August 31, 1870 – May 6, 1952) was an Italian physician and educator best known for the philosophy of education that bears her name, and her writing on scientific pedagogy. At an early age, Montessori broke gender barriers and expectations when she enrolled in classes at an all-boys technical school, with hopes of becoming an engineer. She soon had a change of heart and began medical school at the Sapienza University of Rome, where she graduated – with honors – in 1896. Her educational method is still in use today in many public and private schools throughout the world.

In 1911 and 1912, Montessori's work was popular and widely publicized in the United States; the first North American Montessori school was opened in October 1911, in Tarrytown, New York.

One of Montessori's many accomplishments was the Montessori method. This is a method of education for young children that stresses the development of a child's own initiative and natural abilities, especially through practical play. This method allowed children to develop at their own pace and provided educators with a new understanding of child development. Montessori's book, *The Montessori Method*, presents the method in detail. Educators who followed this model set up special environments to meet the needs of students in three developmentally-meaningful age groups: 2–2.5 years, 2.5–6 years, and 6–12 years. The students learn through activities that involve exploration, manipulations, order, repetition, abstraction, and communication. Teachers encourage children in the first two age groups to use their senses to explore and manipulate materials in their immediate environment. Children in the last age group deal with abstract concepts based on their newly developed powers of reasoning, imagination, and creativity.

The inventor Alexander Graham Bell and his wife became proponents of the method and a second school was opened in their Canadian home. . The first International Training Course in Rome in 1913 was sponsored by the American Montessori Committee, and 67 of the 83 students were from the United States. By 1913 there were more than 100 Montessori schools in the country.

Maria Montessori traveled to the United States in December 1913 on a three-week lecture tour which included films of her European classrooms, meeting with large, enthusiastic crowds wherever she traveled.

Montessori returned to the United States in 1915, sponsored by the National Education Association, to demonstrate her work at the Panama–Pacific International Exposition in San Francisco, California, and to give a third international training course. A glass-walled classroom was put up at the Exposition, and thousands of observers came to see a class of 21 students. Montessori's father died in November 1915, and she returned to Italy. After Maria left in 1915, the Montessori movement in the United States fragmented.

In 1949 Montessori attended the 8th International Montessori Congress in Sanremo, Italy, where a model classroom was demonstrated. The same year, the first training course for birth to three years of age, was established. She was nominated for the Nobel Peace Prize. Montessori was also awarded the French Legion of Honor, Officer of the Dutch Order of Orange Nassau, and received an Honorary Doctorate of the University of Amsterdam. In 1950 she visited Scandinavia, represented Italy at the UNESCO conference in Florence, presented at the 29th international training course in Perugia, and was again nominated for the Nobel Peace Prize. In 1951 she participated in the 9th International Montessori Congress in London, gave a training course in Innsbruck, was nominated for the third time for the Nobel Peace Prize. Montessori died of a cerebral hemorrhage on May 6, 1952, at the age of 81 in Noordwijk aan Zee, the Netherlands.

Maria Montessori created over 4,000 Montessori classrooms across the world and her books were translated into many different languages for the training of new educators. Her methods are installed in hundreds of public and private schools across the United States and are still in use today in many public and private schools throughout the world.

KELLY MILLER

Kelly Miller (July 18, 1863 – December 29, 1939) was the first Black mathematics graduate student.

Born in Winnsboro, South Carolina, Kelly Miller was the sixth of ten children born to Kelly Miller, a free Negro who served in the Confederate Army during the Civil War, and Elizabeth (Roberts) Miller, a slave. Kelly received his early education in one of the local primary schools established during Reconstruction. Based on the recommendation of a missionary (Reverend Willard Richardson) who recognized Miller's mathematical aptitude, Miller attended the Fairfield Institute in Winnsboro, South Carolina from 1878 to 1880.

Awarded a scholarship to Howard University, he completed the Preparatory Department's three-year curriculum in Latin, Greek, and mathematics in two years (1880-1882). Kelly then attended the College Department at Howard University from 1882 to 1886. During that period, he also worked as a clerk for the U.S. Pension

Office for two years. Kelly Miller was appointed to the position in the Pension Office after taking the civil service examination, a test prescribed by the Civil Service Act passed during the administration of President Grover Cleveland. Miller's greatest influence while at Howard University were his professors of Latin (James Monroe Gregory) and History (Howard president William Weston Patton, who also taught philosophy and conducted weekly vesper services required of all students).

Kelly Miller received a Bachelor of Science (B.S.) from Howard University in 1886. He continued to work at the Pension Office after graduation. Kelly also studied advanced mathematics (1886-1887) with Captain Edgar Frisby, an English mathematician at the U.S. Naval Observatory. Frisby's chief at the observatory, Simon Newcomb, who was also a professor of mathematics at Johns Hopkins University, recommended Kelly for admission to Hopkins University president Daniel Coit Gilman.

Johns Hopkins University had recently become the first American school to offer graduate work in mathematics. As Miller was to be the first African American student admitted to the university, the recommendation was decided by the Board of Trustees, who decided to admit him, based on the university founder's known Quaker beliefs.

From 1887 to 1889 Miller performed graduate work in Mathematics, Physics, and Astronomy. When an increase in tuition ($100 to $200) prevented Kelly Miller from continuing his studies, he left (Johns Hopkins closed its doors to Blacks) and taught at the M Street High School in Washington, D.C. (1889-1890), whose principal was Francis L. Cardozo.

After teaching mathematics briefly at the M Street High School in Washington, D.C. (1889-1890), he was appointed to the faculty of Howard University in 1890. Five years later Miller added sociology to Howard's curriculum because he thought that the new discipline was important for developing objective analyses of the racial system in the United States. As dean of the College of Arts and Sciences, he modernized the classical curriculum, strengthening the natural and social sciences.

In 1894 Kelly Miller married Annie May Butler, a teacher at the Baltimore Normal School, with whom he had five children.

Although Miller was a leader at Howard for most of his tenure there, his national importance derived from his intellectual leadership during the conflict between the "accommodationism" of Booker T. Washington and the "radicalism" of the nascent civil rights movement led by W. E. B. Du Bois. Critical of Washington's famous Cotton States Exposition Address (1895) in 1896, Miller later praised Washington's emphasis on self-help and initiative. He remained an opponent of the exaggerated claims made on behalf of industrial education and became one of the most effective advocates of higher education for black Americans when it was attacked as "inappropriate" for a people whose social role was increasingly limited by statute and custom to agriculture, some skilled trades, unskilled labor, and domestic service.

From Howard University, Kelly Miller received a Master of Arts (M.A.) in Mathematics (1901) and a law degree (LL.D.) in 1903. From 1895 to 1907 Miller was professor of mathematics and sociology.

Perhaps Miller's most lasting contribution to scholarship was his pioneering advocacy of the systematic study of black people. In

1901 he proposed to the Howard board of trustees that the university financially support the publications of the American Negro Academy, whose goals were to promote literature, science, art, higher education, and scholarly works by blacks, and to defend them against "vicious assaults." Although the board declined, it permitted the academy to meet on the campus. Convinced that Howard should use its prestige and location in Washington to become a national center for black studies, Miller planned a "Negro-Americana Museum and Library."

Noted for his brilliant mind, Miller rapidly became a major figure in the life of Howard University. In 1907 he was appointed dean of the College of Arts and Sciences. During his twelve-year deanship the college grew dramatically, as the old classical curriculum was modernized and new courses in the natural sciences and the social sciences were added. Miller's recruiting tours through the South and Middle Atlantic states were so successful that the enrollment increased from 75 undergraduates in 1907 to 243 undergraduates in 1911.

In 1914 he persuaded Jesse E. Moorland, a Howard alumnus and Young Men's Christian Association official, to donate to Howard his large private library on blacks in Africa and in the United States as the foundation for the proposed center. This became the Moorland Foundation (reorganized in 1973 as the Moorland-Spingarn Research Center), a research library, archives, and museum that has been vital to the emergence of sound scholarship in this field. Serving from 1915 to 1925 as head of the new sociology department, Professor Miller taught sociology exclusively,

The years after World War I were difficult ones for Miller. J. Stanley Durkee, the last of Howard's white presidents, was appointed in 1918 and set out to curtail the baronial power of the deans by building a new central administration. Miller, a conspicuously powerful dean, was demoted in 1919 to dean of a new junior college, which was later abolished in 1925. A leader in the movement to have a black president of Howard, Miller was a perennial favorite of the alumni but was never selected.

At a time when many younger blacks regarded labor unions as progressive forces, Miller was skeptical of them, citing their history of persistent racial discrimination. He remained an old-fashioned American patriot, despite the nation's many disappointing failures to extend democracy to black Americans. As a weekly columnist in the black press, Miller's views were published in more than one hundred newspapers. By 1923 it was estimated that his columns reached half a million readers. Although his influence at Howard declined significantly by the late 1920s through his retirement in 1934, Miller's stature as a commentator on race relations and politics remained high. He had become alarmed by the vast social changes stimulated by World War I and was seen as increasingly conservative. He opposed the widespread abandonment of farming by black Americans and warned that the mass migration to cities would be socially and culturally destructive.

Miller died at his home on the campus of Howard University on December 29, 1939.

HENRY LOUIS "SKIP" GATES JR.

Henry Louis "Skip" Gates Jr. (born September 16, 1950) is an American literary critic, teacher, historian, filmmaker and public intellectual who serves as the Alphonse Fletcher University Professor and Director of the Hutchins Center for African and African American Research at Harvard University. He discovered what are considered the earliest known literary works of African-American writers, and has published extensively on appreciating African-American literature as part of the Western canon.

Gates was born in Keyser, West Virginia, to Henry Louis Gates Sr. and his wife Pauline Augusta (Coleman) Gates. He grew up in neighboring Piedmont. His father worked in a paper mill and moonlighted as a janitor, while his mother cleaned houses.

At the age of 14, Gates was injured playing touch football, fracturing the ball and socket joint of his hip, resulting in a slipped capital femoral epiphysis. The injury was misdiagnosed by a physician, who told Gates' mother that his problem was psychosomatic. When the physical damage finally healed, his right leg was two inches shorter than his left. Because of the injury, Gates now uses a cane when he walks.

Gates graduated from Piedmont High School in 1968 and attended Potomac State College of West Virginia University before transferring to Yale University, from which he graduated *summa cum laude.* and Phi Beta Kappa with a degree in history. The first African American to be awarded an Andrew W. Mellon Foundation Fellowship, Gates sailed on the *Queen Elizabeth 2* for England and University of Cambridge, where he studied English literature at Clare College and earned his PhD.

After a month at Yale Law School, Gates withdrew from the program. In October 1975 he was hired by Charles Davis as a secretary in the Afro-American Studies department at Yale. In July 1976, Gates was promoted to the post of Lecturer in Afro-American Studies, with the understanding that he would be promoted to assistant professor upon completion of his doctoral dissertation. Jointly appointed to assistant professorships in English and Afro-American Studies in 1979, Gates was promoted to associate professor in 1984. While at Yale, Gates guided Jodie Foster, who majored in African-American Literature there, writing her thesis on writer Toni Morrison.

Gates married Sharon Lynn Adams in 1979. They had two daughters together before they divorced in 1999.

In 1984, Gates was recruited by Cornell University with an offer of tenure; Gates asked Yale if they would match Cornell's offer, but they declined. Gates moved to Cornell in 1985, where he taught until 1989.

Following a two-year stay at Duke University, he was recruited to Harvard University in 1991. At Harvard, Gates teaches undergraduate and graduate courses as the Alphonse Fletcher University Professor, an endowed chair he was appointed to in 2006, and as a professor of English. Additionally, he is the Director of the Hutchins Center for African & African American Research.

His work has rooted African American literary criticism in the African American vernacular tradition. As a literary historian committed to the preservation and study of historical texts, Gates has been integral to the Black Periodical Literature Project, a digital archive of black newspapers and magazines created with financial assistance from the National Endowment for the Humanities. To build Harvard's visual, documentary, and literary archives of African-American texts, Gates arranged for the purchase of *The Image of the Black in Western Art,* a collection assembled by Dominique de Ménil in Houston.

As a result of research as a MacArthur Fellow, Gates discovered *Our Nig*, written by Harriet E. Wilson in 1859, and thought to be the first novel written in the United States by an African American. Later, he acquired and authenticated the manuscript of *The Bondwoman's Narrative* by Hannah Crafts, a novel from the same period that scholars believe may have been written as early as 1853; if so, it would have precedence as the first-known novel written in the

United States by an African American. *The Bondwoman's Narrative* was first published in 2002 and became a bestseller.

As a prominent black intellectual, Gates has concentrated on building academic institutions to study black culture. Additionally, he has worked to bring about social, educational, and intellectual equality for black Americans. His writing includes pieces in *The New York Times* that defend rap music, and an article in *Sports Illustrated* that criticizes black youth culture for glorifying basketball over education. In 1992, he received a George Polk Award for his social commentary in *The New York Times*. Gates's prominence has led to his being called as a witness on behalf of the controversial Florida rap group 2 Live Crew in an obscenity case. He argued that the material, which the government charged was profane, had important roots in African-American Vernacular English, games, and literary traditions, and should be protected.

Since 1995, Gates has been the jury chair for the Anisfield-Wolf Book Award, which honors written works that contribute to society's understanding of racism and the diversity of human culture. Gates was an Anisfield-Wolf prize winner in 1989 for *The Schomburg Library of Women Writers*.

Gates hosted *Faces of America*, a four-part series presented by PBS in 2010. This program examined the genealogy of 12 North Americans of diverse ancestry: Elizabeth Alexander, Mario Batali, Stephen Colbert, Louise Erdrich, Malcolm Gladwell, Eva Longoria, Yo-Yo Ma, Mike Nichols, Queen Noor of Jordan, Mehmet Oz, Meryl Streep, and Kristi Yamaguchi.

In addition to producing and hosting previous series on the history and genealogy of prominent American figures, since 2012 Gates has been host for four seasons of the television series *Finding Your*

Roots on PBS. It combines the work of expert researchers in genealogy, history, and genetics historic research to tell guests about their ancestors' lives and histories.

Henry has learned through contemporary research that his family is descended in part from the Yoruba people of West Africa. He also has learned that he has 50% European ancestry, including Irish; he was surprised it was that much. This notwithstanding, he grew up in the African American community and identifies as such. He has learned that he is also connected to the multiracial West Virginia community of Chestnut Ridge people.

Gates's critically acclaimed six-part PBS documentary series, *The African Americans: Many Rivers to Cross,* traced 500 years of African-American history to the second inauguration of President Barack Obama. Gates wrote, executive produced, and hosted the series, which earned the 2013 Peabody Award and a NAACP Image Award.

MICHAEL MCFARLAND

NABSE President, **Dr. Michael D. McFarland** is an educator who is committed to creating opportunities for success by removing barriers, aligning systems, implementing programs, instituting best practices and building the capacity of people to ensure higher levels of learning for all students.

Originally from Jasper, Texas, he earned a Bachelor of Business Administration in business education from Baylor University, a Master of Education in educational administration and superintendent certification from Stephen F. Austin University, and a Doctorate of Education in educational administration from Baylor.

In 1993, Dr. McFarland began his career in Tyler ISD as an algebra, accounting, and computer science teacher. He then served as principal of John Tyler High School in Tyler, Texas. When McFarland arrived at John Tyler, the school was low performing, academically unacceptable, and plagued with many challenges. Under Dr. McFarland's leadership, the school transformed into a high-performing high school that was recognized by the College Board with the 2006 National Inspiration Award. This award was only received by three schools in the nation and was given due to the increase in student performance and college and career readiness as measured by SAT and college acceptance. More than 92% of the students who graduated from John Tyler High under Dr. McFarland's leadership received letters of acceptance to a college, university, and/or the military.

Dr. McFarland then became principal at Foster Middle School in Longview, Texas. During his tenure as principal there, he was selected as the "Best Principal in East Texas" by the Longview News Journal. And Dr. McFarland relocated to Champaign, Illinois where he served as Assistant Superintendent of Achievement for Champaign Unit 4 Public Schools. While serving in Champaign, he led the development of a high school restructuring model that was adopted by the Illinois Board of Education as a model for transformation of low-performing secondary schools throughout the state. Dr. McFarland also was instrumental in the development and implementation of a collaborative multiagency partnership with the City of Champaign, Park District, and Unit 4 Schools called "Operation Hope in Garden Hills." This multiagency project included the "Lighted Schoolhouse" and was recognized nationally as a model approach for addressing school and community issues.

Dr. McFarland was the superintendent of the Lancaster Independent School District from 2010 to 2017. He led the district from a historically underperforming status to a nationally recognized, award-winning school district. Dr. Michael McFarland has been recognized at the state and national level for his outstanding leadership as a school superintendent. He was honored as the

National Alliance for Black School Educators Superintendent of the Year in 2014 and he was selected as the American Association of School Administrators National Superintendent of the Year from Texas in 2015.

Under his leadership, the district and school board received national recognition as the 2017 Urban School Board Excellence winner, the 2018 HEB Excellence in Education winner, the School Board of the Year winner from National Alliance of Black School Educators, and the Texas Outstanding School Board winner from the Texas Association of School Administrators. Persistent achievement gaps closed, and student performance consistently improved under his leadership.

Dr. McFarland is the current superintendent of the Crowley Independent School District, where he serves more than 15,000 students across 23 campuses. He is married to Cynthia McFarland and has two daughters, Kharis and Michiah, and two sons, Tyler and Jarrett.

There is a source of power in each of us that we don't realize until we take responsibility.
— **Diane Nash**

CHAPTER THREE – THE STUDENT
FEATURING STUDENTS THAT MADE A DIFFERENCE

The formal segregation of blacks and whites in the United States began long before the passage of Jim Crow laws following the end of the Reconstruction Era in 1877. The United States Supreme Court's Dred Scott v. Sandford decision upheld the denial of citizenship to African Americans and found that descendants of slaves are "so far inferior that they had no rights which the white man was bound to respect."

Following the American Civil War and the Emancipation Proclamation, the Fourteenth Amendment, guaranteeing "equal protection under the law", was ratified in 1868 and citizenship was extended to African Americans. Congress also passed the Civil Rights Act of 1875, banning racial discrimination in public accommodations. But in 1883, the Supreme Court struck down the Civil Rights Act of 1875, finding that discrimination by individuals or private businesses is constitutional.

The Reconstruction Era saw efforts at integration in the South, but Jim Crow laws followed and were also passed by state legislatures in the Southwest and Midwest, segregating blacks and whites in all aspects of public life, including attendance of public schools.

The level of racial segregation in schools has important implications for the educational outcomes of minority students. Desegregation efforts of the 1970s and 1980s led to substantial academic gains for black students; as integration increased, blacks' educational attainment increased while that of whites remained largely unchanged. Historically, greater access to schools with higher enrollments of white students helped "reduce blacks' high school dropout rate, reduce the black-white test score gap, and improve outcomes for black students.

Some of the students featured in this chapter were challenged by segregation and discriminative policies within their communities and in their schools; some were inspired by the accomplishments of their parents, politicians or celebrities; and some had personal childhood visions that inspired them to accomplish their dreams. Whatever the reason, these students have set an example that can be admired by others who may also grow up seeking accomplished role models to emulate.

JESSE ERNEST WILKINS JR.

Jesse Ernest Wilkins Jr. (November 27, 1923 – May 12, 2011) attended the University of Chicago at the age of 13, becoming its youngest ever student. His intelligence led to him being referred to as a "negro genius" in the media.

J Ernest Wilkins Jr was born into an African American Methodist family, being the son of J Ernest Wilkins Sr and Lucile Beatrice Robinson. His father J Ernest Wilkins Sr was a lawyer who went on to become President of the Cook County Bar Association in the early 1940s (Cook County is in northeastern Illinois and Chicago is in that County), and Assistant Secretary of Labor in the Eisenhower administration of the 1950s. His mother Lucile Robinson had been educated to the level of a Master's Degree and was trained as a schoolteacher.

In 1940 (at the age of 17) Jesse Ernest Wilkins Jr. completed his B.Sc. in math. In order to improve his rapport with the nuclear engineers reporting to him, Wilkins later received both bachelor's and master's degrees in mechanical engineering from New York University in 1982 and 2001, thus earning five science degrees during his life.

After initially failing to secure a research position at his alma mater in Chicago, Wilkins taught mathematics from 1943 to 1944 at the Tuskegee Institute (now Tuskegee University) in Tuskegee, Alabama.

In 1944 he returned to the University of Chicago where he served first as an associate mathematical physicist and then as a physicist in its Metallurgical Laboratory, as part of the Manhattan Project. Working under the direction of Arthur Holly Compton and Enrico Fermi, Wilkins researched the extraction of fissionable nuclear materials, but was not told of the research group's ultimate goal until after the atomic bomb was dropped on Hiroshima. Wilkins was the co-discoverer or discoverer of a number of phenomena in physics such as the Wilkins effect and the Wigner–Wilkins and Wilkins spectra.

Despite his stature and fame during his various careers he was often the target of unchecked racism. When Wilkins's team was about to be transferred to the Oak Ridge National Laboratory in Oak Ridge, Tennessee (known at the time as site "X"), due to the Jim Crow laws of the Southern United States, Wilkins would have been prevented from working there. When Edward Teller was informed about this, he wrote a letter on September 18, 1944 to Harold Urey (who was the director of war research at Columbia at the time) of Wilkins's abilities, informing him about the problem of Wilkins's race, and recommending his services for a new position.

Wilkins then continued to teach mathematics and conduct significant research in neutron absorption with physicist Eugene Wigner, including the development of its mathematical models. He would also later help design and develop nuclear reactors for electrical power generation, becoming part owner of one such company.

In 1970 Wilkins went on to serve Howard University as its distinguished professor of Applied Mathematical Physics and also founded the university's new PhD program in mathematics. During his tenure at Howard he undertook a sabbatical position as a visiting scientist at Argonne National Laboratory from 1976 to 1977.

From 1974 to 1975 Wilkins served as president of the American Nuclear Society and in 1976 became the second African American to be elected to the National Academy of Engineering.

From 1990 Wilkins lived and worked in Atlanta, Georgia as a Distinguished Professor of Applied Mathematics and Mathematical Physics at Clark Atlanta University, and retired again for his last time in 2003.

Throughout his years of research Wilkins published papers on a variety of subjects, including differential geometry, linear differential equations, integrals, nuclear engineering, gamma radiation shielding and optics, along the way.

Wilkins wrote more than 100 scientific papers, served in various important posts, garnered numerous professional and scientific awards and helped recruit minority students into the sciences. His career spanned seven decades and included significant contributions to pure and applied mathematics, civil and nuclear engineering, and optics.

Jesse Ernest Wilkins Jr. had two children with his first wife Gloria Louise Steward whom he married in June 1947, and subsequently married Maxine G. Malone in 1984. He was married a third time to Vera Wood Anderson in Chicago in September 2003. He had a daughter, Sharon, and a son, Wilkins III during his first marriage.

Jesse Ernest Wilkins Jr. died on May 1, 2011 in Fountain Hills, Arizona. He was survived by his two children, Sharon Wilkins Hill and J. Ernest Wilkins III, plus three grandchildren and two great-grandchildren, and was buried at the National Memorial Cemetery, Cave Creek, Arizona.

DIANE NASH

Diane Judith Nash (born May 15, 1938) is an American civil rights activist, and a leader and strategist of the student wing of the Civil Rights Movement.

Diane was born and raised in Chicago by her father Leon Nash and her mother Dorothy Bolton Nash in a middle-class Catholic area. Her father was a veteran of World War II. Her mother worked as a keypunch operator during the war, leaving Nash in the care of her grandmother, Carrie Bolton, until age 7. Bolton was a cultured woman, known for her refinement and manners.

After the war, Diane's parents' marriage ended. Dorothy married again to John Baker, a waiter on the railroad dining cars owned by the Pullman Company. Baker was a member of the Brotherhood of

Sleeping Car Porters, one of the most powerful black unions in the nation. As Dorothy no longer worked outside the house, Diane saw less of her grandmother Carrie Bolton, but she continued as an important influence in Diane's life. Bolton was committed to making sure her granddaughter understood her worth and value, and didn't discuss race often, believing that racial prejudice was something that was taught to younger generations by their elders. Her grandmother's words and actions instilled Diane with confidence and a strong sense of self-worth, while also creating a bit of a sheltered environment that left her vulnerable to the severity of racism in the outside world as she grew older.

Diane Nash attended Catholic schools, and at one point considered becoming a nun. She also was the runner-up in a regional beauty pageant leading to the competition for Miss Illinois.

After finishing Hyde Park High School in Chicago, Diane went to Washington, D.C. to attend Howard University, a historically black college (HBCU). After a year, she transferred to Fisk University in Nashville, Tennessee, where she majored in English. Diane acknowledged that she looked forward to personal growth during her time in college and wanted to explore the challenging issues of the time. In Nashville, she was first exposed to the full force of Jim Crow laws and customs and their effect on the lives of Blacks. Diane recounted her experience at the Tennessee State Fair when she had to use the "Colored Women" restroom, signifying the first time she had ever seen and been impacted by segregation signage. Outraged by the realities of segregation, Diane began to show signs of leadership and soon became a full-time activist.

Diane's family members were surprised when she joined the Civil Rights Movement. Her grandmother was quoted as saying, "Diane, you've gotten in with the wrong bunch;" she did not know that Diane was the chairwoman of organizing the nonviolent protests at her university. Her family was not familiar with the idea of working for civil rights. Diane Nash spoke of how it took her family time to come around to accept her as a key player in the Civil Rights Movement. But her mother was influenced by Diane's sense of empowerment and she began to use fundraising abilities to raise money for the Freedom Riders.

At Fisk, Nash searched for a way to challenge segregation. She began attending nonviolent civil disobedience workshops led by James Lawson, who, while in India, had studied Mahatma Gandhi's techniques of nonviolent direct action and passive resistance used in his political movement. By the end of her first semester at Fisk, Diane Nash had become one of Lawson's most devoted disciples. Although originally a reluctant participant in nonviolence, she emerged as a leader due to her well-spoken, composed manner when speaking to the authorities and to the press. In 1960 at age 22, Diane became the leader of the Nashville sit-ins, which lasted from February to May. This movement was unique for the time in that it was led by and composed primarily of college students and young people. The Nashville sit-ins spread to 69 cities across the United States.

Though protests would continue in Nashville and across the South, Diane Nash and three other students were first successfully served at the Post House Restaurant on March 17, 1960. Students continued the sit-ins at segregated lunch counters for months, accepting arrest in line with nonviolent principles. Diane Nash, with John Lewis, led the protesters in a policy of refusing to pay bail. In February 1961, Nash served jail time in solidarity with the "Rock Hill Nine"— nine students imprisoned after a lunch counter sit-in. They were all sentenced to pay a $50 fine for sitting at a whites-only lunch counter. Chosen as spokesperson, Nash said to the judge, "We feel that if we pay these fines we would be contributing to and supporting the injustice and immoral practices that have been performed in the arrest and conviction of the defendants."

When Nash asked Nashville's mayor, Ben West, on the steps of City Hall, "Do you feel it is wrong to discriminate against a person solely on the basis of their race or color?", the mayor admitted that he did. Three weeks later, the lunch counters of Nashville were serving blacks. Reflecting on this event, Diane said, "I have a lot of respect for the way he responded. He didn't have to respond the way he did. He said that he felt it was wrong for citizens of Nashville to be discriminated against at the lunch counters solely on the basis of the color of their skin. That was the turning point. That day was very important."

While participating in the Nashville sit-in, Diane Nash first met fellow protester, James Bevel, whom she would later marry. They had two children together, a son and a daughter. The couple divorced after seven years of marriage and Nash never remarried.

In August 1961, Diane Nash participated in a picket line to protest a local supermarket's refusal to hire blacks. When local white youths started egging the picket line and punching various people, police intervened. They arrested 15 people, only five of whom were the white attackers. All but one of the blacks who were jailed accepted the $5 bail and were freed. Nash stayed. The 21-year-old activist had insisted on her arrest with the other blacks, and once in jail, refused bail.

Diane Nash's campaigns were among the most successful of the era. Her efforts included the first successful civil rights campaign to integrate lunch counters (Nashville); the Freedom Riders, who desegregated interstate travel; co-founding the Student Nonviolent

Coordinating Committee (SNCC); and co-initiating the Alabama Voting Rights Project and working on the Selma Voting Rights Movement. This helped gain Congressional passage of the Voting Rights Act of 1965, which authorized the federal government to oversee and enforce state practices to ensure that African Americans and other minorities were not prevented from registering and voting.

In early 1961, Diane Nash and ten fellow students were put under arrest in Rock Hill, South Carolina, for protesting segregation. Once jailed, they would not accept the chance for bail. These dramatic events began to bring light to the fight for racial justice that was beginning to emerge. It also highlighted the idea of "jail, no bail", which was utilized by many other civil rights activists as the fight for rights progressed.

Diane Nash would go on to serve many roles for the SCLC from 1961 through 1965 while it was under Martin Luther King Jr. She cut ties with the SCLC, questioning their leadership structure, including their male- and clergy-dominated ranks. She would also split from SNCC in 1965 when their directives changed under Stokley Carmichael's leadership, taking particular issue with the organization's departure from the founding pillar of nonviolence.

The Freedom Rides, a protest against segregated bus terminals that took place on Greyhound buses from Washington D.C. to Virginia, were initially organized by the Congress of Racial Equality (CORE). However, they encountered a mob of angry segregationists as they entered Anniston, Alabama, and were brutally beaten and unable to finish the route. SNCC—under the direction of Barbara Nash—continued the protest from Birmingham, Alabama, to Jackson, Mississippi.

Before setting off with a group of 10 students from Nashville, Barbara Nash had received a call from John Seigenthaler, assistant to Attorney General Robert Kennedy Jr., who tried to persuade her to end the Freedom Rides, insisting the bloodshed would only continue if they persisted. She was unshaken by the stance of the White House and told Seigenthaler that they knew the risks involved and had already prepared their wills before continuing the Freedom Rides.

After the Civil Rights Movement, Barbara Nash moved back to Chicago where she worked in the fields of education and real estate, continuing as an advocate and championing causes such as fair housing and anti-war efforts. She still lives in Chicago, only a few miles away from her son Douglass Bevel, with whom she remains very close.

Diane Nash's contributions to the success of Civil Rights movement have been increasingly recognized in the years since. During the civil rights era and shortly after, many of the male leaders received most of the recognition for its successes. As the civil rights era has been studied by historians, Nash's contributions have been more fully recognized.

In 1963 President John F. Kennedy appointed Diane Nash to a national committee to promote civil rights legislation. Eventually his proposed bill was passed as the Civil Rights Act of 1964.

In 1965, SCLC gave its highest award, the Rosa Parks Award, to Diane Nash and James Bevel for their leadership in initiating and organizing the Alabama Project and the Selma Voting Rights Movement.

In addition, Diane Nash has received the Distinguished American Award from the John F. Kennedy Library and Foundation (2003), and the LBJ Award for Leadership in Civil Rights from the Lyndon Baines Johnson Library and Museum (2004).

In 2013, Diane Nash expressed her support for Barack Obama, while also sharing her reluctance for his continuing involvement in the wars in Iraq and Afghanistan. While encouraged by the positive implications associated with electing the first Black President of the United States, Diane Nash still believes that the true changes in American society will come from its citizens, not government officials.

Decades after she played a critical role in the Civil Rights Movement, Diane Nash remains committed to the principles of nonviolence that have guided her throughout her life. Although she was a key architect in many of the Movement's most successful efforts, she remains humble upon reflection. "It took many thousands of people to make the changes that we made, people whose names we'll never know. They'll never get credit for the sacrifices they've made, but I remember them.

THE GREENSBORO FOUR

The Greensboro Four were four young black men who staged the first sit-in at Greensboro: Ezell Blair Jr., David Richmond, Franklin McCain and Joseph McNeil. All four were students from North Carolina Agricultural and Technical College. They were influenced by the non-violent protest techniques practiced by Mohandas Gandhi, as well as the Freedom Rides organized by the Congress for Racial Equality (CORE) in 1947, in which interracial activists rode across the South in buses to test a recent Supreme Court decision banning segregation in interstate bus travel.

The Greensboro Four, as they became known, had also been spurred to action by the brutal murder in 1955 of a young black boy, Emmett Till, who had allegedly whistled at a white woman in a Mississippi store.

The **Greensboro sit-ins** were a series of nonviolent protests in Greensboro, North Carolina that started in 1960, when young African-American students staged a sit-in at a segregated Woolworth's lunch counter in Greensboro, North Carolina, and refused to leave after being denied service. The sit-in movement soon spread to college towns throughout the South. Though many of the protesters were arrested for trespassing, disorderly conduct or disturbing the peace, their actions made an immediate and lasting impact, forcing Woolworth's and other establishments to change their segregationist policies. While not the first sit-in of the Civil Rights Movement, the Greensboro sit-ins were an instrumental action, and also the most well-known sit-ins of the Civil Rights Movement. They are considered a catalyst to the subsequent sit-in movement. These sit-ins led to increased national sentiment at a crucial period in US history.

Blair, Richmond, McCain and McNeil planned their protest carefully, and enlisted the help of a local white businessman, Ralph Johns, to put their plan into action. On February 1, 1960, the four students sat down at the lunch counter at the Woolworth's in downtown Greensboro, where the official policy was to refuse service to anyone but whites. Denied service, the four young men refused to give up their seats.

Police arrived on the scene but were unable to take action due to the lack of provocation. By that time, Johns had already alerted the local media, who had arrived in full force to cover the events on television. The Greensboro Four stayed put until the store closed, then returned the next day with more students from local colleges.

By February 5, some 300 students had joined the protest at Woolworth's, paralyzing the lunch counter and other local businesses. Heavy television coverage of the Greensboro sit-ins sparked a sit-in movement that spread quickly to college towns throughout the South and into the North, as young blacks and whites joined in various forms of peaceful protest against segregation in libraries, beaches, hotels and other establishments.

By the end of March, the movement had spread to 55 cities in 13 states. Though many were arrested for trespassing, disorderly conduct or disturbing the peace, national media coverage of the sit-ins brought increasing attention to the civil rights movement.

In response to the success of the sit-in movement, dining facilities across the South were being integrated by the summer of 1960. At the end of July, when many local college students were on summer vacation, the Greensboro Woolworth's quietly integrated its lunch counter. Four black Woolworth's employees—Geneva Tisdale, Susie Morrison, Anetha Jones and Charles Best—were the first to be served.

In 2002, North Carolina A&T commissioned a statue to be sculpted honoring Khazan, along with the three other members of the A&T four: Franklin McCain, Joseph McNeil, and David Richmond. The sculpture named *February One* was unveiled during the 42nd anniversary of the Greensboro Sit-ins. In addition, the four men each have residence halls named for them on the university campus. Also, the section of the lunch counter where McCain and his fellow protesters sat is now preserved at the National Museum of American History.

Ezell Blair (now Jibreel Khazan) and Joseph McNeil are the last two surviving members of the Greensboro Four. Franklin Eugene McCain died January 9, 2014. David Richmond, the fourth member and McCain's freshman college roommate, died in 1990.

MOZIAH BRIDGES

Moziah Bridges was born (November 13, 2001) and raised in Memphis, Tennessee. Moziah is the President and Creative Director of Mo's Bows. Mo's Bows mission is to make you look and feel your best while catering to the sometimes conservative, fun-loving lady or gentleman.

When he was just four years old, Moziah would wear a suit and tie whenever possible and insisted on dressing himself. A few years later, Moziah wanted an accessory to help him look sharp, but didn't see anything out there that fit his style or personality. He liked to wear bow ties, in particular, because they made him look good and feel good; so, with the help of his granny, young Moziah started making his own bow ties.

Moziah's business, Mo's Bows, was born of his love for bow ties and his dissatisfaction with the selection available for kids his age. Even worse than the poor color selection, they were all clip-ons-- Bridges believed real men should tie their own ties. His grandmother taught him to sew by hand and to use a sewing machine, using scraps to create his favorite neckwear.

So, at the age of nine, in 2011 Moziah Bridges began his bowtie company, Mo's Bows. He enlisted the help of both his mother and his grandmother, a retired seamstress, to start selling colorful and expressive bowties online and across Memphis, Tennessee.

Within a few months, he had created his own collection of more than two dozen bow ties. Friends and family fell in love with Moziah's creations. He upped his production, fashioning tidy bow ties from his grandmother's vintage fabrics in an array of floral and African prints, and even scraps of old taffeta dresses.

As if his early success in business weren't enough, Moziah Bridges has also become something of a young philanthropist. He donated $1,600 to send 10 children from his hometown of Memphis to Glenview Summer Camp. Giving back to his community helps him feel humble and it makes him smile because he sees other kids smiling and enjoying the camp.

Word of mouth worked its magic, and soon Bridges was taking orders through Facebook and selling on his own Etsy store. As demand increased, his mother, grandmother, and other family members came on board to help with production. Not yet a teenager, his company had five staff members and received a ton of media attention, from features in *O* magazine and *Vogue*.

Over the next three years, while his classmates were doing homework and playing sports, Moziah Bridges built himself a $150,000 business. At the age of eleven he made an appearance on the TV show *Shark Tank* where he met Daymond John, who became his mentor as a result of Moziah's *Shark Tank* appearance. He never imagined the baby business that he started at his grandmother's kitchen table in South Memphis, Tennessee would one day be an internationally recognized brand.

Today, each bow tie is still sewn from scratch, though Moziah has expanded from vintage materials to tweeds and ginghams, with a formal line of satins and silk. His bow ties are available in his own webstore, on Etsy, and in boutiques throughout Texas, South Carolina, and Tennessee, as well as in stores like Bloomingdales and Neiman Marcus. You can also buy his "Go Mo" bowtie online to support his nonprofit, which provides opportunities to send Memphis children to summer camps. Mo's Bows can also boast that its clients include Barack Obama and Steve Harvey, but his favorite bowtie made for the 2015 NBA Draft was for Willie Caulie-Stein.

Moziah's dream is to become a fashion mogul. When he graduates high school in 2020 he plans to go to college and study fashion design and start a full clothing line by the time he's 20.

Any time, any time while I was a slave, if one minute's freedom had been offered to me, and I had been told I must die at the end of that minute, I would have taken it—just to stand one minute on God's airth a free woman— I would.
– **Elizabeth Freeman**

CHAPTER FOUR - THE COMMUNITY
FEATURING CIVIL RIGHTS LEADERS AND ACTIVISTS
18TH – 19TH CENTURY

Civil rights are designed to achieve equal social opportunities and equal protection for all people under the law, regardless of race, religion, or other personal characteristics. Leaders of the political movement dedicated to securing equal opportunity for members of minority groups are most often defined as civil rights leaders, civil rights workers, or civil rights activists.

Whatever the definition, it should be known that all the men and women who have participated in one phase or another of the civil rights movement in order to gain equal rights for everyone cannot be limited to a specific era, nationality or nation.

Examples of civil rights include the right to vote, the right to a fair trial, the right to government services, the right to a public education, the right to use public facilities; and most importantly, the right to freedom.

For thousands of years the wars, battles and struggles to gain civil rights for people of all colors and cultures has witnessed countless martyrs, many of whom gave up their lives for the cause of freedom and equal opportunities. Most of these notable civil rights leaders changed the course of history through their activism.

Featured in Chapter Four - "The Community," are leaders who have gone above and beyond to protect and or secure the Civil Rights of their fellow citizens. Part One includes those who prevailed in the 18th and 19th Centuries and part Two includes the 20th and 21st Centuries.

ELIZABETH FREEMAN

Elizabeth Freeman (c.1744—December 28, 1829), also known as Bet, Mum Bett, or MumBet, was the first enslaved African American to file and win a freedom suit in Massachusetts.

Freeman was born into slavery around 1744 at the farm of Pieter Hogeboom in Claverack, New York, where she was given the name Bet. When Hogeboom's daughter Hannah married John Ashley of Sheffield, Massachusetts, Hogeboom gave Bet, around seven years old, to Hannah and her husband. Freeman remained with them until 1781, during which time she had a child, Little Bet. She is said to have married, though no marriage record has been located. Her husband (name unknown) is said to have never returned from service in the American Revolutionary War.

Throughout her life, Bet exhibited a strong spirit and sense of self. She came into conflict with Hannah Ashley, who was raised in the strict Dutch culture of the New York colony. In 1780, Bet prevented Hannah from striking a servant girl with a heated shovel; Elizabeth shielded the girl and received a deep wound in her arm. As the wound healed, Bet left it uncovered as evidence of her harsh treatment.

The Massachusetts Supreme Judicial Court ruling, in Freeman's favor, found slavery to be inconsistent with the 1780 Massachusetts State Constitution. Her suit, *Brom and Bett v. Ashley* (1781), was cited in the Massachusetts Supreme Judicial Court appellate review of Quock Walker's freedom suit. When the court upheld Walker's freedom under the state's constitution, the ruling was considered to have implicitly ended slavery in Massachusetts.

Freeman was illiterate and left no written records of her life. Her early history has been pieced together from the writings of contemporaries to whom she told her story or who heard it indirectly, as well as from historical records.

John Ashley was a Yale-educated lawyer, wealthy landowner, businessman and leader in the community. His house was the site of many political discussions and the probable location of the signing of the Sheffield Resolves, which predated the Declaration of Independence.

In 1780, Freeman heard the newly ratified Massachusetts Constitution read at a public gathering in Sheffield, including the following:

All men are born free and equal, and have certain natural, essential, and unalienable rights; among which may be reckoned the right of enjoying and defending their lives and liberties; that of acquiring, possessing, and protecting property; that of seeking and obtaining their safety and happiness. — *Massachusetts Constitution, Article 1.*

Inspired by these words, Bett sought the counsel of Theodore Sedgwick, a young abolition-minded lawyer, to help her sue for freedom in court. According to Catherine Sedgwick's account, she told him, "I heard that paper read yesterday, that says, all men are created equal, and that every man has a right to freedom. I'm not a dumb critter; won't the law give me my freedom?"

After much deliberation Sedgwick accepted her case, as well as that of Brom, another of Ashley's slaves. He enlisted the aid of Tapping Reeve, the founder of Litchfield Law School, one of America's earliest law schools, located in Litchfield, Connecticut. They were two of the top lawyers in Massachusetts, and Sedgwick later served as US Senator.

The case of *Brom and Bett v. Ashley* was heard in August 1781 before the County Court of Common Pleas in Great Barrington. Sedgwick and Reeve asserted that the constitutional provision that "all men are born free and equal" effectively abolished slavery in the state. When the jury ruled in Bett's favor, she became the first African American woman to be set free under the Massachusetts state constitution.

The jury found that "...Brom & Bett are not, nor were they at the time of the purchase of the original writ, the legal Negro of the said John Ashley... The court assessed damages of thirty shillings and awarded both plaintiffs compensation for their labor. Ashley initially appealed the decision, but a month later dropped his appeal, apparently having decided the court's ruling on constitutionality of slavery was "final and binding".

After the ruling, Bett took the name Elizabeth Freeman. Although Ashley asked her to return to his house and work for wages, she chose to work in attorney Sedgwick's household. She worked for his family until 1808 as senior servant and governess to the Sedgwick children, who called her "Mumbet." The Sedgwick children included Catharine Sedgwick, who became a well-known author and wrote an account of her governess's life. Also working at the Sedgwick household during much of this time was Agrippa Hull, a free black man who had served with rebel forces for years during the Revolutionary War.

From the time Freeman gained her freedom, she became widely recognized and in demand for her skills as a healer, midwife and nurse. After the Sedgwick children were grown, Freeman moved into her own house on Cherry Hill in Stockbridge near her daughter, grandchildren and great grandchildren.

Freeman's real age was never known, but an estimate on her tombstone puts her age at about 85 at the time of her death. She died in December 1829 and was buried in the Sedgwick family plot in Stockbridge, Massachusetts. Freeman remains the only non-Sedgwick buried in the Sedgwick plot.

THADDEUS STEVENS

Thaddeus Stevens (April 4, 1792 – August 11, 1868) was born in Danville, Vermont, in poverty. He was the second of four children, all boys, and was named to honor the Polish general who served in the American Revolution, Thaddeus Kościuszko. His parents were Baptists who had emigrated from Massachusetts around 1786. Thaddeus was born with a club foot which left him with a permanent limp, at the time seen as a judgment from God for secret parental sin—and his older brother was born with the condition in both feet. The boys' father, Joshua Stevens, was a farmer and cobbler who struggled to make a living in Vermont. After fathering two more sons (born without disability) Joshua abandoned the children and his wife Sarah. The circumstances of his departure and his subsequent fate are uncertain.

Sarah Stevens struggled to make a living from the farm, with the increasing aid of her sons. She was determined that her sons improve themselves, and in 1807 moved the family to the neighboring town of Peacham, Vermont, where she enrolled young Thaddeus in the Caledonia Grammar School (often called the Peacham Academy). He suffered much from the taunts of his classmates for his disability.

After graduation, Thaddeus enrolled at the University of Vermont but suspended his studies due to the federal government's appropriation of campus buildings during the War of 1812. Stevens then enrolled in the sophomore class at Dartmouth College in Hanover, New Hampshire. At Dartmouth, despite a stellar academic career, he was not elected to Phi Beta Kappa; this was reportedly a scarring experience for him.

Stevens graduated from Dartmouth in 1814, and was chosen as a speaker at the commencement ceremony. Afterwards, he returned to Peacham and briefly taught there. Stevens also began to study law with John Mattocks. In early 1815, correspondence with friend Samuel Merrill, a fellow Vermonter who had moved to York, Pennsylvania to become preceptor of the York Academy, led to an offer for Stevens to join the academy faculty. He moved to York to teach and continued the study of law in the offices of David Cossett.

In Pennsylvania, Stevens taught school at the York Academy and continued his studies for the bar. Local lawyers passed a resolution barring from membership anyone who had "followed any other profession while preparing for admission," a restriction likely aimed at Stevens. Undaunted, he reportedly (according to a story he often retold) presented himself and four bottles of Madeira wine to the examining board in nearby Harford County, Maryland, and few questions were asked but much wine drunk. He left Bel Air the next morning with a certificate allowing him, through reciprocity, to practice law anywhere. Stevens then went to Gettysburg, the seat of Adams County, where he opened an office in September 1816.

He was involved in the first ten cases to reach the Supreme Court of Pennsylvania from Adams County after he began practice, and won nine. One case he later wished he had not won was *Butler v. Delaplaine*, in which he successfully reclaimed a slave on behalf of her owner.

In Gettysburg, Stevens also began his involvement in politics, serving six one-year terms on the borough council between 1822 and 1831 and becoming its president. He took the profits from his practice and invested them in Gettysburg real estate, becoming the largest landowner in the community by 1825, and had an interest in several iron furnaces outside town.

Stevenson quickly became a successful lawyer in Gettysburg, Pennsylvania. He interested himself in municipal affairs, and then in politics. He was elected to the Pennsylvania House of Representatives, where he became a strong advocate of free public education.

At the 1837 Pennsylvania constitutional convention, Stevens, who was a delegate, fought against the disenfranchisement of African-Americans. After he moved to Lancaster, a city not far from the Mason–Dixon line, he became active in the Underground Railroad, not only defending people believed to be fugitive slaves, but coordinating the movements of those seeking freedom. A 2003 renovation at his former home in Lancaster disclosed that there was a hidden cistern, attached to the main building by a concealed tunnel, in which escaped slaves hid.

Financial setbacks in 1842 caused Stevens to move his home and practice to the larger city of Lancaster, Pennsylvania. He knew

Lancaster County was an Anti-Mason and Whig stronghold, which ensured that he retained a political base. Within a short period, he was earning more than any other Lancaster attorney; by 1848 he had reduced his debts to $30,000 and paid them off soon after. It was in Lancaster that he engaged the services of Lydia Hamilton Smith, a housekeeper, whose racial makeup was described as mulatto, and who remained with him the rest of his life.

There, he also joined the Whig Party, and was elected to Congress in 1848. When 31st United States Congress convened in December 1849, Stevens took his seat, joining other newly elected slavery opponents such as Salmon P. Chase. Stevens spoke out against the Compromise of 1850, crafted by Kentucky Senator Henry Clay, that gave victories to both North and South, but would allow for some of the territories of the United States recently gained from Mexico to become slave states.

Stevens was easily re-nominated and reelected in 1850, even though his stance caused him problems among pro-Compromise Whigs. In 1851, Stevens was one of the defense lawyers in the trial of 38 African Americans and three others in federal court in Philadelphia on treason charges. The defendants had been implicated in the so-called Christiana Riot, in which an attempt to enforce a Fugitive Slave Act warrant had resulted in the killing of the slaveowner. Justice Robert Grier of the U.S. Supreme Court, as circuit justice, tried the case, and instructed the jury to acquit on the grounds that though the defendants might be guilty of murder or riot, they were not charged with that, and were not guilty of treason. The well-publicized incident (and others like it) increased polarization over the issue of slavery and made Stevens a prominent face of Northern abolitionism.

Despite this trend, Stevens suffered political problems. He left the Whig caucus in December 1851. His activities as a lawyer and politician in opposition to slavery cost him votes and he did not seek reelection in 1852.

Out of office, Stevens concentrated on the practice of law in Lancaster, remaining one of the leading attorneys in the state. He stayed active in politics, and in 1854, to gain more votes for the anti-slavery movement, he joined the nativist Know Nothing Party. In 1855, Stevens joined the new Republican Party. Other former Whigs who were anti-slavery joined as well, including William H. Seward of New York, Charles E. Sumner of Massachusetts, and Abraham Lincoln of Illinois.

Stevens was a delegate to the 1856 Republican National Convention, where he supported Justice McLean, as he had in 1832. Stevens then returned to the practice of law, but in 1858, with the President and his party unpopular and the nation torn by such controversies as the Dred Scott decision, Stevens saw an opportunity to return to Congress. After a brief flirtation with the Know-Nothing Party, Stevens joined the newly formed Republican Party, and as the Republican nominee, he was easily elected. Democratic papers were appalled. One banner headline read, "Niggerism Triumphant".

Stevens took his seat in the 36th United States Congress in December 1859, only days after the hanging of John Brown, who had attacked the federal arsenal at Harpers Ferry hoping to cause a slave insurrection. Stevens opposed Brown's violent actions at the time, though later, he was more approving. Stevens, until the outbreak of the American Civil War, took the public position that he supported slavery's end and opposed its expansion.

As chairman of the House Ways and Means Committee during the American Civil War, he played a leading role, focusing his attention on defeating the Confederacy, financing the war with new taxes and borrowing, crushing the power of slave owners, ending slavery, and securing equal rights for the Freedmen.

Stevens argued that slavery should not survive the war; he was frustrated by the slowness of U.S. President Abraham Lincoln to support his position. As the war progressed towards a Northern victory, Stevens came to believe that not only should slavery be abolished, but that African Americans should be given a stake in the South's future through the confiscation of land from planters to be distributed to the freedmen. His plans went too far for the Moderate Republicans and were not enacted.

"Forty acres and a mule" is part of Special Field Orders No. 15, a post-Civil War promise proclaimed by Union General William Tecumseh Sherman on January 16, 1865, to allot family units, including freed people, a plot of land no larger than 40 acres. Sherman later ordered the army to lend mules for the agrarian reform effort.

Many freed people believed, after being told by various political figures, that they had a right to own the land they had long worked as slaves and were eager to control their own property. Freed people widely expected to legally claim 40 acres of land and a mule after the end of the war.

Some land redistribution occurred under military jurisdiction during the war and for a brief period thereafter. However, federal and state policy during the Reconstruction era emphasized wage labor, not land ownership, for blacks. Almost all land allocated during the war was restored to its pre-war white owners. Several black communities did maintain control of their land, and some families obtained new land by homesteading. Black land ownership increased markedly in Mississippi during the 19th century, particularly. Most blacks acquired land through private transactions, with ownership peaking at 15,000,000 acres in 1910, before an extended financial recession caused problems that resulted in the loss of property for many.

In July 1861, Stevens secured the passage of an act to confiscate the property, including slaves, of certain rebels. In November 1861, Stevens introduced a resolution to emancipate all slaves; it was defeated. However, the legislation did pass that abolished slavery in the District of Columbia and in the territories.

Stevens quickly adopted the Emancipation Proclamation for use in his successful re-election campaign. The Emancipation Proclamation was a wartime measure, did not apply to all slaves, and might be reversed by peacetime courts; an amendment would be slavery's end.

The Thirteenth Amendment—which outlawed slavery and involuntary servitude except as punishment for crime—easily passed the Senate, but failed in the House in June. The amendment passed narrowly after heavy pressure exerted by Lincoln himself.

After passing the Thirteenth Amendment, Congress debated the economic rights of the freedmen. Urged on by Stevens, it voted to authorize the Bureau of Refugees, Freedmen, and Abandoned Lands, with a mandate (though no funding) to set up schools and to distribute "not more than forty acres" of confiscated Confederate land to each family of freed slaves.

On the evening of April 14, 1865, Lincoln was assassinated by Confederate sympathizer John Wilkes Booth. In May 1865, Andrew Johnson began what came to be known as "Presidential

Reconstruction": Johnson did not push the states to protect the rights of freed slaves, and immediately began to counteract the land reform policies of the Freedmen's Bureau.

Violence against African-Americans was common and unpunished in the South; the new legislatures enacted Black Codes, depriving the freedmen of most civil rights.

Stevens led the delegation of House members sent to inform the Senate of Andrew Johnson's impeachment, though, because of his declining health he had to be carried to its doors by his bearers. During the recess of the impeachment court, the Republicans met in convention in Chicago and nominated Grant for president.

When Congress adjourned in late July, Stevens remained in Washington, too ill to return to Pennsylvania. On the afternoon of August 11, his doctor warned that he would probably not last through the night. His longtime housekeeper and companion, Lydia Hamilton Smith, his nephew Thaddeus, and friends gathered by him. Two black preachers came to pray by him, telling him that he had the prayers of all their people. Thaddeus Stevens died on the night of August 11, 1868.

LUCRETIA MOTT

Lucretia (Coffin) Mott (January 3, 1793 – November 11, 1880) was born in Nantucket, Massachusetts, the second child of Anna Folger and Thomas Coffin. Through her mother, she was a descendent of Peter Folger and Mary Morrell Folger. Her cousin was Framer Benjamin Franklin, while other Folger relatives were Tories.

She was sent at the age of 13 to the Nine Partners School, located in Dutchess County, New York, which was run by the Society of Friends. There she became a teacher after graduation. Her interest in women's rights began when she discovered that male teachers at the school were paid significantly more than female staff. After her family moved to Philadelphia, she and James Mott, another teacher at Nine Partners, followed. On April 10, 1811, Lucretia Coffin married James Mott at Pine Street Meeting in Philadelphia.

Lucretia Mott was a Quaker preacher early in her adulthood. Like many Quakers, Mott considered slavery to be evil. Inspired in part by minister Elias Hicks, she and other Quakers refused to use cotton cloth, cane sugar, and other slavery-produced goods. In 1821, Mott became a Quaker minister. With her husband's support, she traveled extensively as a minister, and her sermons emphasized the Quaker inward light, or the presence of the Divine within every individual. Her sermons also included her free produce and anti-slavery sentiments.

In 1833, Lucretia's husband helped found the American Anti-Slavery Society. By then, an experienced minister and abolitionist, Lucretia Mott was the only woman to speak at the organizational meeting in Philadelphia. She tested the language of the society's Constitution and bolstered support when many delegates were precarious. Days after the conclusion of the convention, at the urging of other delegates, Mott and other white and black women founded the Philadelphia Female Anti-Slavery Society. Integrated from its founding, the organization opposed both slavery and racism, and developed close ties to Philadelphia's Black community. Mott herself often preached at Black parishes. Around this time, Mott's sister-in-law, Abigail Lydia Mott, and brother-in-law, Lindley Murray Moore, were helping to found the Rochester Anti-Slavery Society.

Women's participation in the anti-slavery movement threatened societal norms. Many members of the abolitionist movement opposed public activities by women, especially public speaking. At the Congregational Church General Assembly, delegates agreed on a pastoral letter warning women that lecturing directly defied St. Paul's instruction for women to keep quiet in church.(1 Timothy 2:12) Other people opposed women's speaking to mixed crowds of men and women, which they called "promiscuous." Others were uncertain about what was proper, as the rising popularity of the Grimké sisters and other women speakers attracted support for abolition.

Lucretia attended all three national Anti-Slavery Conventions of American Women (1837, 1838, 1839). During the 1838 convention in Philadelphia, a mob destroyed Pennsylvania Hall, a newly opened meeting place built by abolitionists. Mott and the white and black women delegates linked arms to exit the building safely through the crowd. Afterward, the mob targeted her home and Black institutions and neighborhoods in Philadelphia. As a friend redirected the mob, Mott waited in her parlor, willing to face her violent opponents.

Amidst social persecution by abolition opponents and pain from dyspepsia, Lucretia continued her work for the abolitionist cause. She managed their household budget to extend hospitality to guests, including fugitive slaves, and donated to charities. Lucretia was praised for her ability to maintain her household while contributing to the cause.

In June 1840, Lucretia Mott attended the General Anti-Slavery Convention, better known as the World's Anti-Slavery Convention, in London, England. In spite of Lucretia's status as one of six women delegates, before the conference began, the men voted to exclude the American women from participating, and the female delegates were required to sit in a segregated area. Anti-slavery leaders didn't want the women's rights issue to become associated with the cause of ending slavery worldwide and dilute the focus on abolition. In addition, the social mores of the time generally prohibited women's participation in public political life. Several of the American men attending the convention, including William Lloyd Garrison and Wendell Phillips, protested the women's exclusion. Garrison, Nathaniel Peabody Rogers, William Adam, and African American activist Charles Lenox Remond sat with the women in the segregated area.

Activists Elizabeth Cady Stanton and her husband Henry Brewster Stanton attended the convention while on their honeymoon. Stanton admired Mott, and the two women became united as friends and allies.

Lucretia Mott was among the women included in the commemorative painting of the convention, which also featured female British activists: Elizabeth Pease, Mary Anne Rawson, Anne Knight, Elizabeth Tredgold and Mary Clarkson, daughter of Thomas Clarkson.

Encouraged by active debates in England and Scotland, Lucretia also returned with new energy for the anti-slavery cause in the United States. She continued an active public lecture schedule, with destinations including the major Northern cities of New York City and Boston, as well as travel over several weeks to slave-owning states, with speeches in Baltimore, Maryland and other cities in Virginia. She arranged to meet with slave owners to discuss the morality of slavery. In the District of Columbia, Lucretia timed her lecture to coincide with the return of Congress from Christmas recess; more than 40 Congressmen attended.

In 1848 Lucretia was invited by Jane Hunt to a meeting that led to the first meeting about women's rights. Mott helped write the Declaration of Sentiments during the 1848 Seneca Falls Convention.

Lucretia and James Mott had six children. Their second child, Thomas Mott, died at age two. Their surviving children all became active in the anti-slavery and other reform movements, following in their parents' paths. Her great-granddaughter May Hallowell Loud became an artist. Mott's great-granddaughter served briefly as the

Italian interpreter for American feminist Betty Friedan during a controversial speaking engagement in Rome.

Lucretia's speaking abilities made her an important abolitionist, feminist, and reformer. When slavery was outlawed in 1865, she advocated giving former slaves who had been bound to slavery laws within the boundaries of the United States, whether male or female, the right to vote. She remained a central figure in the abolition and suffrage movement until her death.

Lucretia Mott died on November 11, 1880 of pneumonia at her home, Roadside, in Cheltenham, Pennsylvania. In 1983, Mott was inducted into the National Women's Hall of Fame.

CHARLES LENOX REMOND

Charles Lenox Remond, (February 1, 1810 – December 22, 1873) was the first black professional antislavery lecturer, he devoted his life to lecturing against prejudice and slavery and advocating equal rights for free blacks.

Charles Remond was born in Salem, Massachusetts. His parents, John and Nancy Lenox Remond, had been married by the Rev. Thomas Paul, a prominent African American minister and antislavery activist, in 1807. Nancy Lenox's father was a veteran of the American Revolution, having fought with the Continental Army. John Remond, a descendant of French West Indian immigrants, had emigrated from the Dutch colony of Curacao as a young boy in 1798. In Salem, John Remond was first a barber and, then, with the assistance of his wife, he operated a successful catering business.

The Remonds were also active abolitionists. John became a life-long member of the Massachusetts Anti-Slavery Association.

Charles was the second child and the eldest son of eight children. His siblings included sisters Nancy, Cecilia, Maritchie Juan, Caroline, and Sarah Parker, and a younger brother John Remond. As free blacks, Charles and his sisters, grew up middle class, well educated, and very involved in the abolition movement. Sarah was active in the Salem Female Antislavery Society and the Massachusetts Antislavery Society. In 1856, she became an agent for the American Antislavery Society. Caroline served on the executive committee of the American Antislavery Society.

Charles Remond began his career as a public speaker on behalf of the antislavery movement at the age of seventeen. While in his twenties, Remond started speaking for abolition at public gatherings and conferences in Massachusetts, Rhode Island, Maine, New York and Pennsylvania. Remond proposed resolution at the first national Colored Convention in Philadelphia, PA (1830) calling for blacks to leave "*en masse*" any church "that discriminated against them in seating or at the communion table." Their resolution was adopted.

A supporter of William Lloyd Garrison, in 1832, Remond began work as an agent for The Liberator, and later, the Weekly Advocate and the Colored American. He travelled throughout New England delivering antislavery lectures and drumming up financial support for abolitionist publications.

Charles Remond began his abolitionist career in 1838 as a lecturer for the Massachusetts Antislavery Society when he became one of the original seventeen members of the American Antislavery Society, the first nationwide society. Later, he served as secretary of the American Antislavery Society and vice president of the New

England Antislavery Society, as well as president of his county abolition unit. For several years, Remond was the most distinguished black abolitionist in America, eclipsed only in 1841 by Frederick A. Douglass (with whom he often clashed in the 1840s and 1850s because of Douglass's popularity in the movement). He received recognition as a reformer and an advocate of equality for all people.

Remond spoke at public meetings in Massachusetts, Rhode Island, Maine, New York, and Pennsylvania. While a lecturer for the Massachusetts Antislavery Society, he supported leading white abolitionist William Lloyd Garrison, founder of the American Antislavery Society, concerning the principles of nonviolence and nonvoting. He believed, along with Garrison, in the creation of a totally color-blind society, one in which race had no influence at all.

In 1840, Remond traveled with Garrison on a European tour for nineteen months as a representative at the World's Anti-Slavery Convention in London to gain support for the abolitionist cause and to speak against America's mistreatment of African Americans. Remond gave a lecture at the World Anti-Slavery Convention in London, where he was greeted by repeated applause. While in Great Britain, he appealed to British abolitionist organizations, where his lectures against slavery received high acclaim.

In 1841, Remond traveled to Ireland to gain antislavery support and reduce the influence of Irish proslavery sentiment in America. In his lectures, he described America's slave system and the oppression of free blacks. He helped compose "An Address of the People of Ireland to Their Countrymen and Countrywomen in America." Members of the Hibernian Antislavery Society and other interested volunteers distributed it until it had 60,000 signatures, and 70,000 had been signed by the final count in 1842. He was the first African

American to address the Massachusetts state legislature to protest racial discrimination on railroads and steamboats.

In 1843, Charles Remond spoke at the national antislavery convention in Buffalo, New York, and criticized black abolitionist Henry Highland Garnet's address at the convention advising slaves to liberate themselves through violence.

By 1847, Remond began to abandon his nonviolence stance to end slavery. He advised slaves to take matters in their own hands against their masters to overthrow slavery.

Remond was married in September 1850 to Amy Matilda (Williams) Cassey (1809–56), the daughter of Rev. Peter Williams, Jr. She was the widow of wealthy Philadelphia barber Joseph Cassey, with whom she had eight children and an adopted daughter, Annie E. Wood, the maternal aunt of Charlotte Forten Grimke. After her marriage to Remond, she moved to Salem, where she lived until her death on August 15, 1856.

Remond had a close relationship with his sister Sarah Parker Remond, who also enjoyed a successful career as an abolitionist speaker. During the 1850s, they often travelled together on the lecture circuit. He spoke against the *Dred Scott* Supreme Court decision (1857), which ruled that the Constitution did not include rights for blacks, thus depriving them of citizenship and due process of law.

Remond married again, to Elizabeth Magee, a native of Virginia, in Newton on July 5, 1858. The abolitionist preacher, Rev. Theodore Parker, officiated. Before her death in 1871, Elizabeth and Remond had four children: Amy Matilda (1859–72), Charles Lenox, Jr. (1860–82), Wendell Phillips (1863–66), and Albert Ernest Remond (1866–1903).

At the State Convention of Massachusetts Negroes in New Bedford in 1858, he encouraged convention delegates to support an insurrection among the slaves, declaring that he would rather have them die than live in slavery. He remained vigilant against slavery and supported the upcoming war to end it.

During the Civil War, Remond joined other black abolitionist men, including Frederick Douglass, in the recruitment of African American soldiers into the all-black Massachusetts Fifty-Fourth Regiment of the Union Army, led by Colonel Robert Gould Shaw, a member of a prominent white abolitionist family from Boston. He was active in recruiting black troops for the 54th Massachusetts Infantry, the first northern all-black regiment in the United States Colored Troops (USCT) unit. He was also active in supporting the United States Colored Troops.

After the war, Charles Remond moved to Boston, where he worked as a clerk in the United States Customs House. He also worked as a streetlamp inspector. He later purchased a farm in South Reading (now Wakefield), Massachusetts. Remond also continued to deliver public lectures protesting racism. A staunch opponent of segregation of any kind, Remond joined the American Equal Rights Association in 1867. He embarked on his last lecture tour that year in western New York.

Charles Lenox Remond died in December 22, 1873 at his home in Wakefield, Massachusetts and was buried at Harmony Grove Cemetery in Salem.

HENRY HIGHLAND GARNET

Henry Highland Garnet (December 23, 1815 – February 13, 1882) was an African-American abolitionist, minister, educator and orator. Having escaped with his family as a child from slavery in Maryland, he grew up in New York City.

Henry Highland Garnet was born into slavery in Chesterville (then New Market), Kent County, Maryland. Garnet's father was George Trusty and his enslaved mother was "a woman of extraordinary energy." In 1824, the family, which included a total of 11 members, secured permission to attend a funeral, and from there, they all escaped in a covered wagon, first reaching Wilmington, Delaware.

When Henry was ten years old, his family reunited and moved to New York City, where from 1826 through 1833, he attended the African Free School, and the Phoenix High School for Colored Youth. While in school, Henry began his career in abolitionism.

In 1834, Garnet joined William H. Day and David Ruggles to establish the all-male Garrison Literary and Benevolent Association. It garnered mass support among whites, but the club ultimately had to move due to racist feelings. One year later, in 1835, Henry started studies at the Noyes Academy in Canaan, New Hampshire. Anti-abolitionists and segregationists protested and eventually forced the academy to close after a mob of them attacked it.

Garnett completed his education at the Oneida Institute in Whitesboro, New York, which had recently admitted all races. Here he was acclaimed for his wit, brilliance, and rhetorical skills. In 1839, after graduation, Garnet moved with his family to Troy, New York, where he taught school and studied theology. That same year, he injured his knee playing sports. It never recovered, and two years later, his lower leg had to be amputated.

In 1841 Garnet married abolitionist Julia Williams, whom he had met as a fellow student at the Noyes Academy. She had also completed her education at the Oneida Institute. Together they had three children, only one of whom survived to adulthood.

In 1842, Garnet became pastor of the Liberty Street Presbyterian church, a position he held for six years. During this time, he published papers that combined religious and abolitionist themes. Closely identifying with the church, Garnet supported the temperance movement and became a strong advocate of political antislavery.

He later returned to New York City, where he joined the American Anti-Slavery Society and frequently spoke at abolitionist conferences. One of his most famous speeches, "Call to Rebellion," was delivered August 1843 to the National Negro Convention in Buffalo, New York. Upon the conclusion of the Negro national convention of 1843, Garnet led a state convention of "Negroes" assembled in Rochester.

These conventions by black activists were called to work for abolition and equal rights. Garnet said that slaves should act for themselves to achieve total emancipation. He promoted an armed rebellion as the most effective way to end slavery. Frederick Douglass and William Lloyd Garrison, along with many other abolitionists both black and white, thought Garnet's ideas were too radical and could damage the cause by arousing too much fear and resistance among whites.

By 1849 Garnet began to support emigration of blacks to Mexico, Liberia, or the West Indies, where he thought they would have more opportunities. In support of this, he founded the African Civilization Society. Similar to the British African Aid society, it sought to establish a West African colony in Yoruba (present-day Nigeria). Garnet advocated a kind of black nationalism in the United States, which included establishing separate sections of the nation to be black colonies.

In 1850, Garnet went to Great Britain at the invitation of Anna Richardson of the Free produce movement, which opposed slavery by rejecting the use of products produced by slave labor. He was a popular lecturer and spent two and a half years lecturing.

In 1852 Garnet was sent to Kingston, Jamaica, as a missionary. He and his family spent three years there; his wife Julia Garnet led an industrial school for girls. Henry Garnet had health problems that led to the family returning to the United States.

When the American Civil War started, Garnet's hopes ended for emigration as a solution for African Americans. He worked to organize black army units to aid the Union cause. In the three-day

New York draft riots of July 1863, mobs attacked blacks and black-owned buildings. Garnet and his family escaped attack because his daughter quickly chopped their nameplate off their door before the mobs found them. He organized a committee for sick soldiers and served as almoner to the New York Benevolent Society for victims of the mob.

When the federal government approved creating black units, Garnet helped with recruiting United States Colored Troops. He moved with his family to Washington, DC, so that he could support the black soldiers and the war effort. He preached to many of them while serving as pastor of the prominent Liberty (Fifteenth) Street Presbyterian Church from 1864 until 1866. During this time, Garnet was the first African American minister to preach to the US House of Representatives, addressing them on February 12, 1865 about the end of slavery.

After the war in 1868, Garnet was appointed president of Avery College in Pittsburgh, Pennsylvania. Later he returned to New York City as a pastor at the Shiloh Presbyterian Church (formerly the First Colored Presbyterian Church, and now St. James Presbyterian Church in Harlem).

Henry remained politically active upon his return to New York and was known to provide support to the Cuban independence movement. In 1878, while living at 102 West 3rd Street, in a neighborhood often referred to as Little Africa, Garnet hosted a reception for Cuban revolutionary leader Antonio Maceo.

Henry's first wife Julia died. In 1879, Garnet married Sarah Smith Tompkins, who was a New York teacher and school principal, suffragist, and community organizer.

Garnet's last wish was to go to Liberia to live, even for a few weeks, and to die there. He was appointed as the U.S. Minister to Liberia in late 1881, and died in Africa two months later. Garnet was given a state funeral by the Liberian government and was buried at Palm Grove Cemetery in Monrovia. Frederick Douglass, who had not been on speaking terms with Garnet for many years because of their differences, still mourned Garnet's passing and noted his achievements.

LAURA CORNELIUS KELLOGG

Laura Cornelius Kellogg ("Minnie") ("Wynnogene") (September 10, 1880 – 1947), was an Oneida leader, author, orator, activist and visionary. In 1911, Laura, a descendant of distinguished Oneida leaders, was a founder of the Society of American Indians. SAI was the first national American Indian rights organization run by and for American Indians.

Laura Cornelius Kellogg was born on the Oneida Indian Reservation at Green Bay, Wisconsin, one of five children of Adam Poe and Celicia Bread Cornelius. Her surviving siblings were Chester Poe Cornelius, Alice Cornelius and Frank Ford Cornelius. Kellogg came from a distinguished lineage of Indian tribal leaders, which is said to have contributed a great deal to her racial pride of the Oneida heritage. Her paternal grandfather was John Cornelius, Oneida chief and brother of Jacob Cornelius, chief of the Orchard faction of Oneidas. Her maternal grandfather was Chief Daniel Bread, who helped find land for his people after the Oneidas were forcibly removed from New York State to Wisconsin in the early nineteenth century. Kellogg was also related to Elijah Skenandore, a prominent political figurehead for the Oneida in the nineteenth century, who was well known for his oratorical skills.

Unlike many of her contemporaries on the reservation, Cornelius managed to avoid the usual educational route to distant Indian Eastern boarding schools at Carlisle and Hampton. She was educated at Grafton Hall, a private boarding school administered by the Episcopal Diocese of Fond du Lac, Wisconsin. The school was within 60 miles of her home at Seymour, Wisconsin, and provided a setting that included mostly non-Indian women. Cornelius attributed her education to her "time spent at the soup kettle on the reservation" as well as institutes of higher learning. This experience left Cornelius feeling more enlightened and enabled her to "appreciate the real values of truth".

In 1898, Kellogg graduated with honors; her graduation essay, "The Romans of America," compared the Iroquois Confederacy to the ancient Roman Empire. Her pride in her Iroquois roots provided her with a strong measure of self-confidence.

Between 1898 and 1910 Kellogg continued her education, travelling for two years in Europe and studying at Stanford University, Barnard College, the New York School of Philanthropy, Cornell University, and the University of Wisconsin.

At Barnard, she wrote a short story for the college's literary magazine and was mentioned in the college yearbook. Kellogg never finished her education at any of the aforementioned institutions but is still considered by historians to be "among the very best educated [among] Native American women" in her time.

In 1902, early literary ambitions led to the publication of two stories "The Legend of the Bean" and "The Sacrifice of the White Dog" in a publication of the Episcopal Church Mission to the Oneidas. In 1903, Laura said, "Perhaps it seems strange to an outsider, for I know the ideas that prevail in regards to Indian life, but to do something great when I grew up was impressed upon me from my cradle from my parents, and I've no other ambition and I have known no other ambition."

"Minnie", as she was known to her friends, taught briefly at the Oneida Indian Boarding School, in Oneida, Wisconsin, as well as at the Sherman Institute in Riverside, California, from 1903 to 1905. On May 12, 1903, some 80 miles southeast of Riverside, the Bureau of Indian Affairs evicted a community of Cupeño Indians from their traditional home on the Warner Springs Ranch. Laura Kellogg was reported to have played a crucial role in persuading the Cupeño not to resist relocation to the Pala Reservation, 40 miles away. California newspapers dubbed her "An Indian Heroine" and "The Indian Joan of Arc" for her conciliatory speech reported to have prevented an uprising. The eviction of the Warner Ranch Indians was reported as the crowning crime of the white men against the California Indians who had lawful title to their lands. That year, Kellogg published her only surviving poem, "A Tribute to the Future of My Race", which she recited during the commencement exercises at Sherman Institute.

Originally the Oneida inhabited the area that later became central New York, particularly around Oneida Lake and Oneida County. Today the Oneida have four nationally recognized nations: Oneida Indian Nation in New York, an Oneida Nation, in and around Green Bay, Wisconsin in the United States; and two in Ontario, Canada: Oneida at Six Nations of the Grand River and Oneida Nation of the Thames in Southwold.

Kellogg was an advocate for the renaissance and sovereignty of the Six Nations of the Iroquois, and fought for communal tribal lands, tribal autonomy and self-government. Popularly known as "Indian Princess Wynnogene," Kellogg was the voice of the Oneidas and Haudenosaunee people in national and international forums.

During the 1920s and 1930s, Kellogg and her husband, Orrin J. Kellogg, pursued land claims in New York on behalf of the Six Nations people. Kellogg's "Lolomi Plan" was a Progressive Era alternative to Bureau of Indian Affairs control emphasizing self-sufficiency, cooperative labor and organization, and capitalization of labor. According to historian Laurence Hauptman, "Kellogg helped transform the modern Iroquois, not back into their ancient League, but into major actors, activists and litigants in the modern world of the 20th century Indian politics".

Laura Kellogg's Lolomi Plan was a Progressive Era alternative to Bureau of Indian Affairs control, and presaged subsequent 20th-century movements to reclaim communal lands, institute tribal self-government and promote economic development. Her Lolomi vision is realized in the success of the Oneida Tribe of Indians of Wisconsin. Land holdings by the Oneida Tribe of Indians of Wisconsin have increased since the mid-1980s from approximately 200 acres to more than 18,000 acres. The economic impact on

Brown County, Outagamie County and the metropolitan Green Bay, Wisconsin, area is estimated in excess of $250 million annually.

Other organizations believed that total assimilation into American society was the only way to "save" the Indians, but many Progressive Era Indians and members of SAI fought to preserve Native rights and sovereignty. Laura Kellogg was an advocate against increasingly stringent federal Indian policies that, among other things, sent Native children to boarding schools and sought to eradicate Native languages, cultures, and political, economic and social systems. Kellogg left a controversial legacy — one contemporary called her a "cyclone," while another called her "a woman of brilliance" — but hers is a fascinating story of a Native woman in the late 19th and early 20th centuries.

Kellogg continued her fight for the renaissance and sovereignty of the Six Nations of the Iroquois the rest of her life. By the 1940s, Kellogg was, according to historian Lawrence Hauptman, "a broken woman, who had outlived her time in history and dissipated both her fame and the money that had come with it." Kellogg lived out her remaining days on welfare. She died in New York City in 1947.

ANNA ELEANOR ROOSEVELT

Anna Eleanor Roosevelt (October 11, 1884 – November 7, 1962) was born on October 11, 1884 in Manhattan, New York City, to socialites Anna Rebecca Hall and Elliott Bulloch Roosevelt. From an early age she preferred to be called by her middle name, Eleanor. Through her father, she was a niece of President Theodore Roosevelt. Through her mother, she was a niece of tennis champions Valentine Gill "Vallie" Hall III and Edward Ludlow Hall. Her mother nicknamed her "Granny" because she acted in such a serious manner as a child. Anna was also somewhat ashamed of her daughter's plainness.

Eleanor had two younger brothers: Elliott Jr. and Hall. She also had a half-brother, Elliott Roosevelt Mann, through her father's affair with Katy Mann, a servant employed by the family. Eleanor

Roosevelt was born into a world of immense wealth and privilege, as her family was part of New York high society called the "swells".

Her mother died from diphtheria on December 7, 1892, and Elliott Jr. died of the same disease the following May. Her father, an alcoholic confined to a sanitarium, died on August 14, 1894, after jumping from a window during a fit of delirium tremens. He survived the fall but died from a seizure. Eleanor's childhood losses left her prone to depression throughout her life. Her brother Hall later suffered from alcoholism. Before her father died, he implored her to act as a mother towards Hall, and it was a request she made good upon for the rest of Hall's life.

After the deaths of her parents, Eleanor was raised in the household of her maternal grandmother, Mary Livingston Ludlow of the Livingston family in Tivoli, New York.

Eleanor was tutored privately and with the encouragement of her aunt Anna "Bamie" Roosevelt, she was sent to Allenswood Academy at the age of 15, a private finishing school in Wimbledon, outside London, England, where she was educated from 1899 to 1902. The headmistress, Marie Souvestre, was a noted educator who sought to cultivate independent thinking in young women. Souvestre died in March 1895. Eleanor wished to continue at Allenswood, but she was summoned home by her grandmother in 1902 to make her social debut. At age 17 in 1902, Eleanor completed her formal education and returned to the United States; she was presented at a debutante ball at the Waldorf-Astoria hotel on December 14.

In the summer of 1902, Eleanor encountered her father's fifth cousin, Franklin Delano Roosevelt, on a train to Tivoli, New York. The two began a secret correspondence and romance and became engaged on November 22, 1903.

Franklin's mother, Sara Ann Delano, opposed the union and made him promise that the engagement would not be officially announced for a year, but Franklin remained determined. The wedding date was set to accommodate President Theodore Roosevelt, who was scheduled to be in New York City for the St. Patrick's Day parade, and who agreed to give the bride away.

Eleanor and Franklin Delano Roosevelt were married on March 17, 1905, in a wedding officiated by Endicott Peabody, the groom's headmaster at Groton School. The couple spent a preliminary honeymoon of one week at Hyde Park, then set up housekeeping in an apartment in New York. That summer they went on their formal honeymoon, a three-month tour of Europe. Returning to the U.S., the newlyweds settled in a New York City house that was provided by Franklin's mother, as well as in a second residence at the family's estate overlooking the Hudson River in Hyde Park, New York.

Eleanor and Franklin had six children: Anna Eleanor Roosevelt, James Roosevelt II, Franklin Roosevelt, Elliott Roosevelt, Franklin Delano Roosevelt, Jr., and John Aspinwall Roosevelt II.

After Eleanor discovered her husband's affair with Lucy Mercer in 1918, she resolved to seek fulfillment in leading a public life of her own. She persuaded Franklin to stay in politics after he was stricken with a paralytic illness in 1921, which cost him the normal use of his legs, and began giving speeches and appearing at campaign events in his place. Following Franklin's election as Governor of New York in 1928, and throughout the remainder of his public career in government, Eleanor regularly made public appearances on his behalf.

In 1927, Eleanor joined friends Marion Dickerman and Nancy Cook in buying the Todhunter School for Girls, a finishing school which also offered college preparatory courses, in New York City. Eleanor taught upper-level courses in American literature and history. She continued to teach three days a week while FDR served as governor but was forced to leave teaching after his election as President.

Also in 1927, she established Val-Kill Industries with Cook, Dickerman, and Caroline O'Day. It was located on the banks of a stream that flowed through the Roosevelt family estate in Hyde Park, New York. The women financed the construction of a small factory to provide supplemental income for local farming families who would make furniture, pewter, and homespun cloth, using traditional craft methods.

Eleanor Roosevelt became First Lady of the United States when Franklin was inaugurated on March 4, 1933. Having known all of the twentieth century's previous First Ladies, she was seriously depressed at having to assume the role, which had traditionally been restricted to domesticity and hostessing. She was determined to break the norm. As First Lady, while her husband served as President, she significantly reshaped and redefined the role of First Lady. Eleanor was very outspoken. On a few occasions, she publicly disagreed with her husband's policies. She advocated for expanded roles for women in the workplace, the civil rights of African Americans and Asian Americans, and the rights of World War II refugees.

Eleanor became "the most controversial First Lady in United States history". She was the first presidential spouse to hold regular press conferences and in 1940 became the first to speak at a national party convention. She also wrote a daily and widely syndicated newspaper column, "My Day", became the first Lady to write a monthly magazine column and to host a weekly radio show.

In the first year of her husband's administration, Roosevelt was determined to match his presidential salary, and she earned $75,000 from her lectures and writing, most of which she gave to charity. By 1941, she was receiving lecture fees of $1,000, and was made an honorary member of Phi Beta Kappa at one of her lectures to celebrate her achievements.

Eleanor's chief project during her husband's first two terms was the establishment of a planned community in Arthurdale, West Virginia. On August 18, 1933, Eleanor visited the families of homeless miners in Morgantown, West Virginia, who had been blacklisted following union activities. She proposed a resettlement community for the miners at Arthurdale, where they could make a living by subsistence farming, handicrafts, and a local manufacturing plant.

Families occupied the first fifty homes in June and agreed to repay the government in thirty years' time. Though Eleanor had hoped for a racially mixed community, the miners insisted on limiting membership to white Christians. After losing a community vote, Eleanor recommended the creation of other communities for the excluded black and Jewish miners. The experience motivated Roosevelt to become much more outspoken on the issue of racial discrimination.

During Franklin's administration, Eleanor became an important connection to the African American population in the era of segregation. Despite the President's desire to placate Southern sentiment, Eleanor was vocal in her support of the civil rights movement. After her experience with Arthurdale and her inspections of New Deal programs in Southern states, she concluded that New Deal programs were discriminating against African Americans, who received a disproportionately small share of relief money. Eleanor became one of the only voices in her husband's administration insisting that benefits be equally extended to Americans of all races.

Eleanor Roosevelt also broke with tradition by inviting hundreds of African American guests to the White House. In 1936 she became aware of conditions at the National Training School for Girls, a predominantly black reform school once located in the Palisades neighborhood of Washington, D.C. She visited the school, wrote about it in her "My Day" column, lobbied for additional funding, and pressed for changes in staffing and curriculum. Her White House invitation to the students became an issue in Franklin's 1936 re-election campaign.

When the black singer Marian Anderson was denied the use of Washington's Constitution Hall by the Daughters of the American Revolution in 1939, Eleanor resigned from the group in protest and helped arrange another concert on the steps of the Lincoln Memorial. She later presented Anderson to the King and Queen of the United Kingdom after Anderson performed at a White House dinner. Eleanor also arranged the appointment of African-American educator Mary McLeod Bethune, with whom she had struck up a friendship, as Director of the Division of Negro Affairs of the National Youth Administration. To avoid problems with the staff when Bethune would visit the White House, Roosevelt would meet her at the gate, embrace her, and walk in with her arm-in-arm.

Eleanor lobbied behind the scenes for the 1934 Costigan-Wagner Bill to make lynching a federal crime, including arranging a meeting between Franklin and NAACP president Walter Francis White. Fearing he would lose the votes of Southern congressional delegations for his legislative agenda; however, Franklin refused to publicly support the bill, which proved unable to pass the Senate.

Eleanor's support of African American rights made her an unpopular figure among whites in the South. Rumors spread of "Eleanor Clubs" formed by servants to oppose their employers and "Eleanor Tuesdays" on which African American men would knock down white women on the street, though no evidence has ever been found of either practice. When race riots broke out in Detroit in June 1943, critics in both the North and South wrote that Eleanor Roosevelt was to blame. At the same time, she grew so popular among African Americans, previously a reliable Republican voting bloc, that they became a consistent base of support for the Democratic Party.

Following the Japanese attack on Pearl Harbor on December 7, 1941, Eleanor Roosevelt spoke out against Japanese-American prejudice, warning against the "great hysteria against minority groups." She also privately opposed her husband's Executive Order 9066, which required Japanese-Americans in many areas of the U.S. to enter internment camps. She was widely criticized for her defense of Japanese-American citizens, including a call by the *Los Angeles Times* that she be "forced to retire from public life" over her stand on the issue.

Eleanor supported increased roles for women and African Americans in the war effort and began to advocate for women to be given factory jobs a year before it became a widespread practice. In 1942, she urged women of all social backgrounds to learn trades, saying: "if I were of a debutante age I would go into a factory–any factory where I could learn a skill and be useful." She notably supported the Tuskegee Airmen in their successful effort to become the first black combat pilots, visiting the Tuskegee Air Corps Advanced Flying School in Alabama. She also flew with African-

American chief civilian instructor C. Alfred "Chief" Anderson. Anderson had been flying since 1929 and was responsible for training thousands of rookie pilots; he took her on a half-hour flight in a Piper J-3 Cub. After landing, she cheerfully announced, "Well, you can fly all right." Eleanor used her position as a trustee of the Julius Rosenwald Fund to arrange a loan of $175,000 to help finance the building of Moton Field.

Franklin died on April 12, 1945 after suffering a cerebral hemorrhage at the Little White House in Warm Springs, Georgia. After the funeral, Eleanor temporarily returned to Val-Kill. Franklin left instructions for her in the event of his death; he proposed turning over Hyde Park to the federal government as a museum, and she spent the following months cataloging the estate and arranging for the transfer. She then moved into an apartment at 29 Washington Square West in Greenwich Village.

The Franklin D. Roosevelt Presidential Library and Museum opened on April 12, 1946, setting a precedent for future presidential libraries.

In December 1945, President Harry S. Truman appointed Eleanor Roosevelt as a delegate to the United Nations General Assembly. In April 1946, she became the first chairperson of the preliminary United Nations Commission on Human Rights. Eleanor remained chairperson when the Commission was established on a permanent basis in January 1947. Along with René Cassin, John Peters Humphrey and others, she played an instrumental role in drafting the Universal Declaration of Human Rights (UDHR).

In 1949, she was made an honorary member of the historically black organization Alpha Kappa Alpha. Eleanor Roosevelt also served as the first United States Representative to the United Nations

Commission on Human Rights and stayed on at that position until 1953, even after stepping down as chair of the Commission in 1951. The UN posthumously awarded her one of its first Human Rights Prizes in 1968 in recognition of her work.

Throughout the 1950s, Eleanor Roosevelt embarked on countless national and international speaking engagements. She continued to pen her newspaper column and made appearances on television and radio broadcasts. She averaged one hundred fifty lectures a year throughout the 1950s, many devoted to her activism on behalf of the United Nations.

Eleanor resigned from her UN post in 1953, when Dwight D. Eisenhower became President. She addressed the Democratic National Convention in 1952 and 1956. When John F. Kennedy became President, he reappointed Eleanor Roosevelt to the United Nations, where she served again from 1961 to 1962, and to the National Advisory Committee of the Peace Corps.

Eleanor received the first annual Franklin Delano Roosevelt Brotherhood Award in 1946. Among other notable awards she was the most admired living woman, according to Gallup's most admired man and woman poll of Americans, in 1948, 1949, 1950, 1952, 1953, 1954, 1955, 1956, 1957, 1958, 1959, 1960, and 1961.

In 1961, President Kennedy's undersecretary of labor, Esther Peterson, proposed a new Presidential Commission on the Status of Women. Kennedy appointed Eleanor Roosevelt to chair the commission, with Peterson as director. This was her last public position. She died just before the commission issued its report. It concluded that *female equality was best achieved by recognition of gender differences and needs, and not by an Equal Rights Amendment.*

In April 1960, Eleanor had been diagnosed with aplastic anemia soon after being struck by a car in New York City. In 1962, Eleanor Roosevelt was given steroids, which activated a dormant case of tuberculosis in her bone marrow, and she died of resulting cardiac failure at her Manhattan home at 55 East 74th Street on the Upper East Side on November 7, 1962, at the age of 78. Eleanor's daughter Anna took care of her when she was terminally ill in 1962. President John F. Kennedy ordered all United States flags lowered to half-staff throughout the world on November 8 in tribute to Eleanor Roosevelt.

MARÍA REBECCA LATIGO DE HERNÁNDEZ

María Rebecca Latigo de Hernández (July 29, 1896 – January 8, 1986) was a Mexican-American rights activist. She was born in San Pedro Garza García, near Monterrey, Nuevo León, Mexico. Her father was a professor. As a young adult, she taught at an elementary school while she lived in Monterrey, Mexico.

Maria Hernández was married in 1915 at the age of 19 to Pedro Hernández Barrera. They were married in Hebbronville, Texas and moved to San Antonio in 1918. Maria and Pedro's family eventually grew to include 10 children. The Hernández family owned and ran a grocery store and bakery. Maria fought and wrote against the segregation, racial oppression, and poor education that the Mexican American children were receiving.

In 1929, the Hernández family helped to organize and found the Order of the Knights of America, or the Orden Caballeros de America. The Order of Knights of America was a committee dedicated to political and civil activists in order to help Mexican Americans as well as Mexican immigrants. They helped with matters including educational and social, but the organization was largely focused on educational matters. The main audience targeted by their organization was Mexican American business owners. However, they also set a goal to help both male and female school-aged children.

During the 1930s, Maria spoke publicly and demonstrated on behalf of Mexican Americans about their education in the United States. She and her husband, Pedro Hernandez Barrera, founded Orden Caballeros de America on January 10, 1929. She organized the Asociación Protectora de Madres in 1933.

In 1932 María Rebecca Latigo de Hernández was the first Mexican female announcer on the radio. In 1933 she helped open an association to help expecting mothers, which was known as Asociación Protectora de Madres.

In 1934 María, along with her husband and children, helped to manage an organization which helped to create safe places, and better the education for the West Side Mexican Communities. It was named La Liga de Defensa Pro-Escolar. In connection to her radio career, she spoke to promote Council 16 of the League of United Latin American Citizens on a program called the "Voz de las Americas". During her years with the league, she helped to encourage equality for all Mexican Americans, no matter where they were from or where they were living.

In 1938 Maria began working with the pecan-shellers' strike, with a cause for women workers' rights. The strike had begun as a way for women to obtain safer working conditions as well as increased salaries. In 1939 she was included in a group of women, who were able to visit then Mexican President, Lázaro Cárdenas. The women went to communicate the goodwill between Mexicans from Mexico and Mexican Americans in the United States.

In 1945 "México y Los Cuatro Poderes Que Dirigen al Pueblo" (En: Mexico and the Four Powers that Lead the People) was published. In this essay, she said that domestic sphere founded society. It also stated that mothers were the creators of nations. Close to the time that her essay was published, she was also involved in organizing Club Liberal Pro-Cultura de la Mujer.

In 1968 Maria was a regular guest on San Antonio television, informing the public about education and social progress. In 1969, María Rebecca Latigo de Hernández was appointed the position of Treasurer of the order's board of directors, as well as the President of Circulo Social. In 1970 she grew her political activities by joining the Raza Unida Party. She served as a key-note speaker at the Raza Unida's Statewide Conference, which was held in Austin, Texas.

Maria Hernandez died of pneumonia on January 8, 1986 at the age of 89.. She is buried in the plot of the Orden Caballeros de América outside of Elmendorf, Texas.

CIVIL RIGHTS LEADERS AND ACTIVISTS
20ᵀᴴ CENTURY

Our lives begin to end the day we become silent about things that matter.
– Martin Luther King, Jr.

Civil rights laws attempt to guarantee full and equal citizenship for people who have traditionally been discriminated against on the basis of some group characteristic. When the enforcement of civil rights is found by many to be inadequate, a civil rights movement may emerge in order to call for equal application of the laws without discrimination.

Some Civil Rights leaders are household names; others are not very well known. It is my intention to make you aware of the diversity of the international melting pot and the people who have influenced and instigated equal and civil rights throughout the world, but particularly in America.

Many people protected me and looked out for wrongdoing in my community when I was growing up and they were a great support system. I advise you to do the same whenever the opportunity arises. There are many reasons and many ways you can make a difference. When I happen upon a young mind that is idle or going astray, that is my reason for wanting to serve the community and for my ongoing commitment to Make the Grade.

Today, in this time of COVID-19 the Health Care Workers are, in my opinion, Activists because they have risked their lives by stepping up into the Front Lines during a Pandemic. They are true 21st Century Heroes and Sheroes and have earned a special place in this Chapter.

HARRIETTE VYDA SIMMS AND HARRY TYSON MOORE

Harriette Vyda Simms (June 19, 1902 - October 26, 2015) and her husband Harry Moore were the first martyrs of the Civil Rights Movement when they were fatally injured at their home by a bomb that went off beneath their house.

Harriette was born in West Palm Beach, Florida on, to David Ira Simms (a wood lathe worker) and Annie (Warren) Simms. She had sisters Valerie and Mae, and brothers George, Arnold, Rupert and David, Jr. The family relocated to Mims, Florida. As a youth, Harriette spent summers working in Massillon, Ohio with her father. Simms attended the segregated Daytona Normal Industrial Institute in Daytona Beach, Florida. She later graduated from Bethune-Cookman College, a historically black college in Daytona Beach, with an associate of arts degree in 1941 and a bachelor of science degree in 1950.

Harriette taught elementary school classes for many years, in Merritt Island and Mims in Brevard County, and in Lake Park, Florida until her death. In Mims, she helped to cook lunch every day for the students.

Harriette Simms met Harry Tyson Moore while teaching classes in Brevard County. He was then working as principal of the Titusville Colored School, which offered black students a chance at an equal education. Harriette and Harry married on December 25, 1926, and had two daughters together: Annie Rosalea (known as Peaches, 1928–1972) and Juanita Evangeline (known as Evangeline, 1930-2015).

Soon after the births of their daughters, the Moores founded the Brevard County chapter of the NAACP in 1934. Harry Moore later helped to organize the statewide NAACP organization. In 1946, after he founded a local chapter of the NAACP, Harriette Moore and her husband were both fired by the Brevard County public school system and blacklisted due to their political activities. At the time, segregation was the norm in former Confederate states, and the Moores and other black Southerners had few opportunities for economic or social advancement.

It was a double celebration: Christmas, and the Moores' 25th anniversary. Harry T. and Harriette Moore celebrated the way they had 25 years before, cutting the cake together like newlyweds. They had no idea that the tender moment would be among their last. As they settled into their bed to sleep that evening in 1951, a massive explosion tore through their bedroom.

Harry Tyson Moore (November 18, 1905 – December 25, 1951) was an African-American educator, a pioneer leader of the civil rights movement, founder of the first branch of the National

Association for the Advancement of Colored People (NAACP) in Brevard County, Florida, and president of the state chapter of the NAACP.

Harry T. Moore and his wife, Harriette Moore, also an educator, were the victims of a bombing of their home in Mims, Florida on Christmas night 1951. He died in an ambulance on the way to a black hospital in Sanford, Florida, county seat of Seminole County about 30 miles to the northwest. His wife died nine days later of her wounds on January 3, 1952, at the same hospital. This followed their both having been fired from teaching because of their activism, a form of economic retaliation used by the establishment.

The murder case was investigated, including by the FBI in 1951-1952, but no one was ever prosecuted. Two more investigations were conducted in the 1970s and 1990s. A state investigation and forensic work in 2005-6 resulted in naming the likely perpetrators as four Ku Klux Klan members, all long dead by that time. Harry T. Moore was the first NAACP member and official to be assassinated for civil rights activism; the couple are the only husband and wife to be killed for the movement. Moore has been called the first martyr of this stage of the civil rights movement that expanded in the 1960s.

In the early 1930s, Moore had become state secretary for the Florida chapter of the NAACP. Through his registration activities, he greatly increased the number of members, and he worked on issues of housing and education. He investigated lynchings, filed lawsuits against voter registration barriers and white primaries, and worked for equal pay for black teachers in public schools.

Moore also led the Progressive Voters League. Following a 1944 US Supreme Court ruling against white primaries, between 1944 and 1950, he succeeded in increasing the registration of black voters in Florida to 31 percent of those eligible to vote, markedly higher than in any other Southern state.

The Moores had been murdered, victims of an improvised explosive device made with dynamite and shoved beneath their bedroom floor. It seemed like a simple case: Harry T. Moore had been fighting segregation and racism in the Jim Crow South for years, making plenty of enemies along the way.

The risk to activists and any blacks in the South was high and remained so; according to a later report from the NAACP's Southern Regional Council in Atlanta, the homes of 40 black Southern families were bombed during 1951 and 1952. Some, like the Moores, were activists, but most were either people who had refused to bow to racist convention, or were simply "innocent bystanders, unsuspecting victims of random white terrorism."

Although the story of the Moores' lives faded into obscurity for many years, the late 20th century re-opening of the case provided a new appreciation for their work.

In 1999, Florida approved designation of the homesite of the Moores as a Florida Heritage Landmark. Brevard County started restoring the site. Supplemented by independent funding, by 2004 the county had created the Harry T. and Harriette Moore Memorial Park and Interpretive Center at the homesite in Mims. Brevard County named its Justice Center after the Moores and included material there about their lives and work.

The State of Florida twice returned to the case, but was unable to file charges, as most of the men suspected to have been involved in the crime had died.

In 2005, Florida Attorney General Charlie Crist re-opened a state investigation of Harry and Harriette Moore's deaths. On August 16, 2006, Crist announced the results of the work of the state Office of Civil Rights and the Florida Department of Law Enforcement. Based on extensive evidence, the state concluded that the Moores were victims of a conspiracy by members of a central Florida Klavern of the Ku Klux Klan. *There were eleven other bombings against black families in Florida the year that the Moores were killed.*

The report named the following four individuals, all of whom had reputations for violence, as directly involved:

- Earl J. Brooklyn, a Klansman known for being exceedingly violent, was discovered to have had floor plans of the Moores' home and was recruiting volunteers. He died about a year after the attack, apparently of natural causes.

- Tillman H. Belvin, another violent Klansman, was a close friend of Brooklyn. He also died about a year after the attack, of natural causes.

- Joseph Neville Cox, secretary of the Orange County, Florida chapter of the Klan, was believed to have ordered the attack. In 1952 he committed suicide after being questioned by the FBI.

- As he lay dying of cancer, Klansman Edward L. Spivey claimed to have been at the crime scene in 1951, and he implicated Cox in the attack.

The Moores' younger daughter, Juanita Evangeline Moore, joined former Attorney General Crist in the efforts to uncover the identity of her parents' killers. She was a 1951 graduate of Bethune-Cookman College and a retired government employee. She died on October 26, 2015, in New Carrollton, Maryland.

MARVEL JACKSON COOKE

Marvel Jackson Cooke (April 4, 1903 – November 29, 2000) was a pioneering American journalist, writer, and civil rights activist. She would become the first African American woman to work at a mainstream white-owned newspaper.

Marvel was born in Mankato, Minnesota, to Madison Jackson and Amy Wood Jackson. She was raised in an upper-class, white neighborhood in Minneapolis, where her family moved in 1907. Her father was an Ohio State University law school graduate who was unable to find employment as a black lawyer; her mother was a former teacher who once lived on a Native American reservation.

In 1925, Marvel graduated from the University of Minnesota with a degree in English, at the age of 22. After graduating, she was offered a job as assistant to W. E. B. Du Bois, editor of the NAACP magazine *The Crisis*, and in 1926 moved to New York City, settling in Harlem, during the Harlem Renaissance. Her ability as a writer was recognized by Du Bois, who put her in charge of a column in the magazine, where her brief included writing critiques of works by the literary giants of the day, including Langston Hughes, Zora Neale Hurston and Dorothy Parker.

Mentored by Du Bois, she became friendly with leading writers and artists, including Paul Robeson, Countee Cullen, Elizabeth Catlett and Richard Wright. She broke off her engagement to (later NAACP leader) Roy Wilkins because she thought him too conservative.

In 1928, she went to work on the *New York Amsterdam News*, where she was the first woman reporter in their 40-year history. In 1929, she married Jamaican-born Cecil Cooke – a graduate of Columbia University, who was the world's fastest quarter-miler when she met him. *Their marriage would last until his death in 1978.* After marrying, the Cookes moved to Greensboro, North Carolina, where Marvel taught history, English and Latin in the high-school department of North Carolina Agricultural and Technical College.

Returning to New York and the *Amsterdam News* in 1931, she helped found the first chapter in New York of the Newspaper Guild and was involved in strike action at the *News*, joining the picket for 11 weeks when the editorial workers union was locked out; the strike was finally ended on Christmas Eve 1934. While working at the *Amsterdam News* in the 1930s, Cooke not only helped create a local chapter of the Newspaper Guild, the labor union of newspaper journalists, but held union meetings in her home and subsequently participated in an eleven-week strike, during which she joined the Communist Party. Cooke disliked the crime reports she was assigned by the *News;* she preferred to expand the paper's coverage of the arts. She eventually left the paper for good in 1937.

From 1940 to 1947, Cooke worked on the *People's Voice* (a weekly owned by Adam Clayton Powell), as assistant managing editor. In 1950 she was hired by the New York paper *The Daily Compass*, becoming the first African-American woman to serve as a reporter for a mainstream white-owned newspaper; at the time she was also the only woman employed there, She remained with the paper until its closure in November 1952.

In the 1950s, she served as New York director of the National Council of Arts, Sciences and Professions. In 1953, when she was called twice to testify about her involvement with the Communist Party before Senator Joseph McCarthy, in New York and Washington DC, she pleaded the Fifth Amendment.

She volunteered as national legal defense secretary of the Angela Davis Defense Fund in 1971. In her later years Cooke became national vice-chairman of the American-Soviet Friendship Committee.

Cooke died of leukemia in New York in 2000, at the age of 97, having lived most of her life at 409 Edgecombe Avenue, the legendary apartment building in Sugar Hill, that was home to many other black luminaries.

WILLA BEATRICE BROWN

Willa Beatrice Brown (January 22, 1906 – July 18, 1992) became the first woman in the United States who possessed both a mechanic's license and a commercial license in aviation. Willa had a very positive effect on African Americans as an American aviator, lobbyist, teacher, and civil rights activist.

Willa Beatrice Brown was born to Eric B. Brown, a minister, and Hallie Mae Carpenter Brown on January 22, 1906, in Glasgow, Kentucky. The family first moved to Indianapolis, Indiana, when Willa was six years old and then to Terre Haute, where she received most of her schooling. In 1923 Brown, who was a good student, graduated from Wiley High School.

In 1927, she graduated from Indiana State Teachers College with a degree in business. Immediately upon graduation, Brown found employment as a teacher in Gary, Indiana, where she met and married her first husband, Wilbur Hardaway, an alderman; the marriage was short lived. In 1932 Brown moved to Chicago, where she found employment in the public school system.

As a young high school teacher in Gary, Indiana, and later as a social worker in Chicago, Brown felt that her talents were not being put to their greatest use. Consequently, she sought greater challenges and adventures in life and pushed actively against the limited boundaries of career fields normally open to African Americans.

Brown's years in Chicago were extremely active. After teaching for two years, she returned to school, attending Northwestern University, where she received an MA in business in 1937. During her student days, she taught and worked at a variety of jobs. She worked as a secretary to Calar Paul Page, director of the Chicago Relief Administration and as a social services worker for the Cook County Bureau of Public Welfare. She was also a clerk for the U.S. Department of Immigration and Naturalization and for the United States Post Office and was secretary to Horace Cayton.

In 1934, influenced by the aviatrix, Bessie Coleman, Willa started taking flying lessons from Fred Schumacher at one of Chicago's racially segregated airports, the Harlem Airport in Chicago. It was at the Harlem airport that Brown met Cornelius R. Coffey, an instructor and a mechanic, with whom she shared her passion for flying.

Willa furthered her flying lessons and began studying with Cornelius. In 1935 she earned a masters certificate in aviation mechanics from the Aeronautical University and later joined the

Challenger Air Pilots Association (CAPA), one of the first black pilot organizations. The CAPA was founded by Colonel John C. Robinson, another one of Brown's flight instructors, who was one of the first black graduates of Curtiss Wright Aeronautical University. Willa became a member of the Chicago Girls Flight Club and she also purchased her own airplane. In 1937, the same year she received her pilot's license, she also earned a master's degree from Northwestern University.

On June 22,1938 Willa Beatrice Brown became the first African American woman who earned a private pilot's license in the United States. (Fellow Chicagoan and aviator Bessie Coleman had to go to France for her license in 1921). Later, Brown and Coffey married and established the Coffey School of Aeronautics at Harlem Airport in Chicago, where they trained black pilots and aviation mechanics. It was the first private flight training academy in the United States owned and operated by African Americans.

Willa participated in various flying events such as the Memorial flight for Bessie Coleman and air shows that featured entertaining flight demonstrations. Willa, who, evidently was tall, very good looking, and often wore the typical flight apparel of the day—a jacket, jodphurs, and boots—decided the best way to get the media interested in the show was to go to the media first instead of getting them to come and see her. Hence, she visited the *Chicago Defender* newspaper office.

She was so striking and had such a strong presence that everyone stopped what they were doing and stared at her. She announced who she was, stating that she was an "aviatrix" and described the upcoming show. Her tactic resulted in an audience between two to three hundred people. The event was also covered by Enoch P. Waters, a journalist who, in 1939, along with Brown and Coffey, co-founded the National Airmen's Association of America (NAAA), an organization established and designed to facilitate the acceptance of blacks into the United States Air Force. As the organization's national secretary and the president of the Chicago branch, Brown became an activist for racial equality.

Willa continually lobbied the government for integration of black pilots into the segregated Army Air Corps and the federal Civilian Pilot Training Program (CPTP), the system established by the Civil Aeronautics Authority to provide a pool of civilian pilots for use during national emergencies.

In 1940, Brown and Lieutenant Cornelius R. Coffey started the Coffey School of Aeronautics where approximately 200 pilots were trained in the next seven years. Some of those pilots later became part of the 99th Pursuit Squadron at Tuskegee Institute. They were also known as the legendary "Tuskegee Airmen." *Willa's efforts were directly responsible for the squadron's creation, which led to the integration of the military in 1948.*

Subsequently, when Congress finally voted to allow separate-but-equal participation of blacks in civilian flight training programs, the Coffey School of Aeronautics was chosen for participation in the CPTP. Willa became the coordinator for the CPTP in Chicago. Later, the Coffey School of Aeronautics was also selected by the U.S. Army to provide black trainees for the Air Corps pilot training program at the Tuskegee Institute, which trained hundreds of pilots, several of whom would go on to become Tuskegee Airmen.

Willa Brown eventually became the coordinator of war-training service for the Civil Aeronautics Authority and later was a member of the Federal Aviation Administration's Women's Advisory Board. In 1941, she became the first African American officer in the Civil

Air Patrol (CAP). The U.S. government also named her federal coordinator of the CAP Chicago unit. In 1942, she became a training coordinator for the Civil Aeronautics Administration and a teacher in the Civilian Pilot Training Program.

Well after the Coffey School closed in 1945, Brown remained politically and socially active in Chicago. She organized flight schools for children, she ran for Congress three times (1946, 1948, and 1950, respectively) in Chicago.

In 1955, Brown married her third husband, the Reverend J. H. Chappell and became very active in the West Side Community Church in Chicago. She taught in the Chicago Public School System until 1971, when she retired at the age of 65. In 1972, Willa Brown Chappell was appointed to the Federal Aviation Administration (FAA) Women's Advisory Board in recognition of her contributions to aviation in the United States.

Willa Beatrice Brown did not have any children. She died of a stroke on July 18, 1992. She was 86 years old. A lifelong advocate for gender and racial equality in flight and in the military, in 2010, Willa was posthumously awarded the Distinguished Alumni Award by the Indiana State University Alumni Association.

AMELIA ISADORA PLATTS

Amelia Isadora Platts (August 18, 1911 - August 26, 2015) was the first female African American to run for office in Alabama and the first woman of any race to run for the ticket of the Democratic Party in the state.

Amelia was born in Savannah, Georgia to George and Anna Eliza Platts, both of whom were African-American. She also had Cherokee and German ancestry. Church was central to Amelia and her nine siblings' upbringing. As a young girl, she became involved in campaigning for women's suffrage. Her family encouraged the children to read.

Amelia attended two years at Georgia State Industrial College for Colored Youth (now Savannah State University, a historically black college). She transferred to Tuskegee Institute (now Tuskegee University), earning a degree in home economics in 1927. She later also studied at Tennessee State, Virginia State, and Temple University.

Platts taught in Georgia before starting with the U.S. Department of Agriculture (USDA) in Selma as the home demonstration agent for Dallas County. She educated the county's largely rural population about food production and processing, nutrition, healthcare, and other subjects related to agriculture and homemaking.

She met her future husband Samuel William Boynton in Selma, where he was working as a county extension agent during the Great Depression. They married in 1936 and had two sons, Bill Jr. and Bruce Carver Boynton. Amelia and Samuel had known the noted scholar George Washington Carver at the Tuskegee Institute, from which they both graduated. Their son, Bruce Carver Boynton, was the godson and namesake of George Washington Carver. Later they adopted Amelia's two nieces, Sharon (Platts) Seay and Germaine (Platts) Bowser.

In 1934 Amelia Boynton registered to vote, which was extremely difficult for African Americans to accomplish in Alabama, due to discriminatory practices under the state's disenfranchising constitution passed at the turn of the century. It had effectively excluded most blacks from politics for decades, an exclusion that continued into the 1960s. A few years later she wrote a play, *Through the Years*, which told the story of the creation of Spiritual music and a former slave who was elected to Congress during Reconstruction,. The play was based on her father's half-brother Robert Smalls, in order to help fund a community center in Selma, Alabama. In 1954 the Boyntons met Reverend Martin Luther King,

Jr. and his wife Coretta Scott King at the Dexter Avenue Baptist Church in Montgomery, Alabama, where King was the pastor.

In 1958, her son, Bruce Boynton, was a student at Howard University School of Law when he was arrested for trespassing, while attempting to purchase food at the white section of a bus terminal in Richmond, Virginia. Bruce Boynton was found guilty in state court of a misdemeanor and fined, which he appealed and lost until the case, Boynton v. Virginia, was argued before the U.S. Supreme Court by Thurgood Marshall, reversing lower court decisions.

In 1963, Samuel Boynton died. It was a time of increased activism in the Civil Rights Movement. Amelia made her home and office in Selma a center for strategy sessions for Selma's civil rights battles, including its voting rights campaign. In 1964 Boynton ran for the Congress from Alabama, hoping to encourage black registration and voting. She received 10% of the vote.

In 1964 and 1965 Boynton worked with Martin Luther King, Diane Nash, James Bevel, and others of the Southern Christian Leadership Conference (SCLC) to plan demonstrations for civil and voting rights. While Selma had a population that was 50 percent black, only 300 of the town's African American residents were registered as voters in 1965, after thousands had been arrested in protests. By March 1966, after passage of the Voting Rights Act of 1965, 11,000 were registered to vote.

To protest continuing segregation and disenfranchisement of blacks, in early 1965 Amelia Boynton helped organize a march to the state capital of Montgomery, initiated by James Bevel, which took place on March 7, 1965. Led by John Lewis, Hosea Williams and Bob Mants, and including Rosa Parks and others among the marchers, the event became known as Bloody Sunday when county and state police stopped the march and beat demonstrators after they crossed the Edmund Pettus Bridge into Dallas County. Boynton was beaten unconscious; a photograph of her lying on Edmund Pettus Bridge went around the world.

Amelia suffered throat burns from the effects of tear gas. She participated in both of the subsequent marches. Another short march led by Martin Luther King took place two days later; the marchers turned back after crossing the Pettus Bridge. Finally, with federal protection and thousands of marchers joining them, a third march reached Montgomery on March 24, entering with 25,000 people.

The events of Bloody Sunday and the later march on Montgomery galvanized national public opinion and contributed to the passage of the Voting Rights Act of 1965; Amelia was a guest of honor at the ceremony when President Lyndon Johnson signed the Voting Rights Act into law in August of that year.

Amelia Boynton remarried in 1969, to a musician named Bob W. Billups. He died unexpectedly in a boating accident in 1973. Amelia eventually married a third time, to former Tuskegee classmate James Robinson in 1976. She moved with him to his home in Tuskegee after the wedding. James Robinson died in 1988.

In 1983, Robinson met Lyndon LaRouche, considered a highly controversial political figure in the Democratic Party. A year later she served as a founding board member of the LaRouche-affiliated Schiller Institute. LaRouche was later convicted in 1988 of mail fraud involving twelve counts, over a ten-year period, totaling $280,000. In 1991, the Schiller Institute published a biography of Robinson, who even into her 90s was described as "LaRouche's most high-profile Black spokeswoman."

In 1990, Amelia Robinson was awarded the Martin Luther King, Jr. Freedom Medal.

In 1992, proclamations of "Amelia Boynton Robinson Day" in Seattle and in the state of Washington were rescinded when officials learned of Amelia's involvement in the Schiller Institute. It was the first time the state had pulled back such an honor. A spokesman for the Seattle mayor said, "It was a very difficult decision. The mayor has a lot of respect for her courage during the Civil Rights Movement of the 1960s, but we don't feel her handlers gave us full and accurate information about her current activities."

Amelia said in an interview, "I have had worse things than that done to me when I was fighting for people's right to vote. I have been called rabble-rouser, agitator. But because of my fighting, I was able to hand to the entire country the right for people to vote. To give me an honor and rescind it because I am fighting for justice and for a man who has an economic program that will help the poor and the oppressed ... if that is the reason, then I think they did more good than they did harm."

In 2004 Amelia Robinson sued The Walt Disney Company for defamation, asking for between $1 and $10 million in damages. She contended that the 1999 TV movie *Selma, Lord, Selma*, a docudrama based on a book written by two young participants in Bloody Sunday, falsely depicted her as a stereotypical "black Mammy," whose key role was to "make religious utterances and to participate in singing spirituals and protest songs." She lost the case.

From September to mid-November 2007, Robinson toured Sweden, Denmark, Germany, France and Italy in her capacity as Vice President of the Schiller Institute. She spoke with European youth about her support for LaRouche (who had denied facts about the

9/11 attacks), Martin Luther King, and Franklin Delano Roosevelt, as well as the continuing problem of racism in the United States, which she said was illustrated by the recent events in Jena, Louisiana. Amelia Robinson retired as vice president of the Schiller Institute in 2009.

In February 2011, aged 99, Amelia Robinson returned to her hometown of Savannah, to address students at Savannah State University.

In 2014, the Selma City Council renamed five blocks of Lapsley Street as Boyntons Street to honor Amelia Boynton Robinson and Sam Boynton.

In 2015, Robinson attended the State of the Union Address in January at the invitation of President Barack Obama, and, in her wheelchair, was at Obama's side as he and others walked across the Edmund Pettus Bridge during the Selma Voting Rights Movement 50th Anniversary Jubilee that March.

After suffering a series of strokes, Amelia Robinson died on August 26, 2015 in Montgomery, Alabama, eight days after celebrating her 104th birthday.

FANNIE LOU HAMER TOWNSEND

Fannie Lou Hamer Townsend (October 6, 1917 – March 14, 1977) was born on October 6, 1917, in Montgomery County, Mississippi, the last of the 20 children of Ella and James Lee Townsend.

In 1919 the Townsends moved to Sunflower County, Mississippi to work as sharecroppers on W. D. Marlow's plantation. From age six she picked cotton with her family. During the winters of 1924 through 1930 she attended the one-room school provided for the sharecroppers' children, open between picking seasons. She loved reading and excelled in spelling bees and reciting poetry, but at age 12 she had to leave school to help support her aging parents. By age 13 she could pick 200–300 pounds (90 to 140 kg) of cotton daily, despite having a leg disfigured by polio.

Fannie continued to develop her reading and interpretation skills in Bible study at her church. In 1944, after the plantation owner discovered that she was literate, she was selected as its time and record keeper. The following year she married Perry "Pap" Hamer, a tractor driver on the Marlow plantation, and they remained there for the next 18 years.

The Hamers raised two girls, whom they decided to adopt. One of the girls died of internal hemorrhaging after she was denied admission to the local hospital on account of her mother's activism.

Hamer became interested in the civil rights movement in the 1950s. She heard leaders in the local movement speak at annual Regional Council of Negro Leadership (RCNL) conferences, held in Mound Bayou, Mississippi. The annual conferences discussed black voting rights and other civil rights issues black communities in the area faced.

While having surgery in 1961 to remove a tumor, 44-year-old Hamer was also given a hysterectomy without consent by a white doctor; this was a frequent occurrence under Mississippi's compulsory sterilization plan to reduce the number of poor blacks in the state. Hamer is credited with coining the phrase "Mississippi appendectomy" as a euphemism for the involuntary or uninformed sterilization of black women, common in the South in the 1960s.

Hamer began civil rights activism in 1962, continuing until her health declined nine years later. She was known for her use of spiritual hymnals and quotes and her resilience in leading the civil rights movement for black women in Mississippi. She was extorted, threatened, harassed, shot at, and assaulted by white supremacists and police while trying to register for and exercise her right to vote. She later helped and encouraged thousands of African-Americans in Mississippi to become registered voters, and helped hundreds of disenfranchised people in her area through her work in programs like the Freedom Farm Cooperative.

In 1962, Hamer first learned about the constitutional right to vote from volunteers at the Student Nonviolent Coordinating Committee who had visited her in Mound Bayou. She began to take direct political action in the civil rights movement. On August 31, she traveled with other activists to Indianola, Mississippi, hoping to register to vote. The registration test, crafted to keep blacks from voting, asked her to explain de facto laws. "I knowed as much about a facto law as a horse knows about Christmas Day," she recalled. Rejected, she came home to find the "boss man raisin' Cain." She had better withdraw her registration, she was told, because "we're not ready for that in Mississippi."

"I didn't try to register for you," Hamer told her boss. "I tried to register for myself." She was immediately fired and kicked off the plantation. Her husband was required to stay on the land until the end of the harvest. Hamer moved between homes over the next several days for protection. On September 10, while staying with friend Mary Tucker, Hamer was shot at 16 times in a drive-by shooting by white supremacists. No one was injured in the event. The next day Hamer and her family evacuated to nearby Tallahatchie County for three months, fearing retaliation by the Ku Klux Klan for her attempt to vote. On December 4, just after returning to her hometown, she went to the courthouse in Indianola to take the literacy test again, but failed and was turned away. Hamer told the registrar, "You'll see me every 30 days till I pass".

On January 10, 1963, Hamer took the literacy test a third time. She was successful and was informed that she was now a registered voter in the State of Mississippi. However, when she attempted to vote that fall, she discovered her registration gave her no actual power to vote as the county required voters to have two poll tax receipts. This requirement had emerged in some (mostly former confederate) states after the right to vote was first given to all races by the 1870 ratification of the Fifteenth Amendment to the United States Constitution. These laws along with the literacy tests and local government acts of coercion, were used against blacks and Native Americans. Hamer later paid for and acquired the requisite poll tax receipts.

Hamer had begun to become more involved in the Student Nonviolent Coordinating Committee after these incidents. She attended many Southern Christian Leadership Conferences (SCLC), which she at times taught classes for, and also various SNCC workshops. She traveled to gather signatures for petitions to attempt to be granted federal resources for impoverished black families across the south. In 1963, she also became a field secretary for voter registration and welfare programs for the SNCC. Many of these first actions to attempt to register more black voters in Mississippi met with the same problems Hamer had in trying to register herself.

Hamer decided to attend a pro-citizenship conference by the Southern Christian Leadership Conference (SCLC) in Charleston, South Carolina. Travelling by bus with co-activists, the party stopped for a break in Winona, Mississippi. Some of the activists went inside a local cafe but were refused service by the waitress. Shortly after, a Mississippi State highway patrolman took out his billy club and intimidated the activists into leaving. One of the group decided to take down the officer's license plate number; while doing so the patrolman and a police chief entered the cafe and arrested the party. Hamer left the bus and inquired if they could continue their journey back to Greenwood, Mississippi. At that point the officers arrested her as well.

Once in county jail, Hamer's colleagues were beaten by the police in the booking room (including 15-year-old June Johnson, for not saying "sir" in her replies to the officers). Hamer was then taken to a cell where two inmates were ordered, by the state trooper, to beat her using a blackjack. The police ensured she was held down during the almost fatal beating, and when she started to scream, beat her further. Hamer was groped repeatedly by officers during the assault. When she attempted to resist, she states an officer, "walked over, took my dress, pulled it up over my shoulders, leaving my body exposed to five men." Another in her group was beaten until she was unable to talk; a third, a teenager, was beaten, stomped on, and stripped. An activist from the SNCC came the next day to see if they could help but was beaten until his eyes were shut when he did not address an officer in the expected deferential manner.

Hamer was released on June 12, 1963. She needed more than a month to recuperate from the beatings and never fully recovered. Though the incident had profound physical and psychological effects, including a blood clot over her left eye and permanent damage on one of her kidneys, she returned to Mississippi to organize voter registration drives, including the 1963 Freedom Ballot, a mock election, and the "Freedom Summer" initiative the following year. She was known to the volunteers of Freedom Summer as a motherly figure who believed that the civil rights effort should be multi-racial in nature.

In 1964, Hamer helped co-found the Mississippi Freedom Democratic Party (MFDP), in an effort to prevent the regional all-white Democratic party's attempts to stifle African-American voices, and to ensure there was a party for all people that did not stand for any form of exploitation and discrimination (especially towards minorities). Following the founding of the MFDP, Hamer and other activists traveled to the 1964 Democratic National Convention to stand as the official delegation from the state of Mississippi. Hamer's televised testimony was interrupted because of a scheduled speech that President Lyndon B. Johnson delivered to thirty governors in the East Room of the White House. However, most of the major news networks broadcast her testimony later that evening to the nation, giving Hamer and the MFDP much exposure. In 1964, Hamer also unsuccessfully ran for a seat in the U.S. Senate.

Senator Hubert Humphrey tried to propose a compromise on behalf of the President that would give the Freedom Democratic Party two seats. He stated this would lead to a reformed convention in 1968. The MFDP rejected the compromise, with Hamer saying, "We didn't come all the way up here to compromise for no more than we'd gotten here. We didn't come all this way for no two seats when all of us is tired." Afterwards, all of the white members from the Mississippi delegation walked out.

In 1968 the MFDP was finally seated, after the Democratic Party adopted a clause which demanded equality of representation from their states' delegations. Hamer sought equality across all aspects of society. In Hamer's view, African-Americans were not technically free if they were not afforded the same opportunities as whites, including those in the agricultural industry. Sharecropping was the most common form of post-slavery activity and income in the South. The New Deal era expanded so that many blacks were physically and economically displaced due to the various projects appearing around the country. Hamer did not wish to have blacks be dependent on any group for any longer; so, she wanted to give them a voice through an agricultural movement.

James Eastland, a white senator, was among the groups of people who sought to keep African Americans disenfranchised and segregated from society. His influence on the overarching agricultural industry often suppressed minority groups to keep whites as the only power force in America. Hamer objected to this, and consequently pioneered the Freedom Farm Cooperative (FFC) in 1969, an attempt to redistribute economic power across groups and to solidify an economic standing amongst African-Americans. In the same vein as the Freedom Farm Collective, Hamer partnered with the NCNW to establish an interracial and interregional support program called The Pig Project to provide protein for people who previously could not afford meat.

In 1970 she led legal action against the government of Sunflower County, Mississippi, for continued illegal segregation. Hamer made it her mission to make land more accessible to African Americans. To do this, she started a small "pig bank" with a starting donation from the National Council of Negro Women of five boars and fifty gilts. Through the pig bank, a family could care for a pregnant female pig until it bore its offspring; subsequently, they would raise the piglets and use them for food and financial gain. Within five years, thousands of pigs were available for breeding. Hamer used the success of the bank to begin fundraising for the main farming corporation. She was able to convince the then-editor of the *Harvard Crimson*, James Fallows, to write an article that advocated for donations to the FFC.

Eventually, the FFC had raised around $8,000 which allowed Hamer to purchase 40 acres of land previously owned by a black farmer who could no longer afford to occupy the land. This land became the Freedom Farm. The farm had three main objectives. These were to establish an agricultural organization that could supplement the nutritional needs of America's most disenfranchised people; to provide acceptable housing development; and to create an entrepreneurial business incubator that would provide resources for new companies and re-training for those with limited education but manual labor experience.

Over time, the FFC offered various other services such as financial counseling, a scholarship fund and a housing agency. The FFC aided in securing 35 Federal Housing Administration (FHA) subsidized houses for struggling black families. Through her success, Hamer managed to acquire a new home, which served as inspiration for others to begin building themselves up.

Hamer received countless awards both in her lifetime and posthumously. She received a Doctor of Law from Shaw University, and honorary degrees from Columbia College Chicago in 1970 and Howard University in 1972.

Fannie came out of an extended period in the hospital for nervous exhaustion in January 1972. That same year, she was elected as a national party delegate. She was hospitalized again in January 1974 for a nervous breakdown. By June 1974, Hamer was said to be in extremely poor health.

The FFC ultimately disbanded in 1975 due to lack of funding. In 1976 Fannie was diagnosed with and had surgery for breast cancer.

Hamer died of complications of hypertension and breast cancer on March 14, 1977, aged 59, at Taborian Hospital, Mound Bayou, Mississippi. Fannie Lou Hamer was buried in her hometown of Ruleville, Mississippi. Her tombstone is engraved with one of her famous quotes, "I am sick and tired of being sick and tired."

Fannie was inducted posthumously into the National Women's Hall of Fame in 1993. Fannie Lou Hamer Freedom High School was formed in Bronx, New York, New York, with a focus on humanities and social justice. In 2017 the Fannie Lou Hamer Black Resource Center opened at the University of California at Berkeley. The third annual Women's March, held in Atlantic City, New Jersey on January 19, 2019, was dedicated to Hamer's life and legacy.

MARTIN LUTHER KING JR.

Martin Luther King Jr. (January 15, 1929 – April 4, 1968) was an American Baptist minister and activist who became the most visible spokesperson and leader in the civil rights movement from 1955 until his assassination in 1968.

King was born **Michael King Jr.** on January 15, 1929, in Atlanta, Georgia, the second of three children to the Reverend Michael King Sr. and Alberta (Williams) King Martin's mother named him Michael, which was entered onto the birth certificate by the attending physician. King Sr. stated that "Michael" was a mistake by the physician. Martin's older sister is Christine King Farris and his younger brother was A.D. King. Martin's maternal grandfather Adam Daniel Williams, who was a minister in rural Georgia, moved to Atlanta in 1893, and became pastor of the Ebenezer Baptist Church in the following year. Williams, who was of African-Irish descent, married Jennie Celeste Parks, and they gave birth to King's mother, Alberta. Martin's father was born to sharecroppers, James Albert and Delia King of Stockbridge, Georgia. In his adolescent years, King Sr. left his parents' farm and walked to Atlanta where he attained a high school education. He. then enrolled in Morehouse College and studied to enter the ministry. King Sr. and Alberta began dating in 1920 and married on November 25, 1926. Until Jennie's death in 1941, they lived together on the second floor of her parent's two story Victorian house, where Martin was born.

Shortly after marrying Alberta, King Sr. became assistant pastor of the Ebenezer Baptist Church. Adam Daniel Williams died of a stroke in the spring of 1931. That fall, King's father took over the role of pastor at the church, where he would in time raise the attendance from six hundred to several thousand. In 1934, the church sent King Sr. on a multinational trip to Italy, Tunisia, Egypt, Israel, then Germany for the meeting of the Baptist World Alliance (BWA). The trip ended with visits to sites in Berlin associated with the Protestant reformation leader, Martin Luther. While there, Michael King Sr. witnessed the rise of Nazism. In reaction, the BWA conference issued a resolution which stated, "This Congress deplores and condemns as a violation of the law of God the Heavenly Father, all racial animosity, and every form of oppression or unfair discrimination toward the Jews, toward coloured people, or toward subject races in any part of the world." He returned home in August of 1934, and in that same year began referring to himself as Martin Luther King Sr., and his son as Martin Luther King Jr. Martin's birth certificate was altered to read "Martin Luther King Jr." on July 23, 1957, when he was 28 years old.

At his childhood home, King and his two siblings would read aloud Biblical scripture as instructed by their father. After dinners there, King's grandmother Jennie, who he affectionately referred to as

"Mama", would tell lively stories from the Bible to her grandchildren. King's father would regularly use whippings to discipline his children. At times, King Sr. would also have his children whip each other. King's father later remarked, "[Martin] was the most peculiar child whenever you whipped him. He'd stand there, and the tears would run down, and he'd never cry." Once when King witnessed his brother A.D. emotionally upset his sister Christine, he took a telephone and knocked out A.D. with it. When he and his brother were playing at their home, A.D. slid from a banister and hit into their grandmother, Jennie, causing her to fall down unresponsive. Martin, believing her dead, blamed himself and attempted suicide by jumping from a second-story window. Upon hearing that his grandmother was alive, Martin rose and left the ground where he had fallen.

Martin became friends with a white boy whose father owned a business across the street from his family's home. In September 1935, when the boys were about six years old, they started school. Martin had to attend a school for black children, Younge Street Elementary School, while his close playmate went to a separate school for white children only. Soon afterwards, the parents of the white boy stopped allowing King to play with their son, stating to him "we are white, and you are colored". When Martin relayed the happenings to his parents, they had a long discussion with him about the history of slavery and racism in America. Upon learning of the hatred, violence and oppression that black people had faced in the U.S., Martin would later state that he was "determined to hate every white person". His parents instructed him that it was his Christian duty to love everyone.

King witnessed his father stand up against segregation and various forms of discrimination. Once, when stopped by a police officer who referred to King Sr. as "boy", he responded sharply that Martin was a boy, but he was a man. When Martin's father took him into a shoe store in downtown Atlanta, the clerk told them they needed to sit in the back. King's father refused, stating "we'll either buy shoes sitting here or we won't buy any shoes at all", before taking Martin and leaving the store. He told Martin afterwards, "I don't care how long I have to live with this system, I will never accept it." In 1936, Martin's father led hundreds of African-Americans in a civil rights march to the city hall in Atlanta, to protest voting rights discrimination. Martin later remarked that King Sr. was "a real father" to him.

Martin memorized and sang hymns, and stated verses from the Bible, by the time he was five years old. Over the next year, he began to go to church events with his mother and sing hymns while she played piano. His favorite hymn to sing was *"I Want to Be More and More Like Jesus"*; he moved attendees with his singing. King later became a member of the junior choir in his church. He enjoyed opera, and played the piano. As he grew up, Martin garnered a large vocabulary from reading dictionaries and consistently used his expanding lexicon. He got into physical altercations with boys in his neighborhood, but oftentimes used his knowledge of words to stymie fights. Martin showed a lack of interest in grammar and spelling, a trait which he carried throughout his life. In 1939, Martin sang as a member of his church choir in slave costume, for the all-white audience at the Atlanta premiere of the film *Gone with the Wind*.

On May 18, 1941, when Martin had snuck away from studying at home to watch a parade, he was informed that something had happened to his maternal grandmother. Upon returning home, he found out that she had suffered a heart attack and died while being transported to a hospital. He took the death very hard, and believed that his deception of going to see the parade may have been responsible for God taking her. His father instructed Martin in his bedroom that he shouldn't blame himself for her death, and that she had been called home to God as part of God's plan which could not be changed. Martin struggled with this and could not fully believe that his parents knew where his grandmother had gone. Shortly thereafter, Martin's father decided to move the family to a two-story brick home on a hill that overlooked downtown Atlanta.

In his adolescent years, Martin initially felt resentment against whites due to the "racial humiliation" that he, his family, and his neighbors often had to endure in the segregated South. In 1942, when he was 13 years old, Martin became the youngest assistant manager of a newspaper delivery station for the *Atlanta Journal*. That year, King skipped the ninth grade and was enrolled in Booker T. Washington High School, which was the only high school in the city for African American students. It had been formed after local black leaders including Martin's grandfather (Williams), urged the city government of Atlanta to create it. Martin became known for his public-speaking ability and was part of the school's debate team.

Martin was initially skeptical of many of Christianity's claims. At the age of 13, he denied the bodily resurrection of Jesus during Sunday school. At this point, he stated, "doubts began to spring forth unrelentingly." He concurrently found himself unable to identify with the emotional displays and gestures people would make at his church and started to wonder if he would ever attain personal satisfaction from religion.

During his junior year, Martin Luther King, Jr. won first prize in an oratorical contest sponsored by the Negro Elks Club in Dublin, Georgia. In his speech he stated, "black America still wears chains. The finest negro is at the mercy of the meanest white man." On the ride home to Atlanta by bus, he and his teacher were ordered by the driver to stand so that white passengers could sit down. King initially refused but complied after his teacher told him that he would be breaking the law if he did not submit. During this incident, Martin said that he was "the angriest I have ever been in my life."

Shortly after, Morehouse College—a respected historically black college—announced that it would accept any high school juniors who could pass its entrance exam. At that time, many students had abandoned further studies to enlist in World War II. Due to this, Morehouse was eager to fill its classrooms. At the age of 15, Martin passed the exam and entered Morehouse. He played freshman football there.

The summer before his last year at Morehouse, in 1947, the 18-year-old Martin chose to enter the ministry. He had concluded that the church offered the most assuring way to answer "an inner urge to serve humanity." Martin Luther King's "inner urge" had begun developing, and he made peace with the Baptist Church, as he believed he would be a "rational" minister with sermons that were "a respectful force for ideas, even social protest." In 1948, Martin Luther King, Jr. graduated at the age of 19 from Morehouse with a B.A. in sociology.

Martin enrolled in Crozer Theological Seminary in Chester, Pennsylvania. King Sr. fully supported his son's decision to continue his education and made arrangements for Martin to work with J. Pius Barbour, a family friend who pastored at Calvary Baptist Church in Chester. Martin Luther King, Jr. became known as one of the "Sons of Calvary", an honor he shared with William Augustus Jones Jr. and Samuel D. Proctor who both went on to become well-known preachers in the black church.

While attending Crozer, Martin was joined by Walter McCall, a former classmate at Morehouse. At Crozer, he was elected president of the student body. The African American students of Crozer for the most part conducted their social activity on Edwards Street. Martin became fond of the street because a classmate had an aunt who prepared collard greens for them, which they both relished.

In his third year at Crozer, Martin became romantically involved with the white daughter of an immigrant German woman who worked as a cook in the cafeteria. The woman had been involved with a professor prior to her relationship with Martin. He planned to marry her, but friends advised against it, saying that an interracial marriage would provoke animosity from both blacks and whites, potentially damaging his chances of ever pastoring a church in the South. King tearfully told a friend that he could not endure his mother's pain over the marriage and broke the relationship off six months later. Martin Luther King, Jr. graduated with a B.Div. degree in 1951.

Martin began doctoral studies in systematic theology at Boston University. While pursuing doctoral studies, he worked as an assistant minister at Boston's historic Twelfth Baptist Church with Rev. William Hunter Hester. Hester was an old friend of Martin's father and was an important influence on Martin. In Boston, Martin befriended a small cadre of local ministers his age, and sometimes guest pastored at their churches, including the Reverend Michael Haynes, associate pastor at Twelfth Baptist Church in Roxbury (and younger brother of jazz drummer Roy Haynes). The young men often held bull sessions in their various apartments, discussing theology, sermon style, and social issues.

While studying at Boston University, he asked a friend from Atlanta named Mary Powell, who was a student at the New England

Conservatory Of Music, if she knew any nice Southern girls. Powell asked fellow student Coretta Scott if she was interested in meeting a Southern friend studying divinity. Scott was not interested in dating preachers, but eventually agreed to allow Martin to telephone her based on Powell's description and vouching. On their first phone call, King told Scott "I am like Napoleon at Waterloo before your charms", to which she replied, "You haven't even met me". They went out for dates in his green Chevy. After the second date, King was certain Scott possessed the qualities he sought in a wife. She had been an activist at Antioch in undergrad, where Carol and Rod Serling were schoolmates.

King married Coretta Scott on June 18, 1953, on the lawn of her parents' house in her hometown of Heiberger, Alabama. They became the parents of four children: Yolanda King (1955–2007), Martin Luther King III (b. 1957), Dexter Scott King (b. 1961), and Bernice King (b. 1963). During their marriage, King limited Coretta's role in the civil rights movement, expecting her to be a housewife and mother.

At the age of 25 in 1954, Martin Luther King, Jr. was called as pastor of the Dexter Avenue Baptist Church in Montgomery, Alabama. He received his Ph.D. degree on June 5, 1955, with a dissertation (initially supervised by Edgar S. Brightman and, upon the latter's death, by Lotan Harold DeWolf) titled *A Comparison of the Conceptions of God in the Thinking of Paul Tillich and Henry Nelson Wieman.*

Martin Luthern King, Jr. is best known for advancing civil rights through nonviolence and civil disobedience, inspired by his Christian beliefs and the nonviolent activism of Mahatma Gandhi.

King led the 1955 Montgomery bus boycott and in 1957 became the first president of the Southern Christian Leadership Conference (SCLC). With the SCLC, he led an unsuccessful 1962 struggle against segregation in Albany, Georgia, and helped organize the nonviolent 1963 protests in Birmingham, Alabama. He helped organize the 1963 March on Washington, where he delivered his famous "I Have a Dream" speech.

J. Edgar Hoover considered him a radical and made him an object of the FBI's COINTELPRO from 1963 on. FBI agents investigated him for possible communist ties, recorded his extramarital liaisons and reported on them to government officials, and on one occasion mailed King a threatening anonymous letter, which he interpreted as an attempt to make him commit suicide.

On October 14, 1964, King won the Nobel Peace Prize for combating racial inequality through nonviolent resistance. In 1965, he helped organize the Selma to Montgomery marches. The following year, he and the SCLC took the movement north to Chicago to work on segregated housing. In his final years, he expanded his focus to include opposition towards poverty and the Vietnam War. He alienated many of his liberal allies with a 1967 speech titled "Beyond Vietnam".

In 1968, King was planning a national occupation of Washington, D.C., to be called the Poor People's Campaign, when he was assassinated on April 4 in Memphis, Tennessee. His death was followed by riots in many U.S. cities. Allegations that James Earl Ray, the man convicted of killing King, had been framed or acted in concert with government agents persisted for decades after the shooting. Sentenced to 99 years in prison for King's murder, effectively a life sentence as Ray was 41 at the time of conviction,

Ray served 29 years of his sentence and died from hepatitis in 1998 while in prison.

King was posthumously awarded the Presidential Medal of Freedom and the Congressional Gold Medal. Martin Luther King Jr. Day was established as a holiday in numerous cities and states beginning in 1971; the holiday was enacted at the federal level by legislation signed by President Ronald Reagan in 1986. Hundreds of streets in the U.S. have been renamed in his honor, and a county in Washington State was rededicated for him. The Martin Luther King Jr. Memorial on the National Mall in Washington, D.C., was dedicated in 2011.

RUTH BADER GINSBURG

Ruth Bader Ginsburg (born **Joan Ruth Bader**; March 15, 1933 – September 18, 2020) was an American jurist who served as an associate justice of the Supreme Court of the United States from 1993 until her death in 2020. She was nominated by President Bill Clinton and was generally viewed as a moderate judge who was a consensus builder at the time of her nomination. Ginsburg was the second woman to serve on the U.S. Supreme Court, after Sandra Day O'Connor.

Ginsburg was born and grew up in Brooklyn, New York. Her older sister died when she was a baby, and her mother died shortly before Ginsburg graduated from high school. She earned her bachelor's degree at Cornell University and married Martin D. Ginsburg, becoming a mother before starting law school at Harvard, where she was one of the few women in her class. Ginsburg transferred to Columbia Law School, where she graduated joint first in her class. After law school, Ginsburg entered academia. She was a professor at Rutgers Law School and Columbia Law School, teaching civil procedure as one of the few women in her field.

Ginsburg spent much of her legal career as an advocate for gender equality and women's rights, winning many arguments before the Supreme Court. She advocated as a volunteer attorney for the American Civil Liberties Union and was a member of its board of directors and one of its general counsel in the 1970s. In 1980, President Jimmy Carter appointed her to the U.S. Court of Appeals for the District of Columbia Circuit, where she served until her appointment to the Supreme Court in 1993. Between O'Connor's retirement in 2006 and the appointment of Sonia Sotomayor in 2009, she was the only female justice on the Supreme Court. During that time, Ginsburg became more forceful with her dissents, notably in *Ledbetter v. Goodyear Tire & Rubber Co.* (2007). Ginsburg's dissenting opinion was credited with inspiring the Lilly Ledbetter Fair Pay Act which was signed into law by President Barack Obama in 2009, making it easier for employees to win pay discrimination claims.

Ginsburg received attention in American popular culture for her passionate dissents in numerous cases, widely seen as reflecting paradigmatically liberal views of the law. She was playfully and notably dubbed "The Notorious R.B.G." by a law student, a reference to the late Brooklyn-born rapper The Notorious B.I.G., and she later embraced the moniker. Ginsburg died at her home in Washington, D.C., on September 18, 2020, at the age of 87, from complications of metastatic pancreatic cancer.

Joan Ruth Bader was born on March 15, 1933, at Beth Moses Hospital in Brooklyn, New York City, the second daughter of Celia (née Amster) and Nathan Bader, who lived in the Flatbush neighborhood. Her father was a Jewish emigrant from Odessa,

Russian Empire, and her mother was born in New York to parents who came from Kraków, Poland. The Baders' elder daughter Marylin died of meningitis at age six, when Ruth was 14 months old. The family called Joan Ruth "Kiki", a nickname Marylin had given her for being "a kicky baby". When "Kiki" started school, Celia discovered that her daughter's class had several other girls named Joan, so Celia suggested the teacher call her daughter "Ruth" to avoid confusion. Although not devout, the Bader family belonged to East Midwood Jewish Center, a Conservative synagogue, where Ruth learned tenets of the Jewish faith and gained familiarity with the Hebrew language. Starting as a camper from the age of four, Ruth attended Camp Che-Na-Wah, a Jewish summer program at Lake Balfour near Minerva, New York, where she was later a camp counselor until the age of eighteen.

Celia took an active role in her daughter's education, often taking her to the library. Celia had been a good student in her youth, graduating from high school at age 15, yet she could not further her own education because her family instead chose to send her brother to college. Celia wanted her daughter to get more education, which she thought would allow Ruth to become a high school history teacher. Ruth attended James Madison High School, whose law program later dedicated a courtroom in her honor. Celia struggled with cancer throughout Ruth's high school years and died the day before Ruth's high school graduation.

Bader attended Cornell University in Ithaca, New York, and was a member of Alpha Epsilon Phi. While at Cornell, she met Martin D. Ginsburg at age 17. She graduated from Cornell with a bachelor of arts degree in government on June 23, 1954. She was a member of Phi Beta Kappa and the highest-ranking female student in her graduating class. Bader married Ginsburg a month after her graduation from Cornell. She and Martin moved to Fort Sill,

Oklahoma, where he was stationed as a Reserve Officers' Training Corps officer in the U.S. Army Reserve after his call-up to active duty. At age 21, she worked for the Social Security Administration office in Oklahoma, where she was demoted after becoming pregnant with her first child. She gave birth to a daughter in 1955.

In the fall of 1956, Ginsburg enrolled at Harvard Law School, where she was one of only 9 women in a class of about 500 men. The dean of Harvard Law reportedly invited all the female law students to dinner at his family home and asked the female law students, including Ginsburg, "Why are you at Harvard Law School, taking the place of a man?" When her husband took a job in New York City, Ginsburg transferred to Columbia Law School and became the first woman to be on two major law reviews: the *Harvard Law Review* and *Columbia Law Review*. In 1959, she earned her law degree at Columbia and tied for first in her class.

At the start of her legal career, Ginsburg encountered difficulty in finding employment. In 1960, Supreme Court justice Felix Frankfurter rejected Ginsburg for a clerkship position due to her gender. She was rejected despite a strong recommendation from Albert Martin Sacks, who was a professor and later dean of Harvard Law School. Columbia law professor Gerald Gunther also pushed for Judge Edmund L. Palmieri of the U.S. District Court for the Southern District of New York to hire Ginsburg as a law clerk, threatening to never recommend another Columbia student to Palmieri if he did not give Ginsburg the opportunity and guaranteeing to provide the judge with a replacement clerk should Ginsburg not succeed. Later that year, Ginsburg began her clerkship for Judge Palmieri, and she held the position for two years.

From 1961 to 1963, Ginsburg was a research associate and then an associate director of the Columbia Law School Project on

International Procedure; she learned Swedish to co-author a book with Anders Bruzelius on civil procedure in Sweden. Ginsburg conducted extensive research for her book at Lund University in Sweden. Ginsburg's time in Sweden also influenced her thinking on gender equality. She was inspired when she observed the changes in Sweden, where women were 20 to 25 percent of all law students; one of the judges whom Ginsburg watched for her research was eight months pregnant and still working.

Her first position as a professor was at Rutgers Law School in 1963. The appointment was not without its drawbacks; Ginsburg was informed she would be paid less than her male colleagues because she had a husband with a well-paid job. At the time Ginsburg entered academia, she was one of fewer than twenty female law professors in the United States. She was a professor of law, mainly civil procedure, at Rutgers from 1963 to 1972, receiving tenure from the school in 1969.

In 1970, she co-founded the *Women's Rights Law Reporter*, the first law journal in the U.S. to focus exclusively on women's rights. From 1972 to 1980, she taught at Columbia Law School, where she became the first tenured woman and co-authored the first law school casebook on sex discrimination. She also spent a year as a fellow of the Center for Advanced Study in the Behavioral Sciences at Stanford University from 1977 to 1978.

In 1972, Ginsburg co-founded the Women's Rights Project at the American Civil Liberties Union (ACLU), and in 1973, she became the Project's general counsel. The Women's Rights Project and related ACLU projects participated in more than 300 gender discrimination cases by 1974.

Legal scholars and advocates credit Ginsburg's body of work with making significant legal advances for women under the Equal Protection Clause of the Constitution. Taken together, Ginsburg's legal victories discouraged legislatures from treating women and men differently under the law. She continued to work on the ACLU's Women's Rights Project until her appointment to the Federal Bench in 1980.

Ginsburg was nominated by President Jimmy Carter on April 14, 1980, to a seat on the United States Court of Appeals for the District of Columbia Circuit vacated by Judge Harold Leventhal upon his death. She was confirmed by the United States Senate on June 18, 1980, and received her commission later that day. Her service terminated on August 9, 1993, due to her elevation to the United States Supreme Court.

President Bill Clinton nominated Ginsburg as an Associate Justice of the Supreme Court on June 22, 1993, to fill the seat vacated by retiring Justice Byron White. She was recommended to Clinton by then–U.S. attorney general Janet Reno, after a suggestion by Utah Republican senator Orrin Hatch. At the time of her nomination, Ginsburg was viewed as a moderate, and as a consensus builder in her time on the appeals court. Clinton was reportedly looking to increase the court's diversity, which Ginsburg did as the first Jewish justice since the 1969 resignation of Justice Abe Fortas. She was the second female and the first Jewish female justice of the Supreme Court. She eventually became the longest-serving Jewish justice.

The retirement of Justice Sandra Day O'Connor in 2006 left Ginsburg as the only woman on the court. With the retirement of Justice John Paul Stevens, Ginsburg became the senior member of what was sometimes referred to as the court's "liberal wing". When the court split 5–4 along ideological lines and the liberal justices were in the minority, Ginsburg often had the authority to assign authorship of the dissenting opinion because of her seniority.

At his request, Ginsburg administered the oath of office to Vice President Al Gore for a second term during the second inauguration of Bill Clinton on January 20, 1997. She was the third woman to administer an inaugural oath of office. Ginsburg is believed to have been the first Supreme Court justice to officiate at a same-sex wedding, performing the August 31, 2013, ceremony of Kennedy Center president Michael Kaiser and John Roberts, a government economist.

Despite their ideological differences, Ginsburg considered Antonin Scalia her closest colleague on the court. The two justices often dined together and attended the opera. In addition to befriending modern composers, including Tobias Picker, in her spare time, Ginsburg appeared in several operas in non-speaking supernumerary roles such as *Die Fledermaus* (2003) and *Ariadne auf Naxos* (1994 and 2009 with Scalia), and spoke lines penned by herself in *The Daughter of the Regiment* (2016).

In 2018, Ginsburg expressed her support for the Me Too movement, which encourages women to speak up about their experiences with sexual harassment. She told an audience, "It's about time. For so long women were silent, thinking there was nothing you could do about it, but now the law is on the side of women, or men, who encounter harassment and that's a good thing." She also reflected on her own experiences with gender discrimination and sexual harassment, including a time when a chemistry professor at Cornell unsuccessfully attempted to trade her exam answers for sex.

A few days after Bader graduated from Cornell, she married Martin D. Ginsburg, who later became an internationally prominent tax attorney practicing at Weil, Gotshal & Manges. Upon her accession to the D.C. Circuit, the couple moved from New York City to Washington, D.C., where her husband became a professor of law at Georgetown University Law Center. Their daughter, Jane C. Ginsburg (b. 1955), is a professor at Columbia Law School. Their son, James Steven Ginsburg (b. 1965), is the founder and president of Cedille Records, a classical music recording company based in Chicago, Illinois. Ginsburg was a grandmother of four.

After the birth of their daughter, Ginsburg's husband was diagnosed with testicular cancer. They celebrated their 56th wedding anniversary on June 23, 2010. Martin Ginsburg died of complications from metastatic cancer on June 27, 2010.

In 1999, Ginsburg was diagnosed with colon cancer, the first of her five[117] bouts with cancer. She underwent surgery followed by chemotherapy and radiation therapy. During the process, she did not miss a day on the bench. Ginsburg was physically weakened by the cancer treatment, and she began working with a personal trainer. Bryant Johnson, a former Army reservist attached to the U.S. Army Special Forces, trained Ginsburg twice weekly in the justices-only gym at the Supreme Court. Ginsburg saw her physical fitness improve after her first bout with cancer; she was able to complete twenty push-ups in a session before her 80th birthday.

Nearly a decade after her first bout with cancer, Ginsburg again underwent surgery on February 5, 2009, this time for pancreatic cancer. Ginsburg had a tumor that was discovered at an early stage. She was released from a New York City hospital on February 13 and returned to the bench when the Supreme Court went back into session on February 23, 2009. After experiencing discomfort while exercising in the Supreme Court gym in November 2014, she had a stent placed in her right coronary artery.

Ginsburg's next hospitalization helped her detect another round of cancer. On November 8, 2018, Ginsburg fell in her office at the Supreme Court, fracturing three ribs, for which she was hospitalized. a CT scan of her ribs following her November 8 fall showed cancerous nodules in her lungs. On December 21, Ginsburg underwent a left-lung lobectomy at Memorial Sloan Kettering Cancer Center to remove the nodules. For the first time since joining the Court more than 25 years earlier, Ginsburg missed oral argument on January 7, 2019, while she recuperated. She returned to the Supreme Court on February 15 to participate in a private conference with other justices in her first appearance at the court since her cancer surgery in December 2018.

Months later in August 2019, the Supreme Court announced that Ginsburg had recently completed three weeks of focused radiation treatment to ablate a tumor found in her pancreas over the summer. By January 2020, Ginsburg was cancer-free. By February 2020, Ginsburg was not cancer free, but it was not released to the public. However, by May 2020, Ginsburg was once again receiving treatment for a recurrence of cancer. She reiterated her position that she "would remain a member of the court as long as I can do the job full steam", adding that she remained fully able to do so.

In 2002, Ginsburg was inducted into the National Women's Hall of Fame. Ginsburg was named one of 100 Most Powerful Women (2009), one of *Glamour* magazine's Women of the Year 2012, and one of *Time* magazine's 100 most influential people (2015). She was awarded honorary Doctor of Laws degrees by Willamette University (2009), Princeton University (2010), and Harvard University (2011).

During the presidency of Barack Obama, some progressive attorneys and activists called for Ginsburg to retire so that Obama could appoint a like-minded successor, particularly while the Democratic party held control of the U.S. Senate. They mentioned Ginsburg's age and past health issues as factors making her longevity uncertain. Ginsburg rejected these pleas. She affirmed her wish to remain a justice as long as she was mentally sharp enough to perform her duties. At the time of her death in September 2020, Ginsburg was, at age 87, the fourth-oldest serving U.S. Supreme Court Justice in the history of the country.

Ginsburg's death opened a vacancy on the Supreme Court about six weeks before the 2020 presidential election, initiating controversies regarding the nomination and confirmation of her successor. Ginsburg dictated in a statement through her granddaughter Clara Spera days before her death, stating: "My most fervent wish is that I will not be replaced until a new president is installed."

Ginsburg lay in state at the Capitol. She was both the first Jew and the first woman to lie in state therein.

JOHN ROBERT LEWIS

John Robert Lewis (February 21, 1940 – July 17, 2020) was an American statesman and civil rights leader who served in the United States House of Representatives for Georgia's 5th congressional district from 1987 until his death in 2020. He was the chairman of the Student Nonviolent Coordinating Committee (SNCC) from 1963 to 1966.

Lewis was one of the "Big Six" leaders of groups who organized the 1963 March on Washington. He fulfilled many key roles in the civil rights movement and its actions to end legalized racial segregation in the United States. In 1965, Lewis led the first of three Selma to Montgomery marches across the Edmund Pettus Bridge. In an incident which became known as Bloody Sunday, state troopers and police then attacked the marchers, including Lewis.

A member of the Democratic Party, Lewis was first elected to Congress in 1986 and served 17 terms in the U.S. House of Representatives. Due to his length of service, he became the dean of the Georgia congressional delegation. The district he represented included most of Atlanta.

He was a leader of the Democratic Party in the U.S. House of Representatives, serving from 1991 as a Chief Deputy Whip and from 2003 as Senior Chief Deputy Whip. Lewis received many honorary degrees and awards, including the Presidential Medal of Freedom.

John Robert Lewis was born just outside Troy, Alabama, the third of ten children of Willie Mae (née Carter) and Eddie Lewis. His parents were sharecroppers in rural Pike County, Alabama.

As a boy, Lewis aspired to be a preacher; and at age five, he was preaching to his family's chickens on the farm. As a young child, Lewis had little interaction with white people. In fact, by the time he was six, Lewis had seen only two white people in his life. As he grew older, he began taking trips into town with his family, where he experienced racism and segregation, such as at the public library in Troy. Lewis had relatives who lived in northern cities, and he learned from them that the North had integrated schools, buses, and businesses. When Lewis was 11, an uncle took him to Buffalo, New York, making him more acutely aware of Troy's segregation.

In 1955, Lewis first heard Martin Luther King Jr. on the radio, and he closely followed King's Montgomery bus boycott later that year. At age 15, Lewis preached his first public sermon. Lewis met Rosa Parks when he was 17, and met King for the first time when he was 18. After writing to King about being denied admission to Troy University in Alabama, Lewis was invited to a meeting. King, who referred to Lewis as "the boy from Troy," discussed suing the university for discrimination, but he warned Lewis that doing so could endanger his family in Troy. After discussing it with his parents, Lewis decided to proceed with his education at a small, historically black college in Tennessee.

Lewis graduated from the American Baptist Theological Seminary in Nashville, Tennessee, and was ordained as a Baptist minister. He then received a bachelor's degree in religion and philosophy from Fisk University. He was a member of Phi Beta Sigma fraternity.

As a student, Lewis was dedicated to the civil rights movement. He organized sit-ins at segregated lunch counters in Nashville and took part in many other civil rights activities as part of the Nashville Student Movement. The Nashville sit-in movement was responsible for the desegregation of lunch counters in downtown Nashville. Lewis was arrested and jailed many times in the nonviolent movement to desegregate the city's downtown area. He was also instrumental in organizing bus boycotts and other nonviolent protests to support voting rights and racial equality.

During this time, Lewis expressed the need to engage in "good trouble, necessary trouble" to achieve change, and he held by the phrase and the sentiment throughout his life.

While a student, Lewis was invited to attend nonviolence workshops held at Clark Memorial United Methodist Church by the Rev. James Lawson and Rev. Kelly Miller Smith. There, Lewis and other students became dedicated adherents to the discipline and philosophy of nonviolence, which he practiced for the rest of his life.

In 1961, Lewis became one of the 13 original Freedom Riders. They were seven blacks and six whites determined to ride from Washington, D.C. to New Orleans in an integrated fashion. At that time, several southern states enforced laws prohibiting black and white riders from sitting next to each other on public transportation. The Freedom Ride, originated by the Fellowship of Reconciliation and revived by James Farmer and the Congress of Racial Equality (CORE), was initiated to pressure the federal government to enforce the Supreme Court decision in *Boynton v. Virginia* (1960) that declared segregated interstate bus travel to be unconstitutional. The Freedom Rides also exposed the government's passivity towards violence against law-abiding citizens. The federal government had trusted the notoriously racist Alabama police to protect the Riders, but did nothing itself, except to have FBI agents take notes. The Kennedy Administration then called for a cooling-off period, with a moratorium on Freedom Rides.

In 1963, when Charles McDew stepped down as chairman of the Student Nonviolent Coordinating Committee (SNCC), Lewis, one of the founding members of SNCC, was elected to take over. Lewis's experience at that point was already widely respected. His courage and tenacious adherence to the philosophy of reconciliation and nonviolence made him emerge as a leader. By this time, he had been arrested 24 times in the nonviolent movement for equal justice. He served as chairman until 1966. During his tenure, SNCC opened Freedom Schools, launched the Mississippi Freedom Summer, and organized some of the voter registration efforts during the 1965 Selma voting rights campaign.

In 1963, as chairman of SNCC, Lewis was named one of the "Big Six" leaders who were organizing the March on Washington, the occasion of Dr. Martin Luther King's celebrated "I Have a Dream" speech, along with Whitney Young, A. Philip Randolph, James Farmer, and Roy Wilkins. Lewis and his fellow SNCC workers had experienced the federal government's passivity in the face of Southern violence; Lewis, the youngest speaker that day, begrudgingly acquiesced and delivered the edited speech as the fourth speaker that day, ahead of the "I Have a Dream" speech by King who served as the final speaker that day.

In 1964, Lewis coordinated SNCC's efforts for "Mississippi Freedom Summer," a campaign to register black voters across the South and expose college students from around the country to the perils of African-American life in the South. Lewis traveled the country, encouraging students to spend their summer break trying to help people vote in Mississippi, the most recalcitrant state in the union. Lewis became nationally known during his prominent role in the Selma to Montgomery marches when, on March 7, 1965 – a day that would become known as "Bloody Sunday" – Lewis and fellow activist Hosea Williams led over 600 marchers across the Edmund Pettus Bridge in Selma, Alabama. At the end of the bridge, they were met by Alabama State Troopers who ordered them to disperse. When the marchers stopped to pray, the police discharged tear gas and mounted troopers charged the demonstrators, beating them with nightsticks. Lewis's skull was fractured, but he escaped across the bridge to Brown Chapel, a church in Selma that served as the movement's headquarters. Lewis bore scars on his head from the incident for the rest of his life.

In 1966, Lewis moved to New York City to take a job as the associate director of the Field Foundation. He was there a little over a year before moving back to Atlanta to direct the Southern Regional Council's Community Organization Project. During his time with the SRC, he completed his degree from Fisk University.

Lewis met Lillian Miles at a New Year's Eve party hosted by Xernona Clayton. They married in 1968. Together, they had one son, named John-Miles Lewis. Lillian died on December 31, 2012.

In 1970, Lewis became the director of the Voter Education Project (VEP), a position he held until 1977. Though initially a project of the Southern Regional Council, the VEP became an independent organization in 1971. Despite difficulties caused by the 1973–1975 recession, the VEP added nearly four million minority voters to the rolls under Lewis's leadership. During his tenure, the VEP expanded its mission, including running Voter Mobilization Tours.

In 1981, Lewis ran for an at-large seat on the Atlanta City Council. He won with 69% of the vote and served on the council until 1986.

Soon after, Lewis was elected to represent Georgia's 5th congressional district, one of the most consistently Democratic districts in the nation. In 1988, the year after he was sworn into Congress, Lewis introduced a bill to create a national African American museum in Washington. The bill failed, and for 15 years he continued to introduce it with each new Congress. Each time it was blocked in the Senate, most often by conservative Southern Senator Jesse Helms. In 2003, Helms retired. The bill won bipartisan support, and President George W. Bush signed the bill to establish the museum, with the Smithsonian's Board of Regents to establish the location. The National Museum of African American History and Culture, located adjacent to the Washington Memorial, held its opening ceremony on September 25, 2016.

Lewis was one of the most liberal members of the House and one of the most liberal congressmen to have represented a district in the Deep South.

Lewis drew on his historical involvement in the Civil Rights Movement as part of his politics. He made an annual pilgrimage to Alabama to retrace the route he marched in 1965 from Selma to Montgomery – a route Lewis worked to make part of the Historic National Trails program. That trip became "one of the hottest tickets in Washington among lawmakers, Republican and Democrat, eager to associate themselves with Lewis and the movement. 'We don't deliberately set out to win votes, but it's very helpful," Lewis said of the trip'."

In January 2001, Lewis boycotted the inauguration of George W. Bush by staying in his Atlanta district. He did not attend the swearing-in because he did not believe Bush was the true elected president.

In 2001, the John F. Kennedy Library Foundation awarded Lewis the Profile in Courage Award "for his extraordinary courage, leadership and commitment to civil rights. It is a lifetime achievement award and has been given out only twice, John Lewis and William Winter (in 2008). The next year he was awarded the Spingarn Medal from the NAACP.

In March 2003, Lewis spoke to a crowd of 30,000 in Oregon during an anti-war protest before the start of the Iraq War. In 2006 and 2009 he was arrested for protesting against the genocide in Darfur outside the Sudanese embassy. He was one of eight U.S. Representatives, from six states, arrested while holding a sit-in near the west side of the U.S. Capitol building, to advocate for immigration reform.

At first, Lewis supported Hillary Clinton, endorsing her presidential campaign on October 12, 2007. On February 14, 2008, however, he announced he was considering withdrawing his support from Clinton and might instead cast his superdelegate vote for Barack Obama:

On February 27, 2008, Lewis formally changed his support and endorsed Obama. After Obama clinched the Democratic nomination for president, Lewis said "If someone had told me this would be happening now, I would have told them they were crazy, out of their mind, they didn't know what they were talking about ... I just wish the others were around to see this day. ... To the people who were beaten, put in jail, were asked questions they could never answer to register to vote, it's amazing."

In February 2009, 48 years after he was bloodied in a Greyhound station during a Freedom Ride, Lewis received a nationally televised apology from a white southerner and former Klansman, Elwin Wilson.

In 2010, Lewis was awarded the First LBJ Liberty and Justice for All Award, given to him by the Lyndon Baines Johnson Foundation, and the next year, Lewis was awarded the Presidential Medal of Freedom by President Barack Obama.

On June 22, 2016, House Democrats, led by Lewis and Massachusetts Representative Katherine Clark, began a sit-in demanding House Speaker Paul Ryan allow a vote on gun-safety legislation in the aftermath of the Orlando nightclub shooting. Speaker *pro tempore* Daniel Webster ordered the House into recess, but Democrats refused to leave the chamber for nearly 26 hours.

In a January 2016 interview, Lewis compared Donald Trump, then the Republican front-runner, to former Governor George Wallace. Lewis said that he would not attend Trump's inauguration because he did not believe that Trump was the true elected president. "It will be the first (inauguration) that I miss since I've been in Congress. You cannot be at home with something that you feel that is wrong, is not right," he said. Lewis had failed to attend George W. Bush's inauguration in 2001 because he believed that he too was not a legitimately elected president. Lewis's statement was rated as "Pants on Fire" by PolitiFact.

In 2016, it was announced that a future United States Navy underway replenishment oiler would be named USNS *John Lewis*. Also in 2016, Lewis and fellow Selma marcher Frederick Reese accepted Congressional Gold Medals which were bestowed to the "foot soldiers" of the Selma marchers. The same year, Lewis was awarded the Liberty Medal at the National Constitution Center. The prestigious award has been awarded to international leaders from Malala Yousafzai to the 14th Dalai Lama, presidents George Bush and Bill Clinton and other dignitaries and visionaries. The timing of Lewis's award coincided with the 150th anniversary of the 14th amendment.

Lewis endorsed Joe Biden for president on April 7, 2020, a day before he effectively secured the Democratic nomination. He recommended Biden pick a woman of color as his running mate.

On July 17, 2020, Lewis died at the age of 80 after a six-month battle with the disease in Atlanta, on the same day as his friend and fellow civil rights activist C.T. Vivian. Lewis had been the final surviving "Big Six" civil rights icon.

President Donald Trump ordered all flags to be flown at half-staff in response to Lewis's death. Condolences also came from the international community, with Swedish Prime Minister Stefan Löfven, French President Emmanuel Macron, Irish President Michael D. Higgins among others, all memorializing Lewis.

Public ceremonies honoring Lewis began in his hometown of Troy, Alabama at Troy University, which had denied him admission in 1957 due to racial segregation. Services were then held at the historic Brown Chapel AME Church in Selma, Alabama. Calls to rename the Edmund Pettus Bridge in Selma, in Lewis's honor grew after his death. On July 26, 2020, his casket, carried by a horse-drawn caisson, traveled the same route over the bridge that he walked during the Bloody Sunday march from Selma to

Montgomery, before his lying in state at the Alabama State Capitol in Montgomery.

House Speaker Nancy Pelosi and Senate Majority Leader Mitch McConnell announced that Lewis would lie in state in the United States Capitol Rotunda on July 27 and 28, with a public viewing and procession through Washington, D.C. He is the first African-American lawmaker to be so honored in the Rotunda; in October 2019 his colleague, representative Elijah Cummings, lay in state in the Capitol Statuary Hall. On July 29, 2020, Lewis's casket left the U.S. Capitol and was transported back to Atlanta, Georgia, where he lay in state for a day at the Georgia State Capitol.

Among the distinguished speakers at his final funeral service at Atlanta's Ebenezer Baptist Church were former U.S. Presidents Bill Clinton, George W. Bush, and Barack Obama, who gave the eulogy. Former President Jimmy Carter, unable to travel during the COVID pandemic due to his advanced age, sent a statement to be read during the service. The current President Donald Trump did not attend the service. Lewis's interment followed the service, at Atlanta's historic South-View Cemetery.

Lewis penned an op-ed to the nation that was published in *The New York Times* on the day of his funeral. In it, he called on the younger generation to continue the work for justice and an end to hate.

Lewis was honored by having the 1997 sculpture by Thornton Dial, *The Bridge*, placed at Ponce de Leon Avenue and Freedom Park, Atlanta, dedicated to him by the artist. In 1999, Lewis was awarded the Wallenberg Medal from the University of Michigan in recognition of his courageous lifelong commitment to the defense of civil and human rights. In that same year, he received the Four Freedoms Award for the Freedom of Speech.

Lewis was the only living speaker from the March on Washington present on the stage during the inauguration of Barack Obama. Obama signed a commemorative photograph for Lewis with the words, "Because of you, John. Barack Obama."

In 2020, Lewis was awarded the Walter P. Reuther Humanitarian Award by Wayne State University, the UAW, and the Reuther family.

Lewis's death in July 2020 has given rise to support for renaming the historically significant Pettus bridge in Lewis's honor, an idea previously floated years ago. After his death, the Board of Fairfax County Public Schools announced that Robert E. Lee High School in Springfield, Virginia would be renamed John R. Lewis High School.

KAMALA DEVI HARRIS

Kamala Devi Harris (born October 20, 1964 in Oakland, California) is an American politician and attorney who is the vice president-elect of the United States. A member of the Democratic Party, she is set to assume office on January 20, 2021, alongside President-elect Joe Biden, having defeated incumbent President Donald Trump and Vice President Mike Pence in the 2020 election. She will be the United States' first female vice president and the highest-ranking female elected official in U.S. history. Harris will be also the first Asian-American and the first African-American vice president.

Harris graduated from Howard University and the University of California, Hastings College of the Law. She began her career in the Alameda County District Attorney's Office, before being recruited to the San Francisco District Attorney's Office and later the City Attorney of San Francisco's office. In 2003, she was elected district attorney of San Francisco. She was elected attorney general of California in 2010, and re-elected in 2014.

She defeated Loretta Sanchez in the 2016 Senate election to become the second African-American woman and the first South Asian American to serve in the United States Senate. As a senator, she has advocated for healthcare reform, federal descheduling of cannabis, a path to citizenship for undocumented immigrants, the DREAM Act, a ban on assault weapons, and progressive tax reform. She gained a national profile for her pointed questioning of Trump administration officials during Senate hearings. Harris ran for the 2020 Democratic presidential nomination and attracted national attention before ending her campaign on December 3, 2019.

Kamala Harris' mother, Shyamala Gopalan, a biologist whose work on the progesterone receptor gene stimulated work in breast cancer research, had arrived in the US from India in 1958 as a 19-year-old graduate student in nutrition and endocrinology at the University of California, Berkeley; Gopalan received her PhD in 1964. Kamala's father, Donald J. Harris, is a Stanford University professor emeritus of economics, who arrived in the US from British Jamaica in 1961 for graduate study at UC Berkeley, receiving a PhD in economics in 1966.

Along with her younger sister, Maya, Harris lived in Berkeley, California, until she was twelve years old. They lived briefly on Milvia Street in central Berkeley. Then her family moved to the upper floor of a duplex on Bancroft Way in West Berkeley, an area often called "the flatlands" with a significant Black population.

When Harris began kindergarten, she was bused as part of Berkeley's comprehensive desegregation program to Thousand Oaks Elementary School, a public school in a more prosperous neighborhood in northern Berkeley which previously had been 95 percent white, and after the desegregation plan went into effect became 40 percent Black.

Harris's formative milieu included African-American intellectuals and rights advocates. Mary Lewis, who taught at San Francisco State University for many years and cofounded the field of African-American studies there, was one of her mother's most trusted friends. When her mother worked late at her lab, Kamala was cared for by Regina Shelton, a black woman whose day-care center in the apartment below was decorated with pictures of Harriet Tubman and Sojourner Truth.

Harris grew up going to both a Black church and a Hindu temple. She and her sister visited their mother's family in Madras (now Chennai) – on the southeastern coast of India – several times, the last time in 2009 when Harris returned with her mother's ashes and scattered them in the Indian Ocean waters. She was strongly influenced by her maternal grandfather P. V. Gopalan, a retired Indian civil servant whose progressive views on democracy and women's rights impressed her. She has remained in touch with her Indian aunts and uncles throughout her adult life. She also visited her father's family in Jamaica.

Kamal's parents divorced when she was seven; she has said that when she and her sister visited their father in Palo Alto on weekends, neighbors' kids were not allowed to play with them because they were black. When she was 12, Kamala and her sister moved with their mother to Montreal, Quebec, Canada, where their mother had accepted a research and teaching position at the McGill University-affiliated Jewish General Hospital. Kamala attended a French-speaking middle school, Notre-Dame-des-Neiges, and then

Westmount High School in Westmount, Quebec, graduating in 1981.

After high school, Kamala Harris attended Howard University, a historically black university in Washington, D.C. While at Howard, she interned as a mail room clerk for California senator Alan Cranston, chaired the economics society, led the debate team and joined Alpha Kappa Alpha sorority. Kamala graduated from Howard in 1986 with a degree in political science and economics.

She then returned to California to attend law school at the University of California, Hastings College of the Law. While at UC Hastings, she served as president of its chapter of the Black Law Students Association. She graduated with a Juris Doctor in 1989 and was admitted to the California Bar in June 1990.

In 1990, Kamala Harris was hired as a deputy district attorney in Alameda County, California, where she was noted as being "an able prosecutor on the way up". In 1994, California Assembly speaker Willie Brown appointed Kamala to the state Unemployment Insurance Appeals Board and later to the California Medical Assistance Commission. She took a six-month leave of absence in 1994 from her duties as prosecutor, then afterwards resumed as prosecutor during the years she sat on the boards.

In February 1998, San Francisco district attorney Terence Hallinan recruited Kamala Harris as an assistant district attorney. There, she became the chief of the Career Criminal Division, supervising five other attorneys, where she prosecuted homicide, burglary, robbery, and sexual assault cases – particularly three-strikes cases. In 2000, Harris reportedly clashed with Hallinan's assistant, Darrell Salomon, over Proposition 21 ("Prop 21"), which would have granted prosecutors the option of trying juvenile defendants in Superior

Court rather than juvenile courts. Kamala campaigned against the measure and Salomon opposed directing media inquiries about Prop 21 to Harris and reassigned her, a *de facto* demotion. Harris filed a complaint against Salomon and quit.

In August 2000, Kamala Harris took a new job at San Francisco City Hall, working for city attorney Louise Renne. Kamala ran the Family and Children's Services Division representing child abuse and neglect cases. Renne endorsed Harris during her DA campaign.

In 2004, Harris recruited civil rights activist Lateefah Simon to create San Francisco Reentry Division. The flagship program was the Back on Track initiative, a first-of-its-kind reentry program for first-time nonviolent offenders age 18–30. Initiative participants whose crimes were not weapon or gang-related would plead guilty in exchange for a deferral of sentencing and regular appearances before a judge over a twelve- to eighteen-month period. The program maintained rigorous graduation requirements, mandating completion of up to 220 hours of community service, obtaining a high-school-equivalency diploma, maintaining steady employment, taking parenting classes, and passing drug tests.

At graduation, the court would dismiss the case and expunge the graduate's record. Over six years, the 200 people graduated from the program had a recidivism rate of less than ten percent, compared to the 53 percent of California's drug offenders who returned to prison within two years of release. Back on Track earned recognition from the U.S. Department of Justice as a model for reentry programs. The DOJ found that the cost to the taxpayers per participant was markedly lower ($5,000) than the cost of adjudicating a case ($10,000) and housing a low-level offender ($50,000). In 2009, a state law (the Back on Track Reentry Act, A.B. 750) was enacted, encouraging other California counties to start similar programs.

Adopted by the National District Attorneys Association as a model, prosecutor offices in Baltimore, Philadelphia, and Atlanta have used Back on Track as a template for their own programs.

On November 12, 2008, Kamala Harris announced her candidacy for California attorney general. Both of California's senators, Dianne Feinstein and Barbara Boxer, House speaker Nancy Pelosi, United Farm Workers cofounder Dolores Huerta, and Mayor of Los Angeles Antonio Villaraigosa all endorsed her during the primary. In the June 8, 2010 primary, she was nominated with 33.6 percent of the vote, defeating Alberto Torrico and Chris Kelly.

In the general election, Kamala faced Republican Los Angeles County district attorney Steve Cooley, who led most of the race. Cooley ran as a nonpartisan, distancing himself from the Meg Whitman campaign. The election was held November 2 but after a protracted period of counting mail-in and provisional ballots, Cooley conceded on November 25. Kamala Harris was sworn in January 3, 2011 as the first African American, first Asian American, and first woman to serve as California attorney general.

In February 2012, Kamala Harris announced an agreement with Apple, Amazon, Google, Hewlett-Packard, Microsoft, and Research in Motion to mandate that apps sold in their stores display prominent privacy policies informing users of what private information they were sharing. and with whom. Facebook later joined the agreement. That summer, Kamala announced the creation of a Privacy Enforcement and Protection Unit to enforce laws related to cyber privacy, identity theft, and data breaches.

On November 4, 2014, Harris was re-elected against Republican Ronald Gold, winning 57.5 percent of the vote to 42.5 percent.

In 2015, Kamala Harris secured two settlements with Comcast, one totaling $33 million over allegations that posted online the names, phone numbers and addresses of tens of thousands of customers who had paid for unlisted voice over internet protocol ("VOIP") phone service and another $26 million settlement to resolve allegations that it discarded paper records without first omitting or redacting private customer information. Harris also settled with Houzz over allegations that the company recorded phone calls without notifying customers or employees. Houzz was forced to pay $175,000, destroy the recorded calls, and hire a chief privacy officer, the first time such a provision has been included in a settlement with the California Department of Justice.

Kamala Harris prioritized environmental protection as attorney general, first securing a $44 million settlement to resolve all damages and costs associated with the Cosco Busan oil spill, in which a container ship collided with San Francisco–Oakland Bay Bridge and spilled 50,000 gallons of bunker fuel into the San Francisco Bay. In the aftermath of the 2015 Refugio oil spill, which deposited about 140,000 gallons of crude oil off the coast of Santa Barbara, California,

From 2015 to 2016, Kamala secured multiple multi-million-dollar settlements with fuel service companies Chevron, BP, ARCO, Phillips 66, and ConocoPhillips to resolve allegations they failed to properly monitor the hazardous materials in its underground storage tanks used to store gasoline for retail sale at hundreds of California gas stations. In summer 2016, automaker Volkswagen AG agreed to pay up to $14.7 billion to settle a raft of claims related to so-called "defeat devices" used to cheat emissions standards on its diesel cars while actually emitting up to forty times the levels of harmful nitrogen oxides allowed under state and federal law. Kamala Harris and the chair of the California Air Resources Board, Mary D.

Nichols, announced that California would receive $1.18 billion as well as another $86 million paid to the state of California in civil penalties.

In 2015, Kamala Harris's California Department of Justice was the first statewide agency in the country to require all its police officers to wear body cameras. That same year, Kamala announced a new state law requiring every law enforcement agency in California to collect, report, and publish expanded statistics on how many people are shot, seriously injured or killed by peace officers throughout the state.

In 2016, Kamala Harris announced a patterns and practices investigation into purported civil rights violations and use of excessive force by the two largest law enforcement agencies in Kern County, California, the Bakersfield Police Department and the Kern County Sheriff's Department.

The ACLU found that officers had engaged in patterns of excessive force – including shooting and beating to death unarmed individuals – as well as a practice of filing retaliatory criminal charges against individuals subjected to excessive force. Further analysis also revealed the highest rate of police homicides in the country, as well as excessive use of force, resulting in 17 deaths of unarmed civilians from 2009 to 2013 in the form of dog attacks and tazings.

In 2016, Kamala Harris announced wide-sweeping arrests of more than fifty members of the Mexican Mafia, a.k.a. La Eme, seizing more than sixty firearms, more than $95,000 in cash, and $1.6 million worth of methamphetamine, cocaine, and marijuana in Riverside County. Later that year, Kamala Harris's office coordinated with federal agents in a raid on dozens of businesses in the Los Angeles Fashion District operating as a major money-laundering hub for narcotics traffickers in Mexico, arresting nine people on charges of money laundering through a black market peso exchange scheme and seizing nearly $65 million in illegal proceeds.

After 24 years as California's junior senator, Senator Barbara Boxer (D-CA) announced her intention to retire from the United States Senate at the end of her term in 2016. Kamala Harris was the first candidate to declare her intention to run for Boxer's senate seat. Harris officially announced the launch of her campaign on January 13, 2015.

In February 2016, the California Democratic Party voted at its convention to endorse Harris, who received nearly eighty percent of the vote. Three months later, Governor Jerry Brown endorsed her.

In the June 7 primary, Harris came in first with forty percent of the vote and won by pluralities in most counties. On July 19, President Barack Obama and Vice President Joe Biden endorsed Harris.

Kamala faced congresswoman, and fellow Democrat, Loretta Sanchez, in the general election. It was the first time a Republican did not appear in a general election for the Senate since California began directly electing senators in 1914. In the November 2016 election, Harris defeated Sanchez, capturing over sixty percent of the vote, carrying all but four counties. Following her victory, she promised to protect immigrants from the policies of President-elect Donald Trump and announced her intention to remain Attorney General through the end of 2016.

Harris had been considered a top contender and potential frontrunner for the 2020 Democratic nomination for President. On January 21, 2019, Harris officially announced her candidacy for President of the United States in the 2020 United States presidential election. In the first 24 hours after her candidacy announcement, she tied a record set by Bernie Sanders in 2016 for the most donations raised in the day following an announcement. More than 20,000 people attended her formal campaign launch event in her hometown of Oakland, California, on January 27, according to a police estimate.

In May 2019, senior members of the Congressional Black Caucus endorsed the idea of a Biden–Harris ticket. On December 3, 2019, Harris withdrew from seeking the 2020 Democratic nomination, citing a shortage of funds. A few months later, Harris endorsed Joe Biden for president. In late February, Biden won a landslide victory in the 2020 South Carolina Democratic primary with the endorsement of House whip Jim Clyburn, with more victories on Super Tuesday.

Before the opening of the impeachment trial of Donald Trump on January 16, 2020, Kamala Harris delivered remarks on the floor of the Senate, stating her views on the integrity of the American justice system and the principle that nobody, including an incumbent president, is above the law. Harris later asked Senate Judiciary chairman Lindsey Graham to halt all judicial nominations during the impeachment trial, to which Graham acquiesced. Kamala voted to convict the president on charges of abuse of power and obstruction of Congress.

In early March 2020, Congressman James Clyburn suggested Biden choose a black woman as a running mate, commenting that "African American women needed to be rewarded for their loyalty." That same month Biden committed to choosing a woman for his running mate.

On April 17, 2020, Kamala Harris responded to media speculation and said she "would be honored" to be Biden's running mate. In late

May, in relation to the death of George Floyd and ensuing protests and demonstrations, Biden faced renewed calls to select a black woman to be his running mate, highlighting the law enforcement credentials of Harris and Val Demings.

On June 12, *The New York Times* reported that Harris was emerging as the frontrunner to be Biden's running mate, as she is the only African American woman with the political experience typical of vice presidents. On June 26, CNN reported that more than a dozen people close to the Biden search process considered Harris one of Biden's top four contenders, along with Elizabeth Warren, Val Demings, and Keisha Lance Bottoms.

On August 11, 2020, Biden announced that he had chosen Harris. She is the third woman after Geraldine Ferraro and Sarah Palin to be picked as the vice-presidential nominee for a major party ticket.

Kamala Harris has received numerous honors and awards. In 2005, National Black Prosecutors Association awarded Harris the Thurgood Marshall Award. That year, she was featured along 19 other woman in a Newsweek report profiling "20 of America's Most Powerful Women". In 2006, Harris was elected to the National District Attorneys Association's Board of Directors as vice president and appointed to co-chair its Corrections and Re-Entry Committee. She was also selected to co-chair the California District Attorneys Association's sex crimes committee. Kamala was also selected to serve as a Rodel Fellow with the Aspen Institute along with 24 other elected officials. That same year, Howard University awarded Harris its Outstanding Alumni Award for "extraordinary work in the fields of law and public service". In 2008, she was named an Attorney of the Year by California Lawyer magazine. A *New York Times* article published later that year also identified her as a woman with potential to become President of the United States, highlighting her reputation as a "tough fighter".

In 2010, California's largest legal newspaper *The Daily Journal* designated Kamala Harris as one of the top 75 women litigators in the state, and one of the top 100 lawyers in the state. In 2013, *Time* named Kamala Harris as one of the "100 Most Influential People in the World". In 2016, the 20/20 Bipartisan Justice Center awarded Kamala Harris the Bipartisan Justice Award along with Senator Tim Scott. In 2018, Harris was named the 2018 recipient of the ECOS Environmental Award for her leadership in environmental protection.

Kamala married attorney Douglas Emhoff, who was at one time partner-in-charge at Venable LLP's Los Angeles office, on August 22, 2014, in Santa Barbara, California. Kamala is a stepmother to Emhoff's two children from his previous marriage to Kerstin Emhoff. She is a member of Third Baptist Church of San Francisco, a congregation of the American Baptist Churches USA.

History continues to be made with Kamala Harris and Joe Biden....

> *We live in a society where we may have differences, of course, but we learn to celebrate these differences.*
> **– Bernice King**

CHAPTER FIVE – SPIRITUALITY
FEATURING RELIGIOUS LEADERS

Spirituality is a broad concept with room for many perspectives. In general, it includes a sense of connection to something bigger than ourselves, and it typically involves a search for meaning in life. As such, it is a universal human experience—something that touches us all. People may describe a spiritual experience as *sacred* or *transcendent* or simply a deep sense of aliveness and interconnectedness.

Some may find that their spiritual life is intricately linked to their association with a church, temple, mosque, or synagogue. Others may pray or find comfort in a personal relationship with God or a higher power. Like your sense of purpose, your personal definition of spirituality may change throughout your life, adapting to your own experiences and relationships.

These are some of the religious leaders who have helped people to find comfort in their spiritual journey and have made a positive impact in our society.

RICHARD ALLEN

Richard Allen (February 14, 1760 – March 26, 1831) founded the African Methodist Episcopal Church (AME), the first independent black denomination in the United States.

Richard Allen was born into slavery on February 14, 1760, on the Delaware property of Benjamin Chew. When he was a child Allen and his family were sold to Stokeley Sturgis, who had a plantation in Delaware. When Sturgis had financial problems, he sold Richard's mother and two of his five siblings. Allen had an older brother and sister left with him and the three began to attend meetings of the local Methodist Society, which was welcoming to slaves and free blacks. They were encouraged by their master Sturgis although he was unconverted. Richard taught himself to read and write. He joined the Methodists at 17. He began evangelizing and attracted criticism from local slave owners.

Allen and his brother redoubled their efforts for Sturgis so that no one could say his slaves did not do well because of religion.

The Reverend Freeborn Garrettson, who had freed his own slaves in 1775, began to preach in Delaware. He was among many Methodist and Baptist ministers after the American Revolutionary War who encouraged slaveholders to emancipate their people. When Garrettson visited the Sturgis plantation to preach, Allen's master was touched by this declaration and began to give consideration to the thought that holding slaves was sinful. Sturgis was soon convinced that slavery was wrong and offered his slaves an opportunity to buy their freedom. Allen performed extra work to earn the money and bought his freedom in 1780, when he changed his name from "Negro Richard" to "Richard Allen."

Allen was qualified as a preacher in 1784 at the Christmas Conference, the founding of the Methodist Church in North America in Baltimore, Maryland. He was one of the two black attendees of the conference along with Harry Hosier, but neither could vote during deliberations. Allen was then allowed to lead services at 5 a.m., which were attended mostly by blacks.

In 1786, Allen became a preacher at St. George's Methodist Episcopal Church in Philadelphia, Pennsylvania but was restricted to early-morning services. As he attracted more black congregants, the church vestry ordered them to be in a separate area for worship. Allen regularly preached on the commons near the church, slowly gaining a congregation of nearly 50 and supporting himself with a variety of odd jobs.

Allen and Absalom Jones, also a Methodist preacher, resented the white congregants' segregation of blacks for worship and prayer. They decided to leave St. George's to create independent worship for African Americans. That brought some opposition from the white church as well as the more-established blacks of the community.

In 1787, Allen and Jones led the black members out of St. George's Methodist Church. They formed the Free African Society (FAS), a non-denominational mutual aid society that assisted fugitive slaves and new migrants to the city. Allen, along with Absalom Jones, William Gray and William Wilcher, found an available lot on Sixth Street near Lombard. Allen negotiated a price and purchased this lot in 1787 to build a church, but it was years before they had a building. Now occupied by Mother Bethel African Methodist Episcopal Church, it is the oldest parcel of real estate in the United States that has been owned continuously by African Americans.

Allen's first wife was named Flora. They were married on October 19, 1790. Richard Allen was a minister, educator, writer, and one of America's most active and influential black leaders. He opened his first AME church in 1794 in Philadelphia, Pennsylvania.

Over time, most of the FAS members chose to affiliate with the Episcopal Church, as many blacks in Philadelphia had been Anglicans since the 1740s. They founded the African Church with Absalom Jones. It was accepted as a parish congregation, and opened its doors on July 17, 1794 as the African Episcopal Church of St. Thomas.

Allen and others wanted to continue in the Methodist practice. Allen called their congregation the African Methodist Episcopal Church (AME). Converting a blacksmith shop on Sixth Street, the leaders opened the doors of Bethel AME Church on July 29, 1794. At first affiliated with the larger Methodist Episcopal Church, the church had to rely on visiting white ministers for communion. In recognition of his leadership and preaching, in 1795, Absalom Jones was ordained as a deacon.

Flora worked very closely with Richard during the early years of establishing the church, from 1787 to 1799. They attended church school and worked together purchasing land, which was eventually donated to the church or rented out to families. Richard Allen was ordained as the first black Methodist minister by Bishop Francis Asbury in 1799. He and the congregation still had to continue to negotiate white oversight and deal with white elders of the denomination.

Flora Allen died on March 11, 1801, after a long illness. Scholars do not know if she and Richard had any children. After moving to Philadelphia, Richard Allen married Sarah Bass, a freed slave from Virginia. She had moved to Philadelphia as a child and the couple met around 1800. Richard and Sarah Allen had six children.

Sarah Allen was highly active in what became the AME Church and is called the "Founding Mother." The social themes of Bishop Allen's preaching were abolition, colonization, education, and temperance. Allen and Sara also operated a station on the Underground Railroad for fugitive slaves.

In 1804, Richard Allen became the first black ordained in the United States as an Episcopal priest. A decade after its founding, the AME Church had 457 members, and in 1813, it had 1,272.

Elected the first bishop of the AME Church in 1816, Allen united five African-American congregations of the Methodist Church in Philadelphia; Attleborough, Pennsylvania; Salem, New Jersey; Delaware and Maryland. Together, they founded the independent denomination of the African Methodist Episcopal Church (AME), the first fully independent black denomination in the United States.

Allen focused on organizing a denomination in which free blacks could worship without racial oppression and slaves could find a measure of dignity. He worked to upgrade the social status of the black community, organizing Sabbath schools to teach literacy and promoting national organizations to develop political strategies. On April 10, 1816, the other ministers elected Allen as their first bishop. The African Methodist Episcopal Church is the oldest and largest formal institution in black America.

In September 1830, black representatives from seven states convened in Philadelphia at the Bethel AME church for the first Negro Convention. A civic meeting, it was the first on such a scale organized by African American leaders. Allen presided over the meeting, which addressed both regional and national topics. The convention occurred after the 1826 and 1829 riots in Cincinnati, when whites had attacked blacks and destroyed their businesses. After the 1829 rioting, 1200 blacks had left the city to go to Canada. As a result, the Negro Convention addressed organizing aid to such settlements in Canada, among other issues. The 1830 meeting was the beginning of an organizational effort known as the Negro Convention Movement, part of 19th-century institution building in the black community. National conventions were held regularly.

Richard Allen died at home on Spruce Street on March 26, 1831. He was buried at the church that he founded. His grave remains on the lower level.

JOHN J. JASPER

John Jasper (July 4, 1812 – 1901) is arguably one of the most famous black ministers of nineteenth-century Richmond, Virginia, who gained popularity for his electrifying preaching style and his ability to spiritually move both black and white Baptists. Rev. Jasper's accomplishments are even more remarkable given the fact that he was a slave in the tobacco factories and iron mills of Richmond during the first 25 years of his ministry work during a time when Virginia law expressly prohibited blacks from preaching.

Reverend John Jasper was born into slavery on July 4, 1812 in Fluvanna County, Virginia. He was one of twenty-four children of Philip and Tina Jasper. Philip was a well-known Baptist preacher while Tina was a slave of a Mr. Peachy. John was hired out to various people and when Mr. Peachy's mistress died, he was given to her son, John Blair Peachy, a lawyer who had moved to Louisiana.

John Jasper spent the early years of his life on a farm in Fluvanna County, and was later transferred to Williamsburg. During his time there, he performed the duties of driving and managing oxen. Since he proved to be an efficient worker, his master assigned him to work on the yard and garden, and to wait tables.

In the year 1825, John worked for a new master named Peter McHenry for nearly a year. Afterwards, he worked for Dr. Woldridge in Chesterfield County. John became a servant to Samuel Cosby after he returned to Richmond, Virginia. After Cosby's death, John was eventually owned by Samuel Hargrove, an operator of a tobacco factory in Richmond. After his time with Hargrove, John began his journey as a church organizer. He experienced a personal conversion to Christianity in Capital Square in 1839. He convinced a fellow slave to teach him to read and write and began studying to become a Baptist minister.

John Jasper's father, Phillip Jasper, was a preacher who was permitted by his masters to preach funeral sermons and speak at multiple churches by invitation. Tina Jasper, John Jasper's mother, was in charge of the working women on the Peachy estate.

Although Jasper became a preacher after his conversion to Christianity on the 4th of July 1839, he still remained a slave at the time. He was only allowed to preach whenever a white minister or white delegation was present. Often times, slaves would demand that a "Negro preacher" preach during the funerals of their deceased companions. Funeral services operated at the behest of slave masters. Jasper served as a predominant orator for funerals and was eventually in high demand as a result of his oratory abilities.

John Jasper married three times: first to Elvy Weaden, who left him, secondly, to Candus Jordan in 1844, with whom he had nine children before they divorced, and thirdly to Mary Ann Cole in 1863, who died on August 6, 1874.

John Jasper was known for his unique mode of dress, his manner of walking, and his lofty dignity. For more than two decades, Rev. Jasper traveled throughout Virginia. He often preached at Third Baptist Church in Petersburg, Virginia. He also preached to Confederate Soldiers during the American Civil War (1861–65). After his conversion, Jasper became a passionate student. He eventually learned how to spell words and read. Jasper was typically inclined to read the Bible over any other book. In addition, he would often urge as many members of his race to read whatever it is that they are able to access. As a result of his readings, Jasper was able to nearly recite the content of the Bible from memory. He increased his familiarity with the history of the Hebrews, the inhabitants of the near East, the Amorites, the Babylonians, the Egyptians, and many additional nations of the world. Jasper was able to serve as an invaluable educational resource for his followers and encouraged them to seek more knowledge for their own enrichment.

After his own emancipation following the American Civil War, Rev. Jasper found himself to be a free man. He was able to find a job that involved cleaning bricks and performing specific tasks to rebuild the city of Richmond. Rev. Jasper was not satisfied, seeing as he expected the liberated members of his race to be able to develop their own institutions. He believed that the best way to satisfy this objective was by facilitating leadership. Therefore, Rev. Jasper commenced his most significant journey in his life by founding the Sixth Mount Zion Baptist Church in Richmond. He became a full-time pastor and in 1867 organized the Sixth Mount Zion Baptist Church in Richmond, ministering to hundreds of local black Baptists, but many whites as well.

Rev. Jasper's sermons continued to attract eager audiences, but none seemed to draw more listeners than his famous discourse, "De Sun Do Move" given in 1878. Faithful followers, devoted fans, curious onlookers and even news reporters gathered at the church for a standing-room only lecture on the powers and mysteries of God. His most famous sermon expressed his deep faith in God through the imagery of a flat Earth around which the sun rotates.

By 1887, his church had attracted 2500 members and served as a religious and social center of Richmond's predominately black Jackson Ward—providing a Sunday School and other services. Rev. Jasper's vivid oratory and dramatic speaking style brought renown and calls for him to preach throughout the Eastern United States.

Rev. John Jasper was noted for possessing considerable control over the emotions of his audience. His sermons were influential in such that he was able to create vivid images merely by using words, and he used this ability of his to empower the members of his race. Jasper's sermons were of moral influence as well, seeing as he often detailed the consequences of one's actions, and he encouraged his people to live a dignified life due to the prospects of rich rewards. He served not only as a preacher, but also an educator.

During a time when there were no schools for his people, Rev. Jasper established a Sunday school in his church which educated the younger generations. Although Rev. Jasper yearned to benefit his people, he was never able to address the dilemmas of Africans in a global context. Those who benefited most from his involvement were the members of his church and community. Regardless, he was a prominent figure during a time when formerly enslaved Africans were in need of leadership and stability.

Rev. Jasper's work extended far beyond preaching to the devoted and attempted to minister to all black Richmonders; the Sixth Mount Zion Baptist Church became active in providing community services, including aid to the elderly and the destitute. Rev. Jasper continued in this capacity until 1901 at the age of 88, after half a century of serving God. He delivered his last sermon a few days before his death at the age of 90. The Library of Virginia honored him as one of the African-American trailblazers in its "Strong Men and Women" series in 2012.

IDA B. ROBINSON

Ida B. Robinson (August 3, 1891 – April 20, 1946) was granted a charter for Mount Sinai Holy Church of America, the only organization founded by an African American woman that held consistent female leadership from its founding in 1924 until February 2001.

Ida B. Robinson was born August 3, 1891. She grew up in Pensacola, Florida, the seventh of twelve children born to Robert and Annie Bell. After her conversion as a teenager at an evangelistic street meeting, Ida led prayer services in homes. In 1910 Ida Bell married Oliver Robinson. Though they never had children they adopted a niece, also named Ida Bell; the niece was the daughter of Ida Robinson's brother, Charles.

In 1917 Ida and Oliver left Florida for Philadelphia in hopes of finding better employment opportunities. Upon arrival to the city, Ida joined a small holiness congregation at Seventeenth and South Streets. That congregation was pastored by Elder Benjamin Smith. During her tenure at the church, Ida would at times fill in for Elder Smith when he was unable to minister. Due to her animated preaching style and her singing ability, the membership of the small congregation began to grow.

Complications between her and leadership of the church eventually led to her leaving the church and affiliating herself with the United Holy Church of America where she was consecrated to the ministry through ordination. Ida Robinson was ordained in public as a "Gospel Preacher" by Bishop Henry L. Fisher.

Ida Robinson was appointed as pastor of a small church in 1919. She stressed and preached holiness as a divine requirement; holiness as a work of the Holy Ghost; holiness as a condition to seeing God. The congregation began to grow quickly. However, she began to feel that ministry opportunities for women in United Holy Church were limited.

The year of 1924 was a very important year in the life of Ida Robinson. During the beginning of 1924, Ida Robinson on a number of occasions revealed to a number of persons that God revealed Himself through visions and dreams. It was her belief that God wanted to use her as a vehicle to establish a church that would "loose the women" and allow full clergy rights to them. While fasting and praying in the church for ten days, she stated that she again received a revelation from God. She stated to members of Mount Olive that

"The Holy Ghost spoke and said, 'Come out on Mount Sinai.'" After receiving this message from God, Ida was confident that she understood what God meant for her to do.

On May 20, 1924, the State of Pennsylvania granted her a charter for the new organization. Keeping in mind that the call of the Holy Spirit that she envisioned, the charter for the new church was granted under the name of the Mount Sinai Holy Church of America, Incorporated. At the time of its founding, the church leadership consisted of nine officials. Out of the nine officials, six were women. The growth of Mount Sinai was rapid and quickly spread across the east coast of the United States.

Reverend Robinson was consecrated as bishop at the organization's first Holy Convocation in 1925. Her separation from United Holy Church was one of mutual agreement. Leaders of her parent organization were in attendance at the first Holy Convocation of Mount Sinai and continued to fellowship with the organization during her leadership and after.

On April 6, 1946, Ida Robinson left Philadelphia with a group of missionaries to visit some of the organization's churches in Florida. Her first stop in Florida was Jacksonville. From there she journeyed on to Winter Haven.

Upon arrival to Winter Haven, Florida, she fell very ill. On April 20, Bishop Ida Robinson died. When she died, the denomination consisted of 84 churches, more than 160 ordained ministers of whom 125 were women, an accredited school in Philadelphia, mission work in Cuba and Guyana, and a farm in South Jersey that provided a safe haven away from the city for church members.

FREDERICK K.C. PRICE

Frederick K.C. Price (born January 3, 1932) is the founder and presiding bishop of Crenshaw Christian Center (CCC), located in California. He is known for his *Ever Increasing Faith* ministries broadcast, which is aired weekly on both television and radio.

Price was born in Santa Monica, California, a Los Angeles suburb, the eldest son of Winifred and Frederick Price, Sr., who owned a janitorial service in West Los Angeles. Frederick attended McKinley Elementary School in Santa Monica, Foshay Junior High, Manual Arts High School and Dorsey High School in Los Angeles, and then completed two years of schooling at Los Angeles City College. He later received an honorary diploma from the Rhema Bible Training Center (1976) and an honorary Doctor of Divinity degree from Oral Roberts University (1982).

At old-fashioned tent revivals in the Crenshaw area, Price received Jesus Christ as his personal savior. Soon after becoming born again, he felt the call from God to go into the ministry, serving mostly part-time, while working as a paper cutter, as an assistant pastor in a

Baptist church from 1955 to 1957. He then pastored an African Methodist Episcopal church in Val Verde, California from 1957 to 1959. From there he served in a Presbyterian church and then joined the Christian and Missionary Alliance at West Washington Community Church in 1965.

In February 1970, Price received the baptism of the Holy Spirit with the evidence of "speaking in tongues," an event which he considered the starting point in his own ministry. Shortly thereafter, he encountered the Bible-teaching ministry of late preacher/televangelist Kenneth E. Hagin. Price joined the Neo-charismatic movement Word of Faith and began to teach the messages on speaking in tongues, divine healing, and prosperity teachings. He and his wife Betty co-founded the Crenshaw Christian Center that same year in the Crenshaw section of West Los Angeles, California.

Thus, in November 1973, Price moved with about 300 church members from West Washington in Los Angeles in order to establish the Crenshaw Christian Center in Inglewood, California. Membership continued to grow, and in 1977 the church was forced to hold two services, with another service added in 1982, because the 1,400-seat sanctuary was always filled to capacity. In 1981, the church bought the old Pepperdine University campus. After the purchase, Price oversaw construction of a new sanctuary, called the "FaithDome", which at the time was the largest domed church in the United States.

Ground was broken for the FaithDome on September 28, 1986, and construction began on January 5, 1987. Construction was completed in 1989 on the 10,146-seat dome at a cost of more than $10 million. At the time of its dedication on January 21, 1990, the dome and the church's property were both fully paid for, leaving the ministry debt-free.

In 1990, Price founded the Fellowship of International Christian Word of Faith Ministries (FICWFM), which includes churches and ministers from all over the United States and several other countries. They meet regionally throughout the year and hold a major annual convention. Price is a Word of Faith teacher.

Price also founded the Fellowship of International Christian Word of Faith Ministries to foster and spread the faith message among independent ministries located in urban metropolitan areas of the United States. Price's son Fred Price Jr. has taken over senior-pastor duties, while Price is the center's chairman of the board.

ARCHBISHOP WILTON D. GREGORY

Wilton D. Gregory (born December 7, 1947) is a member of the Board of Trustees at The Catholic University of America. In 2002, in recognition of his handling of the sex abuse scandal with repeated apologies and the defrocking of priests, he was chosen as *Time's* Person of the Week.

Wilton was born in Chicago to Wilton Sr. and Ethel Duncan Gregory. One of three children, he has two sisters, Elaine and Claudia. Gregory's parents divorced when he was quite young, and his grandmother, Etta Mae Duncan, subsequently moved in with the family at their home on the South Side. In 1958, he was enrolled at St. Carthage Grammar School, where he decided to become a priest before even converting to Catholicism. He was baptized and received his First Communion in 1959, and was confirmed by

Bishop Raymond P. Hillinger later that year. Gregory graduated from St. Carthage in 1961, and then attended Quigley Preparatory Seminary South and Niles College in Chicago (now St. Joseph's College Seminary) of Loyola University, and St. Mary of the Lake Seminary in Mundelein.

At the age of 25 Wilton Gregory was ordained a priest of the Archdiocese of Chicago on May 9, 1973, and three years after his ordination began graduate studies at the Pontifical Liturgical Institute (Sant' Anselmo) in Rome. There he earned his doctorate in sacred liturgy in 1980.

After having served as an associate pastor of Our Lady of Perpetual Help Parish in Glenview, IL as a member of the faculty of St. Mary of the Lake Seminary in Mundelein and as a master of ceremonies to Cardinals John Cody and Joseph Bernardin, Bishop Gregory was ordained an auxiliary bishop of Chicago on December 13, 1983. Gregory remained in Chicago until December 29, 1993, when he was appointed the seventh Bishop of Belleville.

On February 10, 1994, Gregory was installed as the seventh bishop of the Diocese of Belleville, IL where he served for the next eleven years. Archbishop Gregory has served in many leading roles in the U.S. church. He has served on the USCCB's Executive and Administrative Committees, the Administrative Board, the Committee on Doctrine and the U.S. Catholic Conference Committee on International Policy. He previously served as the chairman of the Bishops' Committees on Personnel, Divine Worship and the Third Millennium/Jubilee Year 2000 from 1998-2001, and Liturgy from 1991-1993.

In November 2001, he was elected president of the U.S. Conference of Catholic Bishops (USCCB) following three years as vice president under Bishop Joseph Fiorenza of the Diocese of Galveston-Houston. During his tenure in office, the crisis of sex abuse by Catholic clergy escalated; and under his leadership, the bishops implemented the "Charter for the Protection of Children and Young People" in response to Roman Catholic sex abuse cases.

On December 9, 2004, Pope Saint John Paul II, in one of his last episcopal appointments before his death, appointed Bishop Gregory as the sixth archbishop of the Archdiocese of Atlanta, and he was installed on January 17, 2005.

In 2006 he joined an illustrious group of preachers with his induction into the Martin Luther King Board of Preachers at Morehouse College, Atlanta. At the National Pastoral Life Center in Washington, D.C., Archbishop Gregory was honored with the Cardinal Bernardin Award given by the Catholic Common Ground Initiative (2006).

Archbishop Gregory has written extensively on church issues, including pastoral statements on the death penalty, euthanasia/physician-assisted suicide and has published numerous articles on the subject of liturgy, particularly in the African American community.

Archbishop Gregory has been awarded nine honorary doctoral degrees. He received the Great Preacher Award from Saint Louis University in 2002; Doctorate of Humanities from Lewis University in Romeoville, IL (2002-2003); Sword of Loyola from Loyola University of Chicago (2004); Doctorate of Humane Letters from Spring Hill College in Mobile, AL (2005); Doctorate of Humane Letters from Xavier University in Cincinnati, OH; Doctorate of Humane Letters from McKendree College in Lebanon, IL; Doctorate of Humanities from Fontbonne University in St. Louis,

MO; Honorary Law Degree from Notre Dame University (2012); and the Chicago Catholic Theological Union Honorary Doctorate (2013). Gregory was also awarded an honorary degree from Boston College in 2018.

Pope Francis appointed Archbishop Gregory as the seventh Archbishop of the Archdiocese of Washington on April 4, 2019. He was installed on May 21, 2019.

CAPERS C. FUNNYE JR

Capers C. Funnye Jr. (born in 1952) is the first African-American member of the Chicago Board of Rabbis, and serves on the boards of the Jewish Council on Urban Affairs and the American Jewish Congress of the Midwest.

Capers Funnye was born in Georgetown, South Carolina in the Low Country, with paternal ancestry among the GeeChee people (or Gullah) of the Sea Islands. They are an ethnic group that kept strong African traditions. Variations of his surname are common in Nigeria and West Africa.

His family moved to Chicago as part of the Great Migration of African Americans to industrial cities out of the South. He grew up on the South Side. There he got to see more of his mother's extended family in Chicago, including future First Lady of the United States Michelle Robinson Obama, his first cousin once removed. (His mother Verdelle (Robinson) Funnye was a sister of Fraser Robinson Jr., Michelle Robinson's grandfather; their family also was from Georgetown and had Gullah ancestry.)

Capers is one of America's most prominent African American rabbis, known for acting as a bridge between mainstream Jewry and African American Jews. He converted to Judaism after 1970, during years of activism when he regarded Christianity as having been imposed on slaves

Capers Funnye is 12 years older than Michelle Obama. While their families frequently visited when they were young, the two of them got to know each other more as adults. In 1992 she married Barack Obama, the future President of the United States (2009-2017). Funnye and the Obamas were involved in community organizing.

Capers became interested in Judaism while in college at Howard University and has gone through two conversion rituals. He has led efforts to coordinate with both Black Jewish groups and mainline Judaism.

Funnye was raised in the African Methodist Episcopal Church, the first independent black denomination. At 17, he was encouraged by his minister to enter the clergy. Dissatisfied with Christianity during his college years at Howard University and influenced by movements for civil rights and black nationalism, he investigated other religions, including Islam. After meeting with Rabbi Robert Devine, the spiritual leader of the House of Israel Congregation in Chicago, which practiced a kind of messianic Judaism, Funnye joined his congregation. Related Black Jewish movements in the United States had started in the late 19th century in Kansas.

Funnye became drawn to the "more conventional teachings of a black, Brooklyn-based rabbi named Levi Ben Levy, the chief rabbi of the International Israelite Board of Rabbis. This group has its roots in the Commandment Keepers Congregation of the Living God, founded in 1919 by Wentworth Arthur Matthew in Harlem. It incorporated in 1930 and later moved to Brooklyn, where Matthew established a seminary. After Matthew's death in 1973, there had been little dialog with white Jewish congregations, who disagreed with Black Jewish claims of historic descent from ancient Israel. Funnye studied long-distance with Levy for five years, and Levy ordained him in 1985 through the Israelite Rabbinical Academy of Brooklyn, founded by Matthew. The Academy does not have ties to any mainstream Jewish denomination.

With the goal of building bridges to United States Judaism, in 1985 Funnye undertook a second formal conversion to Judaism that was certified by a Conservative rabbinical court. He had also studied Judaism more intensively in Chicago, earning a Bachelor of Arts degree in Jewish Studies and Master of Science in Human Service Administration from the Spertus Institute of Jewish Studies there. Funnye has said that he felt a sense of intellectual and spiritual liberation in the constant examination that Judaism encouraged.

Rabbi Funnye is married to Mary White of Chicago. They have four children and are the proud grandparents of 12 grandchildren, 3 granddaughters and 9 grandsons.

In 1985, Funnye was selected as assistant rabbi at Beth Shalom B'nai Zaken Ethiopian Hebrew Congregation in Chicago; with 200 members, it is now one of the largest black synagogues in the United States. Its congregation is mostly African American.

In 1996, Funnye was the only official black rabbi in the Chicago area recognized by the greater Jewish community. Funnye has been active in the Institute for Jewish and Community Research, reaching out to historically black Jewish communities outside the United States. These include the Beta Israel in Ethiopia, which are formally recognized by Israeli authorities as Jewish, and the Igbo Jews in Nigeria, which are not.

Funnye's current congregation was founded by Rabbi Horace Hasan from Bombay (now Mumbai), India, in 1918 as the Ethiopian Hebrew Settlement Workers Association. Along with African Americans, members include Hispanics and whites who were born Jews; the majority of the congregation has converted to Judaism. As is traditional with Judaism, the congregation does not engage in missionary activity. Members who want to convert must study Judaism for a year before undergoing a traditional conversion, requiring men to be ritually circumcised and women to undergo ritual immersion in a mikvah.

The synagogue is "somewhere between Conservative and Modern Orthodox" with distinctive African-American influences; while men and women sit separately as in Orthodox synagogues, a chorus sings spirituals to the beat of a drum. The congregation occupies a synagogue built by an earlier Ashkenazi congregation in the Marquette Park neighborhood.

In 1995, Rabbi Funnye was a co-founder, with Michelle Stein-Evers of California and Robin Washington of Boston, of the National Conference of Black Jews. Washington is also Jewish and is the editor of the African American newspaper, *Bay State Banner*. They have worked to broaden the conversation among black Jews and Black Hebrews across the country, as well as to build bridges to conventional Judaism, made up predominately of whites. Rabbi

Funnye says, "I am a Jew, and that breaks through all color and ethnic barriers."

On April 2, 2009, Funnye was invited for the first time "to speak at a white, mainstream synagogue in New York", at the Stephen Wise Free Synagogue, a Reform congregation. He called it his "Broadway debut". The congregation had reached out to black Jewish congregations to celebrate Martin Luther King Day, and about one-quarter of the audience were black Jews. Funnye spoke about Rev. Martin Luther King and Barack Obama, the night before the latter's inauguration as president. The next day he and his family went to Washington to join the Obamas in inaugural events.

History was made again on October 24, 2015. On that date Rabbi Funnye was installed as our Chief Rabbi as Chief Rabbi of the International Israelite Board of Rabbis at his home congregation, Beth Shalom Bnai Zaken Ethiopian Hebrew Congregation, in Chicago, Illinois. Over 300 Black Jews attended the events that unfolded over the course of the weekend. Delegation arrived representing Israelite congregations from around the country. Many individuals came who attend White congregations in their hometowns, but simply wanted to enjoy the fellowship and beauty of seeing so many Jews of color.

Letters of congratulations poured in from such dignitaries as Michelle Obama, who wrote to her cousin, Rabbi Funnye, "As you prepare to lead the International Israelite Board of Rabbis, I send my warmest congratulations;" United States Senator Richard Durbin sent a letter praising Rabbi Funnye for his decades of service; and letters were read from the African communities of Jews in South Africa, Uganda, and Nigeria. In August 2016, he was inaugurated to that position. The board is made up of "people who identify themselves as Black Jews or Israelites."

ALPHONSO R. BERNARD, SR

Alphonso R. Bernard, Sr. (born 1957) is founder and CEO of the Christian Cultural Center. As Christian Life Center began experiencing exponential growth — four Sunday services, lines forming at 4:00am, and overflow rooms filled to capacity,

Alphonso's father had disowned him and in 1957, he and his mother moved to the Bedford-Stuyvesant neighborhood of Brooklyn, New York. As part of the 1960s desegregation movement in the public-school system, he was bused to school in Ridgewood, Queens and then attended Grover Cleveland High School. Bernard worked after school in the garment district pushing racks for $2.00 per hour to assist his mother in their single parent household. He landed a clerk position with Bankers Trust Company during his senior year of high school. Bernard earned a number of promotions leading to a position as Operations Specialist in the Consumer Lending Division.

Bernard has been married to his wife Karen since 1972; they met in high school in East New York, when he was 15 and she 16. They have 7 sons and several grandchildren together. His eldest son Alfonso R. Bernard Jr. died from an asthma attack on February 4,

2015 at the age of 39 and is survived by his wife Janel and four children.

Prior to becoming a born again Christian in January 1975, Bernard was a part of the Muslim American movement. In 1978 he and his wife, Karen started a bible study in the kitchen of their Brooklyn railroad apartment. In November 1979, A. R. Bernard, Sr. left a 10-year career with a major New York banking institution and together with his wife, Karen, went into full-time ministry. As the bible study group grew, so did the need for a facility. The Bernards took their savings and rented a small storefront in the Greenpoint section of Brooklyn. Later that year Household of Faith Ministries was incorporated. In 1988, Household of Faith purchased and renovated an abandoned Brooklyn supermarket into a 1000-seat sanctuary, complete with administrative offices and a bookstore. Household of Faith was renamed Christian Life Center and formally moved into its property in June 1989 with a membership of 625. What started as a small storefront church in Williamsburg, Brooklyn has grown into a 37,000+ member megachurch that sits on an 11 ½-acre campus in Brooklyn, New York.

The ministry was quickly outgrowing its home on Linden Boulevard. The need for a larger facility was evident and in 1995 a vacant lot adjacent to Starrett City was purchased and construction followed immediately. On December 31, 2000, under the leadership of Bernard, Christian Cultural Center took its new name and moved into its new home. The 6.5-acre sanctuary and conference center also includes a chapel, bookstore, television production facilities and state of the art youth center. Christian Cultural Center, one of the largest independent churches in the United States, exemplifies a new paradigm in the worship experience. Bernard remains a highly sought-after speaker, teacher and community leader. He has traveled extensively throughout the United States and internationally addressing religious organizations, businessmen and political dignitaries.

Bernard is the founder of Brooklyn Preparatory School in New York City. Formed in 1993, BPS is a premiere early education institution dedicated to serving young children, ages 3–6. Their June 1999 first grade graduates ranked 91st in the national percentile in reading and 96th in the national percentile in mathematics. Bernard is also the founder of the Cultural Arts Academy Charter School established in February 2010.

Bernard has served as the President of the Council of Churches of the City of New York representing 1.5 million Protestants, Anglicans and Orthodox Christians. Bernard founded the Christian Community Relations Council (CCRC, a NY based not-for-profit that will serve as a central resource and coordinating body for congregations and community organizations. He is currently on the Board of Directors for the Commission of Religious Leaders (CORL).

Bernard sat on the NYC Economic Development Corporation Board for current Mayor Bill de Blasio and former Mayor Michael R. Bloomberg; NYC School Chancellor's Advisory Cabinet and served on Mayor Michael Bloomberg's 2001 Transition Team and Mayor Bill de Blasio's 2014 Transition Team.

Bernard was asked to serve on the Board of Directors for the Christian Men's Network (CMN) to help restructure the organization. During his six years on the board, CMN grew to an organization with 74 international offices and with a presence in approximately 150 nations. In addition to serving as Treasurer for the board, Bernard was one of their most requested speakers. With the death of Dr. Edwin Louis Cole in 2002 Bernard became the

President of CMN. ICB began as an assigned project under the leadership of Ed Cole, but after a separation from CMN, Bernard re-launched ICB as his own Men's Ministry.

Bernard has a master's in urban studies and a master's in divinity from Alliance Theological Seminary. He has been awarded an honorary Doctor of Divinity degree from Wagner College and an honorary Doctor of Divinity degree from Nyack College/Alliance Theological Seminary.

BERNICE ALBERTINE KING

Bernice Albertine King (March 28, 1963) was the first official graduate of a joint degree, receiving her Masters of Divinity and J.D. degrees from Emory Candler School of Theology and Emory University Law School. Bernice received her degrees in 1990 from Emory University in the morning, and that evening she was ordained into the ministry. This day would also mark the twenty-fifth anniversary of her father's assassination.

Bernice King was born on March 28, 1963, in Atlanta, Georgia. She is the youngest child of civil rights leaders Martin Luther King Jr. and Coretta Scott King. Bernice has two brothers: Martin Luther King III and Dexter and a sister Yolanda who died in 2007. Bernice Kinge was five years old when her father was assassinated in Memphis in 1968.

The day after Bernice was born, her father, Martin, had to leave for Birmingham, Alabama; but he rushed back when it was time for Bernice and her mother, Coretta, to leave the hospital. He drove them home himself but, in what was all too typical with the work he was doing, had to leave them again within hours.

Following Bernice's birth, Harry Belafonte realized the toll the Civil Rights Movement was taking on her mother's time and energy and offered to pay for a nurse to help Coretta with the Kings' four children. They accepted and hired a person that would help with the children for the next five or six years. Martin died a week after Bernice's fifth birthday.

Other tragedies followed. Bernice's uncle, Alfred Daniel Williams King, drowned in a swimming pool when Bernice was six on July 21, 1969. Five years later, a mentally ill man shot her grandmother, Alberta Williams King, to death during a service at the Ebenezer Baptist Church on June 30, 1974.

Bernice has said that the deaths of her grandmother and uncle caused her to have anger issues since she was 16 years old. At that age, she saw *Montgomery to Memphis*, a documentary film on her father's life from the time of the Montgomery Bus Boycott of 1955 to his assassination in 1968, and "went through almost two hours of crying" and questioning. She had seen the film many times growing up, but that particular viewing "triggered an emotional explosion that later would thrust her into the arms of a loving God. Bernice had a breakdown from watching a documentary about her father. She credited the viewing with influencing her to become a minister like her father, who served as a minister at Ebenezer Baptist Church.

Bernice was with her church youth group in Georgia mountains. King aspired to become the first female President of the United

States at the time of seeing the documentary. King attended Douglass High School in Atlanta and graduated in 1981. Her brother Dexter Scott King attended the school as well and graduated when she was a sophomore. At 17, in her mother's stead, Bernice gave an address advocating against the South African apartheid to the United Nations General Assembly in New York.

At the age of 19, Bernice made her first major speech in Chicago, and stated, "We've come a long way. But we have a long way to go." In early 1983, Bernice King gave a speech at St. Sabina Church in Chicago. Many members of the audience said that she reminded them of her father. Bernice attended Grinnell College in Iowa, and graduated from Spelman College, a historically black college in Atlanta, with a B.A. degree in psychology.

Bernice was arrested with her mother Coretta and her brother Martin Luther King III on June 26, 1985 with the offense of demonstrating in front of an embassy. They were participating in an anti-apartheid demonstration in front of the South African Embassy. The three stayed in jail overnight. The youngest daughter of Martin Luther King, his widow and his eldest son were charged with a misdemeanor, demonstrating within 500 feet of an embassy.

On January 7, 1986, Bernice was arrested with her sister Yolanda and her brother Martin Luther King III for "disorderly conduct." Bernice and her siblings were arrested by officers deployed to the Winn Dixie supermarket. The supermarket had been subject to protest since September 1985, which was when the Southern Christian Leadership Conference began boycotts of South African canned fruit. It was the first time Bernice and her siblings had been arrested together at a protest.

While in graduate school, Bernice King was a student intern who participated in project STEP in one of Atlanta's notorious housing projects, Perry Homes. The program connected the residents to employment. During that time, she also headed demonstrations at Emory University,

On March 27, 1988, nearly 20 years after her father's assassination, King delivered her first sermon at Ebenezer Baptist Church, where both her father and grandfather served as pastors. The sermon's theme was "You've Got to Rise Above the Crowd." King said her decision to deliver the sermon was "affirming a call I received at 17." She also said, "At some point in our lives, comes the moment of decision. For me, that moment is now. I submit myself totally to the will of God." Andrew Young, who attended the sermon, compared her style to her father's and noted their similarities while listening to her speak.

Coretta King said at the time that she was satisfied with her daughter's decision to become a minister and stated that they had become closer than ever in the months leading up to the sermon. She also said listening to her daughter delivering a sermon with the same fervor and intensity her father had "was a joyous occasion; a real thanksgiving." Also in attendance where all three of her elder siblings, Yolanda, Martin Luther King III and Dexter. Bernice King's sermon was delivered the day before her twenty-fifth birthday.

In May 1988, King was among the students of Emory charging that the college should hire more African Americans as teachers and teach the works of African American theologians in its courses.

Bernice served as a student chaplain at the Georgia Retardation Center and Georgia Baptist Hospital as part of the requirements for her theology class and interned at the Atlanta City Attorney's office. She is a member of the Alpha Kappa Alpha sorority, as was her mother.

On May 14, 1990, Bernice King became the second woman to be ordained at Ebenezer Baptist Church. She said, "It was the most humbling moment for me in my life."

On January 18, 1992, President George H. W. Bush visited the Martin Luther King, Jr. Center for Nonviolent Social Change. Bernice King spoke during his visit of the problems of racism, poverty and violence that remained in America since her father was alive; but she did not directly align any of the issues with President Bush.

Bernice king has also received an honorary doctorate of Divinity degree from Wesley college. She was privileged to serve as a law clerk in the Fulton County Juvenile Court System, under Judge Glenda Hatchet, who is Georgia's first African American chief presiding justice of a state court and the department head of one of the largest juvenile court systems in the country. During her tenure, King served as a rehabilitation-outreach coordinator and counseled teens that came through the juvenile court system. She has also served as a mentor to a group of fifth grade girls at an inner-city Atlanta elementary school. Bernice King became a member of the State Bar of Georgia in 1992.

Bernice assisted the pulpit for a number of years before going to Greater Rising Star Baptist Church in 1992, where she developed the praise team women's and youth ministry and the ministers-in-training program. Bernice became assistant pastor in 1995, which was the same year that she attended the inauguration of Nelson Mandela in South Africa.

Bernice King was a minister at New Birth Missionary Baptist Church in Lithonia, Georgia, under the leadership of Bishop Eddie Long. In addition to being a speaker, orator and preacher, Bernice planned and organized numerous conferences, seminars and workshops for all walks of life. Bernice has successfully coordinated women and family conferences, as well as nonviolent conflict resolution conferences for college and university students. She has also conducted a class on race relations at Mississippi College in Jackson, Mississippi, and taught a year-long leadership development class.

Bernice King is a co-founder of Active Ministers Engaged in Nurturing (AMEN) and the Chair of national advisory committee on National King Week College and University Student Conference on Kingian Nonviolence. **Kingian Nonviolence** *is a philosophy of* **nonviolent** *conflict reconciliation, based on the work of Dr. Martin Luther King, Jr, and the organizing strategies he used during the Civil Rights Movement.*

In January 1994, Bernice voiced her opposition to New Hampshire's refusal to recognize Martin Luther King, Jr. Day, calling the decision "racist and separatist." On May 21, 1994, she attended the African-American Women's Conference where she said that parents should not let their children listen to "gangster rap" because of messages in the lyrics. In 1996, Bernice King published a collection of her sermons and speeches called *Hard Questions, Heart Answers*.

Coretta Scott King suffered a stroke in 2005 and she died the following year. Bernice King delivered the eulogy at her mother's funeral. She felt that her mother's death was a "rebirth" for her, "in terms of understanding that I come from roots of greatness and I am called to greatness and there's nothing I can do but try to be my best self."

On May 15, 2007, King's sister Yolanda King died after collapsing and was unable to be revived. King delivered the eulogy at her sister's memorial on May 24, 2007.

On December 14, 2007, at the State Bar of Georgia Headquarters, King was honored by the Georgia Alliance of African American Attorneys with the "Commitment to Community" award for her work as an attorney and community leader.

Bernice supported the presidential campaign of Barack Obama in 2008 and called his nomination part of her father's dream.

On October 7, 2009, King received an award for her "lifetime of service to women and other causes" at the National Coalition of 100 Black Women Convention.

Bernice King was elected president of the Southern Christian Leadership Conference in 2009. Her elder brother Martin III and her father had previously held the position. She was the first woman elected to the presidency in the organization's history. Bernice became upset with the actions of the SCLC, amid feeling that the organization was ignoring her suggestions and declined the presidency in January 2010.

Bernice King became CEO of the King Center only months afterward. Her primary focus as CEO of The King Center and in life is to ensure that her father's nonviolent philosophy and methodology (which The King Center calls Nonviolence 365) is integrated in various sects of society, including education, government, business, media, arts and entertainment and sports. King is also the CEO of First Kingdom Management, a Christian consulting firm based in Atlanta, Georgia.

Bernice King was an elder at New Birth Missionary Baptist Church, but resigned in May 2011. At the time that she chose to leave the church, she planned on starting her own ministry.

On October 16, 2011, King mentioned at the Martin Luther King, Jr. Memorial opening that the memorial had been in the making for a lengthy amount of time and a "priority" for her mother. On March 29, 2012, a month after the shooting death of teenager Trayvon Martin, King released a statement through the King Center. In her remarks, she referred back to the deaths of her father and paternal grandmother, who like Trayvon Martin, were killed by firearms.

She concluded her statement by saying we "are still on the journey to the Mountaintop. Join me on the journey as we pray for Trayvon's family, the community of Sanford and all who are in danger of being victims of violence." She said that Trayvon Martin's death and Zimmerman's acquittal were a wake-up call for Americans.

On November 7, 2013, as part of the "Celebrating the Dream", in commemoration of the 50th anniversary of the I Have a Dream speech done by her father, King received the Legend Award as a tribute to his legacy and after she delivered a speech.

On January 20, 2014, the year's Martin Luther King, Jr. Day, Bernice King spoke at Ebenezer Baptist Church.

On March 19, 2014, Bernice King gave a speech at Seminole State College of Florida as part of the school's Speaker Series. It focused on the 50th anniversary of the March on Washington and the Civil Rights Act of 1964. After her address, King was presented with a key to the city by Sanford Vice Mayor Velma Williams. King spoke at Fontbonne University on September 17, 2014.

Ebony magazine named Bernice King one of their *Ten of Tomorrow* future leaders of the black community.

A black woman can invent something for the benefit of humankind.
— **Bessie Virginia Blount**

CHAPTER SIX — HEALTH & SCIENCE
FEATURING MEDICAL PROFESSIONALS AND SCIENTISTS

A scientist is someone who systematically gathers and uses research and evidence, to make hypotheses and test them, to gain and share understanding and knowledge.

A scientist can be further defined by how they go about this, for instance by use of statistics or data, what they're seeking understanding of, or the elements in the universe (chemists or geologists), or the stars in the sky (astronomers). Or they can be defined by where they apply their science, for instance in the food industry or medical field.

No matter what, all scientists are united by their relentless curiosity and systematic approach to assuaging it. There are countless men and women who have made great contributions to American society throughout the 20th century, advancing health and science. However, in 2020 *Covid-19 Changed How the World Does Science, Together.*

Never before, scientists say, have so many of the world's researchers focused so urgently on a single topic. Nearly all other research has ground to a halt. Therefore, now, more than ever, we realize that the Innovations and advancements of medical professionals and scientists often goes unnoticed or untold. Here are a few of those Medical Professionals and Scientists who are dedicated to finding life-changing solutions.

REBECCA LEE CRUMPLER

Rebecca Lee Crumpler, (February 8, 1831 – March 9, 1895) was named a Doctor of Medicine on March 1, 1864, by the board of trustees, making her the first African-American woman in the United States to earn the degree, and the only African-American woman to graduate from New England Female Medical College.

Born Rebecca Davis on February 8, 1831 in Christiana, Delaware to Matilda Webber and Absolum Davis, she was raised in Pennsylvania by an aunt who cared for infirm neighbors. Rebecca's aunt acted as the doctor in her community and had a huge influence on her. Rebecca later attended the elite West Newton English and Classical School in Massachusetts where she was a "special student in mathematics."

Rebecca moved to Charlestown, Massachusetts, in 1852. While living in Charlestown, she married Wyatt Lee, a Virginia native and former slave. They were married on April 19, 1852.

During the next eight years Rebecca was employed as a nurse until she was accepted into the New England Female Medical College in 1860. This school was founded by Dr. Israel Tisdale and Samuel

Gregory. It was rare for women or black men to be admitted to medical schools during this time. In 1860, due to the heavy demands of medical care for Civil War veterans, there were more opportunities for women physicians and doctors. That year, there were 54,543 physicians in the United States, 300 of whom were women. None of them were African American women. The faculty was hesitant to pass Rebecca because they thought she showed slow progress in learning. They ended up passing her, but they felt pressured to do so. The doctors who Rebecca worked with while in medical school helped persuade the faculty to pass her.

Rebecca was still a medical student when her husband Wyatt died of Phthisis pulmonalis (tuberculosis) on April 18, 1863. Her M.D. degree was awarded under her married name, Rebecca Lee.

Rebecca Lee Crumpler graduated from New England Female Medical College in 1864. Claims have been made that she was "homeopathically trained" and gained a lot of knowledge from other pioneers in her field at the medical college. However, Crumpler and the many other pioneers are not recognized, nor does "history record them as homeopathic practitioners." She won a tuition award from the Wade Scholarship Fund, which was established by the Ohio abolitionist, Benjamin Wade.

After having completed three years of coursework and a thesis, Rebecca gave her final oral examinations in February 1864. The school closed in 1873 due to financial issues, without graduating another black woman. It merged with Boston University School of Medicine and "adopted an exclusively homeopathic allegiance". The school also staffed around 26 new homeopathic faculty members.

Dr. Rebecca Crumpler worked as a general probationer in Boston for various families, and at the end of the Civil War in 1865, she relocated to Richmond, Virginia to work with the Freedmen's Bureau to provide medical care to the newly freed slaves who needed urgent looking-after. Rebecca's loving nature and generous reputation was widely recognized in the Black community for years.

In Saint John, New Brunswick, on May 24, 1865, Rebecca married Arthur Crumpler, a former fugitive slave from Southampton County, Virginia. Born in 1824, he was the son of Samuel Crumpler, a slave of Benjamin Crumpler. Arthur lived on the neighboring estate of a large landowner, Robert Adams. He served with the Union Army at Fort Monroe, Virginia as a blacksmith, based upon his training and experience. He went to Massachusetts in 1862 and was taken in by Nathaniel Allen, founder of the West Newton English and Classical School, called the Allen School.

Rebecca returned to Joy Street in Beacon Hill, Boston with her husband in 1969, where she spent the rest of her days providing help and nutritional advice to impoverished women and children. By the time she moved back to Boston, her neighborhood on Joy Street in Beacon Hill was a predominantly African-American community. She "entered into the work with renewed vigor, practicing outside, and receiving children in the house for treatment; regardless, in a measure, of remuneration."

Rebecca and Arthur were active members of the Twelfth Baptist Church where Arthur was a trustee, and in mid-December, 1870, their daughter, Lizzie Sinclair Crumpler, was born at their 20 Garden Street home.

Crumpler spoke at a service for Massachusetts Senator Charles Sumner upon his death in 1874. She read a poem that she had written for him, where "she touchingly alluded to his love for the gifted Emerson." By 1880, Rebecca and Arthur moved to Hyde Park, Boston.

In 1883, she published *A Book of Medical Discourses* from the notes she kept over the course of her medical career. It was dedicated to nurses and mothers and focused on the medical care of women and children. Though her primary focus was on the health of women and children which seem to be influenced by homeopathy, she "suggested recommendations for treating diseases without mentioning homeopathy". In her book "she did not advocate for the homeopathic approach", even though she was well aware that medicine was dangerous and could cause risk and harm. She "favored conventional amount" of standard medicine usage and recommended many throughout her discourse.

Her medical book is divided into two different sections. In the first half of her book, she focuses on "treatment, prevention, and cure of infantile bowel complaints" that can occur around the teething period until the child is about five years of age. The second portion of the books mainly focuses on womanhood and "distressing complaints" from youth to mature women. Although the book was focused on medical advice, Rebecca Crumpler ties in autobiographical and also describes the progression of experiences that led her to study and practice medicine.

At the time, many early African American authors have had their writings and books include prefaces and introductions that have a white male sounding authentication. Rebecca was able to introduce her own text and is also able to justify her work based on only her authority.

The Rebecca Lee Society, one of the first medical societies for African American women, was named in her honor. Her home on Joy Street is a stop on the Boston Women's Heritage Trail. Dr. Maass Robinson and Dr. Patricia Whitley made this lifelong legacy become reality.

Rebecca Crumpler overcame and challenged the many prejudices towards African Americans in pursuing careers in the medical field. The first African American to hold the job title of a physician was initially credited to a different woman by the name of Dr. Rebecca Cole. In fact, Rebecca Lee Crumpler earned her degree three years before Rebecca Cole.

Rebecca Crumpler died on March 9, 1895, in Fairview, Massachusetts, while still residing in Hyde Park. She and her husband Arthur are both buried at the Fairview Cemetery near their residence in Hyde Park. Arthur died in Boston in 1910.

Dr. Crumpler's achievements and legacy live on forever, remaining an idol and a role model for black physicians, women, and aspiring children, proving anything is possible with hard work and discipline.

WILLIAM AUGUSTUS HINTON

William Augustus Hinton (December 15, 1883 - August 8, 1959), an American bacteriologist, pathologist and educator, was the first black professor in the history of Harvard University.

William Hinton was born in Chicago to Augustus Hinton and Maria Clark, both former slaves freed after the Civil War. William's father Augustus became a farmer and railroad porter, while his mother, Maria, also became a farmer. William grew up in Kansas; and after high school, he studied at the University of Kansas before transferring to Harvard University, where he earned a B.S. degree in 1905. Following his graduation, William taught in Tennessee and Oklahoma. During the summers he continued his studies in bacteriology and physiology at the University of Chicago.

William Hinton married Ada Hawes, a teacher, in 1909. The couple had two daughters, Anne Hinton Jones and Dr. Jane Hinton, a Doctor of Veterinary Medicine.

In 1909, William enrolled in Harvard Medical School and was offered a scholarship reserved for African American students, which he declined. Instead, he competed for and won the prestigious Wigglesworth and Hayden scholarships two years in a row, a scholarship open to all Harvard students. He graduated with honors in 1912 after only 3 years.

William Hinton would later will his $75,000 in savings to be put into a special scholarship fund for Harvard graduate students as a memorial to his parents and the ideals of conduct they passed on to him. He named the scholarship fund after President Dwight D. Eisenhower to recognize the leader who he believed had made great strides in providing equal opportunity employment during his administration. In his book *Mandate for Change*, Eisenhower reflected on this scholarship, writing "I could not recall having been given a personal distinction that had touched me more deeply."

Denied a medical internship due to his race, Hinton worked as a "voluntary assistant" in the Pathology Laboratory at Massachusetts General Hospital from 1913-1915. It was in this position that he became an expert in syphilis, publishing his first paper along with Roger I. Lee. Gaining the respect of his colleagues, he was invited to write a chapter in a leading textbook, *Preventive Medicine and Hygiene*.

In 1915 William was awarded the dual appointments of Director of the Laboratory Department of the Boston Dispensary and Chief of the Wasserman Laboratory of the Massachusetts Department of Public Health, staying at the latter position until his retirement in 1953. Under his supervision, the number of approved laboratories grew from 10 to 117.

After his professional career took off, William returned to Harvard Medical School in 1918 as an instructor in preventive medicine and hygiene. In 1921 he began teaching bacteriology and immunology—subjects he would teach at Harvard for over thirty years. For the majority of his time at Harvard, William Hinton was an assistant and then a Lecturer. He was only made a full professor on the eve of his retirement, when Harvard named him Clinical Professor of Bacteriology and Immunology.

A pioneer in the field of public health, William Hinton developed a flocculation test for syphilis in 1927. He became internationally known as an expert in the diagnosis and treatment of syphilis. Hinton, with a colleague, co-developed another syphilis test using spinal fluid, that would come to be known as the Davies-Hinton test. These tests were considered a boon for medicine, as the treatment for syphilis at the time was long, painful, and hazardous. William's serological test for syphilis, which proved to be more accurate than currently accepted tests and also was simple, quick, and unambiguous, was endorsed by the U.S. Public Health Service in 1934.

In 1936 William Hinton published the first medical textbook by a black American: *Syphilis and Its Treatment*. He was adamant about the role of socioeconomics in health and called syphilis "a disease of the underprivileged."

During his career, William Hinton taught at Simmons College, the Harvard School of Public Health, and the Tufts Medical and Dental Schools. He also started a school for laboratory technicians open only to women, the first of its kind, and saw its graduates get hired quickly throughout the country. This school helped open the field up to women. His daughter, Jane Hinton, would go on to co-develop what would come to be known as the Mueller-Hinton agar.

William Hinton turned down the NAACP's 1938 Spingarn Medal award because he wanted his work to stand on its own merit; he was concerned that his work would not be as well received if it was widely known in his profession that he was black. "Race should never get mixed up in the struggle for human welfare," he would later say. In 1940, William lost a leg after a car accident.

In 1948, in recognition of his contributions as a distinguished scientist, leading serologist and public health bacteriologist, William Hinton was elected a lifetime member of the American Social Science Association. The serology lab at the Massachusetts Department of Public Health's Laboratory Institute Building was named for him.

In 1958, William Augustus Hinton died in in Canton, Massachusetts from complications related to diabetes.

In 1975, the Massachusetts legislature made what had become known as the "Hinton Laboratory" in the scientific community official, passing a bill to rename the state laboratory the "Dr. William A. Hinton Laboratory."

In 2015, the University of South Carolina School of Medicine Greenville named one of its inaugural college societies after Hinton. The Hinton college went on to consistently perform at higher standards than the university's other colleges, such as Hunter, and two other less successful colleges.

On September 13, 2019, a painting of Hinton was unveiled in Harvard Medical School's Waterhouse Room, previously dominated by the portraits of all-white former Deans.

BESSIE VIRGINIA BLOUNT

Bessie Virginia Blount, also known as **Bessie Blount Griffin**, (November 24, 1914 – December 30, 2009) was a writer, physical therapist, inventor and forensic scientist.

Bessie Blount Griffin was born on November 24, 1914. A native of Virginia, Blount was born in the Hickory, Virginia community, in Princess Anne County (now known as the city of Chesapeake).

Blount attended Diggs Chapel Elementary School in Hickory, Virginia, an educational facility built after the Civil War for the opportunity of educational advancement for African American children. While attending Diggs Chapel, Blount's teacher reprimanded her for writing with her left hand by rapping her knuckles, a form of discipline used at the time to teach students proper writing etiquette. Blount took this moment to her advantage, as a challenge to be ambidextrous, among other remarkable skills. Even though her right hand was her primary hand to write with, she still maintained her skill to write with her left hand as well.

In addition, she taught herself the skill to be able to write without the use of her hands by holding a pencil with her teeth and feet. After the sixth grade, all of the academic resources that were being offered to African American children in her location, had been depleted, forcing Blount to stop her education. The family then relocated north to New Jersey, where Blount remained self-taught and obtained her GED. She then attended Community Kennedy Memorial Hospital's nurse's program, in Newark, New Jersey. After obtaining her Nursing degree, she continued her education at Panzer College of Physical Education and Hygiene in East Orange, New Jersey and became a physical therapist.

During her career as a physical therapist, after World War II, many soldiers returned as amputees after being wounded in combat. As a part of Blount's physical therapy exercises, she taught veterans who lost the ability to use their hands new ways to perform everyday tasks by substituting the use of their hands for completing tasks, to the use their teeth and feet. As she worked each day, Blount observed that one of the biggest challenges for patients in this condition was the task of eating without assistance from other people. It was dire to many that they regain the ability to feed themselves. Gaining this ability would give them their sense of independence back and increase their self-esteem.

While working at the Bronx Hospital in New York, Blount invented an electric self-feeding apparatus to help amputees feed themselves. Blount came up with a device that consisted of a tube that transported individual bites of food to the patient's mouth. All the patient would need to do is bite down on the tube and then the food would dispense to the mouthpiece with an attached machine that would dispense the next portion of food to the patients' mouth when prompted. The American Veterans' Administration declined Blount's invention, therefore, she sold it to the French government instead. She stated that this accomplishment showed "that a black woman can invent something for the benefit of humankind."

Her next invention was a way for an injured/ill patient to hold something close to their face using a "portable receptacle support." The device hung around a person's neck with an attachment that supported a cup or a bowl. In April 1951, Blount was granted Patent No. 2,550,554. During her career, Blount was a physical therapist to Thomas Edison's son, Theodore Miller Edison. Blount and Edison became close friends. During the time she spent in the Edison's home she invented the emesis basin. The basin was a disposable cardboard model made out of flour, water, and a newspaper that was baked until the material was hard. Once again, the U.S. showed no interest in Blount's invention. She sold the rights to her invention to a company in Belgium. Her design is still being implemented in Belgian hospitals.

In 1969, Blount began a second career in law enforcement. Blount began conveying forensic science research for police departments in New Jersey and Virginia. As she worked with previous patients, demonstrating how to be ambidextrous, write with their teeth, or write with their feet, she began to observe the close comparison between physical health and handwriting characteristics. From her point of view, she saw how a person's handwriting reflected upon their state of health. This discovery inspired her to publish a technical paper on "medical graphology." After the publication of her technical paper, Blount's career in forensics quickly expanded.

In the late 1960s Blount was assisting police departments in Norfolk, Virginia, Vineland, New Jersey, and then she joined the Portsmouth, Virginia police department as a chief examiner later in her career. In 1977, the Metropolitan Police Forensic Science Laboratory invited Blount to join them in London for advanced studies in graphology. Later, Blount started her own business, using her forensic experience to examine documents and slave papers from the pre-civil war. She operated this business until the age of 83.

Bessie Blount was honored by The American Academy of Physical Therapy, the first African American Physical Therapy Organization. Blount made numerous attempts to spark the interest of the American Veteran's Association in her inventions; however, they were reluctant, despite the devices' evident beneficial impact that they could have on people's lives.

Bessie Blount died at the age of 95 on December 30, 2009, at her home in Newfield, New Jersey.

JAMES EDWARD BOWMAN JR.

James Edward Bowman Jr. (February 5, 1923 – September 28, 2011) was the first tenured African-American professor in the University of Chicago's Biological Sciences Division. He served as the medical school's Assistant Dean of Students for Minority Affairs from 1986 to 1990.

James Bowman was born on February 5, 1923, in Washington, D.C., the eldest of five children of Dorothy Peterson Bowman, a homemaker, and James Edward Bowman Sr., a dentist. James attended Dunbar High School before earning his undergraduate and medical degrees from Howard University in 1943 and 1946.

James Bowman married educator Barbara Taylor, who is an American early childhood education expert/advocate, professor, and author. James and Barbara Bowman had one daughter, Valerie Bowman Jarrett, who was a Senior Advisor to President Barack Obama.

James Bowman did medical internships at Freedmen's Hospital in Washington, D.C. and at Provident Hospital in Chicago. His residency in pathology was at St. Luke's Hospital in Chicago where he was the first African American resident.

Following residency, Bowman served as chair of pathology at Provident Hospital. He was drafted again and spent 1953 to 1955 as chief of pathology for the Medical Nutrition Laboratory at Fitzsimons Army Hospital in Aurora, Colorado. After leaving the military Bowman decided to move overseas. He and his wife decided that they were not going to go back to anything that smacked of segregation. He became chair of pathology at Nemazee Hospital in Shiraz, Iran. They were recently married, so they took a chance and It changed their lives completely. Their daughter, Valerie, was born in Iran.

In Iran, Dr. Bowman saw many diseases for the first time. He saw smallpox, brucellosis, rabies, all sorts of things. One of the most common diseases among certain ethnic groups in Iran was favism, a metabolic disease caused by an enzyme deficiency in red blood cells. The mutation, which is the most common human enzyme defect, renders those who have it unable to break down a toxin found in fava beans. Favism fit with Bowman's lifelong focus on inherited blood diseases and led to a series of important discoveries about the genetics of these diseases and the populations they affect, especially in the Middle East, Africa and America. It enabled him to travel all over the world collecting blood samples for DNA testing. It also led to frequent contacts and collaborations with University of Chicago researchers, who had first described the enzyme deficiency (glucose-6-phosphate dehydrogenase deficiency, or G6PD) and its connection with antimalarial medications.

Bowman joined the faculty of the University of Chicago in 1962 as an assistant professor of medicine and pathology and director of the hospital's blood bank. He was promoted to full professor and director of laboratories in 1971. From 1973 to 1984, he directed the Comprehensive Sickle Cell Center of the University of Chicago, funded by the National Institutes of Health. He was a member of the national advisory group that urged the Nixon administration to initiate the inception of the Comprehensive Sickle Cell Center, which served as a model of patient-centered disease management and research. He also served as assistant dean of students for minority affairs for the Pritzker School of Medicine from 1986 to 1990.

In 1972 Bowman declared that mandatory sickle cell screening laws were "more harmful than beneficial." He stated that these laws could "revive many of the past misadventures and racism of eugenics movements," adding that adult screening programs create "inaccurate, misleading, politically motivated propaganda which has left mothers frantic." In 1973, he was named to two federal review committees designed to oversee sickle cell screening and education and to evaluate laboratory diagnostic techniques.

Bowman was certified by the American Board of Pathology in pathologic anatomy (1951) and clinical pathology (1952). He was a fellow of the Hastings Center, a bioethics research institution.

An American physician and specialist in pathology, hematology, and genetics, as well as a professor of pathology and genetics at the Pritzker School of Medicine at the University of Chicago, Dr. James Bowman died of cancer on September 28, 2011, at the University of Chicago Medical Center, at the age of 88.

NEIL DEGRASSE TYSON

Neil deGrasse Tyson (October 5, 1958) became director of the Hayden planetarium in 1996, and oversaw its $210 million reconstruction project, assisting with its design and helping raise the necessary funds. The project was completed in 2000 and the revamped site offered visitors a cutting-edge look at astronomy.

Tyson was born October 5, 1958 in Manhattan as the second of three children, into a family living in the Bronx. His mother, Sunchita Maria Feliciano Tyson, was a gerontologist for the U.S. Department of Health, Education and Welfare, and is of Puerto Rican descent. His African-American father, Cyril deGrasse Tyson (1927–2016), was a sociologist, human resource commissioner for New York City mayor John Lindsay, and the first Director of Harlem Youth Opportunities Unlimited. Tyson has two siblings: Stephen Joseph Tyson and Lynn Antipas Tyson. Tyson's middle name, deGrasse, is from the maiden name of his paternal grandmother, who was born as Altima de Grasse in the British West Indies island of Nevis.

Tyson grew up in the Castle Hill neighborhood of the Bronx, and later in Riverdale. From kindergarten throughout high school, Tyson attended public schools in the Bronx: P.S. 36, P.S. 81, the Riverdale Kingsbridge Academy (then called "P.S. 141"), and The Bronx High School of Science (1972–1976) where he was captain of the wrestling team and editor-in-chief of the *Physical Science Journal*. His interest in astronomy began at the age of nine after visiting the sky theater of the Hayden Planetarium at the Museum of Natural History where he got his first taste of star-gazing. He recalled that the imprint of the night sky was so strong that he's certain he had no choice in the matter, that in fact, the universe called him.

During high school, Tyson attended astronomy courses offered by the Hayden Planetarium and got his own telescope, which he called "the most formative period" of his life. He credited Dr. Mark Chartrand III, director of the planetarium at the time, as his "first intellectual role model" and his enthusiastic teaching style mixed with humor inspired Tyson to communicate the universe to others the way he did.

Tyson obsessively studied astronomy in his teen years, and he would watch the skies from the roof of his apartment building. He eventually even gained some fame in the astronomy community by giving lectures on the subject at the age of fifteen.

Astronomer Carl Sagan, who was a faculty member at Cornell University, tried to recruit Tyson to Cornell for undergraduate studies. However, Tyson chose to attend Harvard where he majored in physics and lived in Currier House. He was a member of the crew team during his freshman year, but returned to wrestling, lettering in his senior year. He was also active in dance, in styles including jazz, ballet, Afro-Caribbean, and Latin Ballroom.

Tyson studied at Harvard University, the University of Texas at Austin, and Columbia University. He earned an AB degree in physics at Harvard College in 1980 and then began his graduate work at the University of Texas at Austin, from which he received an MA degree in astronomy in 1983. By his own account, he did not spend as much time in the research lab as he should have. His professors encouraged him to consider alternative careers and the committee for his doctoral dissertation was dissolved, ending his pursuit of a doctorate from the University of Texas. From 1986 to 1987 Tyson was a lecturer in astronomy at the University of Maryland .

Tyson had met his wife, Alice Young, in a physics class at the University of Texas at Austin. Alice holds a Ph.D. in mathematical physics. He and Alice got married in 1988 and moved to the Tribeca neighborhood of Lower Manhattan. The couple has two children, Miranda and Travis. Miranda, their first child, is named after the smallest of Uranus' five major moons.

In 1988, Tyson was accepted into the astronomy graduate program at Columbia University, where he earned an MPhil degree in astrophysics in 1989, and a PhD degree in astrophysics in 1991 under the supervision of Professor R. Michael Rich. Rich obtained funding to support Tyson's doctoral research from NASA and the ARCS foundation enabling Tyson to attend international meetings in Italy, Switzerland, Chile, and South Africa and to hire students to help him with data reduction. In the course of his thesis work, he observed using the 0.91 m telescope at the Cerro Tololo Inter-American Observatory in Chile, where he obtained images for the Calán/Tololo Supernova Survey helping to further their work in establishing Type Ia supernovae as standard candles.

During his thesis research at Columbia University, Tyson became acquainted with Professor David Spergel at Princeton University, who visited Columbia University in the course of collaborating with his thesis advisor on the Galactic bulge typically found in spiral galaxies.

From 1991 to 1994, Tyson was a postdoctoral research associate at Princeton University. In 1994, he joined the Hayden Planetarium as a staff scientist and the Princeton faculty as a visiting research scientist and lecturer.

One of Tyson's most controversial decisions at the time was the removal of Pluto from the display of planets. He classified Pluto as a dwarf planet, which invoked a strong response from some visitors. While some asked for the planet Pluto back, the International Astronomical Union followed Tyson's lead in 2006. The organization officially labeled Pluto as a dwarf planet.

From 1995 to 2005, Tyson wrote monthly essays in the "Universe" column for *Natural History* magazine. During the same period, he wrote a monthly column in *StarDate* magazine, answering questions about the universe under the pen name "Merlin".

Tyson served on a 2001 government commission on the future of the U.S. aerospace industry and on the 2004 Moon, Mars and Beyond commission. He was awarded the NASA Distinguished Public Service Medal in the same year. In addition to his work at the planetarium, Tyson has found other ways of improving the nation's scientific literacy. From 2006 to 2011, he hosted the television show *NOVA ScienceNow* documentary series on PBS. One of Tyson's goals is to bring the universe down to Earth in a way that further excites the audience to want more. In addition to breaking down barriers between scientists and the general public, Tyson has brought diversity to astrophysics. He is one of the few African Americans in his field.

Tyson has also served as a presidential advisor. In 2001, President George W. Bush appointed the astrophysicist to serve on the Commission on the Future of the United States Aerospace Industry and in 2004 to serve on the President's Commission on Implementation of United States Space Exploration Policy, the latter better known as the "Moon, Mars, and Beyond" commission. Soon afterward, he was awarded the NASA Distinguished Public Service Medal, the highest civilian honor bestowed by NASA.

In 2001 The Tech 100, voted by editors of *Crain's Magazine* to be among the 100 most influential technology leaders in New York; in 2004 Fifty Most Important African-Americans in Research Science; in 2007 Harvard 100: Most Influential, *Harvard Alumni* magazine, Cambridge, Massachusetts; in 2007 The *Time* 100, voted by the editors of *Time* magazine as one of the 100 most influential persons in the world; in 2008 *Discover Magazine* selected him as one of "The 10 Most Influential People in Science"; and in 2010 elected a Fellow of the American Physical Society.

Since 2009, Tyson has hosted the weekly podcast *StarTalk*. A spin-off, also called *StarTalk*, began airing on National Geographic in 2015. In 2014, he hosted the television series *Cosmos: A Spacetime Odyssey*, The U.S. National Academy of Sciences awarded Tyson the Public Welfare Medal in 2015 for his "extraordinary role in exciting the public about the wonders of science".

In 2017 Tyson received a Grammy Award for Best Spoken Word Album nomination for *Astrophysics for People in a Hurry*

In addition, between 1997 and 2018 Tyson has received 20 Honorary doctorates from colleges and universities throughout the United States.

> *Some people want it to happen, some wish it would happen, others make it happen.*
> **– Michael Jordan**

CHAPTER SEVEN - FINANCIAL LITERACY
FEATURING BUSINESS MOGULS

Financial Literacy is the ability to use knowledge and skills to manage financial resources effectively for a lifetime of financial well-being. Most of us are seeking security and that comes with the knowledge to know how to make it happen.

I had great mentors in Hal Jackson and Percy Sutton. Percy was an Intelligence Officer with the Tuskegee Airmen, an attorney, a politician, cofounder of Inner-City Broadcasting Corporation and my dear friend. One of the things he used to tell me was, "I keep about 5 or 6 or 7 businesses because if 1 or 2 or 3 or even 4 fail I'm still in business." That's a serious quote. To this day, I rely on Percy's wisdom to guide me through many of my financial decisions; and I've learned so much from Hal Jackson who was brilliant in the business of radio and television.

It's never too early to start preparing for your future; but for many of us, too often it's too late. Throughout the various stages of your life, there should be a thought process and an evaluation about what you have, what you want and what you need. Money is the common thread but it's not the end all. How you get it, how you maintain it, how you keep it and how you increase it is not about guessing, it's about planning. To journey through life the best way possible, I advise you to ask questions, read books, attend seminars, talk to a financial advisor, hire an accountant, know your limitations and follow the rules. Follow your dreams. Find out what you want to do in life, and you will Make the Grade.

ROBERT LOUIS JOHNSON

Robert "Bob" Louis Johnson became the first black American billionaire. His companies have counted among the most prominent African-American businesses in the late twentieth and early twenty-first centuries.

Robert L. Johnson was born April 8, 1946 in Hickory, Mississippi, the ninth out of ten children to Edna and Archie Johnson. His mother was a schoolteacher and his father was a farmer. His parents moved the family to Freeport, Illinois when he was a child.

Robert was an honors student in high school. He graduated from the University of Illinois in 1968 with a bachelor's degree in social studies. While at the University of Illinois, Johnson became a member of the Beta chapter of Kappa Alpha Psi fraternity. He married Sheila Johnson in 1969. They divorced in 2001 and have two children.

Robert received a master's degree in public affairs from the Woodrow Wilson School at Princeton University in 1972. After graduating from Princeton, he found a job in Washington, D.C., that introduced him to the television industry. He served as the public affairs director for the Corporation for Public Broadcasting. In this position is where he learned of the power and untapped potential of television.

Around the same time he also worked as the director of communications for the Washington, D.C. office of the National Urban League. Johnson worked as a press secretary for Congressman Walter E. Fauntroy. He later became vice president of government relations at the National Cable and Television Association.

Robert left NCTA in 1979 to create Black Entertainment Television, the first cable television network aimed at African Americans. In 1980, he launched Black Entertainment Television, which became a full-fledged channel in 1983 targeted to African Americans.

When the network launched in 1980, it only aired for two hours on Friday night. BET first turned a profit in 1985 and it became the first black-controlled company listed on the New York Stock Exchange in 1991. In 1998, Robert Johnson and Liberty Media bought all outstanding shares of the company. This purchase gave him 42% of the company. Viacom acquired BET in 2000 for a reported $3 billion. Robert Johnson remained BET CEO until 2006.

Robert Johnson became the first African-American majority club owner of a major American sports league with his 2002 purchase of the Charlotte Bobcats.

By January 2009, Ion Media had another subchannel network, Urban TV, in the works with him. In 2010, Robert sold his majority stake in the Charlotte Bobcats to Michael Jordan.

In 2011, Robert Johnson worked with Morgan Freeman to raise funds for hurricane preparedness in the Bahamas. Robert released a neckwear line in coordination with PVH and The Ella Rose Collection, the RLJ Ella Rose Africa Tie Collection, in 2012 to benefit the charitable organization Malaria No More.

Robert Johnson founded The RLJ Companies, a holding company with a diverse portfolio including hotel real estate investment, private equity, financial services, asset management, automobile dealerships, sports and entertainment, and Video lottery terminal gaming. The RLJ Companies is headquartered in Bethesda, Maryland.

As of 2013, Johnson was a member of the board of directors for RLJ Lodging Trust, RLJ Entertainment, Inc., KB Home, Lowe's Companies, Inc., Strayer Education, Think Finance, Inc., NBA Board of Governors, The Business Council, and the Smithsonian Institution's National Museum of African American History and Culture. Johnson has also served as a member of the board of directors for several other companies and organizations, including US Airways, Hilton Hotels, General Mills, the United Negro College Fund, and Deutsche Bank's Americas Advisory Board.

In 2016, Johnson finalized a partnership agreement with AMC Networks through his RLJ Company after launching his own video on demand streaming service Urban Movie Channel in 2014.

Johnson married Lauren Wooden in May 2016.

CATHERINE LIGGINS HUGHES

Catherine "Cathy" Liggins Hughes was born **Catherine Elizabeth Woods** (April 22, 1947). Along with fellow Howard University student and disc jockey Melvin Lindsey, Hughes created the format known as the "Quiet Storm," which revolutionized urban radio and was aired on over 480 stations nationwide.

Cathy Hughes' mother is Helen Jones Woods, a jazz and swing trombonist widely known for her performances with the International Sweethearts of Rhythm at Piney Woods School, a private boarding school in Mississippi. She was inducted into the Omaha Black Music Hall of Fame in 2007. After World War II, in 1947, Helen moved to Omaha and worked as a licensed practical nurse at Douglas County Hospital. Cathy is her fourth child. Cathy's father is William Alfred Woods, who was the first African American to earn an accounting degree from Creighton University.

The family lived in the Logan Fontenelle Housing Projects while Hughes' father attended college. Hughes was far from an only child, growing up with a household of siblings. She found her love for music at a very young age, while repeatedly each night lying in bed listening to Everly Brothers and the Platters.

In the early life of Cathy Hughes, things were not easy for her because her parents did not have much money. She lied about her age to get her first job at the age of 14. She was married to Alfred Liggins Jr from 1965 to 1967. Together they had one child, Alfred Liggins III, born January 30, 1965, in Omaha, Nebraska. The marriage was terminated after Alfred was born.

Cathy Hughes went to her father's alma mater, the University of Nebraska, Omaha and Creighton University, taking Business Administration courses. In the mid-1960s, Hughes worked for an African American newspaper called the *Omaha Star*. She then began her radio career in 1969 at KOWH in Omaha, but left for Washington, D.C. after she was offered a job as an administrative assistant with Tony Brown at the School of Communications at Howard University's radio station, WHUR-FM. Then, she got a job as a sales manager and in 1973, she became General Sales Manager, increasing station revenue from $250,000 to $3 million in her first year. In 1975, Hughes became the first woman Vice President and General Manager of a station in the nation's capital.

Hughes married Dewey Hughes in 1979, they had no children together. During her marriage with Dewey Hughes in 1979, they set out to purchase a radio station. Successfully finding a lender after being denied thirty-two times by banks, in 1980 Hughes and then-husband Dewey founded Radio One, subsequently buying AM radio station WOL 1450 in Washington, D.C. After the previous employees had destroyed the facility, she faced financial difficulties and subsequently lost her home.

Her fortunes began to change when she revamped the R&B station to a 24-hour talk radio format with the theme, "Information is Power." Hughes served as the station's Morning Show Host for 11 years. In 1982 the bank had threatened to cease payments to Hughes investment unless she agreed to airing music. She decided to keep her station as a talking format in the AM and music throughout the day. WOL is still the most-listened-to talk radio station in the nation's capital.

The debt was overwhelming for her husband Dewey and they divorced in 1987. However, Cathy remained focused and knew she could pay back the 1 million dollars they were able to borrow from their "angel" lender. After her divorce and with looming debt, she ended up moving into the station with her son.

In 1987, Hughes had bought radio station WMMJ with her company Radio One (now Urban One). In 1995, Radio One bought radio station WKYS. She was granted an honorary doctorate from Sojourner Douglass College in Baltimore in 1995. That accomplishment drove Hughes back to school 2 years later. Radio One went on to own 70 radio stations in nine major markets in the U.S. In 1999, Radio One became a publicly traded company, listed under the NASDAQ stock exchange.

Then in January 2004, with her son Alfred C. Liggins III, a Wharton School of Business MBA graduate, as chief executive officer his mother's company, Radio One branched into television by creating TV One. A national cable and satellite network, TV One which bills itself as the "lifestyle and entertainment network for African-American adults reaches more than 40 million African American TV households. Hughes interviews prominent personalities, usually in the entertainment industry, for the network's talk program *TV One on One*.

As of 2007, Hughes's son, Alfred Liggins, III, serves as CEO and president of Radio One, and Hughes as chairperson. Hughes is also a minority owner of BET industries.

Both Cathy Hughes and her son, Alfred Liggins have been named Entrepreneur of the Year by the company Ernst & Young. She is a notable member of Alpha Kappa Alpha sorority.

In 2015, a local business organization unofficially named the corner of 4th Street and H Street NE in Washington, D.C. "Cathy Hughes Corner".

Hughes' life story is featured on the documentary series *Profiles of African-American Success*. In 2016, Hughes was inducted into the National Rhythm & Blues Hall of Fame.

In 2017, TV One changed its name to Urban One after it acquired a collection of Internet media websites, now known as iOne Digital, that focus on news, sports and entertainment stories about and for Black audiences.

Today, Urban One is worth, according to Wall Street estimates based on stock price of about $98 million. The company boasts of reaching 59 million households, 22 million listeners, 40 million video streams, 20 million unique Web visitors. It owns 57 broadcast stations in 15 urban markets, two cable networks and some 80 websites. Hughes works closely with her son, Alfred, who she credits with diversifying Urban One beyond radio and TV.

Cathy Hughes has earned many awards. Hughes is a part of the Maryland Chamber of Commerce Business Hall of Fame. She was also awarded the First Annual Black History Hall of Fame Award. Following that she was presented the National Action Networks "Keepers of the Dream" award, which is an award that spotlights role models who contribute an honor and contribute to Martin Luther King, Jr.'s legacy.

DEBRA L. LEE, ESQ.

Debra Louise Lee, Esq. (born August 8, 1954) was named one of the "100 Most Powerful Women in Entertainment" by The Hollywood Reporter due to her many achievements in her 30-plus year career at BET. According to Wikipedia, Forbes, IMDb & Various Online resources, Debra L Lee's net worth is $106 Million.

Debra L. Lee was born in Fort Jackson, South Carolina and grew up in Birmingham, Alabama. Debra is the youngest of three children of Richard M. and Delma L. Lee. Debra's mother worked as a hospital clerk while her father was an Army tank driver.

Debra attended James B. Dudley High School. In 1976, she graduated from Brown University with a bachelor's degree in political science with an emphasis in Asian politics. She went on to earn a master's degree in public policy from Harvard University's John F. Kennedy School of Government and a J.D. degree at Harvard Law School, where she was a member of the Board of Student Advisers, in 1980.

In 1972, she graduated from Greensboro-James B. Dudley High School and later moved to the East Coast where she attended Brown University. During her junior year, Debra spent a year studying abroad in Southeast Asia in Thailand, Malaysia and Indonesia.

From August 1981 through September 1981, Debra served as a law clerk to Barrington Parker of the U.S. District Court for the District of Columbia. Lee joined BET as Vice President of BET's legal affairs department and general counsel in 1986 after over five years as an attorney with Washington, D.C. based Steptoe & Johnson, a corporate law firm. She has also served as BET's corporate secretary and president and publisher of BET's publishing division, which published *Emerge, YSB, BET Weekend* and *Heart & Soul* magazines.

Debra Lee was married to Randall Coleman from 1985 up to 1987. Debra, together with her former husband Randall Coleman have a son and daughter together, Quinn Coleman and Ava Coleman respectively.

In March 1996, Debra Lee became President and Chief Operating Officer (COO) of BET Holdings, Inc., replacing departing network founder, Robert L. Johnson. In 2005, she was named Chairman and Chief Executive Officer (CEO).

Black Entertainment Television began to move in a different format direction for the network. Debra increased the production budget by 50% and looked into incorporating original programming by getting 16 new shows for the new 2007 season. Lee also redesigned BET's mission statement by supporting families, encouraging their dreams, and presenting fresh talent by creating new shows for its network. She created a new entertainment network, CENTRIC, in September 2009 that features new artists, reality shows, and movies.

During Debra's tenure, BET enjoyed some of its most explosive growth in ratings, revenue and popularity. Debra led the network's evolution beyond its successful music programming into original movies, documentations, concert specials, news, late-night talk shows and public policy coverage. She has also substantially expanded investment in marketing, advertising, digital research and development.

Debra Lee has sat on the board of directors for a number of companies/organizations, including the National Cable & Telecommunications Association, the Ad Council, and the National Cable Television Association, Marriott, and Revlon.

Since 2000 she has also been a director of Washington Gas Light Company, WGL Holdings (since 2000) and the Monsanto subsidiary Genuity. In May 2016, Debra Lee was added to the board of directors of Twitter, following an attempt by returning CEO Jack Dorsey to boost diversity across the social media company's board.

Lee's honors include the 2001 Woman of the Year Award from Women in Cable and Telecommunications, Broadcasting and Cable Hall of Fame and 2002: Women of Vision Award by Women in Film & Video – DC, and the 2003 Distinguished Vanguard Award for Leadership from the NCTA, a first for an African American female executive. Outside of the cable industry, Lee has also received special recognition, including the 2005 Madame C.J. Walker Award from *Ebony* magazine for best exemplifying the entrepreneurial spirit of the pioneering Black businesswoman. In 2014 Debra Lee received an honorary Doctorate of Humane Letters from Brown University.

In May 2018, it was the end of an era at BET Networks, as chairman and CEO Debra Lee stepped down, after 32 years with the company. During her tenure, award shows like **Black Girls Rock, BET Honors** and **The Soul Train Music Awards** were acquired. The flagship BET Awards show was instituted, and The New Edition Story miniseries set viewing records at the network.

ALIKO DANGOTE

Aliko Dangote (born April 10, 1957) has been declared as the wealthiest person in Africa, for the ninth year in a row, with an estimated net worth of $10.1 billion. The Dangote Group is a conglomerate with many of its operations in Benin, Ghana, Nigeria, Zambia and Togo.

Aliko Dangote, an ethnic Hausa Muslim from Kano, Kano State, Nigeria was born on April 10, 1957 into a wealthy Muslim family, the son of Mohammed Dangote and Mariya Sanusi Dantata, who made a fortune, dealing in rice, oats, and groundnuts. Sanusi Aliko's great-grandfather, Alhaji Alhassan Dantata, also happened to be a wealthy man, and at the time of his death in 1955, he was the richest man in Africa.

Aliko's father passed away early, which was followed by his grandfather taking over as his guardian. Soon, Aliko developed a keen interest in business as a career. His first business venture was in primary school and involved purchasing boxes of sweets and selling them off at a little profit.

Aliko received his early education at the 'Sheikh Ali Kumasi Madrasa,' followed by the 'Capital High School' in his home state of Kano. He then headed to Cairo, Egypt, for higher education. Subsequently, he received his bachelor's degree in business studies and administration from 'Al-Azhar University.' He returned to Nigeria in 1977 and started planning his first serious business venture.

The Dangote Group was established as a small trading firm in 1977, the same year Aliko Dangote relocated to Lagos to expand the company. Aliko borrowed a sum equivalent to US$ 2,500 from his grandfather and promised to repay the loan within three years. It was a huge amount at that time, and Aliko used the money to settle in Lagos. He started importing rice and sugar from Thailand and Brazil, respectively, in a deliberately planned business move. He then sold them in Nigeria at a huge profit. The demand for those eatables went through the roof, and Aliko began earning great profits within the very first year of establishing his business venture. Within three months of starting his operations, Aliko was able to return the money he had borrowed from his grandfather.

As Aliko's business grew further, he realized that manufacturing goods was a better option than relying on imports. He pushed all his competitors aside, and by the late 90s, Aliko had established several manufacturing units by himself. The Dangote Group has moved from being a trading company to becoming the largest industrial group in Nigeria.

Additionally, Dangote owns flour mills and is a major importer of rice, fish, pasta, cement, and fertilizer, and the company exports cotton, cashew nuts, cocoa, sesame seeds, and ginger to several countries. Dangote started a polypropylene bagging factory, which provides bags for efficient packaging of goods produced by the company.

Aliko Dangote approached the Central Bank of Nigeria with the idea that it would be cheaper for the bank to allow his transport company to manage their fleet of staff buses, a proposal that was well-received and approved. The 'Dangote Group' owns a vehicle-leasing company. With more than a hundred AC-equipped buses under it, the company aims to grow further in stature.

Dangote also expanded to cover cement manufacturing and freight. An intricate network of 600 trailers work religiously to distribute the company goods to different parts of the country and to the port, from where it is exported.

In Nigeria today, Dangote Group with its dominance in the sugar market and refinery business is the main supplier (70 percent of the market) to the country's soft drinks companies, breweries and confectioners. It is the largest refinery in Africa and the third largest in the world, producing 800,000 tons of sugar annually. Aliko has invested a fortune in the group's 'National Salt Company of Nigeria' and has his own salt-manufacturing units in the country. Dangote Group also has major investments in real estate, banking, transport, textiles, oil, and gas. The company employs more than 11,000 people and is the largest industrial conglomerate in West Africa.

Dangote has diversified into telecommunications and has started building 14,000 kilometres of fibre optic cables to supply the whole of Nigeria. As a result, Dangote was honored in January 2009 as the leading provider of employment in the Nigerian construction industry. In July 2012, Dangote approached the Nigerian Ports

Authority to lease an abandoned piece of land at the Apapa Port, which was approved. He later built facilities for his flour company there.

Aliko Dangote has said, "Let me tell you this and I want to really emphasize it ... nothing is going to help Nigeria like Nigerians bringing back their money. If you give me $5 billion today, I will invest everything here in Nigeria. Let us put our heads together and work."

The 'Dangote Foundation' was established to give shape to the philanthropic endeavors of the company. Millions of dollars are spent by the foundation, each year, for the betterment of the education and the healthcare system in the country. The foundation also works toward repairing roads and houses and indulges in providing scholarships to financially backward students. Dangote has also donated money to the Nigeria sport ministry to renovate the national stadium, Abuja.

In 2014, the Nigerian government said Dangote had donated 150 million naira (US$750,000) to halt the spread of ebola. He was honored by 'Forbes' magazine, with the title of the 2014 'Forbes Africa Person of the Year.' In 2015, Aliko won the 'Clinton Global Citizen Award.'

Africa has 54 nations, but only eight countries have billionaires according to Forbes, with South Africa and Egypt dominating not only the top 10 richest people in Africa list, but in the rankings overall with five billionaires each. Nigeria comes second with four billionaires, including Africa's richest man, Aliko Dangote.

Dangote was awarded Nigeria's second-highest honor, the Grand Commander of the Order of the Niger (GCON) by the former President, Goodluck Jonathan.

MICHAEL JEFFREY JORDAN

Michael Jeffrey Jordan (born February 17, 1963), also known by his initials MJ, Michael is an American former professional basketball player and the principal owner of the Charlotte Hornets of the National Basketball Association (NBA). He played 15 seasons in the NBA, winning six championships with the Chicago Bulls. He was one of the most effectively marketed athletes of his generation and was considered instrumental in popularizing the NBA around the world in the 1980s and 1990s. In 2014, Jordan became the first billionaire player in NBA history. With a net worth of $1.9 billion, he is the fourth-richest African-American, behind Robert F. Smith, David Steward, and Oprah Winfrey.

Michael Jordan was born at Cumberland Hospital in Fort Greene, Brooklyn, to Deloris (Peoples), who worked in banking, and James

R. Jordan Sr., an equipment supervisor. His family moved to Wilmington, North Carolina, when he was a toddler.

Jordan attended Emsley A. Laney High School in Wilmington, where he highlighted his athletic career by playing basketball, baseball, and football. He tried out for the varsity basketball team during his sophomore year, but at 5'11" he was deemed too short to play at that level. His taller friend, Harvest Leroy Smith, was the only sophomore to make the team.

Motivated to prove his worth, Jordan became the star of Laney's junior varsity team, and tallied several 40-point games. The following summer, he grew four inches and trained rigorously. Upon earning a spot on the varsity roster, Jordan averaged more than 25 points per game (ppg) over his final two seasons of high school play. As a senior, he was selected to play in the 1981 McDonald's All-American Game and scored 30 points, after averaging 27 points, 12 rebounds and 6 assists per game for the season.

Jordan was recruited by numerous college basketball programs, including Duke, North Carolina, South Carolina, Syracuse, and Virginia. In 1981, Jordan accepted a basketball scholarship to the University of North Carolina at Chapel Hill, where he majored in cultural geography.

As a freshman, in coach Dean Smith's team-oriented system, he was named ACC Freshman of the Year after he averaged 13.4 ppg on 53.4% shooting (field goal percentage). He made the game-winning jump shot in the 1982 NCAA Championship game against Georgetown, which was led by future NBA rival Patrick Ewing. Jordan later described this shot as the major turning point in his basketball career. During his three seasons with the Tar Heels, he averaged 17.7 ppg on 54.0% shooting, and added 5.0 rpg. He was selected by consensus to the NCAA All-American First Team in both his sophomore (1983) and junior (1984) seasons.

Jordan played on two Olympic gold medal-winning American basketball teams. He won a gold medal as a college player in the 1984 Summer Olympics. The team was coached by Bob Knight and featured players such as Patrick Ewing, Sam Perkins, Chris Mullin, Steve Alford, and Wayman Tisdale. Jordan led the team in scoring, averaging 17.1 ppg for the tournament. His leaping ability, demonstrated by performing slam dunks from the free throw line in Slam Dunk Contests, earned him the nicknames Air Jordan and His Airness. He also gained a reputation for being one of the best defensive players in basketball.

Jordan played three seasons for coach Dean Smith with the North Carolina Tar Heels. As a freshman, he was a member of the Tar Heels' national championship team in 1982. Jordan joined the Bulls in 1984 as the third overall draft pick, and quickly emerged as a league star and entertained crowds with his prolific scoring. Jordan is also known for his product endorsements. He fueled the success of Nike's Air Jordan sneakers which were introduced in 1984 and remain popular today.

Jordan returned to the University of North Carolina to complete his degree in 1986. He graduated the same year with a Bachelor of Arts degree in geography.

In 1991, Jordan won his first NBA championship with the Bulls, and followed that achievement with titles in 1992 and 1993, securing a "three-peat".

In the 1992 Summer Olympics, he was a member of the star-studded squad that included Magic Johnson and Larry Bird that was dubbed the "Dream Team". Jordan was the only player to start all eight games in the Olympics. Jordan and fellow Dream Team members Ewing and Mullin are the only American men's basketball players to win Olympic gold medals as amateurs and professionals.

On October 6, 1993, Jordan announced his retirement, citing a loss of desire to play the game. Jordan later stated that the death of his father three months earlier also shaped his decision.

Jordan abruptly retired from basketball before the 1993–94 NBA season and started a new career in Minor League Baseball, In March 1995, Jordan decided to quit baseball due to the ongoing Major League Baseball strike, as he wanted to avoid becoming a potential replacement player. On March 18, 1995, Jordan announced his return to the NBA through a two-word press release: "I'm back." The next day, Jordan took to the court with the Bulls to face the Indiana Pacers in Indianapolis, scoring 19 points. In 1996, he founded a Chicago area Boys & Girls Club and dedicated it to his father.

Jordan returned to the Bulls and led them to three additional championships in 1996, 1997, and 1998, as well as a then-record 72 regular-season wins in the 1995–96 NBA season. He retired for a second time in January 1999 but returned for two more NBA seasons from 2001 to 2003 as a member of the Washington Wizards.

Playing in his 14th and final NBA All-Star Game in 2003, Jordan passed Kareem Abdul-Jabbar as the all-time leading scorer in All-Star Game history (a record later broken by Kobe Bryant). With the recognition that 2002–03 would be Jordan's final season, tributes were paid to him throughout the NBA. In his final game at the United Center in Chicago, which was his old home court, Jordan received a four-minute standing ovation.

On June 15, 2006, Jordan bought a minority stake in the Charlotte Bobcats, becoming the team's second-largest shareholder behind majority owner Robert L. Johnson. As part of the deal, Jordan took full control over the basketball side of the operation, with the title "Managing Member of Basketball Operations." Despite Jordan's previous success as an endorser, he has made an effort not to be included in Charlotte's marketing campaigns.

Jordan stayed in shape, played golf in celebrity charity tournaments, and spent time with his family in Chicago. He also promoted his Jordan Brand clothing line and rode motorcycles. Since 2004, Jordan has owned Michael Jordan Motorsports, a professional closed-course motorcycle road racing team that competed with two Suzukis in the premier Superbike championship sanctioned by the American Motorcyclist Association (AMA) until the end of the 2013 season.

In February 2010, it was reported that Jordan was seeking majority ownership of the Bobcats, who changed their nickname to the Hornets in 2014. As February wore on, it became apparent that Jordan and former Houston Rockets president George Postolos were the leading contenders for ownership of the team. On February 27, the Bobcats announced that Johnson had reached an agreement with Jordan and his group, MJ Basketball Holdings, to buy the team pending NBA approval. On March 17, the NBA Board of Governors unanimously approved Jordan's purchase, making him the first former player to become the majority owner of an NBA team. It also made him the league's only African American majority owner of an NBA team.

Jordan's individual accolades and accomplishments include six NBA Finals Most Valuable Player (MVP) Awards, ten scoring titles (both all-time records), five MVP Awards, ten All-NBA First Team designations, nine All-Defensive First Team honors, fourteen NBA All-Star Game selections, three All-Star Game MVP Awards, three steals titles, and the 1988 NBA Defensive Player of the Year Award. He holds the NBA records for highest career regular season scoring average (30.12 points per game) and highest career playoff scoring average (33.45 points per game). In 1999, he was named the greatest North American athlete of the 20th century by ESPN, and was second to Babe Ruth on the Associated Press' list of athletes of the century. Jordan is a two-time inductee into the Naismith Memorial Basketball Hall of Fame, having been enshrined in 2009 for his individual career and again in 2010 as part of the group induction of the 1992 United States men's Olympic basketball team ("The Dream Team"). He became a member of the FIBA Hall of Fame in 2015.

JEFFREY PRESTON BEZOS (JORGENSEN)

Jeffrey Preston Bezos (Jorgensen) was born January 12, 1964. He is best known as the founder, chief executive officer, and president of Amazon. The first centi-billionaire on the *Forbes* wealth index, Bezos was named the "richest man in modern history" after his net worth increased to $150 billion in July 2018. He is an American internet and aerospace entrepreneur, media proprietor, and investor.

Bezos was born in Albuquerque, New Mexico, and raised in Houston, Texas. Jeffrey Preston Jorgensen is the son of Jacklyn (Gise) Jorgensen and Ted Jorgensen. At the time of his birth, his mother was a 17-year-old high school student, and his father was a bike shop owner. After Jacklyn divorced Ted, she married Cuban immigrant Miguel "Mike" Bezos in April 1968. Shortly after the wedding, Mike adopted four-year-old Jorgensen, whose surname was then changed to Bezos. The family moved to Houston, Texas, where Mike worked as an engineer for Exxon after he received a degree from the University of New Mexico. Bezos attended River Oaks Elementary School in Houston from fourth to sixth grade.

Bezos' maternal grandfather was Lawrence Preston Gise, a regional director of the U.S. Atomic Energy Commission (AEC) in Albuquerque. Gise retired early to his family's ranch near Cotulla, Texas, where Bezos would spend many summers in his youth. Bezos would later purchase this ranch and expand it from 25,000 acres to 300,000 acres. His maternal grandmother was Mattie Louise Gise, through whom he is a cousin of country singer George Strait. Bezos often displayed scientific interests and technological proficiency; he once rigged an electric alarm to keep his younger siblings out of his room.

The family moved to Miami, Florida, where Bezos attended Miami Palmetto High School. While Bezos was in high school, he worked at McDonald's as a short-order line cook during the breakfast shift. He attended the Student Science Training Program at the University of Florida. He was high school valedictorian, a National Merit Scholar, and a Silver Knight Award winner in 1982. In the graduation speech Bezos told the audience he dreamed of the day when the people of earth would colonize space.

Bezos graduated from Princeton University in 1986 with a degree in electrical engineering and computer science. In 1986, he graduated *summa cum laude* from Princeton University with a 4.2 grade point average and a Bachelor of Science in Engineering in electrical engineering and computer science; he was also a member of Phi Beta Kappa. In addition, he was elected to Tau Beta Pi and was the president of the Princeton chapter of the Students for the Exploration and Development of Space. After his graduation, Bezos had numerous offers on his table from several different major tech companies of the time. He worked on Wall Street as a hedge fund manager and in a variety of related fields.

He was offered jobs at Intel, Bell Labs, and Andersen Consulting, among others. He first worked at Fitel, a fintech telecommunications start-up, where he was tasked with building a network for international trade. Bezos was promoted to head of development and director of customer service thereafter. He transitioned into the banking industry when he became a product manager at Bankers Trust; he worked there from 1988 to 1990. He then joined D. E. Shaw & Co, a newly founded hedge fund with a strong emphasis on mathematical modelling, in 1990 and worked there until 1994. Bezos became D. E. Shaw's fourth senior vice-president at the age of 30.

He founded the online retailer Amazon in late 1994 on a cross-country road trip from New York City to Seattle. The company began as an online bookstore and has since expanded to a wide variety of other e-commerce products and services, including video and audio streaming, cloud computing, and artificial intelligence. It is currently the world's largest online sales company, the largest internet company by revenue, as well as the world's largest provider of AI assistance and cloud infrastructure services through its Amazon Web Services arm. Amazon recently bought out the grocery chain Whole Foods.

In late 1993, Bezos decided to establish an online bookstore. He left his job at D. E. Shaw and founded Amazon in his garage on July 5, 1994, after writing its business plan on a cross-country drive from New York City to Seattle. Bezos initially named his new company *Cadabra* but later changed the name to *Amazon* after the Amazon River in South America, in part because the name begins with the letter *A*, which is at the beginning of the alphabet. He accepted an estimated $300,000 from his parents and invested in Amazon. He warned many early investors that there was a 70% chance that Amazon would fail or go bankrupt.

Although Amazon was originally an online bookstore, Bezos had always planned to expand to other products. Three years after Bezos founded Amazon, he took it public with an initial public offering (IPO). In response to critical reports from *Fortune* and *Barron's*, Bezos maintained that the growth of the Internet would overtake competition from larger book retailers such as Borders and Barnes & Noble.

Bezos founded the aerospace manufacturer and sub-orbital spaceflight services company Blue Origin in 2000. A Blue Origin test flight successfully first reached space in 2015, and the company has upcoming plans to begin commercial suborbital human spaceflight. Bezos also purchased the major American newspaper *The Washington Post* in 2013 for US $250 million in cash and manages many other investments through his venture capital firm, Bezos Expeditions.

He meets with Amazon investors for a total of only six hours a year. Instead of using PowerPoints, Bezos requires high-level employees to present information with six-page narratives. Starting in 1998, Bezos publishes an annual letter for Amazon shareholders wherein he frequently refers to five principles: focus on customers not competitors, take risks for market leadership, facilitate staff morale, build a company culture, and empower people. Bezos maintains the email address "jeff@amazon.com" as an outlet for customers to reach out to him and the company. Although he does not respond to the emails, he forwards some of them with a question mark in the subject line to executives who attempt to address the issues. Bezos has cited Warren Buffett (of Berkshire Hathaway), Jamie Dimon (of JPMorgan Chase), and Bob Iger (of Walt Disney) as major influences on his leadership style.

PART TWO
MORE NOTABLE PEOPLE WHO HAVE DONE EXTRAORDINARY THINGS TO MAKE THE GRADE

PEOPLE TO KNOW IN BLACK HISTORY & BEYOND

MORE EDUCATORS WHO MAKE THE GRADE...

Nellie May Quander (February 11, 1880 - September 24, 1961) served as an educator in Washington, DC public schools for 30 years. Early in her career, she earned an M.A. at Columbia University. Later she earned a degree in social work at New York University, plus a diploma at the University of Uppsala, Sweden.

Nellie Quander was born in Washington, D.C. to John Pierson Quander and Hannah Bruce Ford Quander. Her family could trace its lineage and sense of purpose for three hundred years in Maryland and Virginia. They are considered to be one of oldest free African-American families whose ancestors had once been enslaved in America. Her father was a descendant of Nancy Quander, one of the slaves freed by President of the United States George Washington in his last will and testament.

During her early years, Nellie Quander attended Washington, D.C.'s public schools. She graduated from Miner Normal School with honors. It was established in 1851 as the Normal School for Colored Girls to train teachers.

While enrolled at Howard University, Quander also taught students at the Garrison School in Washington D.C.'s public school system. Nellie Quander became a member of Alpha Kappa Alpha at Howard in 1910.

In June 1912, Nellie graduated with a Bachelor of Arts degree, magna cum laude, in history, economics, and political science. After graduation, Quander became an educator for the public-school system in Washington, D.C., where she served generations of students for 30 years.

With Quander's help, Alpha Kappa Alpha was nationally incorporated in Washington, D.C., as a non-profit under the name Alpha Kappa Alpha Sorority, Incorporated on January 29, 1913. After leading the initiative to incorporate the sorority, Quander served as president of Alpha Kappa Alpha.

From 1914 to 1915, Quander studied at Columbia University to earn her Master of Arts degree. Quander furthered her education by attaining a degree in social work at New York University, and studied economics for two summers at the University of Washington.

From 1916 to 1917, Quander was a special field agent for the Children's Bureau for the Department of Labor. After having served six years as AKA's president, in 1919, Nellie Quander resigned. She continued to act as graduate advisor to Alpha chapter, and was a member of the Xi Omega chapter in Washington, D.C. Later, Quander was the first director of the North Atlantic Region of AKA.

In 1936, Quander earned a diploma at Uppsala University in Uppsala, Sweden. She attended the International Conference on Social Work in London, England during the same year. In the public schools, Quander established and supported the School Safety Patrol Unit for twenty-five years.

Nellie Quander devoted her life to education and civic activities. She died on September 24, 1961.

Elder Watson Diggs (December 23, 1883 – November 8, 1947), principal founder of Kappa Alpha Psi Fraternity, Incorporated was born on December 23, 1883 in Christian County, Kentucky (in the city of Hopkinsville), and raised in Madisonville by his mother Cornelia Diggs along with his younger brother and sister. He attended Indiana State Normal School (now Indiana State University), graduating in spring 1908. In 1909, he enrolled in Howard University. It was here that, in 1910, he met Byron Kenneth Armstrong. In the fall of that year, Diggs and Armstrong left Howard University to attend Indiana University.

While Diggs attended Indiana University, he was one of 10 African American students enrolled. University life was not particularly kind to African American students, as they were barred from engaging in activities permitted to white students.

Unhappy with the plight of African Americans on Indiana University's campus, Diggs met with eight other men and on January 5, 1911, he and the other founders of Kappa Alpha Psi officially formed this new fraternity, with Diggs being made the chairman, a position later termed Polemarch. He served as the Grand Polemarch, chairman of the entire fraternity, for the first six years of Kappa Alpha Psi.

In June 1912, after the end of the school year, Diggs, Byron K. Armstrong, and Irven Armstrong, the current Grand Keeper of Records, continued to develop the various aspects of the fraternity while working as waiters in Fort Wayne, Indiana. Diggs completed the fraternity's constitution and initiation ceremony, and with the help of the others, completed the fraternity's coat of arms.

Diggs served as a high school principal at Vincennes, Indiana, in 1913 and 1914, and continued to work toward expanding the fraternity to other universities. He also worked to improve the academic and cultural opportunities for blacks.

Diggs graduated from the Indiana University School of Education in 1916, becoming the first African American to do so. In 1917, he resigned as principal in order to enter the United States' first Officer's Training Camp at Fort Des Moines, Iowa, thereby becoming one of the first members of Kappa Alpha Psi to join the armed forces. He served with the 368th Infantry in Europe, after which he became a captain in the Reserve Officers' Training Corps.

In 1924, Diggs, for his incessant efforts to improve and expand the fraternity and commitment to the fraternity's ideals, received the Laurel Wreath, the highest recognition of achievement in Kappa Alpha Psi.

Diggs died on November 8, 1947 and was buried in Crown Hill Cemetery in Indianapolis, Indiana. After Diggs' death, the Indianapolis Public School #42 (the school where he served as a teacher and principal for 26 years) was changed in his honor to the "Elder W. Diggs IPS School #42".

Lucy Diggs Slowe (July 4, 1885 – October 21, 1937) was the first black woman to serve as Dean of Women at any American university and the first Dean of Women at Howard University.

Lucy Diggs Slowe was born in Berryville, Virginia to Henry Slowe and Fannie Porter Slowe. At thirteen, Lucy and her family moved to Baltimore, Maryland, where she attended the Baltimore Colored School. She graduated second in her class in 1904 from the Baltimore Colored High School.

Slowe was the first person from her school to attend Howard University, the top historically black college in the nation, at a time when only 1/3 of 1% of African Americans and 5% of whites of eligible age attended any college. She was one of the original sixteen founders of Alpha Kappa Alpha Sorority, Incorporated, the first sorority founded by African-American women. She was one of the nine original founders of the sorority in 1908 at Howard University. She was instrumental in drafting the sorority's constitution. She also served as the chapter's first president.

Slowe also founded the National Association of College Women, which she led for several years as first president, as well as the Association of Advisors to Women in Colored Schools.

After graduation in 1908, Slowe returned to Baltimore to teach English in high school. During the summers, she started studying at Columbia University in New York, where she earned her Masters of Arts degree in 1915.

After earning her M.A., she returned to Washington, DC to teach. Because the District was run as part of the Federal government, African American teachers in the public schools were part of the civil service and paid on the same scale as European Americans. The system attracted outstanding teachers, especially for Dunbar High School, the academic high school for African Americans. Slowe was also a tennis champion, winning the national title of the American Tennis Association's first tournament in 1917, the first African-American woman to win a major sports title.

In 1919, the District of Columbia asked Lucy Slowe to create the first junior high school in its system for blacks and then appointed her as principal. She led the school until 1922, creating the first integrated in-service training for junior high school teachers in the District.

In 1922, Howard University selected Lucy Slowe as its first Dean of Women. Slowe was the first African American female to serve in that position at any university in the United States. Slowe continued to serve as a College Dean at Howard for the rest of her career, another 15 years until her death on October 21, 1937.

Lawrence D. Bobo (born February 18, 1958) is the W. E. B. Du Bois Professor of the Social Sciences at Harvard University. He holds appointments in the Department of Sociology and the Department of African and African American Studies. His research focuses on the intersection of social inequality, politics, and race.

Professor Bobo is an elected member of the National Academy of Science as well as a Fellow of the American Academy of Arts and Sciences and the American Association for the Advancement of Science. He is a Guggenheim Fellow, an Alphonse M. Fletcher Sr. Fellow, a Fellow of the Center for Advanced Study in the Behavioral Sciences, and a Russell Sage Foundation Visiting Scholar.

Bobo has received research grants from the National Science Foundation, the Russell Sage Foundation, the Ford Foundation, and the Spencer Foundation. He has held tenured appointments in the sociology departments at the University of Wisconsin, Madison, the University of California, Los Angeles, and at Stanford University where he was Director of the Center for Comparative Studies in Race and Ethnicity. In September 2018 Bobo was appointed Dean of Social Science in the Faculty of Arts and Sciences at Harvard University.

Brian Keith Price (January 28, 1959) joined Harvard Law School in 1997 as Senior Clinical Instructor of the Community Enterprise Project at the WilmerHale Legal Services Center in Jamaica Plain, Massachusetts.

Professor Price was appointed Director of the WilmerHale Legal Services Center in July 2006 and appointed Clinical Professor of Law in November 2007. In July 2009 he became Director of the

Transactional Law Clinics, consisting of the Business and Non-Profit Clinic, Real Estate Clinic, Entertainment Law Clinic and Community Enterprise Project (CEP). The clinics educate and train 2L and 3L students in the practice of law as they render legal services to hundreds of clients every year.

Professor Price oversaw the founding of the Harvard Recording Artist Project (RAP), a student practice organization engaged in music law, and is its faculty director and supervising attorney. Additionally, Professor Price oversaw the founding of and is the faculty advisor for the Harvard Law Entrepreneurship Project (HLEP), a student practice organization at Harvard Law School providing legal advice to start-up enterprises.

Brian Price received his B. A. from Princeton University and his J.D. from the University of Pennsylvania Law School.

John Stauffer (born 1965) is the Summer R. and Marshall S. Kates Professor of English and of African and African American Studies at Harvard University. He is also chair and professor of the History of American Civilization at Harvard University.

John received his PhD from Yale in 1999 and won the Ralph Henry Gabriel Prize for the best dissertation in American Studies. He began teaching at Harvard that year and was tenured in 2004. He teaches courses on protest literature, Emancipation, southern literature, Douglass and Lincoln, the Civil War, autobiography, the nineteenth-century novel and historical fiction. In 2009 Harvard named him the Walter Channing Cabot Fellow for "achievements and scholarly eminence in the fields of literature, history or art."

John Stauffer has received two teaching awards from Harvard: the Everett Mendelsohn Excellence in Mentoring Award and the Jan Thaddeus Teaching Prize. He served as Chair of American Studies at Harvard from 2006-2012. John came to Yale and Harvard from an unlikely and circuitous route. He was raised in Iowa, Nebraska, and North Dakota and educated in public schools. After receiving a BSE in Mechanical Engineering from Duke University and working briefly in finance, he received an MA in Humanities from Wesleyan University and an MA in American Studies from Purdue University before pursuing his PhD.

MORE CIVIL RIGHTS LEADERS AND ACTIVISTS WHO MAKE THE GRADE ...

George Mason IV (December 11, 1725 – October 7, 1792) was an American planter, politician and delegate to the U.S. Constitutional Convention of 1787, one of three delegates who refused to sign the Constitution. His writings, including substantial portions of the Fairfax Resolves of 1774, the Virginia Declaration of Rights of 1776, and his *Objections to this Constitution of Government* (1787) opposing ratification, have exercised a significant influence on American political thought and events. The Virginia Declaration of Rights, which Mason principally authored, served as a basis for the United States Bill of Rights, of which he has been deemed the father.

Mason was born in 1725, most likely in what is now Fairfax County, Virginia. His father died when he was young, and his mother managed the family estates until he came of age. He married in 1750, built Gunston Hall and lived the life of a country squire, supervising his lands, family and slaves. He briefly served in the House of Burgesses and involved himself in community affairs, sometimes serving with his neighbor George Washington. As tensions grew between Britain and the American colonies, Mason came to support the colonial side, using his knowledge and experience to help the revolutionary cause, finding ways to work around the Stamp Act of 1765 and serving in the pro-independence Fourth Virginia Convention in 1775 and the Fifth Virginia Convention in 1776.

Mason prepared the first draft of the Virginia Declaration of Rights in 1776, and his words formed much of the text adopted by the final Revolutionary Virginia Convention. He also wrote a constitution for the state; Thomas Jefferson and others sought to have the convention adopt their ideas, but they found that Mason's version could not be stopped. During the American Revolutionary War, Mason was a member of the powerful House of Delegates of the Virginia General Assembly but, to the irritation of Washington and others, he refused to serve in the Continental Congress in Philadelphia, citing health and family commitments.

In 1787, Mason was named one of his state's delegates to the Constitutional Convention and traveled to Philadelphia, his only lengthy trip outside Virginia. Many clauses in the Constitution bear his stamp, as he was active in the convention for months before deciding that he could not sign same. He cited the lack of a bill of rights most prominently in his *Objections*, but also wanted an immediate end to the slave trade and a supermajority for navigation acts, which might force exporters of tobacco to use more expensive American ships. He failed to attain these objectives, and again at the Virginia Ratifying Convention of 1788, but his prominent fight for a bill of rights led fellow Virginian James Madison to introduce same during the First Congress in 1789; these amendments were ratified in 1791, a year before Mason died. Obscure after his death, Mason has come to be recognized, in the 20th and 21st centuries, for his contributions to the early United States and to Virginia.

Paul Cuffe (January 17, 1759 – September 7, 1817) was born free into a Native American, African American family on Cuttyhunk Island, Massachusetts. He became a successful businessman, merchant, sea captain, whaler and Abolitionist. His mother, Ruth Moses, was a Wampanoag from Harwich on Cape Cod and his father an Ashanti, captured as a child in West Africa and sold into slavery in Newport about 1720. In the mid-1740s the father was manumitted by his Quaker master, John Slocum, in Massachusetts and his parents married in 1747 in Dartmouth, Massachusetts.

Cuffe's father died when was thirteen. He and his older brother, John, inherited the family farm (with life rights to their mother) and resided there with their mother and three younger sisters. The following year Cuffe signed on to the first of three whaling voyages to the West Indies. During the Revolutionary War, Cuffe delivered urgently needed goods to the people of Nantucket by slipping through a British Naval blockade on a small sailboat. After the war, he built a lucrative shipping business along the Atlantic Coast and in other parts of the world. He also built his own ships in a boatyard on the Westport River. Paul Cuffe established in Westport, Massachusetts the first racially integrated school in North America.

He became involved in the British effort to develop a colony in Sierra Leone, to which the British had transported many former slaves from America. Some were slaves who had sought refuge and freedom with British military units during the war. After the British were defeated, they took those freed slaves first to Nova Scotia and then in 1792 to Sierra Leone where they were settled in the new colony.

in 1815–16, he transported nine families of free blacks from Massachusetts to Sierra Leone to assist and work with the former slaves and other local residents to be more productive. This voyage has been cited by some as the beginning of a "Back to Africa" movement that was being promoted at that time through the American Colonization Society (ACS) that was mainly led by Southern slave owners who were more interested in removing freed slaves from the US and preserving slavery than in helping the people of Africa. After some hesitation, and strong objections by the free blacks in Philadelphia and New York City, Cuffe chose not to support the ACS and saw his efforts very differently as providing training and machinery and boats to the people of Africa so that they could improve their condition and rise in the world.

In early 1817, Cuffe's health deteriorated. He never returned to Africa and died in Westport on September 7, 1817. Cuffe left an estate with an estimated value of almost $20,000 (equivalent to $313,708 in 2018). His will bequeathed property and money to his widow, siblings, children, grandchildren, a poor widow, and the Friends Meeting House in Westport. He is buried in the graveyard behind the Westport Friends Meeting House.

Geronimo (Mescalero-Chiricahua: "the one who yawns)," (June 1829 – February 17, 1909) was a prominent leader and medicine man from the Bedonkohe band of the Apache tribe. From 1850 to 1886, Geronimo joined with members of three other Chiricahua Apache bands — the Tchihende, the Tsokanende and the Nednhi — to carry out numerous raids, as well as fight against Mexican and U.S. military campaigns in the northern Mexico states of Chihuahua and Sonora and in the southwestern American territories of New Mexico and Arizona. Geronimo's raids and related combat actions were a part of the prolonged period of the Apache–United States conflict, which started with American settlement in Apache lands following the end of the war with Mexico in 1848.

While well known, Geronimo was not a chief of the Chiricahua or the Bedonkohe band. However, since he was a superb leader in raiding and warfare, he frequently led large numbers of men beyond his own following. At any one time, he would be in command of about 30 to 50 Apaches.

During Geronimo's final period of conflict from 1876 to 1886, he "surrendered" three times and accepted life on the Apache reservations in Arizona. Reservation life was confining to the free-moving Apache people, and they resented restrictions on their customary way of life.

In 1886, after an intense pursuit in northern Mexico by American forces that followed Geronimo's third 1885 reservation "breakout," Geronimo surrendered for the last time to Lt. Charles Bare Gatewood, an Apache-speaking West Point graduate who had earned Geronimo's respect a few years before. Geronimo was later transferred to General Nelson Miles at Skeleton Canyon, just north of the Mexican/American boundary. Miles treated Geronimo as a prisoner of war and acted promptly to move Geronimo, first to Fort Bowie, then to the railroad at Bowie Station, Arizona, where he and 27 other Apaches were sent to join the rest of the Chiricahua tribe, which had been previously exiled to Florida.

While holding him as a prisoner, the United States capitalized on Geronimo's fame among non-Indians by displaying him at various events. For the United States, this provided proof of the superiority of American ways. For Geronimo, it provided him with an opportunity to make a little money. In 1898, for example, Geronimo was exhibited at the Trans-Mississippi and International Exhibition in Omaha, Nebraska. Following this exhibition, he became a frequent visitor to fairs, exhibitions, and other public functions. He made money by selling pictures of himself, bows and arrows, buttons off his shirt, and even his hat. In 1905, the Indian Office provided Geronimo for the inaugural parade for President Theodore Roosevelt. Later that year, the Indian Office took him to Texas, where he shot a buffalo in a roundup staged by 101 Ranch Real Wild West for the National Editorial Association. Geronimo was escorted to the event by soldiers, as he was still a prisoner. The teachers who witnessed the staged buffalo hunt were unaware that Geronimo's people were not buffalo hunters.

Geronimo married Chee-hash-kish, and they had two children, Chappo and Dohn-say. Then he took another wife, Nana-tha-thtith, with whom he had one child. He later had a wife named Zi-yeh at the same time as another wife, She-gha, one named Shtsha-she and later a wife named Ih-tedda. Geronimo's ninth and last wife was Azul.

The great-great-grandson of Geronimo, Harlyn Geronimo teaches Apache language lessons at Mescalero Apache Reservation as of 2019.

In February 1909, Geronimo was thrown from his horse while riding home, and had to lie in the cold all night until a friend found him extremely ill. He died of pneumonia on February 17, 1909, as a prisoner of the United States at Fort Sill, Oklahoma. On his deathbed, he confessed to his nephew that he regretted his decision to surrender. His last words were reported to be said to his nephew, "I should have never surrendered. I should have fought until I was the last man alive." He was buried at Fort Sill, Oklahoma in the Apache Indian Prisoner of War Cemetery.

Robert Smalls (April 5, 1839 – February 23, 1915) was an American businessman, publisher, and politician. Born into slavery in Beaufort, South Carolina, he freed himself, his crew, and their families during the American Civil War by commandeering a Confederate transport ship, CSS *Planter*, in Charleston harbor, on May 13, 1862, and sailing it from Confederate-controlled waters of the harbor to the U.S. blockade that surrounded it. He then piloted the ship to the Union-controlled enclave in Beaufort-Port Royal-Hilton Head area, where she became a Union warship. His example and persuasion helped convince President Abraham Lincoln to accept African-American soldiers into the Union Army.

After the American Civil War he returned to Beaufort and became a politician, winning the election as a Republican to the South Carolina State legislature and the United States House of Representatives during the Reconstruction era. Smalls authored state legislation providing for South Carolina to have the first free and compulsory public school system in the United States. He founded the Republican Party of South Carolina. Smalls was the last Republican to represent South Carolina's 5th congressional district until 2010.

Smalls died of malaria and diabetes in 1915 at the age of 75. He was buried in his family's plot in the churchyard of the Tabernacle Baptist Church in downtown Beaufort. The monument to Smalls in this churchyard is inscribed with a statement he made to the South Carolina legislature in 1895: "My race needs no special defense, for the past history of them in this country proves them to be the equal of any people anywhere. All they need is an equal chance in the battle of life."

Hin-mah-too-yah-lat-kekt popularly known as **Chief Joseph**, **Young Joseph**, or **Joseph the Younger** (March 3, 1840 – September 21, 1904), was a leader of the Wal-lam-wat-kain (Wallowa) band of Nez Perce, a Native American tribe of the interior Pacific Northwest region of the United States, in the latter half of the 19th century. He succeeded his father Tuekakas (Chief Joseph the Elder) in the early 1870s.

Chief Joseph led his band of Nez Perce during the most tumultuous period in their history, when they were forcibly removed by the United States federal government from their ancestral lands in the

Wallowa Valley of northeastern Oregon onto a significantly reduced reservation in the Idaho Territory. A series of violent encounters with white settlers in the spring of 1877 culminated in those Nez Perce who resisted removal, including Joseph's band and an allied band of the Palouse tribe, to flee the United States in an attempt to reach political asylum alongside the Lakota people, who had sought refuge in Canada under the leadership of Sitting Bull.

At least 700 men, women, and children led by Joseph and other Nez Perce chiefs were pursued by the U.S. Army under General Oliver O. Howard in a 1,170-mile fighting retreat known as the Nez Perce War. The skill with which the Nez Perce fought and the manner in which they conducted themselves in the face of incredible adversity earned them widespread admiration from their military opponents and the American public, and coverage of the war in U.S. newspapers led to popular recognition of Chief Joseph and the Nez Perce.

In October 1877, after months of fugitive resistance, most of the surviving remnants of Joseph's band were cornered in northern Montana Territory, just 40 miles from the Canadian border. Unable to fight any longer, Chief Joseph surrendered to the Army with the understanding that he and his people would be allowed to return to the reservation in western Idaho. He was instead transported between various forts and reservations on the southern Great Plains before being moved to the Colville Indian Reservation in the state of Washington.

In 1903, Chief Joseph visited Seattle, a booming young town, where he stayed in the Lincoln Hotel as guest to Edmond Meany, a history professor at the University of Washington. It was there that he also befriended Edward Curtis, the photographer, who took one of his most memorable and well-known photographs. Joseph also visited

President Theodore Roosevelt in Washington, D.C. the same year. Everywhere he went, it was to make a plea for what remained of his people to be returned to their home in the Wallowa Valley, but it never happened.

Chief Joseph's life remains iconic of the American Indian Wars. For his passionate, principled resistance to his tribe's forced removal, Joseph became renowned as a humanitarian and peacemaker.

An indomitable voice of conscience for the West, still in exile from his homeland, Chief Joseph died on September 21, 1904, according to his doctor, "of a broken heart". Meany and Curtis helped Joseph's family bury their chief near the village of Nespelem, Washington, where many of his tribe's members still live. The Chief Joseph band of Nez Perce who still live on the Colville Reservation bear his name in tribute to their prestigious leader.

Nellie Stone Johnson (December 17, 1905 – April 2, 2002) was an American civil rights activist and union organizer. She was the first black elected official in Minneapolis and shaped Minnesota politics for 70 years.

Nellie Saunders Allen was born, the oldest of eight children, in Dakota County, Minnesota, near Lakeville, to William and Gladys Allen, one of the few black farming families in Minnesota in the early 1900s. When she was 13, she distributed literature for the Nonpartisan League on her way to school. Nellie attended public schools in both Dakota and Pine Counties. The family moved to a larger farm east of Hinckley in 1919. There, Nellie attended school in Clover Township, which only taught up to the 10th grade. She joined the NAACP as a teenager.

In September 1922, Nellie moved to Minneapolis where she was a live-in nanny for a white family that lived close to Loring Park.

Nellie then moved into her aunt and uncle's house in north Minneapolis. She took extension courses at the University of Minnesota, initially at the agriculture school. She took chemistry, intending to become a pharmacist, before gravitating towards social and political science. While at the University Nellie met Paul Robeson.

In 1924, she had been hired as an elevator attendant at the all-male Minneapolis Athletic Club, earning $15 per week. After her wages were cut to $12.50, she began quietly organizing workers with the Minneapolis Hotel and Restaurant Workers union. In the 1930s Nellie joined the University of Minnesota's Young Communist League. In 1936, she became a member and then vice president of AFL's Local 665, Hotel and Restaurant Workers union.

Johnson met future Vice President Hubert Humphrey in 1941 at Duluth State College. She would later mentor him in civil rights issues. In 1944, she was on the committee that merged the moderate Minnesota Democratic Party with the more radical Farmer–Labor Party, forming the Minnesota Democratic–Farmer–Labor Party (DFL). In 1945, Nellie was elected to the Library Board and became the first black person to be elected to a citywide office in Minneapolis.

Nellie was the main force behind the creation of state and local Fair Employment Practices departments, which later became the Minneapolis Civil Rights Commission and the state Human Rights Department. In the 1940s she spearheaded the drive to create the Minneapolis Fair Employment Practices department, which was the first of its kind in the nation.

She also authored the 1950 initiative from the Minneapolis NAACP that led to the desegregation of the US armed forces. She was fired from her job at the Minneapolis Athletic Club in 1950 and in October, she resigned her position as Chair of the Hennepin County Progressive Party. She lost a union election for the Local 665 in January 1951, at a time when left wing officers in the union were on the wane. In February 1951, Johnson formally severed her relations with the Progressive and Communist Parties. In 1955, she led the initiative to create a statewide version of the Minneapolis legislation, the Employment Practices Act of 1955.

In the 1960s, she raised money for the Freedom Marches of Martin Luther King.

Johnson traveled to Africa for the State Department with Vice President Walter Mondale in 1980 and Governor Rudy Perpich appointed her to the Minnesota State University Board in 1982. She was a member of the Democratic National Committee for two terms.

Johnson helped form the Minnesota Democratic–Farmer–Labor Party (DFL) and spearheaded the effort to create the first Fair Employment Practices department in the nation.

She received a lifetime achievement award from the Black Caucus of the American Association for Higher Education in 2000. Nellie Stone Johnson died on April 2, 2002, in Minneapolis. She was 96.

Elizabeth Jean Peratrovich (July 4, 1911 – December 1, 1958) of the Tlingit nation, was an important civil rights activist; she worked on behalf of equality for Alaska Natives.

In 1941, while living in Juneau, the Peratroviches found much discrimination, having difficulty finding housing and seeing signs banning Native entry to public facilities. They petitioned the territorial governor, Ernest Gruening, to ban the "No Natives Allowed" signs then common at public accommodations in that city and elsewhere. The Anti-Discrimination Act was defeated by the territorial legislature in 1943. As leaders of the Alaska Native Brotherhood and the Alaska Native Sisterhood, the Peratroviches lobbied the territory's legislators and represented their organizations in their testimony.

Elizabeth Peratrovich was the last to testify before the territorial Senate voted on the bill in 1945, and her impassioned testimony was considered decisive. She was credited with advocacy that gained the passage of the territory's Anti-Discrimination Act of 1945, the first anti-discrimination law in the United States.

Peratrovich talked about herself, her friends, her children, and the cruel treatment that consigned Alaska Natives to a second-class existence. She described to the Senate what it means to be unable to buy a house in a decent neighborhood because Natives aren't allowed to live there. She described how children feel when they are refused entrance into movie theaters or see signs in shop windows that read "No dogs or Natives allowed". She also stated, "I would not have expected that I, who am barely out of savagery, would have to remind gentlemen with five thousand years of recorded civilization behind them, of our Bill of Rights."

She was responding to earlier comments by territorial senator Allen Shattuck of Juneau, who had earlier asked, "Who are these people, barely out of savagery, who want to associate with us whites, with 5,000 years of recorded civilization behind us?" The Senate voted 11-5 for House Resolution 14, providing "...full and equal accommodations, facilities, and privileges to all citizens in places of public accommodations within the jurisdiction of the Territory of Alaska; to provide penalties for violation." The bill was signed into law by Governor Gruening, nearly 20 years before the US Congress passed the Civil Rights Act of 1964. Acts of the territorial legislature required final approval from the U.S. Congress, which affirmed it.

Elizabeth Peratrovich died December 1, 1958. In March 2019, her obituary was added to the New York Times as part of their "Overlooked No More" series.

Marie Frankie Muse Freeman (November 24, 1916 – January 12, 2018) was an American civil rights attorney.

The daughter of William Brown Muse and Maude Beatrice Smith Muse, Frankie came from a college-educated family. She was born and grew up in Danville, Virginia, where she attended Westmoreland School and learned to play the piano. At age sixteen, Muse enrolled in her mother's alma mater, Hampton Institute, which she attended between 1933 and 1936. In 1944, she was admitted to Howard University Law School and received a law degree in 1947. While a student at Howard Law, Freeman became a member of Epsilon Sigma Iota sorority, the first American legal sorority for women of color.

In 1948, after writing to several law firms and not hearing back from them, Muse decided to establish her own private practice. She began her practice with pro bono, divorce and criminal cases. After two years, Freeman began her work in civil rights when she became legal counsel to the NAACP legal team that filed suit against the St. Louis Board of Education in 1949.

In 1954, Freeman was the lead attorney for the landmark NAACP case *Davis et al. v. the St. Louis Housing Authority*, which ended legal racial discrimination in public housing with the city. Settling in St. Louis, Freeman worked as staff attorney for the St. Louis Land Clearance and Housing Authorities from 1956–70, first as associate general counsel and later as general counsel of the St. Louis Housing Authority.

In March 1964, she was nominated by President Lyndon Johnson as a member of the United States Commission on Civil Rights. On September 15, 1964, the Senate approved Freeman's nomination and she was officially appointed as the first black woman on the civil rights commission, a federal fact-finding body that investigates complaints alleging discrimination. Freeman was subsequently reappointed by presidents Richard Nixon, Gerald Ford and Jimmy Carter, and held the position until July 1979.

Freeman was also appointed as Inspector General for the Community Services Administration during Jimmy Carter's presidential administration in 1979. A year later, the Republican Ronald Reagan was elected president and demanded the resignation of Democratic inspectors general appointed by previous presidents.

Freeman returned to St. Louis, where she practiced law. In 1982, she joined 15 other former high federal officials who formed a bipartisan Citizens Commission on Civil Rights, a group committed to ending racial discrimination and devising remedies that would counteract its harmful effects.

In 2003, she published her memoir, *A Song of Faith and Hope*. She was the 14th National President of Delta Sigma Theta Sorority, Incorporated.

In 2007, Marie Freeman was inducted in the International Civil Rights Walk of Fame at the Martin Luther King Jr. National Historic Site, Atlanta, Georgia, for her leadership role in the Civil Rights Movement.

On February 5, 2015, President Barack Obama appointed Freeman to serve as a Member of the Commission on Presidential Scholars.

At age 90, she was still practicing law with Montgomery Hollie & Associates, L.L.C. in St. Louis, a three-attorney firm. Marie Freeman celebrated her 100th birthday in November 2016 and died January 12, 2018 at the age of 101.

Humberto Noé "Bert" Corona (May 29, 1918 – January 15, 2001) was an American labor and civil rights leader. Throughout his long career, he worked with nearly every major Mexican-American organization, founding or co-founding several. He organized workers for the Congress of Industrial Organizations and fought on the behalf of immigrants. By the time of the Chicano Movement of the 1960s and 1970s, he was known as *El Viejo* ("the Old Man"), and was well-known and respected as a veteran activist.

In April 1960, Corona was one of the founders of the Mexican American Political Association, which was organized as a result of the view that the Democratic Party had failed to genuinely address concerns of Mexican-Americans. Corona led MAPA's Northern Californian operations, serving as the organization's president from 1966 to 1971.

Corona was also closely associated with *Hermandad Mexicana Nacional*, which emphasized organizing unions and defending and providing social services to undocumented workers. He met fellow activist Soledad Alatorre during the latter's work with labor organizations. The two of them made connections to the HMN, which was at the time one of the only organizations working for Mexican Americans that was also run by Mexican Americans. The HMN was facing difficulties due to the activities of the House Un-American Activities Committee, so Corona and Alatorre took charge of the organization, and in 1968 moved it to Los Angeles, where its local chapters came to be known as *Centro de Accion Social Autonomo*, or "CASA". CASA began to work for the rights of immigrant workers, and also provided them social services, including legal help and education. It also advocated for policies in their favor.

From the late 1960s to the 1980s, Corona taught as a part-time instructor in the controversial emerging field of Chicano Studies at California State University, Northridge and California State University, Los Angeles.

In 1968, Dr. Martin Luther King, Jr. invited Corona, along with Corky Gonzales, Reies Tijerina to Atlanta to plan for the March on Poverty. King, however, was assassinated before the march took place.

James Leonard Farmer, Jr. (January 12, 1920 - July 9, 1999) was an American civil rights activist. Farmer, who sought racial justice by means of nonviolence, was often a target of racial violence himself.

Farmer was educated at Wiley College in Marshall, Texas (1938), and at Howard University in Washington, D.C. (1941), where his father taught divinity. A conscientious objector on religious grounds, he received a military deferral in World War II, and joined the pacifist Fellowship of Reconciliation (FOR).

In 1942, Farmer co-founded the Committee of Racial Equality in Chicago along with George Houser, James R. Robinson, Samuel E. Riley, Bernice Fisher, Homer Jack, and Joe Guinn. It was later called the Congress of Racial Equality (CORE), and was dedicated to ending racial segregation in the United States through nonviolence. Farmer served as the national chairman from 1942 to 1944.

Within a year, CORE had a national membership, and within a few years a roster of more than 60,000 members in more than 70 chapters, coast to coast. *In its heyday in the 1960's, it claimed a membership of 82,000 in 114 local groups.*

By the 1960s, Farmer was known as "one of the Big Four civil rights leaders in the 1960s, together with King, NAACP chief Roy Wilkins and Urban League head Whitney Young."

In 1963, Louisiana state troopers hunted him door to door for trying to organize protests. A funeral home director had Farmer play dead in the back of a hearse that carried him along back roads and out of town. He was arrested that August for disturbing the peace.

After serving as the national chairman of CORE Farmer was later elected the national director of the organization. He organized and led the Freedom Ride, which originated integrated bus trips through the South and immensely contributed to the desegregation of interstate transportation in the United States.

As the Director of CORE, Farmer was considered one of the "Big Six" of the Civil Rights Movement who helped organize the March on Washington for Jobs and Freedom in 1963. (The press also used the term "Big Four", ignoring John Lewis and Dorothy Height.) Growing disenchanted with emerging militancy and black nationalist sentiments in CORE, Farmer resigned as director in 1966. By that time, Congress had passed the Civil Rights Act of 1964, ending segregation, and the Voting Rights Act of 1965, authorizing federal enforcement of registration and elections.

Farmer took a teaching position at Lincoln University, a historically black college (HBCU) near Philadelphia, Pennsylvania. He also lectured around the country. In 1968, Farmer ran for U.S. Congress as a Liberal Party candidate backed by the Republican Party, but lost to Shirley Chisholm. In 1969, the newly elected Republican President Richard Nixon offered Farmer the position of Assistant Secretary of the Department of Health, Education, and Welfare (now Health and Human Services). Frustrated by the Washington bureaucracy, Farmer resigned from the position. He retired from politics in 1971 but remained active, lecturing and serving on various boards and committees. He was one of the signers of the Humanist Manifesto II in 1973.

In 1975, he co-founded Fund for an Open Society. Its vision is a nation in which people live in stably integrated communities, where political and civic power is shared by people of different races and ethnicities. He led this organization until 1999. Farmer was named an honorary vice chairman of the Democratic Socialists of America.

In 1984, Farmer began teaching at Mary Washington College (now The University of Mary Washington) in Fredericksburg, Virginia. He retired from his teaching position in 1998. That same year, James Leonard Farmer, Jr. was awarded the Presidential Medal of Freedom by President Bill Clinton.

James Leonard Farmer, Jr. died on July 9, 1999, of complications from diabetes in Fredericksburg, Virginia.

Golden Asro Frinks (August 15, 1920 – July 19, 2004) was an American civil rights activist and a Southern Christian Leadership Conference (SCLC) field secretary who represented the New Bern, North Carolina SCLC chapter. He is best known as a principal civil rights organizer in North Carolina during the 1960s which landed him a reputation as "The Great Agitator", having been jailed eighty-seven times during his lifetime.

Frinks was also a United States Army veteran who fought in World War II and worked at the U.S. naval base in Norfolk, Virginia. After his military career, he began promoting equality for African Americans through organized demonstrations.

After becoming a field secretary of the SCLC, Frinks built a close relationship with Martin Luther King Jr. and often worked with the civil rights leader in organizing desegregation movements until King's death in 1968. Frinks' work as a field secretary and his direct actions against the Jim Crow Laws began a new era for the civil rights movement in North Carolina and the desegregation of the South.

When Martin Luther King Jr. received the Nobel Peace Prize on December 10, 1964, he alluded to Frinks during his acceptance speech when he stated "I am always mindful of the many people who make a successful journey possible- the known pilots and the unknown ground crew." While Frinks was not a nationally known figure, he was a crucial shadow in the civil rights movement and was partially responsible for King's success. In 1977, Frinks officially ended his employment with the SCLC but continued to support the SCLC's activities. Frinks' commitment and dedication to the civil rights movement landed him numerous awards and recognitions.

Golden Asro Frinks died on July 19, 2004, in Edenton, North Carolina, at the age of 84. In the end, Frinks' lifelong dedication to civil rights activism and desegregation inspired countless others to stand up in pursuit of social justice and equality.

Ruth M. Batson (August 3, 1921–2003), was an American civil rights activist and outspoken advocate of equal education. She spoke out about the desegregation of Boston Public Schools, served on the Public Education Committee of the NAACP Boston Branch and later served as the executive director of the Metropolitan Council for

Educational Opportunity (METCO). Throughout her life, in various professional roles, she championed fair and equal public education.

Ruth Marion (Watson) Batson was born in Roxbury, Massachusetts to Jamaican immigrants, Joel R. Watson and Cassandra D. Buchanan. She attended the Everett School in Dorchester, Massachusetts. Ruth graduated from the Girls Latin School in 1939. She attended the Nursery Training School of Boston, which was associated with Boston University and later received a Master of Education degree from Boston University in 1976. At age nineteen, Watson married John C. Batson. They had three daughters together: Cassandra Way, Susan Batson, and Dorothy Owusu. John Batson died in 1971.

Inspired by her mother's interest in civil rights, Ruth Batson became the chairman of the Public Education Sub-Committee of the National Association for the Advancement of Colored People (NAACP) in 1953. In April 1957, she became the chairwoman of the New England Regional Conference of the NAACP, where she worked as a civil rights lobbyist. In the early 1960s, Ruth challenged the Boston School Committee, charging that Boston Public Schools were largely segregated. She also pointed out that schools with high black enrollments received inadequate facilities. Batson accused school administrators with ignoring "a basic American concept that equal opportunity should be available to all people regardless of race, color, or creed."

Batson was the first black woman on the Democratic National Committee and the first woman elected president of NAACP's New England Regional Conference, a role in which she served from 1957 to 1960.

After serving as chairwoman of the Massachusetts Commission Against Discrimination from 1963 to 1966, she helped launched the Metropolitan Council for Educational Opportunity (METCO) voluntary desegregation program. As associate director, then director, Ruth helped guide METCO's growth from transporting 225 black urban children to several suburbs to 1,125 children to 28 communities. She stepped down in 1969.

She served in several roles at Boston University: director of the consultation and education program (1970–1975), director of the school desegregation research project (1975–1981), coordinator of the clinical task force, and associate professor at the School of Medicine's Division of Psychiatry.

In 1989 Batson received an honorary Doctorate of Pedagogy from Northeastern University. In 1993, she received an honorary degree from the University of Massachusetts Boston. She was a member of the board of visitors of Boston University's School of Medicine; trustees, Boston City Hospital; member, Corporation of the Massachusetts General Hospital and former member of its board of trustees; and board member of Roxbury Community College Foundation. Ruth Batson died on October 28, 2003, at the age of 82.

Whitney Moore Young Jr. (July 31, 1921 – March 11, 1971) was an articulate American civil rights leader who spearheaded the drive for equal opportunity for blacks in U.S. industry and government service.

After army service in World War II, Young switched his career interest from medicine to social work, in which he took his M.A. from the University of Minnesota (1947). Starting as director of industrial relations for the Urban League at St. Paul, Minnesota (1947–50), he moved to Omaha, Nebraska, where he served as executive secretary (1950–54). Becoming dean of the School of Social Work of Atlanta (Georgia) University in 1954, he was instrumental in improving relations between the city and the university.

Young later spent most of his career working to end employment discrimination in the United States. He won an impressive reputation as a national black activist who helped bridge the gap between white political and business leaders and poor blacks and militants. His advocacy of a "Domestic Marshall Plan"—massive funds to help solve America's racial problems—was felt to have strongly influenced federal poverty programs sponsored by Democratic Party administrations in Washington (1963–69).

During his 10 years as executive director of the National Urban League (1961–71), the world's largest social-civil rights organization, Young turned the National Urban League from a relatively passive civil rights organization into one that aggressively worked for equitable access to socioeconomic opportunity for the historically disenfranchised.

Under Young's direction the organization grew from 60 to 98 chapters and shifted its focus from middle-class concerns to the needs of the urban poor. He was particularly credited with almost singlehandedly persuading corporate America and major foundations to aid the civil rights movement through financial contributions in support of self-help programs for jobs, housing, education, and family rehabilitation.

Young also served as President of the National Association of Social Workers (NASW), from 1969 to 1971. He took office at a time of fiscal instability in the association and uncertainty about President

Nixon's continuing commitment to the "War on Poverty" and to ending the war in Vietnam.

On March 11, 1971, Whitney Young drowned while swimming with friends in Lagos, Nigeria, where he was attending a conference sponsored by the African American Institute. President Nixon sent a plane to Nigeria to collect Young's body and traveled to Kentucky to deliver the eulogy at Young's funeral.

James Charles Evers (born September 11, 1922) is an American civil rights activist, disc jockey and former politician. Evers was known for his role in the civil rights movement along with his younger brother Medgar Evers. After serving in World War II, Evers began his career as a disc jockey at WHOC in Philadelphia, Mississippi. In 1954, he was made the National Association for the Advancement of Colored People (NAACP) State Voter Registration chairman. After his brother's assassination in 1963, Evers took over his position as field director of the NAACP in Mississippi. As field director, Evers organized and led many demonstrations for the rights of African Americans.

In 1969, Evers was named "Man of the Year" by the NAACP. On June 3, 1969, Evers was elected in Fayette, Mississippi, as the first African-American mayor of a *biracial* town in the state in the post-Reconstruction era, following passage of the Voting Rights Act of 1965 which enforced constitutional rights for citizens.

At the time of Evers's election as mayor, the town of Fayette had a population of 1,600 of which 75% was African American and almost 25% White. According to the Associated Press, the white officers on the Fayette city police "resigned rather than work under a black administration." Evers told reporters "I guess we will just have to operate with an all-black police department for the present.

But I am still looking for some whites to join us in helping Fayette grow." Evers then outlawed the carrying of firearms within city limits.

He unsuccessfully ran for governor in 1971 and the United States Senate in 1978, both times as an Independent candidate. In 1989, Evers was defeated for re-election after serving sixteen years as mayor. After his political career ended, he returned to radio and hosted his own show, "Let's Talk."

Hosea Lorenzo Williams (January 5, 1926 – November 16, 2000), was an American civil rights leader, activist, ordained minister, businessman, philanthropist, scientist, and politician. He may be best known as a trusted member of fellow famed civil rights activist and Nobel Peace Prize winner Martin Luther King, Jr.'s inner circle. Under the banner of their flagship organization, the Southern Christian Leadership Conference,

King depended on Hosea Williams to organize and stir masses of people into nonviolent direct action in myriad protest campaigns they waged against racial, political, economic, and social injustice. King alternately referred to Hosea, his chief field lieutenant, as his "bull in a china closet" and his "Castro". Hosea's famous motto was "Unbought and Unbossed."

On January 17, 1987, Hosea Williams led a "March Against Fear and Intimidation" in Forsyth County, Georgia, which at the time (before becoming a major exurb of northern metro Atlanta) had no non-white residents. The ninety marchers were assaulted with stones and other objects by several hundred counter-demonstrators led by the Nationalist Movement and Ku Klux Klan. The following week 20,000, including senior civil rights leaders and government officials marched.

Forsyth County began to slowly integrate in the following years with the expansion of the Atlanta suburbs. Vowing to continue King's work for the poor, Hosea Williams is well known in his own right as the founding president of one of the largest social services organizations in North America. in 1971, he founded a non-profit foundation, Hosea Feed the Hungry and Homeless, widely known in Atlanta for providing hot meals, haircuts, clothing, and other services for the needy on Thanksgiving, Christmas, Martin Luther King, Jr. Day and Easter Sunday each year. Williams' daughter Elizabeth Omilami serves as head of the foundation. In 1974, Williams organized the International Wrestling League (IWL), based in Atlanta, with Thunderbolt Patterson serving as president. Among other entrepreneurial endeavors, he founded Hosea Williams Bail Bonds, Inc., a bail bond agency.

In 1974, Williams was also elected to the Georgia Senate where he served five terms as a Democrat, until 1984. In 1985 he was elected to the Atlanta City Council, serving for five years, until his election in 1989 when he ran for Mayor of Atlanta but lost to Maynard Jackson. That same year Williams successfully campaigned for a seat on the DeKalb County, Georgia County Commission which he held until 1994. Williams supported former Georgia Governor Jimmy Carter for president in 1976, but surprised many black civil rights figures in 1980 by joining Ralph Abernathy and Charles Evers in endorsing Ronald Reagan. By 1984, however, he had soured on Reagan's policies, and returned to the Democrats to support Walter F. Mondale.

Williams died at Piedmont Hospital in Atlanta, after a three-year battle with cancer on November 16, 2000.

Edison Uno (1929–1976) was a Japanese American civil rights advocate, best known for opposing laws used to implement the mass detention of Japanese Americans during World War II and for his role in the early stages of the movement for redress after the war. To many Japanese American activists, Uno was the father of the redress movement.

Edison Uno was born in Los Angeles in 1929 into a family of 11. He was the son of George and Riki Uno. In 1942, Uno was interned with his parents and siblings at the Granada War Relocation Center in Colorado. Then, he was subsequently transferred to the Crystal City internment Camp in Texas. He stayed at the internment camp even after the war was over, and he was told that he was the last American citizen to be released, after 1,647 days in prison

Following the war, Uno graduated from Los Angeles State College with a degree in political science. Later, he married Rosalind Kido, daughter of wartime national JACL president Saburo Kido. He later became involved in academia, teaching at the University of California, San Francisco, and various civil rights issues. Uno was active in grand jury reform, as well as in such civil rights issues as the Wendy Yoshimura Defense Fund, Title II Repeal, Redress for Evacuation, and worked on Farewell to Manzanar television program. in 1950 Edison became the youngest chapter president of JACL. Uno died of a heart attack in 1976.

Dolores Clara Fernández Huerta (born April 10, 1930) is an American labor leader and civil rights activist, who, with Cesar Chavez, is a co-founder of the National Farmworkers Association, which later became the United Farm Workers (UFW). Huerta helped organize the Delano grape strike in 1965 in California and was the lead negotiator in the workers' contract that was created after the strike.

Huerta has received numerous awards for her community service and advocacy for workers', immigrants', and women's rights, including the Eugene V. Debs Foundation Outstanding American Award, the United States Presidential Eleanor Roosevelt Award for Human Rights and the Presidential Medal of Freedom. She was the first Latina inducted into the National Women's Hall of Fame, in 1993.

In California, April 10 is Dolores Huerta day.

Gloria Marie Steinem (born March 25, 1934) is an American feminist, journalist, and social political activist who became nationally recognized as a leader and a spokeswoman for the American feminist movement in the late 1960s and early 1970s.

Steinem was a columnist for *New York* magazine. In 1969, Steinem published an article, "After Black Power, Women's Liberation", which brought her to national fame as a feminist leader.

In 1972, she co-founded the feminist-themed magazine *Ms.* with Dorothy Pitman Hughes; it began as a special edition of *New York*, and Clay Felker funded the first issue. Its 300,000 test copies sold out nationwide in eight days. Within weeks, *Ms.* had received 26,000 subscription orders and over 20,000 reader letters. The magazine was sold to the Feminist Majority Foundation in 2001; Steinem remains on the masthead as one of six founding editors and serves on the advisory board.

In 2005, Steinem, Jane Fonda, and Robin Morgan co-founded the Women's Media Center, an organization that "works to make women visible and powerful in the media".

As of May 2018, Steinem traveled internationally as an organizer and lecturer, and was a media spokeswoman on issues of equality.

Roy Emile Alfredo Innis (June 6, 1934 – January 8, 2017) was an American activist and politician. He had been National Chairman of the Congress of Racial Equality (CORE) since his election to the position in 1968. In 1973 Roy Innis became the first American to attend the Organization of African Unity (OAU) in an official capacity.

Roy Innis was born in Saint Croix, U.S. Virgin Islands in 1934. In 1947, Innis moved with his mother from the U.S. Virgin Islands to New York City, where he graduated from Stuyvesant High School in 1952. At age 16, Innis joined the U.S. Army, and at age 18 he received an honorable discharge. He entered a four-year program in chemistry at the City College of New York. He subsequently held positions as a research chemist at Vick Chemical Company and Montefiore Hospital.

Innis joined CORE's Harlem chapter in 1963. In 1964 he was elected Chairman of the chapter's education committee and advocated community-controlled education and black empowerment. In 1965, he was elected Chairman of Harlem CORE, after which he campaigned for the establishment of an independent Board of Education for Harlem. White CORE activists, according to James Peck, were removed from CORE in 1965, as part of a purge of whites from the movement then under the control of Innis.

In early 1967, Innis was appointed the first resident fellow at the Metropolitan Applied Research Center (MARC), headed by Dr. Kenneth Clark. In the summer of 1967, he was elected Second National Vice-Chairman of CORE. Innis co-drafted the Community Self-Determination Act of 1968 and garnered bipartisan sponsorship of this bill by one-third of the U.S. Senate and over 50 congressmen. This was the first time in U.S. history that CORE or any civil rights organization drafted a bill and introduced it into the United States Congress

Innis was selected National Chairman of CORE in 1968. Innis and a CORE delegation toured seven African countries in 1971. He met with several heads of state, including Kenya's Jomo Kenyatta, Tanzania's Julius Nyerere, Liberia's William Tolbert and Uganda's Idi Amin, who was awarded a life membership of CORE. Innis met with Amin and the aforementioned African statesmen as part of his CORE campaign drive for finding jobs in Africa for black Americans. Under Innis' leadership, CORE supported the presidential candidacy of Richard Nixon in 1972. This was the beginning of a sharp rightward turn in the organization.

Innis was long active in criminal justice matters, including the debate over gun control and the Second Amendment. After losing two sons to young black criminals with guns, he became an advocate for the rights of law-abiding citizens to self-defense. His eldest son, Roy Innis, Jr., was killed at the age of 13 in 1968. His next oldest son Alexander, 26, was shot and slain in 1982.

A Life Member of the National Rifle Association, he also served on its governing board. Innis also chaired the NRA's Urban Affairs Committee and was a member of the NRA Ethics Committee and continued to speak publicly in the US and around the world in favor of individual civilian ownership of firearms, gun issues, and individual rights.

In 1986, Innis challenged incumbent Major Owens in the Democratic primary for the 12th Congressional District, representing Brooklyn. He was defeated by a three-to-one margin.

In the 1993, New York City Democratic Party mayoral primary, Innis challenged incumbent David Dinkins, the first African-

American to hold the office. Innis lost to Dinkins, who then lost to Giuliani in the general election.

Innis served as New York State Chair in Alan Keyes' 2000 presidential campaign. Roy Innis died on January 8, 2017, at the age of 82, from Parkinson's disease.

Kwame Ture (June 29, 1941 – November 15, 1998) born **Stokely Standiford Churchill Carmichael**, was a prominent African-American organizer in the civil rights movement in the United States and the global Pan-African movement. Born in Trinidad, he grew up in the United States from the age of 11 and became an activist while attending Howard University. He eventually developed the Black Power movement, first while leading the Student Nonviolent Coordinating Committee (SNCC), later serving as the "Honorary Prime Minister" of the Black Panther Party (BPP), and lastly as a leader of the All-African People's Revolutionary Party (A-APRP).

Carmichael was one of the original SNCC freedom riders of 1961 under Diane Nash's leadership. Inspired by Malcolm X's example, he articulated a philosophy of "black power. Carmichael became one of the most popular and controversial Black leaders of the late 1960s.

In May 1967, Carmichael stepped down as chairman of SNCC and was replaced by H. Rap Brown. Carmichael accepted the position of Honorary Prime Minister in the Black Panther Party, but also remained on the staff of SNCC. He tried to forge a merger between the two organizations.

J. Edgar Hoover, director of the FBI, secretly identified Carmichael as the man most likely to succeed Malcolm X as America's "black messiah". The FBI targeted him for personal destruction through its COINTELPRO program, which focused on black activists.

In July 1968, Hoover stepped up his efforts to divide the black power movement. Declassifed documents show he launched a plan to undermine the SNCC-Panther merger, as well as to "bad-jacket" Carmichael as a CIA agent. Both efforts were largely successful: Carmichael was expelled from SNCC that year, and the rival Panthers began to denounce him, putting him at grave personal risk.

In 1968, he married Miriam Makeba, a noted singer from South Africa. They left the US for Africa in 1968. Carmichael re-established himself in Ghana, and then Guinea by 1969. He changed his name to "Kwame Ture", to honor the African leaders Nkrumah and Sékou Touré, who had become his patrons and he began campaigning internationally for revolutionary socialist Pan-Africanism.

Miriam Makeba was appointed Guinea's official delegate to the United Nations. Three months after his arrival in Guinea, in July 1969, Kwame Ture published a formal rejection of the Black Panthers, condemning them for not being separatist enough and for their "dogmatic party line favoring alliances with white radicals". Kwame remained in Guinea after his separation from the Black Panther Party. He continued to travel, write, and speak in support of international leftist movements. In 1973, Makeba and Kwame divorced in Guinea after separating.

Later Kwame married Marlyatou Barry, a Guinean doctor. They divorced some time after having a son, Bokar, in 1981

In 1986, two years after Sékou Touré's death, the military regime that took his place arrested Carmichael for his past association with Touré, and jailed him for three days on suspicion of attempting to overthrow the government.

After his diagnosis of prostate cancer in 1996, Ture was treated for a period in Cuba, while receiving some support from the Nation of Islam. Benefit concerts for Ture were held in Denver; New York; Atlanta; and Washington, D.C., to help defray his medical expenses. The government of Trinidad and Tobago, where he was born, awarded him a grant of $1,000 a month for the same purpose. He went to New York, where he was treated for two years at the Columbia-Presbyterian Medical Center, before returning to Guinea.

In 1998 Kwame Ture died of prostate cancer at the age of 57 in Conakry, Guinea.

The civil rights leader Jesse Jackson spoke in celebration of Ture's life, stating: "He was one of our generation who was determined to give his life to transforming America and Africa. He was committed to ending racial apartheid in our country. He helped to bring those walls down".

Fredrick Allen Hampton (August 30, 1948 – December 4, 1969) was an American activist and revolutionary socialist. He came to prominence in Chicago as chairman of the Illinois chapter of the Black Panther Party (BPP), and deputy chairman of the national BPP. In this capacity, he founded a prominent multicultural political organization, the Rainbow Coalition that initially included the Black Panthers, Young Patriots and the Young Lords, and an alliance among major Chicago street gangs to help them end infighting, and work for social change.

Because of his strong leadership, in 1967 the FBI identified Hampton as a radical threat and began to try to subvert his activities in Chicago, sowing disinformation among these groups and placing a counterintelligence operative in the local Panthers. In December 1969, Hampton was shot and killed in his bed during a predawn raid at his Chicago apartment by a tactical unit of the Cook County State's Attorney's Office in conjunction with the Chicago Police Department and the Federal Bureau of Investigation; during the raid, another Panther was killed and several seriously wounded. In January 1970, a coroner's jury held an inquest and ruled the deaths of Hampton and Mark Clark to be justifiable homicide.

A civil lawsuit was later filed on behalf of the survivors and the relatives of Hampton and Clark. It was resolved in 1982 by a settlement of $1.85 million; the City of Chicago, Cook County, and the federal government each paid one-third to a group of nine plaintiffs. Given revelations about the illegal COINTELPRO program and documents associated with the killings, scholars now widely consider Hampton's death an assassination under the FBI's initiative.

MORE RELIGIOUS LEADERS WHO MAKE THE GRADE...

John Boyd (1927 – July 11, 2012) started New Greater Bethel Ministries in 1972. He erected a small tent on the corner of Linden and Francis Lewis boulevards in Cambria Heights that over the years grew into a thriving ministry with more than 2,000 members. In 1975, the church acquired the Cambria Heights theater complex and that became its new home.

The congregation established a food pantry and a soup kitchen, giving free meals to hundreds of homeless individuals. Boyd also created the Set Free Prison Ministry, to help meet the spiritual needs of the incarcerated.

Greater Bethel created a 24-hour prayer line, with counselors ready to minister to those in need, even in the middle of the night. The church also spread its message of faith through the Voice of Bethel radio broadcast, reaching nearly 150 million listeners worldwide.

In 1993, the congregation expanded to include a location at 215-32 Jamaica Ave. in Queens Village, which could accommodate 1,500 people, and contained a Christian literature and media center, a drama center and recording and television studios.

Boyd was married to his wife, Margie, for 65 years and the couple has five children, all of whom pursued careers in ministry. Boyd studied at the Manhattan Bible Institute and earned his Doctrine of Divinity from the United Christian College.

In January 2000, he had a massive stroke while preaching at the pulpit. Three years later he suffered a heart attack. But despite those medical setbacks, he was able to make a full recovery and soon returned to preaching.

Rev. John Boyd, pastor of New Greater Bethel Ministries, died of natural causes at Bellevue Hospital on July 11 at the age of 85. He left behind a legacy of religious dedication, community service and a thriving church.

The ministry, which was established in 1972 by its founder, the Late Apostle John H. Boyd, Sr. is now under the leadership of his son, Rev. John Boyd II Senior Pastor of the New Greater Bethel Ministries (NGBM), located in Queens, New York.

Anthony Tyrone "Tony" Evans (born September 10, 1949), is a Christian pastor, speaker, author, and widely syndicated radio and television broadcaster in the United States. Dr. Evans serves as senior pastor to the over-9,500-member Oak Cliff Bible Fellowship in Dallas, Texas. He has served as chaplain for the NFL's Dallas Cowboys and is currently the longest-serving NBA chaplain, a position he holds with the Dallas Mavericks.

Dr. Evans earned a BA at Carver College in 1972, Th.M. in 1976, and a Th.D. at Dallas Theological Seminary in 1982.

He founded the Oak Cliff Bible Fellowship in Dallas, Texas, in 1976 with 10 members meeting at his home. He also founded The Urban Alternative, a national organization that seeks to restore hope and transform lives through the proclamation and the application of the Word of God. The Urban Alternative radio broadcast, *The Alternative with Dr. Tony Evans*, can be heard over 1,400 outlets daily throughout the U.S. and in over 130 countries worldwide.

In 1992 Dr. Evans became president of the National Black Church Initiative, working with churches and religious leaders across the country on issues of social and economic justice. The organization, which reports an affiliation with 34,000 churches across the country, has a mission that includes fighting health disparities, promoting financial responsibility and protecting babies from abuse and neglect.

In 2017, Dr. Evans launched the Tony Evans Training Center, an online learning platform providing quality seminary-style courses to equip Christian leaders who cannot attend seminary.

Dr. Evans holds the honor of writing and publishing the first full-Bible commentary and study Bible by an African American. He is also the author of over 100 books.

Fred J. Luter Jr. (November 11. 1956) in New Orleans) is a former president of the Southern Baptist Convention (SBC).

Luter had begun his ministry in 1977 in New Orleans' Lower Ninth Ward after he suffered a motorcycle accident. He has credited his motorcycling misadventure as his "road to Damascus moment"—his analogy to the conversion of Saul of Tarsus. He began as a street preacher at the corner of Caffin and Galvez.

During his street-preaching days Luter observed a need to draw men, particularly fathers, into his evangelistic appeal by urging events which attract male interest, on one occasion, in 1981, hosting a gathering for a pay-per-view televised boxing match between Thomas Hearns and Sugar Ray Leonard. His first sermon in a church building was in 1983 at New Orleans' Law Street Missionary Baptist Church. He was a staff minister at the city's Greater Liberty Baptist Church when he learned of the opening at Franklin Avenue and sought the job.

Luter is senior minister of the Franklin Avenue Baptist Church in New Orleans, which had been a predominantly white Southern Baptist congregation, in transition because of changing neighborhood demographics. Luter has been with the congregation since 1986, when it had 65 members.

Before Hurricane Katrina struck in 2005, the congregation had grown to over 7000 members, making it the largest congregation affiliated with SBC in Louisiana. Luter led the rebuilding of the membership after the diaspora from Katrina, and as of his election to the Southern Baptist presidency the congregation had 5000 members. Luter's strategy for congregational growth is rooted in his concept "FRANgelism"—the acronym "FRAN" standing for *friends*, *relatives*, *associates*, and *neighbors* in acts of networking people into the life of the congregation. He was elected on June 19, 2012 and is SBC's first African-American president. According to Southeastern Baptist Theological Seminary president Daniel L. Akin, ". . . the most significant event to happen in our [SBC's] history since our formation" is Luter's election.

On June 20, the day after electing Luter, SBC voted to permit use of the designation "Great Commission" as an alternative to "Southern" for congregations desiring a break from the geographical and historical eponym. Nominated by David Crosby of New Orleans' First Baptist Church, Luter succeeded Bryant Wright of Johnson Ferry Baptist Church in Marietta, Georgia.

Today the Franklin Avenue Baptist church has a majority African American congregation and is one of the largest Southern Baptist churches in Louisiana.

MORE BUSINESS MOGULS WHO MAKE THE GRADE...

S teven Allan Spielberg (born December 18, 1946) is an American filmmaker. He is considered one of the founding pioneers of the New Hollywood era and one of the most popular directors and producers in film history. Steven Spielberg is not only an Oscar-winning director but is also the highest-grossing director of all time.

Spielberg was born on December 18, 1946 in Cincinnati, Ohio. His mother, Leah was a restaurateur and concert pianist, and his father, Arnold Spielberg, was an electrical engineer involved in the development of computers. His family was Orthodox Jewish. Spielberg's paternal grandparents were Jewish Russian immigrants who settled in Cincinnati in the 1900s; his grandmother was from Sudylkiv, while his grandfather was from Kamianets-Podilskyi. In 1950, his family moved to Haddon Township, New Jersey, when his father took a job with RCA. Three years later, the family moved to Phoenix, Arizona. Spielberg attended Hebrew school from 1953 to 1957, in classes taught by Rabbi Albert L. Lewis.

At age 12, he made his first home movie: a train wreck involving his toy Lionel trains. Throughout his early teens, and after entering high school, Spielberg continued to make amateur, 8 mm, "adventure" films.

In 1958, he became a Boy Scout and fulfilled a requirement for the photography merit badge by making a nine-minute, 8 mm film entitled *The Last Gunfight*. Years later, Spielberg recalled to a magazine interviewer, "My dad's still-camera was broken, so I asked the scoutmaster if I could tell a story with my father's movie camera. He said yes, and I got an idea to do a Western. I made it and got my merit badge. That was how it all started." At age 13, while living in Phoenix, Spielberg won a prize for a 40-minute, war film he titled *Escape to Nowhere*, using a cast composed of other high school friends. That motivated him to make 15 more amateur, 8 mm films.

In 1963, at age 16, Spielberg wrote and directed his first independent film, a 140-minute science fiction adventure called *Firelight*, which would later inspire *Close Encounters*. The film was made for $500, most of which came from his father, and was shown in a local cinema for one evening, which earned back its cost.

After attending Arcadia High School in Phoenix for three years, his family later moved to Saratoga, California where he attended and graduated from Saratoga High School in 1965. He attained the rank of Eagle Scout. His parents divorced while he was still in school, and, soon after, he graduated. Spielberg moved to Los Angeles, staying initially with his father. His long-term goal was to become a film director. His three sisters and mother remained in Saratoga. In Los Angeles, he applied to the University of Southern California's film school but was turned down because of his "C" grade average. He then applied and was admitted to California State University, Long Beach where he became a brother of Theta Chi Fraternity. Spielberg attended Brookdale Community College for his undergrad.

While still a student, he was offered a small, unpaid, intern job at Universal Studios with the editing department. He was later given the opportunity to make a short film for theatrical release, the 26-minute, 35 mm *Amblin'*, which he wrote and directed. Studio vice president Sidney Sheinberg was impressed by the film, which had won a number of awards, and offered Spielberg a seven-year directing contract. It made him the youngest director ever to be signed for a long-term deal with a major Hollywood studio. He subsequently dropped out of college to begin professionally directing TV productions with Universal. Spielberg later returned to California State University, Long Beach and completed his BA degree in Film and Electronic Arts in 2002.

Spielberg started in Hollywood directing television and several minor theatrical releases. His first professional TV job came when he was hired to direct one of the segments for the 1969 pilot episode of *Night Gallery*, written by Rod Serling and starring Joan Crawford. Crawford, however, was "speechless, and then horrified" at the thought of a twenty-one-year-old newcomer directing her, one of Hollywood's leading stars. "Why was this happening to me?" she asked the producer. Her attitude changed after they began working on her scenes:

He became a household name as the director of *Jaws* (1975), which was critically and commercially successful and is considered the first summer blockbuster. His subsequent releases focused typically on science fiction/adventure films such as *Close Encounters of the Third Kind* (1977), *Raiders of the Lost Ark* (1981), *E.T. the Extra-Terrestrial* (1982), and *Jurassic Park* (1993), which became archetypes of modern Hollywood escapist filmmaking.

Spielberg transitioned into addressing serious issues in his later work with *The Color Purple* (1985), *Empire of the Sun* (1987), *Schindler's List* (1993), *Amistad* (1997), and *Saving Private Ryan* (1998). He has largely adhered to this practice during the 21st century, with *Munich* (2005), *Lincoln* (2012), *Bridge of Spies* (2015), and *The Post* (2017).

Spielberg and his wife made numerous real estate investments throughout the years and managed to turn them into a huge profit. They co-founded Amblin Entertainment and DreamWorks Studios, which is a mini-studio compared to other Hollywood studios. There Spielberg has also served as a producer or executive producer for several successful film trilogies, tetralogies and more including the *Gremlins*, *Back to the Future*, *Men in Black*, and the *Transformers* series. He later transitioned into producing several video games.

Spielberg is one of the American film industry's most critically successful filmmakers, with praise for his directing talent and versatility, and he has won the Academy Award for Best Director twice. Some of his movies are also among the highest-grossing films, while his total work makes him the highest-grossing film director in history. Spielberg along with his wife Kate Capshaw and their children hold on to a wealth of about $3.7 billion.

In November 24, 2015, Spielberg was awarded the Presidential Medal of Freedom from President Barack Obama in a ceremony at the White House.

Janice Bryant Howroyd (born September 1, 1952) is an entrepreneur, educator, ambassador, businesswoman, author, and mentor. She is founder and chief executive officer of The ActOne Group, the largest privately held, minority-woman-owned personnel company founded in the U.S. Howroyd is most well known as being the first African American woman to build and own a billion dollar company.

Janice Bryant was born in Tarboro, North Carolina, the fourth of 11 children. Janice's parents, John and Elretha K. Bryant, weaved proven principles of success and significance into the strong fabric of family, business, and life experiences. While her dad went out to work, her mother stayed home and ran things. Janice witnessed entrepreneurship without knowing and understanding what it actually was. Her mother's family ran a barbecue shop. They opened the formal dining room of their home to accommodate the locals to stop in for a midday meal. Most would go to the rear of the home for "take and carry" similar to today's fast food carry out.

Janice's mother laid the foundation for her success as an entrepreneur by executing with the highest levels of quality, organization, and administration. The children knew what time it was to carry out a task. They knew what belonged where in their home. They clearly understood roles and responsibilities. Her mom actually taught the children different skill sets by rotating roles appropriately around timelines. There were checkoff lists when an assignment was completed. Then her mother inspected and everything had to be legit before it was passed on for the next assignment.

As a teen, Janice was one of the first African American students to desegregate her town's previously segregated high school. She was educated at North Carolina A&T State University, where she earned a degree in English.

In 1976, Janice moved to Los Angeles, California, and worked as a temporary secretary for her brother-in-law Tom Noonan at Billboard magazine. While at Billboard, Noonan introduced Howroyd to business executives, celebrities, travel, diversity in the workplace, and decision-making in ways she had not previously been exposed to.

Armed with industry experience and knowledge, and with little more than $1,000 Janice continued to focus on employment services and launched her own company, The ACT•1 Group, in a small

Beverly Hills, California office in 1978, with Tom Noonan as her first client.

According to Bloomberg L.P., "ActOne Group, Inc. provides employment, workforce management, and procurement solutions to Fortune 500 organizations, local and mid-market companies, and government agencies." ActOne Group companies include AppleOne, All's Well, AT-Tech, ACT-1 Personnel Services, Agile-1, ACT-1Govt, ACheck GLobal, which provide personnel and recruiting services to different industries, and DSSI, which provides document management services. ACT-1 Group, raked in $2.8 billion in revenues and placed as No. 2 on Black Enterprise's annual BE 100s list of the nation's largest black businesses in 2019.

Nicholas "Nick" Scott Cannon (born October 8, 1980) is an American actor, comedian, rapper, director, writer, producer, and television host.

On television, Cannon began as a teenager on *All That* before going on to host *The Nick Cannon Show*, *Wild 'N Out*, *America's Got Talent*, *Lip Sync Battle Shorties* and *The Masked Singer*. He acted in the films *Drumline*, *Love Don't Cost a Thing* and *Roll Bounce*.

As a rapper he released his debut self-titled album in 2003 with the single "Gigolo", a collaboration with singer R. Kelly. In 2007 he played the role of the fictional footballer TJ Harper in the film *Goal II: Living the Dream*.

Nick Cannon is certainly one of the youngest elite individuals out there, but this award-winning rapper, actor and producer is amongst the richest. Much of his fortune comes from his music. He was a member of a rap group called Da G4 Dope Bomb Squad in his early beginnings.

He soon became famous thanks to his hits like "Nick's Story," "Can I Live?" and "Teach Me How to Dougie." He then decided that it was time for him to start his own label, and shortly after he opened up his own small record company.

Cannon is also known for his marriage to singer Mariah Carey, with whom he had two children (twins). Cannon married Mariah in 2008; the pair separated and filed for divorce in December 2014. The divorce was finalized in 2016, and they co-parent their children.

Nick is now the mastermind behind TeenNick for the Nickelodeon TV network. He also signed an exclusive deal with NBC. When he hosted America's Got Talent, he earned $70,000 per episode. **Nick Cannon** has a net **worth** of $30 million. During his career, **Nick** has found success on television, films radio and as an entrepreneur/producer.

Robyn Rihanna Fenty (born February 20, 1988) is a Barbadian singer, songwriter, actress, and businesswoman, who has been recognized for embracing various musical styles and reinventing her image throughout her career.

Rihanna was born in Saint Michael, Barbados, the daughter of accountant Monica (Braithwaite) and warehouse supervisor Ronald Fenty. Rihanna has two brothers, Rorrey and Rajad Fenty, and two half-sisters and a half-brother from her father's side. She grew up in a three-bedroom bungalow in Bridgetown and sold clothes with her father in a stall on the street. Her childhood was deeply affected by her father's alcoholism and crack cocaine addiction, which contributed to her parents' strained marriage. Rihanna's father used to physically abuse her mother and she would try to get in between them to break up fights. By the time she was 14, her parents had divorced.

Rihanna grew up listening to reggae music. She attended Charles F. Broome Memorial Primary School and Combermere School, where she studied alongside future international cricketers Chris Jordan and Carlos Brathwaite. Rihanna was an army cadet in a sub-military programme, where the later Barbadian singer-songwriter Shontelle was her drill sergeant. Although she initially wanted to graduate from high school, she chose to pursue a musical career instead.

In 2003, Rihanna formed a musical trio with two of her classmates. She was discovered in her home country of Barbados by American record producer Evan Rogers. Without a name or any material, the girl group managed to land an audition with Rogers. He scheduled a second meeting with Rihanna's mother present and then invited Rihanna to his hometown in the United States to record some demo tapes that could be sent to record labels. That same year, Rihanna was signed to Rogers's and Carl Sturken's production company, Syndicated Rhythm Productions.

Rihanna moved to the US in 2005, when she signed with Def Jam Recordings. She earned significant recognition following the release of her first two studio albums, *Music of the Sun* (2005) and *A Girl like Me* (2006), both of which were influenced by Caribbean music and peaked within the top ten of the US *Billboard* 200 chart. Rihanna's third studio album, *Good Girl Gone Bad* (2007), incorporated more elements of dance-pop and catapulted her to greater stardom, establishing her status as a sex symbol and a leading figure in the music industry. Its international chart-topping single "Umbrella" earned Rihanna her first Grammy Award, winning Best Rap/Sung Collaboration.

Among her many music awards, Rihanna has won 9 Grammy Awards, 12 Billboard Music Awards, 13 American Music Awards (including the Icon Award), and 7 MTV Video Music Awards (including the Michael Jackson Video Vanguard Award).

In 2007, around the time Rihanna released the hit "Umbrella," she had a net worth close to $50 million, according to Money Nation. Since then she has scaled her career to new heights via entrepreneurship despite a few personal bumps in the road along the way. She used her voice, eye for fashion, business acumen, and bounce back mentality to grow her empire.

At just 31 years old, Rihanna is officially the wealthiest female musician on the planet, according to *Forbes*. Her net worth is estimated at $600 million. A large part of Rihanna's wealth has been generated through her cosmetics company, Fenty Beauty, which launched in collaboration with luxury giant LVMH (Moët Hennessy Louis Vuitton). in September 2017. Noted for its inclusive range of 40 shades of foundation, Fenty reportedly racked up $100 million in sales within weeks due to Rihanna's mass appeal and social media following. Since then, sales for the beauty brand have continued to soar.

"Fenty Beauty generated an estimated $570 million in revenue in 2019, after only 15 months in business. In May 2019 LVMH announced that it was opening a fashion house under the Fenty name. This makes Rihanna the first black woman to head a major luxury fashion house. Her new clothing line with LVMH, which includes high-end clothes, shoes, accessories, and jewelry, launched in Paris on May 24. In addition, Rihanna co-owns the Savage X Fenty lingerie line with TechStyle Fashion Group.

Rihanna's hard work has garnered her nearly 80 million Instagram followers and the 2020 NAACP President's Award which she received at the NAACP Image Awards on February 22.

INVENTORS AND SCIENTISTS WHO MAKE THE GRADE...

Saint Elmo Brady (December 22, 1884 – December 25, 1966) was the first African American to obtain a Ph.D. degree in chemistry in the United States. He received his doctorate at the University of Illinois in 1916.

Saint Elmo Brady was born on December 22, 1884 in Louisville, Kentucky, the eldest of three children. At the age of 20 he left home to attend Fisk University, an all-black college in Nashville, Tennessee, where he was encouraged by his chemistry teacher, Thomas Talley. Greatly influenced by Thomas W. Talley, a pioneer in the teaching of science, Brady received his bachelor's degree from Fisk University in 1908 at the age of 24, he took a teaching position at Tuskegee Normal and Industrial Institute (now Tuskegee University) in Alabama. Brady also had a close relationship with and was mentored by Booker T. Washington and the agricultural chemist George Washington Carver.

In 1912, after four years at Tuskegee University, he was offered a graduate scholarship to the University of Illinois to engage in graduate studies. There he earned a master's degree in chemistry in 1914 and his doctorate in 1916.

During his time at the University of Illinois, Brady became the first African American admitted to the university's national chemical honor society, Phi Lambda Upsilon, (1914), and he was one of the first African Americans to be inducted into Sigma Xi, the science honorary society (1915).

Dr. Brady went on to become highly regarded for his impressive teaching career at four historically black colleges, where he energized the chemistry curricula and established new programs for young African American scientists. Dr. Brady returned to teaching at Tuskegee University in 1916, this time heading up the science division. He married Myrtle Travers August. 28, 1917 and they had two sons, Robert and St. Elmo Brady, Jr. who worked as a physician.

In 1920, seeking better research facilities, Dr. Brady accepted a teaching position at Howard University in Washington, D.C. and headed north to the nation's capital.

In 1927 Dr. Brady moved to Fisk University to chair the school's Chemistry department, during which he developed the undergraduate curricula and founded the first ever graduate studies program at a Black College/University. Talley-Brady Hall on the Fisk campus is named for two pioneers in science education, Fisk alumni and Professor Thomas Talley and his former student, Saint Elmo Brady. He remained at Fisk for 25 years until his retirement in 1952.

After his retirement from Fisk, Dr Brady taught at Tougaloo College in Jackson, Mississippi.

He also spent several years collaborating with educators at Tougaloo College, helping them build their chemistry department.

Saint Elmo Brady's legacy was his establishment of strong undergraduate curricula, graduate programs, and fundraising development for four historically black colleges and universities. In conjunction with faculty from the University of Illinois, he established a summer program in infrared spectroscopy, which was open to faculty from all colleges and universities. St. Elmo Brady eventually moved back to Washington, D.C., where he died in 1966 on Christmas Day.

Marjorie Stewart Joyner (October 24, 1896 – December 27, 1994) was an American businesswoman. She was also a leader in developing new products, such as her permanent wave machine.

She was born in Monterey, Virginia, the granddaughter of a slave and a white slave-owner. Marjorie moved to Chicago in 1912, and shortly thereafter, she began studying cosmetology. She graduated A.B. Molar Beauty School in Chicago in 1916, the first African American to achieve this. That year, at the age of 20, she married podiatrist Robert E. Joyner and opened her salon. That was where she met Madam C. J. Walker, an African American beauty entrepreneur, and the owner of a cosmetic empire. Joyner went to work for her and oversaw 200 of Madame Walker's beauty schools as the national adviser.

In 1939, Marjorie started looking for an easier way for women to curl their hair, taking her inspiration from a pot roast cooking with paper pins to quicken preparation time. Joyner experimented initially with these paper rods and soon designed a table that could be used to curl or straighten hair by wrapping it. This method allowed hairstyles to last several days. At the beginning of her invention, there were complaints from users that it was uncomfortable. That was when Marjorie improved it with the simple idea of having a scalp protector while the lady is curling her hair. Her patent for this design, (U.S. pat. #1,693,515) established her as the first African American woman to receive a patent.

Joyner taught some 15,000 stylists over her fifty-year career. She helped write the first cosmetology laws for the state of Illinois, and founded a sorority and fraternity, Alpha Chi Pi Omega on October 27, 1945 as well as a national association for black beauticians.

Joyner was friends with Eleanor Roosevelt, and helped found the National Council of Negro Women. She was an advisor to the Democratic National Committee in the 1940s, and advised several New Deal agencies trying to reach out to black women.

Joyner's design was popular in salons with both African American and white women. The patent was credited to Madame Walker's company and she received almost no money for it. In 1967, she co-founded the United Beauty School Owners and Teachers Association. In 1973, at the age of 77, she was awarded a bachelor's degree in psychology from Bethune-Cookman College in Daytona Beach, Florida.

In 1987 the Smithsonian Institution in Washington opened an exhibit featuring Joyner's permanent wave machine and a replica of her original salon. Marjorie Stewart Joyner died of heart failure at her South Side Chicago home on December 27, 1994, at the age of ninety-eight.

Marie Maynard Daly (April 16, 1921 – October 28, 2003) was an American biochemist. She was the first Black American woman in the United States to earn a Ph.D. in chemistry (awarded by Columbia University in 1947). Daly made important contributions in four areas of research: the chemistry of histones, protein synthesis, the relationships between cholesterol and hypertension, and creatine's uptake by muscle cells.

Marie Daly's interest in science was also influenced by her father, who had attended Cornell University with intentions of becoming a chemist, but had been unable to complete his education due to a lack of funds. His daughter continued her father's legacy by majoring in chemistry.

Dr. Daly worked as a physical science instructor at Howard University, from 1947 to 1948 while simultaneously conducting research under the direction of Herman Branson. After being awarded an American Cancer Society grant to support her postdoctoral research, she joined Dr. A. E. Mirsky at the Rockefeller Institute, where they studied the cell nucleus and its constituents. At the time, the structure and function of DNA were not yet understood.

Dr. Daly began working in the College of Physicians and Surgeons at Columbia University in 1955. In collaboration with Dr. Quentin B. Deming, she studied arterial metabolism. She continued this work as an assistant professor of biochemistry and of medicine at the Albert Einstein College of Medicine at Yeshiva University, where she and Deming moved in 1960. From 1958 to 1963, Daly also served as an investigator for the American Heart Association.. In 1971 she was promoted to associate professor.

Dr. Daly was a member of the prestigious board of governors of the New York Academy of Sciences for two years. Additional fellowships that Daly received throughout her career include the American Cancer Society, American Association for the Advancement of Science and Council on Arteriosclerosis of the American Heart Association.

Dr. Daly was designated as a career scientist by the Health Research Council of the City of New York. She retired in 1986 from the Albert Einstein College of Medicine, and in 1988 established a scholarship for African American chemistry and physics majors at Queens College in memory of her father. In 1999, she was recognized by the National Technical Association as one of the top 50 women in Science, Engineering and Technology. Marie Maynard Daly Clark died on October 28, 2003.

Annie J. Easley (April 23, 1933 – June 25, 2011) was an African-American computer scientist, mathematician, and rocket scientist. She worked for the Lewis Research Center (now Glenn Research Center) of the National Aeronautics and Space Administration (NASA) and its predecessor, the National Advisory Committee for Aeronautics (NACA). She was a leading member of the team which developed software for the Centaur rocket stage, and was one of the first African Americans to work as a computer scientist at NASA. Easley's work with the Centaur project helped lay the technological foundations for future space shuttle launches and launches of communication, military and weather satellites.

From the fifth grade through high school, Annie attended Holy Family High School, and was valedictorian of her graduating class. In 1950 she went to Xavier University in New Orleans, which was then an African American Roman Catholic University, and majored in pharmacy for about two years.

In 1954, she returned to Birmingham. As part of the Jim Crow laws that maintained racial inequality, African Americans were required to pass a literacy test and pay a poll tax in order to vote. Subsequently, she helped other African Americans prepare for the test.

In 1964, the Twenty-fourth Amendment outlawed the poll tax in federal elections. The following year the Voting Rights Act eliminated the literacy test.

Shortly thereafter, Annie moved to Cleveland for personal reasons. In 1955, she read a story in a local newspaper about twin sisters who worked for She the National Advisory Committee for Aeronautics (NACA) as a "computer" and was hired two weeks later - one of four African Americans of about 2500 employees. She began her career as a mathematician and computer engineer at the NACA Lewis Flight Propulsion Laboratory (which became NASA Lewis Research Center, 1958–1999, and subsequently the John H. Glenn Research Center) in Cleveland, Ohio. Throughout the 1970s, Easley advocated for and encouraged female and minority students at college career days to work in STEM careers. In 1977, Annie obtained a Bachelor of Science in Mathematics from Cleveland State University.

Annie's 34-year career included developing and implementing computer code that analyzed alternative power technologies, supported the Centaur high-energy upper rocket stage, determined solar, wind and energy projects, identified energy conversion systems and alternative systems to solve energy problems. Annie's computer applications have been used to identify energy conversion systems that offer the improvement over commercially available technologies. She retired in 1989. Her prior work contributed to the 1997 flight to Saturn of the Cassini probe, the launcher of which had the Centaur as its upper stage.

Walter Lincoln Hawkins (March 21, 1911 – August 20, 1992) was an American chemist and engineer widely regarded as a pioneer of polymer chemistry. For thirty-four years he worked at Bell Laboratories, where he was instrumental in designing a long-lasting plastic to sheath telephone cables, so assisting the introduction of telephone services to thousands of Americans.

Walter Hawkins was born in Washington, D.C. His father was a lawyer for the U.S. Census Bureau and his mother was a science teacher in the District of Columbia school system.

After graduating from Washington's Dunbar High School Hawkins went to Rensselaer Polytechnic Institute in Troy, New York. In 1932 he graduated with a chemical engineering degree. Unable to find a job during the Great Depression, he enrolled in graduate school at Howard University, where in 1934, he earned a master's degree in chemistry. Professor Howard Blatt, Hawkins' friend and mentor at Howard, informed him of a special scholarship at McGill University in Montreal, Canada. Hawkins enrolled at McGill, earned his Doctorate in Chemistry, and left to continue his research at Columbia University when he received a fellowship from the National Research Council.

In 1942, Hawkins became the first African American to join the technical staff of Bell Laboratories. By controlling much of the Pacific theater in World War II, the Japanese had cut off much of America's rubber supply from Southeast Asia. Hawkins contributed to the development of a rubber substitute made from petroleum stock.

After the war, Hawkins began work on an important project, a new and improved insulation for telephone cables. Underground and underwater cables, which were laid over incredibly long distances, were covered with fiber wrapped in heavy, expensive lead sheathing. Hawkins and Vincent Lanza in 1956 invented a plastic coating that could withstand extreme fluctuations in temperature, last up to seventy years, and was less expensive than lead. Telephone lines were subsequently installed in rural areas, bringing affordable phone service to thousands of people.

Hawkins, who worked at Bell Labs for thirty-four years, became assistant director of their chemical research lab in 1974. His work with polymers, primarily plastics, focused on the development of new products and recycling. The extremely durable nature of plastic becomes a huge problem when it must be discarded. Hawkins became an expert, not only in making plastics last longer, but in recycling these seemingly indestructible products.

Upon his retirement from Bell Labs in 1976, Hawkins began teaching and encouraging college students to study science and engineering. In 1981, he became the first chairman of Project SEED (Support of the Educationally & Economically Disadvantaged), an American Chemical Society program designed to promote science careers for minority students. He also helped to set up a program at Bell Labs and AT&T to recruit African-American scientists and engineers.

Hawkins was frequently honored as a polymer chemistry pioneer. The first African-American to become a member of the National Academy of Engineering, Hawkins also won the International Medal of the Society of Plastics. In a 1992 White House ceremony, he received the National Medal of Technology from President George H. W. Bush.

On August 20, 1992, Hawkins died in San Marcos, California due to heart failure. He was 81 years old.

ATHLETES WHO MAKE THE GRADE...

Frederick Douglass "Fritz" Pollard (January 27, 1894 – May 11, 1986) was an American football player and coach. He was the first African American head coach in the National Football League (NFL).

Pollard attended Albert G. Lane Manual Training High School in Chicago, also known as "Lane Tech," where he played football, baseball, and ran track. He then went to Brown University, majoring in chemistry. Pollard played halfback on the Brown football team, which went to the 1916 Rose Bowl. He was the first black football player at Brown. He became the first black running back to be named to Walter Camp's All-America team.

Pollard coached Lincoln University (Pennsylvania)'s football team during the 1918 to 1920 seasons and served as athletic director of the school's World War I era Students' Army Training Corps. During 1918–1919, he led the team to a victorious season defeating Howard University's Bisons 13–0 in the annual Thanksgiving classic as well as Hampton (7–0) on November 9, 1918, and teams of military recruits at Camp Dix (19–0) on November 2, 1918, and Camp Upton (41–0).

Fritz later played pro football with the Akron Pros, the team he would lead to the NFL (APFA) championship in 1920. A total of nine black people suited up for NFL teams between 1920 and 1926, including future attorney, black activist, and internationally acclaimed artist Paul Robeson, as well as famed race record producer J. Mayo Williams. Fritz Pollard and Bobby Marshall were the first black players in what is now the NFL in 1920.

Fritz Pollard became the first (and until 1989, only) black coach in 1921; during the early-to-mid-1920s, the league used player-coaches and did not have separate coaching staffs. In 1921, he became the co-head coach of the Akron Pros, while still maintaining his roster position as running back. He also played for the Milwaukee Badgers, Hammond Pros, Gilberton Cadamounts, Union Club of Phoenixville and Providence Steam Roller. Some sources indicate that Pollard also served as co-coach of the Milwaukee Badgers with Budge Garrett for part of the 1922 season. He also coached the Gilberton Cadamounts, a non-NFL team. In 1923 and 1924, he served as head coach for the Hammond Pros.

Pollard, along with all nine of the black players in the NFL at the time, were removed from the league at the end of the 1926 season, never to return again. With a large number of available, talented white players, black players were generally the first to be removed. Many observers will attribute the subsequent lockout of black players to the entry of George Preston Marshall into the league in 1932. Marshall openly refused to have black athletes on his Boston Braves/Washington Redskins team, and reportedly pressured the rest of the league to follow suit. Marshall, however, was likely not the only reason: the Great Depression had stoked an increase in racism and self-inflicted segregation across the country, and internal politics likely had as much of an effect as external pressure. By 1934, there were no more black players in the league. The NFL did not have another black player until after World War II, when in 1946 the Rams signed Kenny Washington, making him the first African-American to sign a contract with a National Football League (NFL) team in the modern (post-World War II) era.

After their systematic removal from the NFL starting in 1926 most black players either ended up in the minor leagues or found themselves onto all-black barnstorming teams such as the Harlem Brown Bombers. Fritz Pollard spent some time organizing all-black barnstorming teams, including the Chicago Black Hawks in 1928 and the Harlem Brown Bombers in the 1930s. However, the Depression ended the Brown Bombers' run in 1938, and Pollard went on to other ventures. Football pioneer Walter Camp ranked Pollard as "one of the greatest runners these eyes have ever seen." Fritz" Pollard died in 1986 at the age of 92.

Leroy Robert "Satchel" Paige (July 7, 1906 – June 8, 1982) was an American Negro league baseball and Major League Baseball (MLB) pitcher who is notable for his longevity in the game, and for attracting record crowds wherever he pitched.

Satchel Paige, who received his distinctive nickname as a young railroad porter, honed his baseball skills at the age of twelve, while in reform school. He first played for the semi-professional Mobile Tigers from 1924 to 1926.

Then he began his professional baseball career in 1926 with the Chattanooga Black Lookouts of the Negro Southern League and became one of the most famous and successful players from the Negro leagues. He was a pitcher for various teams in the Negro Southern Association and the Negro National League. Wearing a false red beard, he also played for the House of David team (a team fielded by a communal Christian religious sect that forbade its male members to shave or cut their hair). A true "iron man," he pitched in the Dominican Republic and Mexican leagues during the northern winter. As a barnstormer, he would travel as many as 30,000 miles a year while pitching for any team willing to meet his price. He is reputed to have pitched a total of 2,500 games during his nearly 30-year career, winning 2,000 of them.

Despite the color bar, Paige faced the best major league players in exhibition games before 1948. He once struck out Rogers Hornsby, probably the greatest right-handed hitter in baseball history, five times in one game. In Hollywood in 1934 Paige scored a spectacular 1–0 victory in 13 innings over Dizzy Dean, who won 30 games for the St. Louis Cardinals that year.

At age 42 in 1948, Satchel Paige was the oldest major league rookie while playing for the Cleveland Indians. He finally was allowed to enter the major leagues after the unwritten rule against black players was abolished. He was the first player who had played in the Negro leagues to pitch in the World Series. Paige had considerable pitching speed, but he also developed a comprehensive mastery of slow-breaking pitches and varied deliveries. He is rated as one of the greatest players in the history of baseball.

Paige was well past his prime in 1948 when team owner Bill Veeck signed him for the Cleveland Indians; he was the oldest rookie ever to play in the major leagues. He helped to spark that team to American League pennant and World Series victories that year Satchel Paige played with the team until age 47. He was its most effective relief pitcher from 1951 through 1953 and represented the St Louis Browns in the All-Star Game in 1952 and 1953.

He also pitched three scoreless innings for the Kansas City Athletics in 1965, which made him the oldest to pitch in the major leagues. He played his last professional game on June 21, 1966 for the Peninsula Grays of the Carolina League.

Satchel Paige pitched professionally for 30 years. He threw exclusively fastballs for the first 15 years of his career—and was still by far the best pitcher in his league. Paige made his MLB debut at *age 42* and still made two All-Star teams. He mastered every single pitch—from his looping curveball to a knuckleball to a changeup—and had precise, never-before-seen control. In 1971 Satchel Paige became the first electee of the Committee on Negro Baseball Leagues to be inducted into the National Baseball Hall of Fame,.

Charles Luther Sifford (June 2, 1922 – February 3, 2015) was a professional golfer who was the first African American to play on the PGA Tour.

Sifford began golfing professionally in 1948. He competed in the golf tournaments that black golfers organized for themselves as they were excluded from the Professional Golfers' Association of America (PGA). Sifford won the United Golf Association's National Negro Open six times, including consecutive wins from 1952 through 1956. Sifford later worked as a valet and golf instructor to the singer Billy Eckstine, who also financially supported his career when he was unable to find sponsorship.

Charles Sifford first attempted to qualify for a PGA Tour event at the 1952 Phoenix Open, using an invitation obtained by former World heavyweight boxing champion Joe Louis. Sifford was subjected to threats and racial abuse there and at other tournaments.

In 1957, Sifford won the Long Beach Open, which was not an official PGA Tour event, but was co-sponsored by the PGA and had some well-known white players in the field. Sifford competed in the U. S. Open in 1959 for the first time, and tied for 32nd place. He became a member of the Tour in 1961.

He won the 1963 Puerto Rico Open, Greater Hartford Open in 1967 and the Los Angeles Open in 1969 and finished in the top 60 in overall winnings in his first nine years as a member of the PGA Tour. He also won the United Golf Association's National Negro Open six times; and in 1975, the PGA Seniors' Championship, then the leading tournament for golfers over fifty.

Lee Trevino referred to Sifford as the "Jackie Robinson" of golf, and Tiger Woods acknowledged that Sifford paved the way for his career. Tiger Woods named his son Charlie after him and referred to Sifford as "the Grandpa I never had."

For his contributions to golf, Charles Sifford became the first African American inducted into the World Golf Hall of Fame in 2004. On June 22, 2006, he received an honorary degree from the University of St Andrews as a Doctor of Laws. In 2007 he was awarded the Old Tom Morris Award from the Golf Course Superintendents Association of America (GCSAA), the GCSAA's highest honor. In 2009, the Northern Trust Open created an exemption for a player who represents the advancement of diversity in golf; it is named in honor of Sifford and is referred to as the Charlie Sifford Exemption. In 2011, Mecklenburg County Park and Recreation changed the name of Revolution Park Golf Course to Dr. Charles L. Sifford Golf Course at Revolution Park.

President Barack Obama awarded him the 2014 Presidential Medal of Freedom. Charles Luther Sifford died in 2015 at the age of 92.

Willie Howard Mays, Jr. (born May 6, 1931), nicknamed "**The Say Hey Kid**", is an American former professional baseball center fielder, who spent almost all of his 22-season Major League Baseball (MLB) career playing for the New York/San Francisco Giants, before finishing with the New York Mets (1972-1973).

Mays shares the record of most All-Star Games played (24), with Hank Aaron and Stan Musial. In appreciation of his All-Star record,

Ted Williams said "They invented the All-Star Game for Willie Mays."

Between 1951-1973 Willie Mays played for the Giants, but during that time he was drafted into the US Army in 1952 and missed most of that season and all of the 1953 season.

In 1954, Mays returned to the Giants and hit for a league-leading .345 batting average while slugging 41 home runs enroute to his only World Series championship. Mays won the National League Most Valuable Player Award and the Hickok Belt as top professional athlete of the year. He also became the first player in history to hit 30 home runs before the All-Star Game and was selected as an All-Star for the first of 19 consecutive seasons (20 total). The Giants won the National League pennant and the 1954 World Series, sweeping the Cleveland Indians in four games.

Willie Mays led the league with 51 home runs. In 1956, he hit 36 homers and stole 40 bases, being only the second player, and first National League player, to join the "30–30 club". In 1957, the first season the Gold Glove award was presented, he won the first of 12 consecutive Gold Glove Awards. In 1957, Mays became the fourth player in major league history to join the 20–20–20 club (2B, 3B, HR), something no player had accomplished since 1941. Mays also stole 38 bases that year, making him the second player in baseball history (after Frank Schulte in 1911) to reach 20 in each of those four categories (doubles, triples, homers, steals) in the same season.

Mays hit over 50 home runs in 1955 and 1965, representing the longest time span between 50-plus home run seasons for any player in Major League Baseball history.

Mays played a season and a half with the Mets before retiring; he appeared in 133 games. In 1972 and 1973, Mays was the oldest regular position player in baseball. The Mets honored him on September 25, 1973 (Willie Mays Night), where he thanked the New York fans and said goodbye to baseball. He finished his career in the 1973 World Series, which the Mets lost to the Oakland Athletics in seven games.

At age 42, Willie Mays became the oldest position player to appear in a World Series game. Mays got the first hit of the Series but had only seven at-bats (with two hits). The final hit of his career came in Game 2, a key single to help the Mets win.

Mays retired after the 1973 season with a lifetime batting average of .302 and 660 home runs. His lifetime total of 7,095 outfield putouts remains the major league record. Mays is the only major league player to have hit a home run in every inning from the 1st through the 16th innings. He finished his career with a record 22 extra-inning home runs. He has the third-highest career power–speed number, behind Barry Bonds and Rickey Henderson, at 447.1.

Mays won two National League (NL) Most Valuable Player (MVP) awards, ended his career with 660 home runs—third at the time of his retirement and currently fifth all-time—and won a record-tying 12 Gold Glove awards beginning in 1957, when the award was introduced.

Willie Mays is regarded as one of the greatest baseball players of all time and on January 23, 1979, he was elected to the Baseball Hall of Fame in his first year of eligibility. He garnered 409 of the 432 ballots cast (94.68%).

In 1999, Mays placed second on *The Sporting News'* "List of the 100 Greatest Baseball Players", making him the highest-ranking living player. Later that year, he was also elected to the Major League

Baseball All-Century Team. Mays is one of five National League players to have had eight consecutive 100-RBI seasons.

In November 2015, Mays was awarded the Presidential Medal of Freedom by President Barack Obama during a ceremony at the White House.

In September 2017, Major League Baseball announced their decision to rename the World Series Most Valuable Player Award after Mays, and it has since been referred to as the Willie Mays World Series Most Valuable Player Award. The first recipient of the rechristened award was Houston Astros Outfielder, George Springer.

William Felton Russell (born February 12, 1934) aka **Bill Russell** was the first outstanding defensive center in the history of the National Basketball Association (NBA) from 1956 to 1969 and one of the sport's greatest icons. He was the first black player to achieve superstar status in the NBA, winning 11 NBA titles in the 13 seasons that he played with the Boston Celtics. He also served a three-season (1966–69) stint becoming the first African American coach of a modern major professional sports team in in North American professional sports and the first to win a championship. when he was named the player-coach of the Celtics in 1966.

A five-time NBA Most Valuable Player and a twelve-time All-Star, Bill Russell was the centerpiece of the Celtics dynasty that won eleven NBA championships during his thirteen-year career. Russell led the University of San Francisco to two consecutive NCAA championships in 1955 and 1956, and he captained the gold-medal winning U.S. national basketball team at the 1956 Summer Olympics.

Bill Russell is regarded by many as one of the greatest basketball players of all time. He led the NBA in rebounds four times, had a dozen consecutive seasons of 1,000 or more rebounds, and remains second all-time in both total rebounds and rebounds per game. He is one of just two NBA players (the other being prominent rival Wilt Chamberlain) to have grabbed more than 50 rebounds in a game.

Russell is one of seven players in history to win an NCAA Championship, an NBA Championship, and an Olympic gold medal. He was inducted into the Naismith Memorial Basketball Hall of Fame and the National Collegiate Basketball Hall of Fame. He was selected into the NBA 25th Anniversary Team in 1971 and the NBA 35th Anniversary Team in 1980, and named as one of the 50 Greatest Players in NBA History in 1996, one of only four players to receive all three honors. In 2007, he was enshrined in the FIBA Hall of Fame. In Russell's honor the NBA renamed the NBA Finals Most Valuable Player trophy in 2009: it is now the Bill Russell NBA Finals Most Valuable Player Award.

In 2011, Barack Obama awarded Russell the Presidential Medal of Freedom for his accomplishments on the court and in the Civil Rights Movement.

James "Jim" Nathaniel Brown (born February 17, 1936) is an American former professional football player, sports analyst and actor. He was a fullback for the Cleveland Browns of the National Football League (NFL) from 1957 through 1965.

Jim Brown earned unanimous All-America honors playing college football at Syracuse University, where he was an all-around player for the Syracuse Orangemen football team. In addition to his football accomplishments, Jim Brown excelled in basketball, track, and especially lacrosse. As a sophomore, he was the second-leading scorer for the basketball team and earned a letter on the track team. In 1955, he finished in fifth place in the Nation Championship decathlon. His junior year, he averaged 11.3 points in basketball, and was named a second-team All-American in lacrosse. His senior year, he was named a first-team All-American in lacrosse (43 goals in 10 games to rank second in scoring nationally). He is in the Lacrosse Hall of Fame. He was inducted into the College Football Hall of Fame in 1995.

Brown was taken in the first round of the 1957 NFL draft by the Cleveland Browns, the sixth overall selection. In the ninth game of his rookie season, against the Los Angeles Rams he rushed for 237 yards, setting an NFL single-game record that stood unsurpassed for 14 years and a rookie record that remained for 40 years. Brown broke the single-season rushing record in 1958.

In his professional career, Jim Brown carried the ball 2,359 times for 12,312 rushing yards and 106 touchdowns, which were all records when, after nine years in the NFL, he retired as the league's record holder for both single-season (1,863 in 1963) and career rushing. Jim was the first player ever to reach the 100-rushing-touchdowns milestone and is the only player in NFL history to average over 100 rushing yards per game for his career.

Every season he played, Brown was voted into the Pro Bowl, despite not playing past 29 years of age. Brown's six games with at least four touchdowns remains an NFL record. He was also recognized as the AP NFL Most Valuable Player three times, and won an NFL championship with the Browns in 1964. He led the league in rushing yards in eight out of his nine seasons, and by the time he retired, he shattered most major rushing records as the first NFL player ever to rush for over 10,000 yards. Shortly before the end of his football career, Brown became an actor, and had several leading roles throughout the 1970s.

Jim Brown was enshrined in the Pro Football Hall of Fame in 1971. He was named to the NFL 75th Anniversary All-Time Team, and later to the NFL 100th Anniversary All-Time Team, comprising the best players in NFL history. In 2002, Jim Brown was named by *The Sporting News* as the greatest professional football player ever. In 2020, Jim Brown was honored at CFP championship game as the greatest college football player of all time. His number 32 jersey is retired by the Browns.

Wilma Glodean Rudolph (June 23, 1940 – November 12, 1994) was an African-American sprinter born in Saint Bethlehem, Tennessee, who became a world-record-holding Olympic champion and international sports icon in track and field following her successes in the 1956 and 1960 Olympic Games.

Rudolph competed in the 200-meter dash and won a bronze medal in the 4 × 100-meter relay at the 1956 Summer Olympics at Melbourne, Australia. She also won three gold medals, in the 100- and 200-meter individual events and the 4 x 100-meter relay at the 1960 Summer Olympics in Rome, Italy. Rudolph was acclaimed the fastest woman in the world in the 1960s and became the first American woman to win three gold medals in a single Olympic Games.

Due to the worldwide television coverage of the 1960 Summer Olympics, Rudolph became an international star along with other Olympic athletes such as Cassius Clay (later known as Muhammad Ali), Oscar Robertson, and Rafer Johnson who competed in Italy.

As an Olympic champion in the early 1960s, Rudolph was among the most highly visible black women in America and abroad. She became a role model for black and female athletes and her Olympic successes helped elevate women's track and field in the United States. Rudolph is also regarded as a civil rights and women's rights pioneer. In 1962 Rudolph retired from competition at the peak of her athletic career as the world record-holder in the 100- and 200-meter individual events and the 4 × 100-meter relays.

After competing in the 1960 Summer Olympics, the 1963 graduate of Tennessee State University became an educator and coach. Rudolph died of brain and throat cancer in 1994, and her achievements are memorialized in a variety of tributes, including a U.S. postage stamp, documentary films, and a made-for-television movie, as well as in numerous publications, especially books for young readers.

John Wesley Carlos (born June 5, 1945) is an American former track and field athlete and professional football player. He was the bronze-medal winner in the 200-meters at the 1968 Summer Olympics, and his Black Power salute on the podium with Tommie Smith caused much political controversy.

The 1968 Olympic Trials were held on the Californian side of Lake Tahoe at Echo Summit trailhead, which at 7,377 feet above sea level is approximately the same altitude as Mexico City. He went on to tie the world record in the 100-yard dash and beat the 200 meters world record (although the latter achievement was never certified). Carlos won the 200-meter dash in 19.92 seconds, beating world-record holder Tommie Smith and surpassing his record by 0.3 seconds. Though the record was never ratified because the spike formation on Carlos' shoes ("brush spikes") was not accepted at the time, the race reinforced his status as a world-class sprinter.

Carlos became a founding member of the Olympic Project for Human Rights (OPHR), and originally advocated a boycott of the 1968 Mexico City Olympic Games unless four conditions were met: withdrawal of South Africa and Rhodesia from the games, restoration of Muhammad Ali's world heavyweight boxing title, Avery Brundage to step down as president of the IOC, and the hiring of more African-American assistant coaches. As the boycott failed to achieve support after the IOC withdrew invitations for South Africa and Rhodesia, he decided, together with Smith, to participate but to stage a protest in case he received a medal. Following his third-place finish behind fellow American Smith and Australian Peter Norman in the 200 at the Mexico Olympics, Carlos and Smith made headlines around the world by raising their black-gloved fists at the medal award ceremony. Both athletes wore black socks and no shoes on the podium to represent African-American poverty in the United States. In support, Peter Norman, the silver medalist who was a white athlete from Australia, participated in the protest by wearing an OPHR badge.

In response to their actions, International Olympic Committee (IOC) president Avery Brundage ordered Smith and Carlos suspended from the US team and banned from the Olympic Village.

John Carlos was also the gold medalist at 200 meters at the 1967 Pan American Games in Winnipeg, Manitoba, Canada and set indoor world bests in the 60-yard dash (5.9) and the indoor 220-yard dash (21.2).

Following his retirement from football, John Carlos worked for Puma, the United States Olympic Committee, the Organizing Committee of the 1984 Summer Olympics and the City of Los Angeles.

In 1985, Carlos became a counselor and in-school suspension supervisor, as well as the track and field coach, at Palm Springs High School in California. In 2003, he was elected to the National Track & Field Hall of Fame. In 2003, he was elected to the National Track & Field Hall of Fame.

On July 16, 2008, John Carlos and Tommie Smith accepted the Arthur Ashe Award for Courage for their salute, at the 2008 ESPY Awards held at NOKIA Theatre L.A. LIVE in Los Angeles, California.

Michael Spinks (born July 13, 1956) is an American former professional boxer who competed from 1977 to 1988. He held world championships in two weight classes, including the undisputed light heavyweight title from 1983 to 1985, and the lineal heavyweight title from 1985 to 1988. As an amateur he won a gold medal in the middleweight division at the 1976 Summer Olympics.

Spinks is the brother of former world heavyweight champion Leon Spinks, and uncle of Cory Spinks, a former welterweight and light middleweight champion.

After a successful amateur career, which culminated in his Olympic gold medal win, Spinks went undefeated in his first 31 professional fights.

After 10 successful title defenses, Spinks moved up to heavyweight, and as an underdog defeated long-reigning IBF heavyweight champion Larry Holmes; in doing so, Spinks became the first reigning light heavyweight world champion to win the heavyweight title. In his final fight, Spinks was knocked out by Mike Tyson in 91 seconds, the only defeat of his professional career.

Spinks has been inducted into the International Boxing Hall of Fame and the World Boxing Hall of Fame. The International Boxing Research Organization and BoxRec rank Spinks among the 10 greatest light heavyweights of all time.

Florence Delorez Griffith Joyner (born **Florence Delorez Griffith**; December 21, 1959 – September 21, 1998), also known as **Flo-Jo**, was an American track and field athlete.

She is considered the fastest woman of all time based on the fact that the world records she set in 1988 for both the 100 m and 200 m still stand. During the late 1980s she became a popular figure in international track and field because of her record-setting performances and flashy personal style.

Griffith-Joyner was born and raised in California. She was athletic from a young age and began running track meets as a child. While attending California State University, Northridge (CSUN) and University of California, Los Angeles (UCLA), she continued to compete in track and field. While still in college, Griffith-Joyner qualified for the 100 m 1980 Olympics, although she did not actually compete due to the U.S. boycott. She made her Olympic debut four years later, winning a silver medal in the 200 meter distance at the 1984 Olympics held in Los Angeles. At the 1988 U.S. Olympic trials, Griffith set a new world record in the 100 meter sprint. She went on to win three gold medals at the 1988 Olympics.

In February 1989, she abruptly retired. After her retirement from athletics, Griffith-Joyner remained a pop culture figure through endorsement deals, acting, and designing. She died in her sleep as the result of an epileptic seizure in 1998 at the age of 38.

Frederick Carlton "Carl" Lewis (born July 1, 1961) is an American former track and field athlete who won nine Olympic gold medals, one Olympic silver medal, and 10 World Championships medals, including eight gold. His career spanned from 1979 to 1996, when he last won an Olympic event. He is one of only three Olympic athletes who won a gold medal in the same individual event in four consecutive Olympic Games.

Lewis was a dominant sprinter and long jumper who topped the world rankings in the 100 m, 200 m and long jump events frequently from 1981 to the early 1990s. He set world records in the 100 m, 4 × 100 m and 4 × 200 m relays, while his world record in the indoor long jump has stood since 1984. His 65 consecutive victories in the long jump achieved over a span of 10 years is one of the sport's longest undefeated streaks. Over the course of his athletics career, Lewis broke ten seconds for the 100 meters 15 times and 20 seconds for the 200 meters 10 times. Lewis also long jumped over 28 feet 71 times.

Carl Lewis' accomplishments have led to numerous accolades, including being voted "World Athlete of the Century" by the International Association of Athletics Federations and "Sportsman of the Century" by the International Olympic Committee, "Olympian of the Century" by *Sports Illustrated* and "Athlete of the Year" by *Track & Field News* in 1982, 1983, and 1984.

After retiring from his athletics career, Lewis became an actor and has appeared in a number of films.

Jerry Lee Rice Sr. (born October 13, 1962) is an American former professional football player who was a wide receiver in the National Football League (NFL), primarily with the San Francisco 49ers. Due to his numerous records, accomplishments, and accolades, he is widely regarded as the greatest wide receiver in NFL history.

Rice had a record-setting 1983 campaign, including NCAA marks for receptions (102) and receiving yards (1,450), and was named a first-team Division I-AA All-American. He also set a single-game NCAA record by catching 24 passes against Louisiana's Southern University. As a senior in 1984, he broke his own Division I-AA records for receptions (112) and receiving yards (1,845). His 27 touchdown receptions in that 1984 season set the NCAA record for all divisions. In 1999, *The Sporting News* listed Rice second behind Jim Brown on its list of "Football's 100 Greatest Players".

At the conclusion of the 2004 season—his 20th in the NFL—Rice initially opted to join the Denver Broncos for a one-year deal, but ultimately decided he would rather retire than be at the bottom of any team's depth chart. In August 2006, the 49ers announced that Rice would sign a contract with them, allowing him to retire as a member of the team where his NFL career began. On August 24, he officially retired as a 49er, signing a one-day contract for $1,985,806.49. The number represented the year Rice was drafted (1985), his number (80), the year he retired (2006), and the 49ers (49). The figure was ceremonial, and Rice received no money. There was a halftime ceremony to honor him during the 49ers' match-up with the Seattle Seahawks on November 19, 2006.

Over the course of his career, Rice played more games than any non-placekicker or punter in NFL history, playing 303 games overall. (Quarterback George Blanda played 340 games, but he was also a placekicker.)

Rice was selected for induction in the Pro Football Hall of Fame class of 2010 in his first year of eligibility. He was inducted in Canton, Ohio on August 7, 2010. On September 20, 2010, during halftime of a game against the Saints, the 49ers retired Rice's No. 80 jersey.

Rice has scored more points than any other non-kicker in NFL history with 1,256. Rice was selected to the Pro Bowl 13 times (1986–1996, 1998, 2002) and named All-Pro 12 times in his 20 NFL seasons. He won three Super Bowls with the 49ers and an AFC Championship with the Oakland Raiders.

Jerry Rice was inducted into the College Football Hall of Fame in 2006. He was also inducted into the Mississippi Sports Hall of Fame in 2007, and in that same year inducted into the Bay Area Sports Hall of Fame. In 2010, he was chosen by NFL Network's NFL Films production *The Top 100: NFL's Greatest Players* as the greatest player in NFL history. He was also inducted into the Pro Football Hall of Fame in 2010As of 2017, Jerry Rice holds over 100 NFL records, the most of any player by a wide margin.

Emmitt James Smith III (born May 15, 1969) is an American former professional football player who was a running back for fifteen seasons in the National Football League (NFL) during the 1990s and 2000s, primarily with the Dallas Cowboys. A three-time Super Bowl champion with the Cowboys, he is the league's all-time leading rusher.

Smith grew up in Pensacola, Florida and became the second-leading rusher in American high school football history while playing for Escambia High School. Smith played three years of college football for the Florida Gators, where he set numerous school rushing records. After being named a unanimous All-American in 1989, Smith chose to forgo his senior year of eligibility and play professionally.

The Cowboys selected Smith in the first round of the 1990 NFL draft. He holds the record for career rushing touchdowns with 164. Smith is the only running back to ever win a Super Bowl championship, the NFL Most Valuable Player award, the NFL rushing crown, and the Super Bowl Most Valuable Player award all in the same season (1993).

Emmett Smith is also one of four running backs to lead the NFL in rushing three or more consecutive seasons, joining Steve Van Buren, Jim Brown and Earl Campbell. Smith led the league in rushing and won the Super Bowl in the same year three times (1992, 1993, and 1995) when to that point it had never been done.

In 1996, Smith scored his 100th career rushing touchdown and surpassed 10,000 career rushing yards, becoming just the twelfth player in league history and the youngest one to reach this milestone.

In 1998, he became the Cowboys' all-time leading rusher (passing Dorsett) and the NFL's all-time rushing touchdown leader (surpassing Marcus Allen). The next year, he became the NFL's all-time leader in career postseason rushing yards (1,586) and postseason rushing touchdowns (19).

With 1,021 rushing yards in 2001, Smith became the first player in NFL history with 11 consecutive 1,000-yard seasons and the first to post eleven 1,000-yard rushing seasons in a career.

In 2002, he reached the goal he set as a rookie, finishing the season with 17,162 career yards and breaking the NFL rushing record previously held by Walter Payton against the Seattle Seahawks. After the season, the Cowboys hired head coach Bill Parcells who wanted to go with younger running backs and released Smith on February 26, 2003.

On March 26, 2003, Smith signed a two-year contract as a free agent with the Arizona Cardinals. On October 5, in a highly anticipated game, he returned to Texas Stadium to play against the Cowboys, but suffered a broken left shoulder blade after safety Roy Williams hit him in the second quarter. The injury forced him to miss 6 games, and he eventually finished the season with 256 rushing yards and averaged just 2.8 yards per carry.

In 2004, new head coach Dennis Green was hired and named Smith as the team's starter at running back. He posted 937 rushing yards and 9 touchdowns. He also became the oldest player in NFL history ever to throw his first touchdown pass.

Three days before Super Bowl XXXIX on February 3, 2005, Smith announced his retirement from the NFL. He was not re-signed by the Cardinals and signed a one-day contract for one dollar with the Dallas Cowboys, after which he immediately retired with the team he had played with for most of his career.

Smith is one of only two non-kickers in NFL history to score more than 1,000 career points (the other being Jerry Rice). Smith was inducted into the College Football Hall of Fame in 2006 and the Pro Football Hall of Fame in 2010.

Dwayne Douglas Johnson (born May 2, 1972), also known by his ring name, **The Rock**, is an American actor, producer, investor and retired professional wrestler. Johnson was a professional wrestler for the World Wrestling Federation (WWF, now WWE) for eight years prior to pursuing an acting career. His films have grossed over $3.5 billion in North America and over $10.5 billion worldwide, making Johnson one of the most successful and highest-grossing box-office stars of all time.

Dwayne Johnson was a college football player for the University of Miami, with whom he won a national championship in 1991. He initially aspired for a professional career in football and entered the 1995 NFL Draft, but he went undrafted. As a result, Dwayne signed with the Calgary Stampeders of the Canadian Football League (CFL), but was cut from the team in the middle of his first season. Shortly after, he began training as a professional wrestler.

In 1996, Dwayne Johnson secured a contract with the WWF and was promoted as the first third-generation wrestler in the company's history, as he is the son of Rocky Johnson and grandson of Peter Maivia. He subsequently won his first WWF Championship in 1998 and helped usher the WWF into the "Attitude Era", a boom period in the company's business in the latter 1990s and early 2000s which still hold professional wrestling records for television ratings. In 2004, he left the WWE to pursue an acting career and went on a seven-year hiatus before returning in 2011 as a part-time performer until 2013, before wholly retiring in 2019.

Considered to be one of the greatest professional wrestlers and biggest draws of all-time, The Rock headlined the most-bought professional wrestling pay-per-view event ever, WrestleMania XXVIII, and was featured in among the most watched episodes of WWE's television shows, *WWE Raw* and *WWE SmackDown*. He has won several championships, being a two-time Intercontinental Champion, a five-time tag team champion, and a ten-time world champion. He was also a Royal Rumble match winner and WWE's sixth Triple Crown champion.

The Rock made the *Time* 100 Most Influential People in the World list in both 2016 and 2019. He is a dual citizen of both the United States and Canada.

Alexander Emmanuel Rodriguez (born July 27, 1975), nicknamed "**A-Rod**", is an American former professional baseball shortstop and third baseman who played 22 seasons in Major League Baseball (MLB). He played seven seasons with Seattle Mariners, three seasons with the Texas Rangers and twelve seasons with the New York Yankees. Rodriguez began his professional career as one of the sport's most highly touted prospects and is considered to be one of the greatest baseball players of all time. Rodriguez amassed a .295 batting average, over 600 home runs (696), over 2,000 runs batted in (RBI), over 2,000 runs scored, over 3,000 hits, and over 300 stolen bases, the only player in MLB history to achieve all of those feats. He was also a 14-time All-Star, winning three American League (AL) Most Valuable Player (MVP) Awards, ten Silver Slugger Awards, and two Gold Glove Awards. Rodríguez is also the career record holder for grand slams with 25. He signed two of the most lucrative sports contracts in baseball.

After retiring as a player, Rodriguez became a media personality, serving as a broadcaster for Fox Sports 1, a cast member of *Shark Tank* and a member of the ABC News network.

Thomas Edward Patrick Brady Jr. (born August 3, 1977) aka **Tom Brady** is an American football quarterback for the New England Patriots of the National Football League (NFL). Brady has played in a record nine Super Bowls, winning six of them (XXXVI, XXXVIII, XXXIX, XLIX, LI, and LIII), the most of any player in NFL history. He has won a record four Super Bowl MVP awards (XXXVI, XXXVIII, XLIX, and LI) as well as three NFL MVP awards (2007, 2010, 2017). Due to his numerous records and accolades, many sports writers, commentators, players (current and former) consider Brady to be the greatest quarterback of all time.

After playing college football for the University of Michigan, Brady was drafted 199th overall by the Patriots in the sixth round of the 2000 NFL Draft. Due to his late selection, Brady is considered the biggest "steal" in the history of the NFL Draft. He went on to become the team's starting quarterback in his second season after an injury to Drew Bledsoe, and has been with the Patriots for 20 seasons, the NFL record for seasons as quarterback for one team. He is one of only two quarterbacks to win a Super Bowl in their first season as a starter.

The only quarterback to reach 200 regular-season wins, Brady is the winningest quarterback in NFL history, and has never had a losing season as a starting quarterback. He has led his team to more division titles (16) than any other quarterback in NFL history. With a postseason record of 30–11, he is first all-time in playoff wins and appearances for an NFL player. Brady has led the Patriots to an NFL-record eight consecutive AFC championship games since 2011 (and 13 overall). Brady has also been selected to 14 Pro Bowls, which ties the NFL record for most selections.

For regular season and postseason combined, Brady is first all-time in career passing yards and touchdown passes. He is one of only two players in NFL history to amass 70,000 passing yards and 1,000 rushing yards. Brady is second all-time in career regular season passing yards, second in career touchdown passes, and tied for fifth in career passer rating. He is first in postseason career completions, passing yards, and passing touchdowns, tied for 14th in postseason career passer rating. He also tied the record for the longest touchdown pass at 99 yards to Wes Welker.

Brady's two-year deal with the Buccaneers includes $50 million guaranteed along with another $9 million in incentives, Adam Schefter of ESPN reports.

Schefter also notes that the agreement includes a clause that prevents the team from franchise tagging the QB after two years, which suggests that Brady -- who turns 43 in August -- "has ideas of playing beyond this contract." In the meantime, he'll look forward to working with a talented group of pass-catchers in Tampa Bay that currently includes wide receivers Mike Evans and Chris Godwin, as well as tight ends O.J. Howard and Cameron Brate.

Tom Brady, at the age of 42, completed a 2019 season with the New England Patriots, which drafted him in 2000. Brady retired from the Patriots, thus becoming a Free Agent, and then he finalized a contract on March 18, 2020 with the Tampa Bay Buccaneers. Brady's two-year deal with the Buccaneers includes $50 million guaranteed along with another $9 million in incentives. Brady will have former Patriots teammate Rob Gronkowski as his No. 1 tight end in Tampa Bay during the 2020 season following Rob's trade acquisition.

Patrick Lavon Mahomes II (born September 17, 1995) is an American football quarterback for the Kansas City Chiefs of the National Football League (NFL). Patrick Mahomes is the third African-American quarterback to win the Super Bowl after Doug Williams and Russell Wilson. He is the second youngest quarterback (24 years and 138 days) to win the Super Bowl after Ben Roethlisberger (23 years and 320 days) and is the youngest quarterback to win Super Bowl MVP.

He is the son of former Major League Baseball (MLB) pitcher Pat Mahomes. He initially played college football and college baseball at Texas Tech University. Following his sophomore year, Mahomes quit baseball to focus solely on football. In his junior year, he led all NCAA Division I FBS players in multiple categories including passing yards (5,052 yards) and passing touchdowns (53 touchdowns). He then entered the 2017 NFL Draft where he was the tenth overall selection by the Kansas City Chiefs.

Mahomes spent his rookie season as the backup to Alex Smith. After the Chiefs traded Smith to the Washington Redskins the following season, Mahomes was named the starter. That season, Mahomes threw for 5,097 yards, 50 touchdowns, and 12 interceptions. He became the only quarterback in history to throw for over 5,000 yards in a season in both college and the NFL. He also joined Peyton Manning as the only players in NFL history to throw 50 touchdown passes and 5,000 yards in a single season.

For his performance in his first season as starter, Mahomes was named to the Pro Bowl, named First Team All-Pro, and won the NFL Offensive Player of the Year and NFL Most Valuable Player awards. Mahomes, along with Lamar Jackson, Cam Newton, and Steve McNair, is one of only four African-American quarterbacks to win the AP MVP award.

During the 2019–20 playoffs, Mahomes led the Chiefs to Super Bowl LIV, their first Super Bowl appearance in 50 years, where they defeated the San Francisco 49ers for their first Super Bowl victory since 1970. Mahomes was awarded the Super Bowl Most Valuable Player for his performance, becoming the second African-American quarterback to win the award after Doug Williams.

Gabrielle "Gabby" Christina Victoria Douglas (born December 31, 1995) is an American artistic gymnast. Gabby Douglas is the first African American and the first of African descent of any nationality in Olympic history to become the individual all-around champion. She is also the first U.S. gymnast to win gold in both the individual all-around and team competitions at the same Olympics as well as the 2016 AT&T American Cup all-around champion.

Gabby began training in gymnastics at age six when her older sister convinced their mother to enroll her in gymnastics classes. In

October 2002, Douglas began her training at Gymstrada. At the age of eight, Douglas won the Level 4 all-around gymnastics title at the 2004 Virginia State Championships.

Gabby Douglas made her international debut in 2008 at the US Classic in Houston, Texas, where she placed 10th place in the all-around rankings. She went on to compete at the 2008 Visa Championships in Boston, Massachusetts. Placing 16th in that competition, Douglas was not eligible for the 2008 Junior Women's National Team.

At fourteen, she moved to Des Moines, Iowa, to train full-time with coach Liang Chow. Because her family had to stay in Virginia while her siblings finished school, she lived with Travis and Missy Parton and their four daughters, one of whom also trained at Chow's gym. However, Gabby struggled to fit in because of the separation from her family and hometown.

In 2009, Gabby suffered a fracture in the growth plate of her wrist. Due to this injury, she was not able to compete and missed the 2009 Covergirl US Classic. While she competed at the 2009 Visa Championships in Dallas, Texas, Gabby was unable to perform her full routines and competed only on balance beam and floor exercise.

In 2011 at the City of Jesolo Trophy in Italy, Gabby Douglas was part of the US team that won gold. She also placed second on floor, tied for third on beam, and placed fourth in the all-around and on vault. That same year, Douglas earned the silver medal in uneven bars at the CoverGirl Classic in Chicago.

At the 2011 U.S. National Championships in St. Paul, Minnesota, Gabby tied for third on bars and placed seventh all-around. That same year, at the 2011 World Championships in Tokyo, Japan,

Gabby shared in the team gold medal won by the U.S. Douglas also placed fifth in uneven bars.

At the 2012 AT&T American Cup at Madison Square Garden in March, Gabby Douglas received the highest total all-around score in the women's competition, ahead of her teammate and current world champion Jordyn Wieber. However, her scores did not count towards winning the competition because she was an alternate.

At the 2012 U.S. National Championships in June, Gabby won the gold medal in uneven bars, silver in the all-around, and bronze in floor. Márta Károlyi, the National Team Coordinator for USA Gymnastics, nicknamed Douglas the "Flying Squirrel" for her aerial performance on the uneven bars.

At the 2012 Olympic Trials held in San Jose, California on July 1, Gabby placed first in the all-around rankings, securing the only guaranteed spot on the women's Olympic gymnastics team. She was part of the gold-winning U.S. team at the Pacific Rim Championships, where she also won gold in uneven bars. She is the 2012 Olympic all-around champion, the 2015 World all-around silver medalist, and also a member of the 2015 World Championships.

Gabby was a member of the 2016 Summer Olympics. She helped the United States win a second consecutive gold medal in the team event, which was also her third Olympic gold medal. When the team final scores were announced, Gabby and her teammates called themselves the "Final Five" in honor of coach Marta Karolyi's retirement and the team size being reduced to four beginning in 2020.

ACTORS AND ACTRESSES WHO MAKE THE GRADE ...

Hattie McDaniel (June 10, 1895 – October 26, 1952) was an American actress of stage and screen, professional singer-songwriter, and comedian. She is best known for her role as "Mammy" in *Gone with the Wind* (1939), for which she won the Academy Award for Best Supporting Actress, the first Oscar won by a black entertainer.

McDaniel was born to former slaves in Wichita, Kansas. She was the youngest of 13 children. Her mother, Susan Holbert, was a singer of gospel music, and her father, Henry McDaniel, fought in the Civil War with the 122nd United States Colored Troops. In 1900, the family moved to Colorado, living first in Fort Collins and then in Denver, where Hattie attended Denver East High School. Her brother, Sam McDaniel, played the butler in the 1948 Three Stooges' short film *Heavenly Daze*. Her sister Etta McDaniel was also an actress.

McDaniel was a songwriter as well as a performer. She honed her songwriting skills while working with her brother's minstrel show. After the death of her brother Otis in 1916, the troupe began to lose money, and Hattie did not get her next big break until 1920. From 1920 to 1925, she appeared with Professor George Morrison's *Melody Hounds*, a black touring ensemble. In the mid-1920s, she embarked on a radio career, singing with the Melody Hounds on station KOA in Denver. From 1926 to 1929, she recorded many of her songs for Okeh Records and Paramount Records in Chicago.

McDaniel recorded seven sessions: one in the summer of 1926 on the rare Kansas City label Meritt; four sessions in Chicago for Okeh from late 1926 to late 1927 (of the 10 sides recorded, only four were issued), and two sessions in Chicago for Paramount in March 1929.

After the stock market crashed in 1929, McDaniel could find work only as a washroom attendant and waitress at Club Madrid in Milwaukee. Despite the owner's reluctance to let her perform, she was eventually allowed to take the stage and soon became a regular performer.

In 1931, McDaniel moved to Los Angeles to join her brother and two sisters. When she could not get film work, she took jobs as a maid or cook. Sam was working on a KNX radio program, *The Optimistic Do-Nut Hour*, and was able to get his sister a spot. She performed on radio as "Hi-Hat Hattie", a bossy maid who often "forgets her place". Her show became popular, but her salary was so low that she had to continue working as a maid.

She made her first film appearance in *The Golden West* (1932), in which she played a maid. Her second appearance came in the highly successful Mae West film *I'm No Angel* (1933), in which she played one of the black maids with whom West camped it up backstage. She received several other uncredited film roles in the early 1930s, often singing in choruses.

In addition to acting in many films, McDaniel recorded 16 blues sides between 1926–1929 (10 were issued), was a radio performer and television star; she was the first black woman to sing on radio in the United States. She appeared in over 300 films, although she received screen credits for only 83.

McDaniel has two stars on the Hollywood Walk of Fame in Hollywood: one at 6933 Hollywood Boulevard for her contributions to radio and one at 1719 Vine Street for acting in motion pictures. In 1975, she was inducted into the Black Filmmakers Hall of Fame and in 2006 became the first black Oscar winner honored with a US postage stamp. In 2010, she was inducted into the Colorado Women's Hall of Fame.

Harry Belafonte (March 1, 1927) is an American singer, songwriter, activist, and actor. One of the most successful Jamaican-American pop stars in history, he was dubbed the "King of Calypso" for popularizing the Caribbean musical style with an international audience in the 1950s. His breakthrough album *Calypso* (1956) is the first million-selling LP by a single artist. Belafonte is known for his recording of "The Banana Boat Song", with its signature lyric "Day-O".

Belafonte was born Harold George Bellanfanti Jr. at Lying-in Hospital on March 1, 1927, in Harlem, New York, the son of Melvine Love, a housekeeper, and Harold George Bellanfanti Sr., who worked as a chef. His mother was born in Jamaica, the child of a Scottish white mother and a black father. His father also was born in Jamaica, the child of a black mother and Dutch Jewish father of Sephardi origins. Belafonte has described his grandfather, whom he never met, as "a white Dutch Jew who drifted over to the islands after chasing gold and diamonds, with no luck at all". From 1932 to 1940, he lived with one of his grandmothers in her native country of Jamaica, where he attended Wolmer's Schools.

When he returned to New York City, he attended George Washington High School after which he joined the Navy and served during World War II. In the 1940s, he was working as a janitor's assistant in NYC when a tenant gave him, as a gratuity, two tickets to see the American Negro Theater. He fell in love with the art form and also met Sidney Poitier. The financially struggling pair regularly purchased a single seat to local plays, trading places in between acts, after informing the other about the progression of the play. At the end of the 1940s, he took classes in acting at the Dramatic Workshop of The New School in New York with the influential German director Erwin Piscator alongside Marlon Brando, Tony Curtis, Walter Matthau, Bea Arthur, and Sidney Poitier, while performing with the American Negro Theatre. He subsequently received a Tony Award for his participation in the Broadway revue *John Murray Anderson's Almanac*.

Harry Belafonte has recorded and performed in many genres, including blues, folk, gospel, show tunes, and American standards. He has also starred in several films, including Otto Preminger's hit musical *Carmen Jones* (1954), *Island in the Sun* (1957), and Robert Wise's *Odds Against Tomorrow* (1959).

Belafonte was an early supporter of the Civil Rights Movement in the 1950s and 1960s and was a confidant of Martin Luther King Jr.. Throughout his career, he has been an advocate for political and humanitarian causes, such as the Anti-Apartheid Movement and USA for Africa. Since 1987, he has been a UNICEF Goodwill Ambassador. He was a vocal critic of the policies of the George W. Bush presidential administrations. Belafonte acts as the American Civil Liberties Union celebrity ambassador for juvenile justice issues.

Belafonte has won three Grammy Awards (including a Grammy Lifetime Achievement Award), an Emmy Award, and a Tony Award. In 1989, he received the Kennedy Center Honors. He was awarded the National Medal of Arts in 1994. In 2014, he received the Jean Hersholt Humanitarian Award at the Academy's 6th Annual Governors Awards.

Diahann Carroll born **Carol Diann Johnson** (July 17, 1935 – October 4, 2019) was an American actress, singer, model, and activist. She rose to prominence in some of the earliest major studio films to feature black casts, including *Carmen Jones* (1954) and *Porgy and Bess* (1959). In 1962, Carroll won a Tony Award for best actress, a first for an African American woman, for her role in the Broadway musical *No Strings.*

Carol Diahann Johnson was born in the Bronx, New York City, to John Johnson, a subway conductor, and Mabel (Faulk), a nurse. While Carroll was still an infant, the family moved to Harlem, where she grew up. She attended Music and Art High School, and was a classmate of Billy Dee Williams. In many interviews about her childhood, Carroll recalls her parents' support, and their enrolling her in dance, singing, and modeling classes. By the time Carroll was 15, she was modeling for *Ebony*. She also began entering television contests, including *Arthur Godfrey's Talent Scouts,* under the name Diahann Carroll.

Carroll's big break came at age 18, when she appeared as a contestant on the DuMont Television Network program, *Chance of a Lifetime*, hosted by Dennis James. On the show, which aired January 8, 1954, she took the $1,000 top prize for a rendition of the Jerome Kern/Oscar Hammerstein song, "Why Was I Born?" She went on to win the following four weeks. Engagements at Manhattan's Café Society and Latin Quarter nightclubs soon followed.

Carroll's film debut was a supporting role in *Carmen Jones* (1954), as a friend to the sultry lead character played by Dorothy Dandridge. That same year, she starred in the Broadway musical, *House of Flowers*. A few years later, she played Clara in the film version of George Gershwin's *Porgy and Bess* (1959), but her character's singing parts were dubbed by opera singer Loulie Jean Norman. The following year, Carroll made a guest appearance in the series *Peter Gunn*, in the episode "Sing a Song of Murder" (1960). In the next two years, she starred with Sidney Poitier, Paul Newman, and Joanne Woodward in the film *Paris Blues* (1961) and won the 1962 Tony Award for best actress (the first time for a Black woman) for portraying Barbara Woodruff in the Samuel A. Taylor and Richard Rodgers musical *No Strings*.

Twelve years later, she was nominated for an Academy Award for Best Actress for her starring role alongside James Earl Jones in the film *Claudine* (1974), which part had been written specifically for actress Diana Sands (who had made guest appearances on *Julia* as Carroll's cousin Sara), but shortly before filming was to begin, Sands learned she was terminally ill with cancer. Sands attempted to carry on with the role, but as filming began, she became too ill to continue and recommended her friend Carroll take over the role. Sands died in September 1973, before the film's release in April 1974.

Her 1968 debut in *Julia*, the first series on American television to star a Black woman in a non-stereotypical role, was a milestone both in her career and the medium. In the 1980s, she played the role of Dominique Deveraux, a mixed-race diva, in the prime time soap opera *Dynasty*. Carroll was the recipient of numerous stage and screen nominations and awards, including the Golden Globe Award for Best Actress In a Television Series in 1968. She received an Academy Award for Best Actress nomination for the film *Claudine* (1974). Diahann Carroll died on October 4, 2019 after a battle with breast cancer.

Lynn (Butler-Smith) Whitfield (born February 8, 1953) is an American actress and producer. She began her acting career in television and theatre, before progressing to supporting roles in film.

She won a Primetime Emmy Award for Outstanding Lead Actress in a Limited Series or Movie and received a Golden Globe Award nomination for her performance as Josephine Baker in the HBO biographical drama film *The Josephine Baker Story* (1991).

Whitfield spent her career after her breakthrough performance as Josephine Baker, playing the leading roles in a number of made for television movies in the 1990s, and had several starring roles in films, include performances in *A Thin Line Between Love and Hate* (1996), *Gone Fishin'* (1997), *Eve's Bayou* (1997), *Stepmom* (1998), *Head of State* (2003), *Madea's Family Reunion* (2006) and *The Women* (2008). Whitfield also starred in a number of smaller movies in the 2000s and 2010s. In 2016, she began starring as villainous Lady Mae Greenleaf in the Oprah Winfrey Network drama series, *Greenleaf*. Whitfield has won seven NAACP Image Awards.

Whitfield was born in Baton Rouge, Louisiana, the daughter of Jean Butler, who is African-American, an officer of a finance agency, and Valerian Smith who is Creole, a dentist. She is the eldest of four children and a third-generation BFA graduate from Howard University. Her dentist father was instrumental in developing Lynn's initial interest in acting as he was a prime figure in forming community theater in her native Baton Rouge.

First garnering attention on the stage by studying and performing with the Black Repertory Company in Washington, D.C, Lynne married one of the company's co-founders and pioneers of black theatre, playwright/director/actor Vantile Whitfield in 1974. She eventually moved to New York and appeared off-Broadway in such shows as *The Great Macdaddy* and *Showdown* before earning acclaim in the 1977 Los Angeles production of the landmark play 'for colored girls who have considered suicide / when the rainbow is enuf' co-starring alongside Alfre Woodard.

Lynn Whitfield won an NAACP Image Award for Outstanding Supporting Actress in a Drama Series in 2019 and well as Gracie Award for Outstanding Female Actor in a Supporting Role in a Drama Series in 2017. In 2018, she co-starred opposite Sanaa Lathan in the romantic comedy film *Nappily Ever After*, the film was released on Netflix.

Clifton Powell (born March 16, 1956) is an American actor, who primarily plays supporting roles in films, such as in *Ray* (2004), for which he received an NAACP Image Award for Outstanding Supporting Actor in a Motion Picture nomination.

Powell was born in Washington, D.C., and grew up in Mayfair Mansions in Northeast D.C. Powell is a graduate of the Duke Ellington School of the Arts. Powell was married to Kimberly, with whom he has two children.

Clifton Powell has appeared in more than one hundred films, beginning in the 1980s. His credits include *Menace II Society* (1993), *Dead Presidents* (1995), *Why Do Fools Fall in Love* (1998), *Rush Hour* (1998), *Next Friday* (2000), and its 2002 sequel, *Friday After Next*, *Woman Thou Art Loosed* (2004), and *Ray* (2004). He played Martin Luther King, Jr. in the 1999 television film *Selma, Lord, Selma*. Powell also has had many supporting roles in smaller direct-to-video films in 2000s and 2010s.

On television, Powell had the recurring roles on *Roc*, *South Central*, and *Army Wives*, as well as guest-starred on *In the Heat of the Night*, *Murder, She Wrote*, *NYPD Blue*, and *CSI: Crime Scene Investigation*. In 2016, Powell was cast as main antagonist in the Bounce TV first prime time soap opera, *Saints & Sinners* opposite Vanessa Bell Calloway and Gloria Reuben.

Powell is also known for his voice acting role as the antagonist Big Smoke from the video game *Grand Theft Auto: San Andreas*. In 2017, he appeared in the second season of *My Step Kidz*.

Angela Evelyn Bassett (born August 16, 1958) is an American actress and activist known for her biographical film roles, most notably her performance as Tina Turner in the biopic *What's Love Got to Do with It* (1993), for which she was nominated for the Academy Award for Best Actress and won the Golden Globe Award for Best Actress – Motion Picture Comedy or Musical. Bassett has additionally portrayed real life figures Betty Shabazz in both *Malcolm X* (1992) and *Panther* (1995), Katherine Jackson in *The Jacksons: An American Dream* (1992), Voletta Wallace in *Notorious* (2009) and Coretta Scott King in *Betty & Coretta* (2013). Her other notable film roles include Reva Styles in *Boyz n the Hood* (1991), Bernie Harris in *Waiting to Exhale* (1995), Rachel Constantine in *Contact* (1997), Lynne Jacobs in *Olympus Has Fallen* (2013) and *London Has Fallen* (2016), and Queen Ramonda in *Black Panther* (2018) and *Avengers: Endgame* (2019).

Angela Bassett was born in the Harlem neighborhood of New York City, the daughter of Betty Jane Gilbert and Daniel Benjamin Bassett. Angela's parents divorced and she was raised with her sister, D'nette, in St. Petersburg, Florida by her single mother, Betty, a social worker.

After graduating from Jordan Park Elementary School, Angela began being bused out of her neighborhood to attend Disston Middle School for seventh grade. The year she began attending was 1970, the first year busing was implemented to integrate public schools in St. Petersburg. After completing seventh grade, she was bused to Azalea Middle School for eighth and ninth grade. On a high school trip, Angela became inspired to act after seeing a Kennedy Center production of the classic story *Of Mice and Men*, starring James Earl Jones.

Encouraged by a teacher, Angela went on to study at Yale on a scholarship, earning a B.A. in Afro-American Studies and an M.F.A. in drama. While there, she studied under the renowned stage director Lloyd Richards, who cast her in the Broadway productions of two August Wilson plays: *Ma Rainey's Black Bottom* and *Joe Turner's Come and Gone*.

At Boca Ciega High School, Angela was a cheerleader and a member of the Upward Bound college prep program, the debate team, student government, drama club and choir. During high school, Angela became the first African American from Boca Ciega to be admitted to the National Honor Society.

Bassett attended Yale University and received her B.A. degree in African-American studies in 1980. In 1983, she earned an M.F.A. degree from the Yale School of Drama, despite opposition from her father's sister who warned her to not "waste" her "Yale education on theater." She was the only member of Bassett's family to have gone to both college and graduate school. At Yale, Angela met her future husband Courtney B. Vance, a 1986 graduate of the drama school. She was also classmates with actor Charles S. Dutton.

After graduation, Angela worked as a receptionist for a beauty salon and as a photo researcher. She soon looked for acting work in the New York theater. One of her first New York performances came in 1985 when she appeared in J. E. Franklin's *Black Girl* at Second Stage Theatre. She appeared in two August Wilson plays at the Yale Repertory Theatre under the direction of her long-time instructor Lloyd Richards. The Wilson plays featuring Bassett were *Ma Rainey's Black Bottom* (1984) and *Joe Turner's Come and Gone*

(1986). In 2006, she had the opportunity to work on the Wilson canon again, starring in *Fences* alongside longtime collaborator Laurence Fishburne at the Pasadena Playhouse in California.

Bassett began her film career in the 1980s, after earning a bachelor of arts degree from Yale University and a master of fine arts degree from the Yale School of Drama. In the 1990s, she appeared in films nearly every year. The 2000s saw a succession of films starring Bassett, with her appearing in at least one film every year. Bassett's success has continued into the 2010s. Bassett earned nominations for her roles in films such as *The Score* (2001), *Akeelah and the Bee* (2006), *Meet the Browns* (2008) and *Jumping the Broom* (2011) and won awards for her performances in *How Stella Got Her Groove Back* (1998) and *Music of the Heart* (1999), among others. Bassett's performance as Rosa Parks in the 2002 film *The Rosa Parks Story* was honored with her first Primetime Emmy Award nomination.

In 2013, Bassett had a recurring role on the FX horror anthology series *American Horror Story: Coven*, earning her second Primetime Emmy Award nomination for her performance as Voodoo queen Marie Laveau. She returned for *Freak Show*, the series' fourth season, portraying a three-breasted woman named Desiree Dupree, for which she received another Emmy Award nomination. In 2018, Bassett began producing and starring in the Fox first responder drama series *9-1-1*, playing LAPD patrol sergeant Athena Grant.

That same year, Angela Basset was awarded an honorary D.F.A. degree from her alma mater, Yale University.

Forest Steven Whitaker III (born July 15, 1961) is an American actor, producer, and director. Whitaker has earned a reputation for intensive character study work for films such as *Bird*, *The Crying*

Game, *Platoon*, *Ghost Dog: The Way of the Samurai*, *The Great Debaters*, *The Butler*, and *Arrival*. He has also appeared in blockbusters such as *Rogue One: A Star Wars Story* as Saw Gerrera and *Black Panther* as Zuri.

Forest Steven Whitaker III was born on July 15, 1961, in Longview, Texas, the son of Laura Francis, a special education teacher who put herself through college and earned two master's degrees while raising her children, and Forest Steven Whitaker Jr., an insurance salesman. When Whitaker was four, his family moved to Carson, California. He has two younger brothers, Kenn and Damon, and an older sister, Deborah. His first role as an actor was the lead in Dylan Thomas' play *Under Milk Wood*.

Whitaker attended Palisades Charter High School, where he played on the football team and sang in the choir, graduating in 1979. He entered California State Polytechnic University, Pomona on a football scholarship, but a back injury made him change his major to music (singing). He toured England with the Cal Poly Chamber Singers in 1980. While still at Cal Poly, he briefly changed his major to drama. He was accepted to the Music Conservatory at the University of Southern California to study opera as a tenor and was subsequently accepted into the university's Drama Conservatory. He graduated from USC with a BFA in acting in 1982. He was pursuing a degree in "The Core of Conflict: Studies in Peace and Reconciliation" at New York University's Gallatin School of Individualized Study in 2004.

For his performance as Ugandan dictator Idi Amin in the 2006 film *The Last King of Scotland*, Whitaker won the Academy Award, BAFTA Award, Golden Globe Award, National Board of Review Award, Screen Actors Guild Award, and various critics groups' awards for a lead acting performance.

William Bradley "Brad" Pitt (born December 18, 1963) is an American actor and film producer. He has received multiple awards, including two Golden Globe Awards and an Academy Award for his acting, in addition to another Academy Award and a Primetime Emmy Award as producer under his production company, Plan B Entertainment.

Pitt was born in Shawnee, Oklahoma, to William Alvin Pitt, the proprietor of a trucking company, and Jane Etta Hillhouse, a school counselor. The family soon moved to Springfield, Missouri, where he lived along with his younger siblings, Douglas Mitchell (born 1966) and Julie Neal (born 1969). Born into a conservative Christian household, he was raised as Southern Baptist.

Pitt attended Kickapoo High School, where he was a member of the golf, swimming and tennis teams. He participated in the school's Key and Forensics clubs, in school debates, and in musicals. Following his graduation from high school, Pitt enrolled in the University of Missouri in 1982, majoring in journalism with a focus on advertising. As graduation approached, Pitt did not feel ready to settle down. He loved films—"a portal into different worlds for me"—and, since films were not made in Missouri, he decided to go to where they were made. Two weeks short of completing the coursework for a degree, Pitt left the university and moved to Los Angeles, where he took acting lessons and worked odd jobs. He has named his early acting heroes as Gary Oldman, Sean Penn and Mickey Rourke.

Pitt first gained recognition as a cowboy hitchhiker in the road movie *Thelma & Louise* (1991). His first leading roles in big-budget productions came with the drama films *A River Runs Through It* (1992) and *Legends of the Fall* (1994), and the horror film *Interview with the Vampire* (1994). He gave critically acclaimed performances in the crime thriller *Seven* (1995) and the science fiction film *12 Monkeys* (1995), the latter earning him a Golden Globe Award for Best Supporting Actor and an Academy Award nomination.

Pitt starred in *Fight Club* (1999) and the heist film *Ocean's Eleven* (2001), as well as its sequels, *Ocean's Twelve* (2004) and *Ocean's Thirteen* (2007). His greatest commercial successes have been *Ocean's Eleven* (2001), *Troy* (2004), *Mr. & Mrs. Smith* (2005), *World War Z* (2013), and *Once Upon a Time in Hollywood* (2019), for which he won a second Golden Globe Award and the Academy Award for Best Supporting Actor. Pitt's other Academy Award nominated performances were in *The Curious Case of Benjamin Button* (2008) and *Moneyball* (2011).

He produced *The Departed* (2006) and *12 Years a Slave* (2013), both of which won the Academy Award for Best Picture, and also *The Tree of Life* (2011), *Moneyball* (2011), and *The Big Short* (2015), all of which were nominated for Best Picture.

As a public figure, Pitt has been cited as one of the most influential and powerful people in the American entertainment industry. For a number of years, he was cited as the world's most attractive man by various media outlets, and his personal life is the subject of wide publicity. From 2000 to 2005, he was married to the actress Jennifer Aniston, and from 2014 to 2019, he was married to the actress Angelina Jolie. Pitt and Jolie have six children together, three of whom were adopted internationally.

Blair Erwin Underwood (born August 25, 1964) is an American television, film, and stage actor and director. He played attorney Jonathan Rollins on the NBC legal drama *L.A. Law* for seven years. He has received two Golden Globe Award nominations, three NAACP Image Awards and one Grammy Award. In recent years, he has appeared in *The New Adventures of Old Christine*, *Dirty Sexy Money* and *In Treatment*, *The Event*, *Quantico*, *When They See Us* and as Andrew Garner in *Agents of S.H.I.E.L.D.*.

Blair was born in Tacoma, Washington, the son of Marilyn Ann Scales, an interior decorator, and Frank Eugene Underwood, Sr., a United States Army colonel. Owing to his father's military career, Blair lived on bases and Army Posts in the United States and Stuttgart, Germany, during his childhood. Blair attended Petersburg High School in Petersburg, Virginia. He went on to attend the Carnegie Mellon School of Drama in Pittsburgh, Pennsylvania, and is an honorary member of the Phi Beta Sigma fraternity.

After his film debut, *Krush Groove*, Underwood's 1985 appearance on *The Cosby Show* landed him a short stint on the ABC soap opera *One Life to Live* as Bobby Blue, which eventually led to his performance on the TV series *L.A. Law*, where he appeared from 1987 to 1994. In 1996 he was featured in the July issue of *Playgirl*. Blair also appeared in the 1987 TV series 21 Jump Street aside a young Johnny Depp on episode "Gotta Finish the Riff."

On September 17, 1994, he married Desiree DaCosta, with whom he has three children, Paris, Brielle, and Blake .

Underwood's film career began with roles in *Just Cause* (1995), *Set It Off* (1996) and *Deep Impact* (1998). He also had a supporting role as a geneticist in *Gattaca*. In 2000, he played the lead role in the short-lived television series *City of Angels*. In 2003, he guest starred in four episodes on the HBO series *Sex and the City* playing Cynthia Nixon's love interest. In 2004, he played the role of Roger De Souza opposite Heather Locklear in NBC's *LAX*. He gained acclaim as the sexy grade school teacher in the CBS sitcom *The New Adventures of Old Christine* opposite Julia Louis-Dreyfus for two years. In

2007, he guest starred in an episode of the NBC series *Law & Order: Special Victims Unit*. He played the character Alex in the first season of the HBO series *In Treatment*, for which he was nominated for best supporting actor at the 2009 Golden Globes.

Underwood has received six NAACP Image Awards, for his film work in *Rules of Engagement*, and his television work in *L.A. Law*, *City of Angels*, *Murder in Mississippi*, *Mama Flora's Family*, and *The Trip to Bountiful*. Underwood was voted one of *People* magazine's "50 Most Beautiful People" in 2000, and one of *TV Guide* magazine's "Most Influential Faces of the 90s".

He supported President Barack Obama's candidacy and spoke at campaign rallies for Obama. Underwood got to know Obama while researching his *L.A. Law* role at Harvard Law School, when Obama was president of the *Harvard Law Review*.

Viola Davis (born August 11, 1965) is an American actress and producer. Having won an Academy Award, an Emmy Award, and two Tony Awards, she is the first black thespian to achieve the Triple Crown of Acting. *Time* magazine named her one of the 100 most influential people in the world in 2012 and 2017.

Born in St. Matthews, South Carolina, Davis began her acting career in Central Falls, Rhode Island, starring in minor theater productions. After graduating from the Juilliard School in 1993, she won an Obie Award in 1999 for her performance as Ruby McCollum in *Everybody's Ruby*. She played minor roles in several films and television series in the late 1990s and early 2000s, before winning the Tony Award for Best Featured Actress in a Play for her role as Tonya in August Wilson's *King Hedley II* in 2001. Davis's film breakthrough came in 2008, when her role as a troubled mother in

Doubt earned her a nomination for the Academy Award for Best Supporting Actress.

Greater success came to Davis in the 2010s. She won the 2010 Tony Award for Best Actress in a Play for playing Rose Maxson in the revival of August Wilson's play *Fences*. For starring as a 1960s housemaid in the comedy-drama *The Help* (2011), Davis received a nomination for the Academy Award for Best Actress and won a SAG Award. In 2014, Davis began playing lawyer **Anna Julia Cooper** lise Keating in the ABC television drama series *How to Get Away with Murder*, and in 2015, she became the first black woman to win the Primetime Emmy Award for Outstanding Lead Actress in a Drama Series. In 2016, Davis played Amanda Waller in the superhero film *Suicide Squad* and reprised the role of Maxson in the film adaptation of *Fences*, winning the Academy Award for Best Supporting Actress. She went on to receive a BAFTA nomination for starring in the heist film *Widows* (2018).

Davis and her husband, Julius Tennon, are founders of production company, JuVee Productions. Davis is also widely recognized for her advocacy and support of human rights and equal rights for women and women of color. She identifies as a feminist.

Chadwick Aaron Boseman (born November 29, 1976) is an American actor known for his portrayals of real-life historical figures such as Jackie Robinson in *42* (2013), James Brown in *Get on Up* (2014) and Thurgood Marshall in *Marshall* (2017), and for his portrayal of the superhero Black Panther in the Marvel Cinematic Universe films *Captain America: Civil War* (2016), *Black Panther* (2018), *Avengers: Infinity War* (2018) and *Avengers: Endgame* (2019).

Boseman was born and raised in South Carolina, to Carolyn and Leroy Boseman. His mother was a nurse and his father worked at a textile factory, managing an upholstery business as well. Boseman graduated from T. L. Hanna High School in 1995. In his junior year, he wrote his first play, *Crossroads*, and staged it at the school after a classmate was shot and killed.

Boseman attended college at Howard University in Washington, D.C. and graduated in 2000 with a Bachelor of Fine Arts in directing. One of his teachers was Phylicia Rashad, who became a mentor. She helped raise funds so that Boseman and some classmates could attend the Oxford Mid-Summer Program of the British American Drama Academy in London, to which they had been accepted. One of the supporters was Denzell Washington.

Boseman wanted to write and direct, and initially began studying acting to learn how to relate to actors. After he returned to the U.S., he graduated from New York City's Digital Film Academy.

He lived in Brooklyn at the start of his career. Boseman worked as the drama instructor in the Schomburg Junior Scholars Program, housed at the Schomburg Center for Research in Black Culture in Harlem, New York. In 2008, he moved to Los Angeles to pursue an acting career.

Boseman got his first television role in 2003, in an episode of *Third Watch*. His early work included episodes of the series *Law & Order*, *CSI:NY*, and *ER*. He also continued to write plays, with his script for *Deep Azure* performed at the Congo Square Theatre Company in Chicago; it was nominated for a 2006 Joseph Jefferson Award for New Work. In 2008, he played a recurring role on the television series *Lincoln Heights* and appeared in his first feature film, *The*

Express: The Ernie Davis Story. He landed a regular role in 2010 in another television series, *Persons Unknown*.

Boseman had his first starring role in the 2013 film *42*, in which he portrayed baseball pioneer and star Jackie Robinson. He had been directing an off-Broadway play in East Village when he auditioned for the role, and was considering giving up acting and pursuing directing full-time at the time. About 25 other actors had been seriously considered for the role, but director Brian Helgeland liked Boseman's bravery and cast him after he had auditioned twice. In 2013, Boseman also starred in the indie film *The Kill Hole*, which was released in theaters a few weeks before the film *42*.

In 2014, Boseman appeared opposite Kevin Costner in *Draft Day*, in which he played an NFL draft prospect. Later that year, he starred as James Brown in *Get on Up*. In 2016, he starred as Thoth, a deity from Egyptian mythology, in *Gods of Egypt*.

In 2016 he started portraying the Marvel Comics character T'Challa / Black Panther, with *Captain America: Civil War* being his first film in a five-picture deal with Marvel. He headlined *Black Panther* in 2018, which focused on his character and his home country of Wakanda in Africa. The film opened to great anticipation, becoming one of the highest-grossing films of the year in the United States. He reprised the role in both *Avengers: Infinity War* and *Avengers: Endgame*, which were released in 2018 and 2019, respectively. Both films were the highest grossing of the year they were released, with *Endgame* going on to become the highest-grossing film of all time.

PROFESSIONAL DANCERS WHO MAKE THE GRADE

Bill "Bojangles" Robinson (May 25, 1878 – November 25, 1949) was an American tap dancer, actor, and singer, the best known and most highly paid black American entertainer in America during the first half of the twentieth century. His long career mirrored changes in American entertainment tastes and technology.

Bojangles began in the age of minstrel shows and moved to Vaudeville, Broadway theatre, the recording industry, Hollywood films, radio and television.

His signature routine was the Stair Dance, in which he would tap up and down a set of stairs in a rhythmically complex sequence of steps, a routine that he unsuccessfully attempted to patent. He is also credited with having coined the word *copasetic* in popular culture via his repeated use of it in Vaudeville and radio appearances.

Bojangles was a popular figure in both the black and white entertainment worlds of his era. In his career, Bojangles appeared in a total of 14 films and six Broadway shows, sometimes in prominent roles – an enormous triumph for a black actor in his day. He is best known today for his dancing with Shirley Temple in a series of films during the 1930s, and for starring in the musical *Stormy Weather* (1943), loosely based on his own life and selected for preservation in the National Film Registry.

Bojangles was the first black solo performer to star on white vaudeville circuits, overcoming vaudeville's two-colored rule where he was a headliner for four decades. He used his popularity to challenge and overcome numerous racial barriers, including becoming one of the first minstrel and Vaudeville performers to appear without the use of blackface makeup; the first black performer to appear in a Hollywood film in an interracial dance team (with Shirley Temple in *The Little Colonel*, 1935); and the first black performer to headline a mixed-race Broadway production.

Bojangles co-founded the New York Black Yankees baseball team in Harlem in 1936 with financier James "Soldier Boy" Semler. The team was a successful member of the Negro National League until it disbanded in 1948, after Major League Baseball was desegregated.

Gregory Hines produced and starred in a biographical movie about Robinson for which he won the NAACP Best actor Award.

Bojangles' final public appearance in 1949, a few weeks before his death, was as a surprise guest on a TV show, Ted Mack's The Original Amateur Hour, in which he emotionally embraced a competitor on the show who had tap-danced for the audience.

Despite being the highest-paid black performer of the first half of the twentieth century, earning more than US$2 million during his lifetime, Robinson died penniless in 1949, at the age of 71 from heart failure. His funeral was arranged and paid for by longtime friend and television host Ed Sullivan.

Bojangles Robinson was inducted into the National Museum of Dance's Mr. & Mrs. Cornelius Vanderbilt Whitney Hall of Fame in 1987. In 1989, a joint U.S. Senate/House resolution declared "National Tap Dance Day" to be May 25, the anniversary of Bill Robinson's birth.

Howard "Sandman" Sims (January 24, 1917 – May 20, 2003) was an African-American tap dancer who began his career in vaudeville. He was skilled in a style of dancing that he performed in a wooden sandbox of his own construction and acquired his nickname from the sand he sprinkled to alter and amplify the sound of his dance steps.

Born in Fort Smith, Arkansas, Sims was one of 12 children. The family soon relocated to Los Angeles, California, where he was raised. He learned to dance from his father, and said he was dancing as soon as he could walk. He began tap-dancing at the age of 3. He attributed some of his early love for tap dancing in particular to his mother, exasperated that he kept wearing out the toes of his shoes, putting steel taps on the shoes. Along with his brothers, Sims was dancing on the sidewalks of Los Angeles from a young age. At the age of 14, peeping in the windows of a dance school got Sims arrested for loitering, but he was able to dance his way to freedom, convincing a judge that his reason for being on that street was legitimate.

Despite performing at various vaudeville venues, Sims found neither fame nor success as a dancer in Los Angeles. In 1947, he tagged along on one of his professional-boxer friend Archie Moore's cross-country drives, and settled in New York City.

A significant change to Sims's dancing style came about as a result of his interaction with Harlem's hoofers, practitioners of a variation on the tap he had learned on the west coast.

After arriving in Harlem, Sims began performing on the street as he had done in California, but faced stiff competition from other innovative dancers. He performed on corners in between working whatever jobs he could find, and then discovered the "Amateur

Night" stage on Wednesdays at the Apollo Theater, where he soon gained local notoriety. He eventually won the Amateur Night competition a record-breaking 25 times, after which a rule was instituted that performers could no longer compete once they had earned four first prizes.

By the mid-1950s, he had been hired as the Apollo's stage manager, and soon began his role as the Apollo's famed "executioner", chasing Amateur Night contestants the crowd disapproved of off the stage with a shepherd's crook (known since vaudeville times as "the hook") a broom, or other props, while dressed in a variety of wacky costumes, whether long underwear, a clown suit, or even a diaper. Sims would play "executioner" until shortly after Time Warner took over the Apollo in 1999. He was also involved in New York City's Hoofers Club, a venue primarily for black tap dancers.

In 1949, motivated by the death of Bill "Bojangles" Robinson, Sims became a founding member of the Original Copasetics, another fellowship of tap dancers that became a source of mentor-student relationships. With paying gigs harder to find and paying less, Sims turned to other sources of income. Despite not having had any formal instruction himself, he taught dance, including to such later stars as Gregory Hines and Ben Vereen. He also taught footwork to boxing greats Sugar Ray Robinson and Muhammad Ali.

The late 1960s brought the beginning of a wave of nostalgia for tap, and Sims found his dance skills in demand again. In 1969, he was part of the all-star cast of *Tap Happening*, a revue that played Off-Broadway. *Tap Happening* was popular enough to run for several years.

As part of New York's leg of the 1981 Newport Jazz Festival (which spanned both NYC and its home city of Newport, Rhode Island, that year), he performed with former Cotton Club bandleader Cab Calloway in a production called *Stompin' at the Savoy*. A few weeks later, Sims was on stage at the American Dance Festival, dancing both with and without his sandbox.

The National Endowment for the Arts granted Sims a $5,000 National Heritage Fellowship in 1984. That same year, clogger Ira Bernstein received an NEA Folk Arts Apprenticeship grant "to study traditional Black tap dance with master dancer Howard 'Sandman' Sims."

Sims performed before a crowd of 2,600 fans at the Lincoln Center during the Newport Jazz Festival. As part of the resurgence of interest in tap dancing in the 1980s, Sandman Sims served as a cultural ambassador, representing the United States on behalf of the U.S. State Department, traveling to over 50 countries in a span of 11 months with dance performances around the world.

He was also featured in the 1989 dance film *Tap*, along with Sammy Davis Jr., Gregory Hines and Savion Glover, demonstrating classic challenge dancing. Sims was a featured performer at the third annual celebration of National Tap Dance Day on May 30, 1993. In 1998, the New York Committee to Celebrate National Tap Dance Day and the Young People's Tap Conference honored Sandman Sims for his contributions to the art of hoofing.

While Sims had a first marriage which produced his first child Diane Sims, he later married his second wife, Solange. They would have 1 son together, Howard Sims Jr., as well as 5 grandchildren and 1 great-grandchild. Sims died on May 20, 2003 in New York City. He had suffered from Alzheimer's disease. A memorial service for Sims was held May 28, 2003 at the Apollo Theater.

Geoffrey Lamont Holder (August 1, 1930 – October 5, 2014) was a Trinidadian-American actor, voice actor, dancer, choreographer, singer, director and painter. A multifaceted performer and creator, he is best remembered by audiences for his performance as the villainous Baron Samedi in the 1973 Bond-movie *Live and Let Die* and as the pitchman for 7 Up.

Born in Port of Spain, Trinidad, to parents of Bajan and Trinidadian descent, Holder was one of four children. He was educated at Tranquility School and Queen's Royal College in Port of Spain. He made his performance debut at the age of seven in his brother Boscoe Holder's dance company.

After seeing him perform in St. Thomas, the choreographer Agnes de Mille invited Holder to work with her in New York. Upon arriving he joined Katherine Dunham dance school where he taught folkloric forms for two years.

From 1955 to 1956, he performed with the Metropolitan Opera Ballet as a principal dancer. He left the ballet to make his Broadway debut in the Harold Arlen and Truman Capote musical *House of Flowers*. While working on *House of Flowers*, Holder met Alvin Ailey, with whom he later worked extensively, and Carmen de Lavallade, his future wife. Holder married Carmen in 1955. They spent their lives in New York City and had one son, Léo. They were the subject of a 2004 film, *Carmen & Geoffrey*.

After the show closed he starred in an all-black production of *Waiting for Godot* in 1957.

Holder began his movie career in the 1962 British film *All Night Long*, a modern remake of Shakespeare's *Othello*.

In addition to his movie appearances, Holder was a spokesman in advertising campaigns for the soft drink 7 Up in the 1970s and 1980s.

In 1975, Holder won two Tony Awards for direction and costume design of *The Wiz*, the all-black musical version of *The Wizard of Oz*. Holder was the first black man to be nominated in either category. He won the *Drama Desk Award for Outstanding Costume Design*. The show ran for 1672 performances.

As a choreographer, Holder created dance pieces for many companies, including the Alvin Ailey American Dance Theater and the Dance Theatre of Harlem. In 1978, Holder directed and choreographed the Broadway musical *Timbuktu*. Holder's 1957 piece "Bele" is also part of the Dance Theater of Harlem repertory.

Geoffrey Holder died in Manhattan of complications from pneumonia on October 5, 2014, aged 84.

Paul Lawrence Kennedy (1940 - March 16, 2002) was born in Boston, Massachusetts. He and his sister Arlene Kennedy were tap dancers, choreographers, and directors who trained some of the most talented dancers in their Universal Dance Design Studio in Los Angeles,.

Their mother, Mildred Kennedy Bradic, was a renowned dance teacher who introduced her children to the art at an early age, her motto, "If you can walk you can dance." Mildred began her dancing career at the age of seven and earned 35 cents weekly for offering dance classes at the Boston Community Center. When Mildred tried to enroll her children, Paul and Arlene, in dance school she was told they were too young. In 1946 she opened her own school at the Lenox Street Projects Social Hall where she taught ballet, toe, tap and acrobatics, charging 50 cents a class. After three years, she moved the Kennedy School of Dance to Massachusetts Avenue.

When Mildred moved to Washington, D.C. with Arlene, Paul-- who found he could pick up steps faster than most-- remained in Boston and ran the Kennedy School of Dance from 1963 to 1979. Paul was the first black male dancer at the Boston School of Ballet. He received a B.F.A. in Dance from the Boston Conservatory.

In the 1960s and 70s, he arranged dances for bands and singing groups, touring with Gladys Knight and the Pips. He also choreographed moves to the songs from Marvin Gaye's album "From Here, My Dear" for performances, and worked with Michael Jackson on tap dancing. In 1977 he went on the road with Kool and the Gang as choreographer of their shows. He went to Los Angeles with Gladys Knight and the Pips and worked with such Motown groups as High Energy, the Commodores, and Temptations. Arlene, meanwhile, toured Europe with dance groups. She later joined her mother in Washington D.C. to teach at the Academy of Theatrical Arts and her mother's dance school.

In 1980 Paul signed a two-year contract as Marvin Gaye's choreographer. He sent for Arlene and they began to teach in Victoria Park in Carson, California with 500 students in the Parks and Recreation Department, from 1980 to 1983. In 1988 they moved the studio to the west side of Los Angeles and called it the Universal Design Dance Studio. They also founded the Kennedy Tap Company.

They were known for training students to have beautiful footwork; for staging recitals that were like Broadway shows; for teaching students with no money and the children of celebrities, among them Dormeshia Sumbry Edwards, Derick K. Grant; the son of Sammy

Davis, Jr., the grandson of Al Williams (of the Four Step Brothers), and the granddaughters of Fayard Nicholas.

In the meantime, he continued to work in the commercial dance world and choreographed an episode of the TV series "A Different World" in 1993. During his career, Paul received a number of awards from the dance community. In 1998 he received special recognition when the legendary Cuban ballerina Alicia Alonso invited the Kennedy tap company to perform in Havana at the 50th anniversary celebration of the National Ballet of Cuba. Pop dance choreographer and teacher, Paul Lawrence Kennedy, died at the age of 61 on March 16, 2002 of heart failure.

Deborah (Debbie) Kaye Allen (born January 16, 1950) is an American actress, dancer, choreographer, television director, television producer, and a former member of the President's Committee on the Arts and Humanities. Debbie Allen is a three-time Emmy Award winner for Choreography for the series *Fame* and *The Motown 25th Anniversary Special*. She has won 10 Image Awards as a director, actress, choreographer and producer for *Fame*, *A Different World*, *Motown 25*, *The Academy Awards*, *The Debbie Allen Special* and *Amistad*.

Allen was born in Houston, Texas, the third child to orthodontist Andrew Arthur Allen and Pulitzer Prize-nominated artist, poet, playwright, scholar, and publisher, Vivian (Ayers) Allen. She is the younger sister of actress/director/singer Phylicia Rashad.

Debbie earned a B.A. degree in classical Greek literature, speech, and theater from Howard University and studied acting at HB Studio in New York City. She holds *honoris causa* Doctorates from Howard University and the University of North Carolina School of the Arts. She also taught choreography to former Los Angeles

Lakers dancer-turned-singer, Paula Abdul currently teaches young dancers..

Debbie Allen auditioned at the Houston Ballet Academy at the age of twelve. Even though her audition performance exceeded beyond the qualifications of admission, Debbie Allen was denied admission to the school due to systemic racism that had corrupted the process.

This is not the only time Allen had experienced racism. When she was sixteen, she had a successful audition for the North Carolina School of the Arts and was given an opportunity to demonstrate dance techniques to other prospective students applying to the institution. Unfortunately, Allen was rejected acceptance due to her body not being suited for ballet. After receiving numerous rejections, Allen decided to mainly focus on her academics and, from then on, was well on her way to the start of her career.

Debbie Allen was also selected to appear in the 1979 miniseries *Roots: The Next Generations* by Alex Haley where she plays the wife of Haley.

Debbie Allen had her Broadway debut in the chorus of *Purlie*. She also created the role of Beneatha in the Tony Award-winning musical *Raisin*. She first began receiving critical attention in 1980 for her appearance in the role of Anita in the Broadway revival of *West Side Story* which earned her a Tony Award nomination and a Drama Desk Award, she would receive a second Tony Award nomination in 1986 for her performance in the title role of Bob Fosse's *Sweet Charity*.

Allen was first introduced as Lydia Grant in the 1980 film *Fame*. Although her role in the film was relatively small, Lydia would become a central figure in the television adaptation, which ran from 1982 to 1987. She is perhaps best known for her work on the 1982 musical-drama television series *Fame*, where she portrayed dance teacher Lydia Grant, and served as the series' principal choreographer. Debbie was nominated for the Emmy Award for Best Actress four times during the show's run. She is the only actress to have appeared in all three screen incarnations of *Fame*, playing Lydia Grant in both the 1980 film and 1982 television series and playing the school principal in the 2009 remake. She currently portrays Catherine Fox on *Grey's Anatomy*.

For her contributions to the television industry, Debbie Allen was honored in 1991 with a star on the Hollywood Walk of Fame at 6904 Hollywood Boulevard in the center of Hollywood directly opposite the Dolby Theatre at Hollywood & Highland Center. She was presented with the George and Ira Gershwin Award for Lifetime Musical Achievement, at the 1992 UCLA Spring Sing.

Debbie Allen is married to former NBA player Norm Nixon, and they have three children: dancer Vivian Nichole Nixon, basketball player Norman Ellard Nixon Jr. (Wofford College & Southern University), and DeVaughn Nixon.

In 2001, Debbie Allen founded the Debbie Allen Dance Academy, a 501(c)3 nonprofit organization. She was awarded an honorary doctorate from the North Carolina School of the Arts, as well as from her alma mater, Howard University.

Debbie Allen was appointed by President George W. Bush in 2001 as a member of the President's Committee on the Arts and Humanities. On February 4, 2009, she was honored for her contributions to dance and was presented with a Lifetime Achievement Award by Nia Peeples at The Carnival: Choreographer's Ball 10th anniversary show.

Stephen Laurel "Twitch" Boss (born September 29, 1982) is a freestyle hip hop dancer, choreographer, entertainer, actor, television producer and television personality from Montgomery, Alabama.

In 2003, Twitch was a semifinalist on MTV's *The Wade Robson Project* and a runner-up on the television talent competition *Star Search*. In 2007 he was a Maybelle's Store Dancer in *Hairspray*.

Twitch first auditioned in 2007 for Season 3 of *So You Think You Can Dance* but was not selected to be in the Top Twenty. Twitch returned to audition again in Season 4 in 2008, where he was not only selected to compete in the Top Twenty, but placed runner-up in the competition after fellow hip-hop dancer Joshua Allen. During Season 4, Twitch danced with fellow contestant Katee Shean to a Contemporary piece choreographed by Mia Michaels. The dance was nominated for an Emmy for Choreography in the 61st Primetime Emmy Awards. In season 5, Twitch returned to *So You Think You Can Dance* with fellow season 4 contestant Katee Shean to perform their Emmy-nominated piece "Mercy", choreographed by Mia Michaels. He was one of the 11 "All Stars" for season 7.Twitch served as a frequent All Star in Seasons 7, 8 and Season 9 of *So You Think You Can Dance*, performing many memorable routines, including the hip hop number "Outta Your Mind" with ballet dancer Alex Wong, which was then reprised by comedian Ellen DeGeneres in Season 7's finale. Twitch was the Team Captain for "Team Street" in Season 12 of *So You Think You Can Dance*.

After competing in *So You Think You Can Dance*, Twitch went on to teach at South County Classical Ballet with fellow finalist Katee Shean. He has also choreographed for South Korean pop/R&B singer, Seven. On April 30, 2013, he and Allison Holker performed a dance routine on *Dancing with the Stars*. They danced to Crystallize, which was being performed live by Lindsey Stirling.

On December 10, 2013, Twitch and fellow SYTYCD alum Allison Holker married at Nigel Lythgoe's Villa San Juliette Vineyard and Winery in Paso Robles, California. He also adopted Holker's daughter, Weslie Renae Boss. On March 27, 2016, Holker gave birth to their son, Maddox Laurel Boss. The couple recently gave birth to their third child, a baby girl, Zaia Boss.

Since 2014, he has been featured on *The Ellen DeGeneres Show* as a DJ. He is also featured in *Ellen's Game of Games* as a sidekick to DeGeneres.

SINGERS AND MUSICIANS WHO MAKE THE GRADE

Samuel "Sammy" George Davis Jr. (December 8, 1925 – May 16, 1990) was an American singer, musician, dancer, actor, vaudevillian, comedian and activist known for his impressions of actors, musicians and other celebrities. At age three, Davis Jr. began his career in vaudeville with his father Sammy Davis Sr. and the Will Mastin Trio, which toured nationally.

After military service, Davis Jr. returned to the trio and became an overnight sensation following a nightclub performance at Ciro's (in West Hollywood) after the 1951 Academy Awards. With the trio, he became a recording artist. In 1954, at the age of 29, he lost his left eye in a car accident. Several years later, he converted to Judaism, finding commonalities between the oppression experienced by African-American and Jewish communities.

After a starring role on Broadway in Mr. (1956), he returned to the stage in 1964's *Golden Boy.* Davis Jr.'s film career began as a child in 1933. In 1960, he appeared in the Rat Pack film *Ocean's 11.*

In 1966, he had his own TV variety show, titled *The Sammy Davis Jr. Show*. While Davis' career slowed in the late 1960s, he did have a hit record with "The Candy Man" in 1972 and became a star in Las Vegas, earning him the nickname "Mister Show Business".

Davis had a complex relationship with the black community and drew criticism after publicly supporting President Richard Nixon in 1972. One day on a golf course with Jack Benny, he was asked what his handicap was. "Handicap?" he asked. "Talk about handicap. I'm a one-eyed Negro Jew." This was to become a signature comment, recounted in his autobiography and in many articles.

After reuniting with Frank Sinatra and Dean Martin in 1987, Davis toured with them and Liza Minnelli internationally. He was also the recipient of the Kennedy Center Honors in 1987. Sammy Davis Jr. died of complications from throat cancer at his home in Beverly Hills, California, on May 16, 1990, aged 64. He was interred in the Forest Lawn Memorial Park. On May 18, 1990, two days after his death. The neon lights of the Las Vegas Strip were darkened for ten minutes as a tribute.

Sammy Davis Jr. was awarded the Spingarn Medal by the NAACP and was nominated for a Golden Globe Award. In 2001, he was posthumously awarded the Grammy Lifetime Achievement Award. In 2017, he was inducted into the Rhythm & Blues Hall of Fame for being the Greatest Entertainer in the World. Sammy Davis, Jr.

William "Smokey" Robinson Jr. (born February 19, 1940) is an American singer, songwriter, record producer, and former record executive. Smokey was the founder and front man of the Motown vocal group the Miracles, for which he was also chief songwriter and producer. Smokey Robinson led the group from its 1955 origins as "the Five Chimes" until 1972, when he announced a retirement from the group to focus on his role as Motown's vice president. However, Smokey returned to the music industry as a solo artist the following year. Following the sale of Motown Records in 1988, he left the company in 1990.

Smokey Robinson was inducted into the Rock and Roll Hall of Fame in 1987, and was awarded the 2016 Library of Congress Gershwin Prize for his lifetime contributions to popular music.

Smokey Robinson was born to an African-American father and a mother of African-American and French ancestry into a poor family in the North End area of Detroit, Michigan, His uncle Claude gave him the nickname "Smokey Joe" when he was a child. He attended Northern High School, where he was above average academically and a keen athlete, though his main interest was music and he formed a doo-wop group named the Five Chimes. At one point, he and Aretha Franklin lived several houses from each other on Belmont; he knew Franklin since she was about five.

Smokey said his interest in music started after hearing the groups Nolan Strong & the Diablos and Billy Ward and his Dominoes on the radio as a child. He later listed Barrett Strong, a Detroit native, as a strong vocal influence. In 1955, he formed the first lineup of the Five Chimes with childhood friend Ronald White and classmate Pete Moore. Two years later, in 1957, they were renamed the Matadors and included Bobby Rogers. Another member, Emerson Rogers, was replaced by Bobby's cousin Claudette Rogers. The group's guitarist, Marv Tarplin, joined them sometime in 1958. The Matadors began touring Detroit venues around this time. They later changed their name to the Miracles.

In August 1957, Robinson and the Miracles met songwriter Berry Gordy after a failed audition for Brunswick Records. At that time during the audition, Smokey had brought along with him a "Big 10" notebook with 100 songs he wrote while in high school. Gordy was impressed with Robinson's vocals and even more impressed with Robinson's ambitious songwriting. During this time, Smokey attended college and started classes in January 1959, studying electrical engineering. He dropped out after only two months.

Between 1960 and 1970, Robinson would produce 26 top forty hits with the Miracles as lead singer, chief songwriter and producer, including several top ten hits such as "You've Really Got a Hold on Me",[6] "Mickey's Monkey", "I Second That Emotion", "Baby Don't Cry" and the group's only number-one hit during their Robinson years, "The Tears of a Clown". In 1965, the Miracles were the first Motown group to change their name when they released their 1965 album *Going to a Go-Go* as Smokey Robinson & the Miracles.

Between 1962 and 1966, Smokey Robinson was also one of the major songwriters and producers for Motown, penning many hit singles such as "Two Lovers", "The One Who Really Loves You", "You Beat Me to the Punch" and "My Guy" for Mary Wells; "The Way You Do The Things You Do", "My Girl", "Since I Lost My Baby" and "Get Ready" for the Temptations; "Stillwater" for the Four Tops; "When I'm Gone" and "Operator" for Brenda Holloway; "Don't Mess With Bill", "The Hunter Gets Captured by the Game" and "My Baby Must Be a Magician" for the Marvelettes; and "I'll Be Doggone" and "Ain't That Peculiar" for Marvin Gaye.

By 1969, Smokey wanted to retire from touring to focus on raising his two children with his wife Claudette and on his duties as Motown's vice president, a job he had taken on by the mid-1960s after Esther Gordy Edwards had left the position. However, the success of the group's "Tears of a Clown" made Robinson stay with the group until 1972. Robinson's last performance with the group was in July 1972 in Washington, D.C.

After a year of retirement, Robinson announced his comeback with the release of the eponymous *Smokey* album, in 1973. The album included the Miracles tribute song, "Sweet Harmony" and the hit ballad "Baby Come Close". In 1974, Robinson's second album, *Pure Smokey*, was released but failed to produce hits.

Robinson answered his critics the following year with *A Quiet Storm*, released in 1975. The album launched three singles – the number-one R&B hit "Baby That's Backatcha", "The Agony & The Ecstasy" and "Quiet Storm". However, Robinson's solo career suffered from his work as Motown's vice president, and his own music took the backseat.

In 1981, Robinson topped the charts again with another sensual ballad, "Being with You", which was another number one hit in Cash Box and peaked at number two on the *Billboard* Hot 100. It also hit number one in the UK Singles Chart, becoming his most successful single to date. In 1983, Robinson teamed up with fellow Motown label mate Rick James recording the R&B ballad, "Ebony Eyes".

In 1987, following a period of personal and professional issues, Robinson made a comeback with the album, *One Heartbeat* and the singles, "Just to See Her" and "Heartbeat", which were Top 10 hits on *Billboard*'s Pop, Soul, and Adult Contemporary charts. They were aided by popular music videos. "Just to See Her" won Robinson his first Grammy Award in 1988. The album became one of his most successful ever, selling over 900,000 copies in the United States alone. He was inducted as a solo artist to the Rock and Roll Hall of Fame in 1988, later igniting controversy as the committee had inducted only Robinson and not members of his group, the Miracles, which Robinson was personally offended by. In 2012, however, the committee rectified the mistake announcing that the group would be inducted on their own merit.

After Motown was sold off to MCA in 1988, Robinson relinquished his position as vice president.

Barry Eugene Carter (born September 12, 1944 – July 4, 2003), better known by his stage name **Barry White**, was an American singer-songwriter, musician, record producer and composer.

A two-time Grammy Award–winner known for his distinctive bass-baritone voice and romantic image, his greatest success came in the 1970s as a solo singer and with The Love Unlimited Orchestra, crafting many enduring soul, funk, and disco songs such as his two biggest hits: "You're the First, the Last, My Everything" and "Can't Get Enough of Your Love, Babe".

During the course of his career in the music business, White achieved 112 gold albums worldwide, 41 of which also attained platinum status. White had 20 gold and 10 platinum singles, with worldwide record sales in excess of 100 million records, and is one of the best-selling music artists of all time.

In 1973, White created The Love Unlimited Orchestra, a 40-piece orchestral group to be used originally as a backing band for the girl-group Love Unlimited. However, White had other plans, and in 1973 he released a single with "Love's Theme" (written by him and played by the Orchestra). That same track reached #1 on the *Billboard* Pop charts. Later, in 1974, he made the first album of the Love Unlimited Orchestra, *Rhapsody in White*, containing "Love's Theme". White is sometimes credited with ushering in the "disco" sound, seamlessly combining R&B music with classical music. Some[also regard "Love's Theme" as the first hit in the actual "disco era".

White would continue to make albums with the Orchestra, however. The Orchestra ceased to make albums in 1983 but continued to support White as a backing band.

White wanted to work with another act but decided to work with a solo male artist. While working on a few demos for a male singer, he made three song demos of himself singing and playing, White was finally persuaded to release the songs himself, although he was initially reluctant to step out behind the microphone.

He then wrote several other songs and recorded them for what eventually became an entire album of music. It eventually became White's first solo album, 1973's *I've Got So Much to Give*. It included the title track and his first solo chart hit, "Baby", which also rose to #1 on the *Billboard* R&B charts as well as #3 on the *Billboard* Pop charts in 1973 and stayed in the top 40 for many weeks.

Other chart hits by White included "Never, Never Gonna Give You Up" (#2 R&B, #7 Pop in 1973), "Can't Get Enough of Your Love, Babe" (# 1 Pop and R&B in 1974), "You're the First, the Last, My Everything" (#1 R&B, #2 Pop in 1974), "What Am I Gonna Do with You" (#1 R&B, #8 Pop in 1975), "Let the Music Play" (#4 R&B in 1976), "It's Ecstasy When You Lay Down Next to Me" (#1 R&B, #4 Pop in 1977) and "Your Sweetness Is My Weakness" (#2 R&B in 1978) and others. White also had a strong following in the UK, where he scored five Top 10 hits and a #1 for "You're the First, the Last, My Everything".

After six years White left 20th Century in 1979 to launch his own label, Unlimited Gold, with CBS/Columbia Records.

White was nominated for 11 Grammy Awards; winning two for *Staying Power* at the 42nd Annual Grammy Awards in 2000.

White was overweight for most of his adult life and suffered from related health problems. White was hospitalized with kidney failure attributed to chronic diabetes mellitus and high blood pressure.

While undergoing dialysis and awaiting a kidney transplant in May 2003, White suffered a severe stroke, which forced him to retire from public life. On July 4, 2003, Barry White died at Cedars-Sinai Medical Center in Los Angeles at the age of 58. His remains were cremated, and the ashes were scattered in the ocean off the Californian coast.

On September 20, 2004, Barry White was posthumously inducted into the Dance Music Hall of Fame at a ceremony held in New York. On September 12, 2013, which would have been White's 69th birthday, he was posthumously awarded the 2,506th star on the Hollywood Walk of Fame at 6914 Hollywood Blvd in the category of recording.

On June 25, 2019, *The New York Times Magazine* listed Barry White among hundreds of artists whose material was reportedly destroyed in the 2008 Universal fire.

Robert "Bob" Nesta Marley, OM (February 6, 1945 – May 11, 1981) was a Jamaican singer, songwriter and musician. Considered one of the pioneers of reggae, his musical career was marked by fusing elements of reggae, ska, and rocksteady, as well as his distinctive vocal and songwriting style. Marley's contributions to music increased the visibility of Jamaican music worldwide, and made him a global figure in popular culture for over a decade.

Born in Nine Mile, British Jamaica, Marley began his professional musical career in 1963, after forming Bob Marley and the Wailers. The group released its debut studio album *The Wailing Wailers* in 1965, which contained the single "One Love/People Get Ready"; the song was popular worldwide, and established the group as a rising figure in reggae. The Wailers subsequently released eleven further studio albums; while initially employing louder instrumentation and singing, the group began engaging in rhythmic-based song construction in the late 1960s and early 1970s, which coincided with the singer's conversion to Rastafarianism. During this period Marley relocated to London, and the group typified their musical shift with the release of the album *The Best of The Wailers* (1971).

The group attained international success after the release of the albums *Catch a Fire* and *Burnin'* (both 1973), and forged a reputation as touring artists. Following the disbandment of the Wailers a year later, Marley went on to release his solo material under the band's name. His debut studio album *Natty Dread* (1974) received positive reception, as did its follow-up *Rastaman Vibration* (1976). A few months after the album's release Marley survived an assassination attempt at his home in Jamaica, which prompted him to permanently relocate to London. During his time in London he recorded the album *Exodus* (1977); it incorporated elements of blues, soul, and British rock, enjoyed widespread commercial and critical success.

In 1977, Marley was diagnosed with acral lentiginous melanoma; he died as a result of the illness in 1981. His fans around the world expressed their grief, and he received a state funeral in Jamaica. The greatest hits album *Legend* was released in 1984, and became the best-selling reggae album of all time. Marley also ranks as one of the best-selling music artists of all time, with estimated sales of more than 75 million records worldwide. He was posthumously honored by Jamaica soon after his death with a designated Order of Merit by his nation. In 1994, he was inducted into the Rock and Roll Hall of Fame. *Rolling Stone* ranked him No. 11 on its list of the 100 Greatest Artists of All Time.

Natalie Maria Cole (February 6, 1950 – December 31, 2015) was an American singer, songwriter, and actress.

Natalie Cole was born at Cedars of Lebanon Hospital in Los Angeles, to American singer and jazz pianist Nat King Cole and former Duke Ellington Orchestra singer Maria Hawkins Ellington, and raised in the affluent Hancock Park district of Los Angeles. Regarding her childhood, Cole referred to her family as "the black Kennedys" and was exposed to many great singers of jazz, soul and blues. At the age of 6, Natalie sang on her father's Christmas album The Magic of Christmas and later started performing at age 11.

Cole grew up with an older adopted sister, Carole "Cookie" Cole (1944–2009) (her mother Maria's younger sister's daughter), adopted brother Nat "Kelly" Cole (1959–95), and younger twin sisters Timolin and Casey (born 1961). Through her mother, Cole was a grandniece of educator Charlotte Hawkins Brown.

Her paternal uncle, Freddy Cole, is a singer and pianist with numerous albums and awards. Cole enrolled in Northfield School for Girls, an elite New England preparatory school (since 1971 known as Northfield Mount Hermon School after merging with another school) before her father died of lung cancer in February 1965. Soon afterwards she began having a difficult relationship with her mother. She enrolled in the University of Massachusetts Amherst. She transferred briefly to University of Southern California where she pledged the Upsilon chapter of Delta Sigma Theta sorority. She later transferred back to the University of Massachusetts, where she majored in Child Psychology and minored in German, graduating in 1972.

Natalie Cole rose to success in the mid-1970s as an R&B singer with the hits "This Will Be", "Inseparable" (1975), and "Our Love" (1977). She returned as a pop singer on the 1987 album *Everlasting* and her cover of Bruce Springsteen's "Pink Cadillac". In the 1990s, she sang traditional pop by her father, resulting in her biggest success, *Unforgettable... with Love*, which sold over seven million copies and won her seven Grammy Awards. She sold over 30 million records worldwide.

On December 31, 2015, Cole died at the age of 65 at Cedars-Sinai Medical Center in Los Angeles, California, due to congestive heart failure.

Jennifer Lynn Lopez (born July 24, 1969), also known by her nickname **J.Lo**, is an American actress, singer, dancer, fashion designer, producer, and businesswoman. In 1991, Lopez began appearing as a Fly Girl dancer on *In Living Color*, where she remained a regular until she decided to pursue an acting career in 1993. For her first leading role in the 1997 Selena biopic of the same name, Lopez received a Golden Globe nomination and became the first Latin actress to earn over US$1 million for a film. She went on to star in *Anaconda* (1997) and *Out of Sight* (1998), later establishing herself as the highest-paid Latin actress in Hollywood.

Lopez ventured into the music industry with her debut studio album *On the 6* (1999), which helped propel the Latin pop movement in American music. With the simultaneous release of her second studio album *J.Lo* and her romantic comedy *The Wedding Planner* in 2001, Lopez became the first woman to have a number one album and film in the same week. Her 2002 remix album, *J to tha L–O! The Remixes*, became the first in history to debut at number one on the U.S. *Billboard* 200. Later that year, she released her third studio album *This Is Me... Then*, and starred in the US box office number-one *Maid in Manhattan*.

After starring in *Gigli* (2003), a critical and commercial failure, Lopez subsequently starred in the successful romantic comedies *Shall We Dance?* (2004) and *Monster-in-Law* (2005). Her fifth studio album, *Como Ama una Mujer* (2007), received the highest first-week sales for a debut Spanish album in the United States. Following an unsuccessful period, she returned to prominence in 2011 with her appearance as a judge on *American Idol*, and released her seventh studio album *Love?*.

In 2012, *Forbes* ranked her as the most powerful celebrity in the world, as well as the 38th most powerful woman in the world.

From 2016 to 2018, she starred in the crime drama series *Shades of Blue* and performed a residency show, Jennifer Lopez: All I Have, at Planet Hollywood Las Vegas.

Since 2017, Lopez has produced and served as a judge on *World of Dance*. In 2019, she received critical praise for starring as a stripper in the crime drama *Hustlers*, for which she earned Golden Globe and Screen Actors Guild Award nominations.

Time listed her among the 100 most influential people in the world in 2018. Her most successful singles on the US *Billboard* Hot 100 include: "If You Had My Love", "I'm Real", "Ain't It Funny", "All I Have", and "On the Floor", which is one of the best-selling singles of all time. For her contributions to the music industry, Lopez has received a landmark star on the Hollywood Walk of Fame, the *Billboard* Icon Award, and the Michael Jackson Video Vanguard Award among other honors. Her other ventures include clothing lines, fragrances, a production company, and a charitable foundation.

With a cumulative film gross of US$3.1 billion and estimated global sales of 80 million records, Lopez is regarded as the most influential Latin performer in the United States.

AUTHORS WHO MAKE THE GRADE

Gwendolyn Elizabeth Brooks (June 7, 1917 – December 3, 2000) was an American poet, author, and teacher. Her work often dealt with the personal celebrations and struggles of ordinary people in her community. Brooks was the poet laureate of Illinois. On May 1, 1950 Gwendolyn Brooks won the Pulitzer Prize for Poetry, for *Annie Allen*, making her the first African American to receive a Pulitzer Prize.

Brooks published her first poem, "Eventide", in a children's magazine, *American Childhood*, when she was 13 years old. By the age of 16, she had already written and published approximately 75 poems. In her early years, she received commendations on her poetic work and encouragement from James Weldon Johnson, Richard Wright and Langston Hughes. James Weldon Johnson sent her the first critique of her poems when she was only sixteen years old.

At 17, she started submitting her work to "Lights and Shadows," the poetry column of the *Chicago Defender*, an African-American newspaper. Gwendolyn Brooks' keen insight and musical language make her writing required reading for students of poetry today. "We Real Cool" is a good place to begin. Her poems, many published while she attended Wilson Junior College, ranged in style from traditional ballads and sonnets to poems using blues rhythms in free verse.

In 1939, Gwendolyn Brooks married Henry Lowington Blakely, Jr., whom she met after joining Chicago's NAACP Youth Council.

They had two children: Henry Lowington Blakely III, and Nora Brooks Blakely.

Brooks' published her first book of poetry, *A Street in Bronzeville* (1945), with Harper & Brothers, after a strong show of support to the publisher from author Richard Wright. The book earned instant critical acclaim for its authentic and textured portraits of life in Bronzeville. Brooks received her first Guggenheim Fellowship in 1946 and was included as one of the "Ten Young Women of the Year" in *Mademoiselle* magazine.

Brooks' second book of poetry, *Annie Allen* (1949), focused on the life and experiences of a young Black girl growing into womanhood in the Bronzeville neighborhood of Chicago. The book was awarded the 1950 Pulitzer Prize for poetry, and was also awarded *Poetry* magazine's Eunice Tietjens Prize.

In 1953, Brooks published her first and only narrative book, a novella titled *Maud Martha,* which in a series of 34 vignettes follows the life of a black woman named Maud Martha Brown as she moves about life from childhood to adulthood. Throughout her prolific writing career, Brooks received many more honors. A lifelong resident of Chicago, she was appointed Poet Laureate of Illinois in 1968, a position she held until her death 32 years later. She was also named the Poet Laureate Consultant in Poetry to the Library of Congress for the 1985–86 term. In 1976, she became the first African-American woman inducted into the American Academy of Arts and Letters. Gwendolyn Brooks died at her Chicago home on December 3, 2000, aged 83.

Chloe Anthony Wofford Morrison born **Chloe Ardelia Wofford**; (February 18, 1931 – August 5, 2019), known as **Toni Morrison**, was an American novelist, essayist, editor, teacher, and professor emeritus at Princeton University. Her first novel, *The Bluest Eye*, was published in 1970. The critically acclaimed *Song of Solomon* (1977) brought her national attention and won the National Book Critics Circle Award. In 1988, she won the Pulitzer Prize and the American Book Award for *Beloved* (1987).

Born and raised in Lorain, Ohio, Morrison graduated from Howard University in 1953 and went to graduate school at Cornell University. She later taught English at Howard University and also married and had two children before divorcing in 1964. In the late 1960s, she became the first black female editor in fiction at Random House in New York City. In the 1970s and 1980s, she developed her own reputation as an author.

Morrison was awarded the Nobel Prize in Literature in 1993. In 1996, the National Endowment for the Humanities selected her for the Jefferson Lecture, the U.S. federal government's highest honor for achievement in the humanities. Her perhaps most celebrated work, *Beloved*, was made into a 1998 film.

When Barack Obama won the Presidential election, Morrison said she felt like an American for the first time. She felt very powerfully patriotic when she went to the inauguration of Barack Obama. On May 29, 2012, President Barack Obama presented Morrison with the Presidential Medal of Freedom. Also that year, she was honored with the National Book Foundation's Medal of Distinguished Contribution to American Letters. . In 2016, she received the PEN/Saul Bellow Award for Achievement in American Fiction.

After the 2016 election of Donald Trump as President of the United States, Morrison wrote an essay, "Mourning for Whiteness," published in the November 21, 2016 issue of *The New Yorker*. In it she argues that white Americans are so afraid of losing privileges afforded them by their race that white voters elected Trump, whom she described as being "endorsed by the Ku Klux Klan" in order to keep the idea of white supremacy alive.

Morrison died at Montefiore Medical Center in The Bronx, New York City, on August 5, 2019, from complications of pneumonia. She was 88 years old.

August Wilson (April 27, 1945 – October 2, 2005) was an American playwright whose work included a series of ten plays, *The Pittsburgh Cycle*, for which he received two Pulitzer Prizes for Drama. Each work in the series is set in a different decade, and depicts comic and tragic aspects of the African-American experience in the 20th century.

Frederick August Kittel Jr. changed his name to August Wilson to honor his mother, Daisy Wilson, after his father's death in 1965. That same year, he discovered the blues as sung by Bessie Smith, and he bought a stolen typewriter for $10, which he often pawned when money was tight. At 20, he decided he was a poet and submitted work to such magazines as *Harper's*.

He began to write in bars, the local cigar store, and cafes—longhand on table napkins and on yellow notepads, absorbing the voices and characters around him. He would then gather the notes and type them up at home. Gifted with a talent for catching dialect and accents, Wilson had an "astonishing memory", which he put to full use during his career. He slowly learned not to censor the language he heard when incorporating it into his work.

Malcolm X's voice influenced Wilson's life and work (such as *The Ground on Which I Stand,* 1996). Both the Nation of Islam and the Black Power spoke to him regarding self-sufficiency, self-defense, and self-determination, and he appreciated the origin myths that

Elijah Muhammad supported. In 1969 Wilson married Brenda Burton, a Muslim, and converted to Islam. He and Brenda had one daughter, Sakina Ansari-Wilson, and divorced in 1972. In 1981 he married Judy Oliver, a social worker; they divorced in 1990. He married again in 1994 and was survived by his third wife, costume designer Constanza Romero, whom he met on the set of *The Piano Lesson*. They had a daughter, Azula Carmen Wilson.

Wilson's best known plays are *Fences* (1985) (which won a Pulitzer Prize and a Tony Award), *The Piano Lesson* (1990) (a Pulitzer Prize and the New York Drama Critics' Circle Award), *Ma Rainey's Black Bottom*, and *Joe Turner's Come and Gone*.

Wilson reported that he had been diagnosed with liver cancer in June 2005 and been given three to five months to live. He died on October 2, 2005, at Swedish Medical Center in Seattle, and was interred at Greenwood Cemetery, Pittsburgh, on October 8, 2005, aged 60.

On October 16, 2005, fourteen days after Wilson's death, the Virginia Theatre in New York City's Broadway Theater District was renamed the August Wilson Theatre. It is the first Broadway theatre to bear the name of an African American.

Ta-Nehisi Paul Coates (born September 30, 1975) is an American author and journalist. Coates gained a wide readership during his time as national correspondent at *The Atlantic*, where he wrote about cultural, social, and political issues, particularly regarding African Americans and white supremacy.

Coates has worked for *The Village Voice*, *Washington City Paper*, and *Time*. He has contributed to *The New York Times Magazine*, *The Washington Post*, *The Washington Monthly*, *O*, and other publications. He has published three books, a memoir and *Between the World and Me*, which won the 2015 National Book Award for

Nonfiction. He has also written a Black Panther series and a Captain America series for Marvel Comics. In 2015 he received a "Genius Grant" from the MacArthur Foundation.

Coates' first book, *The Beautiful Struggle,* was published in 2008. His first fiction novel, *The Water Dancer*, was published in 2019.

Coates was born in Baltimore, Maryland. His father, William Paul "Paul" Coates, was a Vietnam War veteran, former Black Panther, publisher, and librarian. His mother, Cheryl Lynn (Waters), was a teacher. Coates' father founded and ran Black Classic Press, a publisher specializing in African-American titles. The Press grew out of a grassroots organization, the George Jackson Prison Movement (GJPM). Initially the GJPM operated a Black bookstore called the Black Book.

Coates' interest in books was instilled at an early age when his mother, in response to bad behavior, would require him to write essays. His father's work with the Black Classic Press was a huge influence: Coates has said that he read many of the books his father published.

Coates attended a number of Baltimore-area schools, including William H. Lemmel Middle School and Baltimore Polytechnic Institute, before graduating from Woodlawn High School.

He then attended Howard University. In mid-2014, Coates attended an intensive program in French at Middlebury College to prepare for a writing fellowship in Paris, France.

Coates became a senior editor at *The Atlantic*, for which he wrote feature articles as well as maintaining his blog. Topics covered by the blog included politics, history, race, culture as well as sports, and music. His writings on race, such as his September 2012 *The*

Atlantic cover piece "Fear of a Black President" and his June 2014 feature "The Case for Reparations" have been especially praised and won his blog a place on the Best Blogs of 2011 list by *Time* magazine and the 2012 Hillman Prize for Opinion & Analysis Journalism from The Sidney Hillman Foundation.

In 2008, Coates published *The Beautiful Struggle*, a memoir about coming of age in West Baltimore and its effect on him. In the book, he discusses the influence of his father, a former Black Panther" the prevailing street crime of the era and its effects on his older brother; his own troubled experience attending Baltimore-area schools; and his eventual graduation and enrollment in Howard University.

Coates' second book, *Between the World and Me*, was published in July 2015. One of the origins of the book was the death of a college friend, Prince Carmen Jones Jr., who was shot by police in a case of mistaken identity.

Coates is the writer of the comic book series about the Black Panther drawn by Brian Stelfreeze and published by Marvel Comics. Issue #1 went on sale April 6, 2016, and sold an estimated 253,259 physical copies, the best-selling comic for the month of April 2016.

Coates' first novel and work of fiction, *The Water Dancer*, was published in 2019, and is a surrealist story set in the time of slavery. The novel is also an official Oprah's Book Club selection.

Coates was the 2012–14 MLK visiting professor for writing at the Massachusetts Institute of Technology. He joined the CUNY Graduate School of Journalism as its journalist-in-residence in late 2014. In 2017, Coates joined the faculty of New York University's Arthur L. Carter Journalism Institute as a Distinguished Writer in Residence.

PUBLISHERS WHO MAKE THE GRADE

Col. Leon H. Washington Jr. (c. 1907 – June 17, 1974) was an American newspaper publisher. He was the founder and first publisher of the *Los Angeles Sentinel*, an African-American newspaper in Los Angeles, California.

Washington was born in Kansas City, Kansas. He attended Washburn University and began his career in journalism by working for several newspapers. He quickly built a reputation as an activist among the Black community in Los Angeles. Washington founded the *Sentinel* newspaper in 1933, during the Depression and most of its readers lived on the Eastside in a section anchored by Central Avenue. The *Sentinel* was an outgrowth of Washington's work as an advertising salesman of the old *California Eagle*. His friends called him "Wash" and he epitomized "personalized" journalism in that the stamp of his personality was discernible on every page of the *Sentinel*.

Knowing the reach the *Sentinel* had with African American readers, Washington ran the "Don't Spend Where You Can't Work" campaign in the newspaper during the Great Depression to encourage readers to fight for their rights and demand fair treatment. Washington also published reports to shed light on the discrimination and racism against African Americans in Los Angeles. By 1974, the *Sentinel* had a circulation of 50,000.

Washington married Ruth Brumell, a photographer. He used the Sentinel as a potent vehicle to gain respect for the Black community from the larger society by targeting acts of discrimination and launching protests against merchants who mistreated Blacks, especially in the Black community.

The Sentinel is Washington's most important monument; and today, it is the largest Black newspaper in the West. Public appreciation of Washington and the Sentinel is exemplified by such tributes as the Leon H. Washington Post Office, the Leon H. Washington Public Library and the Leon H. Washington County Park.

Leon H. Washington died June 17, 1974, in a Pasadena, California, hospital after a brief illness. He was survived by his wife, who took over as publisher of the newspaper.

Ruth Washington operated her own photography shop prior to becoming the business manager of the Sentinel, When Col. Washington died, Ruth assumed the role of publisher of the newspaper and carried on the tradition he started as the voice of the Black community.

Like her husband, Ms. Washington was deeply involved in the social affairs of the Black community and often led the charge in the areas of social change and unbiased coverage of the news relevant to the Black Community. Along with Congresswoman Maxine Waters and Ethel Bradley (the first lady of Los Angeles) Ruth Washington formed the Black Women's Forum, dedicated to promoting issues affecting the Black woman, particularly in the Southern California region. Her unwavering determination kept her going and when the paper's fiscal picture appeared dismal, she reached out to her attorney, Kenneth Thomas, who, along with Ms. Washington devised a plan to keep the paper solvent. She remained publisher until her death in 1990.

When **Kenneth R. Thomas** became the publisher of the Sentinel, the paper was nearly 60 years old and had been known as the "Voice of the Black Community"; he took it to another level. "Ken" was a licensed probate attorney and had served in the U.S. Air Force where he attained the rank of First Lieutenant and received two medals for distinguished service: the Korean Service and the United Nations Medals. After leaving the military, he earned his bachelors and law degrees from Ohio State University and College of Laws. He was a member of the Ohio and the California Bar Associations, and was admitted to practice in the District Federal Courts for Central and Southern California. In 1968, he was admitted to practice before the U.S. Supreme Court, a distinction that only a few lawyers attain.

As Ken relocated the Sentinel offices to a new building at 3800 Crenshaw Boulevard, Los Angeles – the hub of the Black community – he said, "We're moving, not leaving. There he maintained an active legal practice, in addition to being the publisher of the Sentinel. The move signaled Thomas' recognition that if the paper was to remain in the eye of the Black community, it had to travel along the same path as most of its readership.

Under his leadership, the paper was given the responsibility of representing the Black press at the O.J. "trial of the century" by the National Newspaper Publishers Association (NNPA).As an activist and advocate of minority rights since his early days in college, he was a member of the N.A.A.C.P., the American Civil Liberties Union, C.O.R.E., the Fair Housing Counsel of Los Angeles and many other civil rights organizations.

Kenneth R. Thomas died in 1933.He was married to Jennifer Thomas, who assumed the role of publisher of the Sentinel when her husband passed.

Jennifer Thomas made a smooth transition and despite the obvious void that occurs when the leader of an institution dies, Mrs. Thomas did not have the "luxury" to mourn in private. She arranged her affairs and continued as the publisher, never missing an issue. Under Jennifer's leadership, the *Sentinel* continued its mission to report the news and views while championing the causes of the African American community and promoting cooperation, understanding and goodwill throughout Los Angeles.

During her time as publisher, Mrs. Thomas incorporated an annual fashion show, which supplemented the paper's activities within the community and provided it with additional artistic exposure. The *Sentinel* was also involved in the Los Angeles Black Business Expo, an annual event that promoted and showcased Black businesses, employers, government and service-oriented community businesses.

Danny Joseph Bakewell (born 1946) is an American civil rights activist and entrepreneur. He is the owner of *The Bakewell Company*, which includes among its holdings the New Orleans radio station WBOK and the Los Angeles Sentinel newspaper. He is currently Chairman of the National Newspaper Publishers Association.

Bakewell was born and raised in New Orleans, graduating from St. Augustine High School.

Described by the Los Angeles Times as "one of the most dynamic leaders in America today," the Bakewell Family took over the reins of the Sentinel with Danny J. Bakewell, Sr. as the publisher in 2004.

Prior to assuming the role of publisher, Blackwell served as President of *The Brotherhood Crusade*, a civil rights advocate organization and the largest Black philanthropic institution in America, for over thirty years. He was also co-founder of the National Black United Fund (NBUF), the advocacy organization which directs African American philanthropy to Black-led organizations nationally. In addition, Bakewell was also named as "one of the leading proponents of urban bootstrap economics" by Time magazine.

In recent years, Bakewell has been focused on expanding and diversifying his firm *The Bakewell Company*, which is the largest minority-owned development firm on the West Coast. He purchased the Los Angeles Sentinel, the city's oldest and largest Black newspaper, in 2004. Soon after, in 2007, he purchased the WBOK radio station in New Orleans, Louisiana. Both the Sentinel and WBOK have added to his emergence into the media market. In 2009, Bakewell was elected Chairman of the National Newspaper Publishers Association (NNPA).

Bakewell and his wife Aline have two adult children (Danny Jr. and Brandi) and four grandchildren. Bakewell and his family currently reside in Bradbury, California.

POLITICIANS, LAWYERS AND OTHER LEADERS WHO MAKE THE GRADE

Harold Lee Washington (April 15, 1922 – November 25, 1987) was an American lawyer and politician who was the 51st Mayor of Chicago. Washington became the first African American to be elected as the city's mayor in February 1983.

Born in Chicago and raised in the Bronzeville neighborhood, Washington became involved in local 3rd Ward politics under Chicago Alderman and future Congressman Ralph Metcalfe after graduating from Roosevelt University and Northwestern University School of Law. Washington was a member of the U.S. House of Representatives from 1981 to 1983, representing Illinois's first district. Washington had previously served in the Illinois State Senate and the Illinois House of Representatives from 1965 until 1976.

Harold Lee Washington was born on April 15, 1922 at Cook County Hospital in Chicago, Illinois, to Roy and Bertha Washington. Harold Washington grew up in Bronzeville, a Chicago neighborhood that was the center of black culture for the entire Midwest in the early and middle 20th century. After attending St Benedict, the Moor Boarding School in Milwaukee from 1928 to 1932, Washington attended DuSable High School, then a newly established racially segregated public high school, and was a member of its first graduating class. In a 1939 citywide track meet, Washington placed first in the 110-meter-high hurdles event, and second in the 220-meter low hurdles event. Between his junior and senior year of high school, Washington dropped out, claiming that he no longer felt challenged by the coursework. He worked at a meatpacking plant for a time before his father helped him get a job at the U.S. Treasury branch in the city. There he met Nancy Dorothy Finch, whom he married soon after; Washington was 19 years old and Dorothy was 17 years old. Seven months later, the U.S. was drawn into World War II with the bombing of Pearl Harbor by the Japanese on Sunday, December 7, 1941.

In 1942, Washington was drafted into the United States Army for the war effort and after basic training, sent overseas as part of a racially segregated unit of the U.S. Army Air Corps unit of Engineers. After the American invasion of the Philippines in 1944, on Leyte Island and later the main Luzon island, Washington was part of a unit building runways for bombers, protective fighter aircraft, refueling planes, and returning damaged aircraft. Eventually, Washington rose to the rank of First Sergeant in the Army Air Corps (later in the war renamed the U.S. Army Air Forces).

In the summer of 1946, Washington, aged 24 and a war veteran, enrolled at Roosevelt College (now Roosevelt University). Washington joined other groups of students not permitted to enroll in other local colleges. He chaired a fund-raising drive by students, and then was named to a committee that supported citywide efforts to outlaw "restrictive covenants" in housing.

In 1948, after the college had moved to the Auditorium Building, Washington was elected the third president of Roosevelt's student council. He graduated in August 1949, with a Bachelor of Arts (B.A.) degree. In addition to his activities at Roosevelt, he was a member of Phi Beta Sigma fraternity.

Washington then applied and was admitted to study law at the Northwestern University School of Law in Chicago. During this time, Washington was divorced from Dorothy Finch.

At Northwestern Law School, Washington was the only black student in his class. As at Roosevelt, he entered school politics. In 1951, his last year, he was elected treasurer of the Junior Bar Association (JBA). Overall, Washington stayed away from the activism that defined his years at Roosevelt. During the evenings and weekends, he worked to supplement his GI Bill income. He received his J.D. in 1952.

From 1951 until he was first slated for election in 1965, Washington worked in the offices of the 3rd Ward Alderman, former Olympic athlete Ralph Metcalfe. While working under Metcalfe, Washington began to organize the 3rd Ward's Young Democrats (YD) organization. At YD conventions, the 3rd Ward would push for numerous resolutions in the interest of blacks. Washington avoided radicalism and preferred to work through the party to engender change.

While working with the Young Democrats, Washington met Mary Ella Smith. They dated for the next 20 years, and in 1983 Washington proposed to Smith.

During his time as an Illinois legislator (1965-1980), Washington backed fair-housing codes and the establishment of a statewide Martin Luther King Jr. Day. In 1980, Washington was elected to the U.S. House of Representatives in Illinois's 1st congressional district. He defeated incumbent Representative Bennett Stewart in the Democratic primary.

When Washington graduated to the United States House of Representatives in 1981, he used his congressional seat to condemn proposals seeking to weaken affirmative action, and the Congressional Black Caucus also tapped Washington to oversee enhancements to the Voting Rights Act of 1965.

Anticipating that the Democratic Party would challenge him in his bid for re-nomination in 1982, Washington spent much of his first term campaigning for re-election, often travelling back to Chicago to campaign. Washington missed many House votes, an issue that would come up in his campaign for mayor in 1983.

During hearings in the South regarding the Voting Rights Act, Washington asked questions that shed light on tactics used to prevent African Americans from voting After the amendments were submitted on the floor, Washington spoke from prepared speeches that avoided rhetoric and addressed the issues. As a result, the amendments were defeated, and Congress passed the Voting Rights Act Extension. By the time Washington faced re-election in 1982, he had cemented his popularity in the 1st Congressional District.

He had collected 250,000 signatures to get on the ballot, although only 610 signatures were required. With his re-election to Congress locked up, Washington turned his attention to the next Chicago mayoral election.

Upon exiting Congress, Washington went on to become Chicago's first black mayor. In the February 22, 1983, Democratic mayoral primary, more than 100,000 new voters registered to vote led by a coalition that included the Latino reformed gang Young Lords led by Jose Cha Jimenez. Washington won with 37% of the vote, versus 33% for Byrne and 30% for Daley. Washington was sworn in as mayor on April 29, 1983 and resigned his Congressional seat the following day. He served as mayor from April 29, 1983 until his death, just a few weeks into his second mayoral term.

On November 25, 1987, thousands of Chicagoans attended his wake in the lobby of City Hall between November 27 and November 29, 1987. On November 30, 1987, Reverend B. Herbert Martin officiated Washington's funeral service in Christ Universal Temple at 119th Street and Ashland Avenue in Chicago. After the service, Washington was buried in Oak Woods Cemetery on the South Side of Chicago.

In later years, various city facilities and institutions were named or renamed after the late mayor to commemorate his legacy.

Barbara Charline Jordan (February 21, 1936 – January 17, 1996) was an American lawyer, educator and politician who was a leader of the Civil Rights Movement.

Barbara Jordan was born in her parents' home in Houston, Texas' Fifth Ward. Barbara's childhood was centered on church life. Her mother Arlyne Patten Jordan was a maid, housewife and church teacher, and her father Benjamin Jordan, was a Baptist minister and warehouse clerk. Barbara was the youngest of three children, with siblings, Rose Mary Jordan McGowan and Bennie Jordan Creswell. Barbara Jordan attended Roberson Elementary School. She then attended the segregated Phillis Wheatley High School, where a career day speech by Edith Sampson, a black lawyer, inspired her to become an attorney. Barbara graduated from Phillis Wheatley High School in 1952 with honors.

Because of segregation, Barbara could not attend The University of Texas at Austin and instead she became a member of the inaugural class at Texas Southern University, the historically-black institution hastily created by the Texas legislature to avoid having to integrate The University of Texas. There, Barbara majored in political science and history. At Texas Southern University, Jordan joined the debate team and helped lead it to national renown, defeating opponents from Yale and Brown and famously tying Harvard's debaters when they came to Houston.

Barbara graduated magna cum laude from Texas Southern University in 1956 and was accepted at Boston University's School of Law. Three years later, in 1959, Barbara Jordan earned her law degree as one of only two African American women in her class. She passed the Massachusetts and Texas bars and then taught political science at Tuskegee Institute in Alabama for a year. In 1960, she returned to Houston to open a law office in the Fifth Ward.

Jordan campaigned unsuccessfully in 1962 and 1964 for the Texas House of Representatives. She won a seat in the Texas Senate in 1966, becoming the first African-American state senator since 1883 and the first black woman to serve in that body. Re-elected to a full term in the Texas Senate in 1968, she served until 1972. She was the first African-American female to serve as president *pro tem* of the state senate and served one day, June 10, 1972, as acting governor of Texas. To date, Jordan is the only African American woman to serve as governor of a state (excluding lieutenant governors). During her time in the Texas Legislature, Jordan sponsored or cosponsored some 70 bills.

In 1972, she was elected to the U.S. House of Representatives, the first woman elected in her own right to represent Texas in the House. She also received extensive support from former President Lyndon B. Johnson, who helped her secure a position on the House Judiciary Committee.

On July 25, 1974, Jordan gave the 15-minute opening statement of the Judiciary Committee's impeachment hearing for Richard Nixon. The impeachment speech helped lead to Nixon's resignation over the Watergate scandal and won Jordan national acclaim for her rhetoric, intellect and integrity. Two years later she was asked to deliver the keynote address at the 1976 Democratic National Convention—another first for an African American woman.

Jordan retired from Congress in 1979 to become an adjunct professor teaching ethics at the Lyndon Baines Johnson School of Public Affairs at the University of Texas. She became an active public speaker and advocate, amassing 25 honorary doctorates.

From 1994 until her death, Jordan chaired the U.S. Commission on Immigration Reform. Her work as chair of the U.S. Commission on Immigration Reform, which recommended reducing legal immigration by about one-third, is frequently cited by American immigration restrictionists.

In 1994 Bill Clinton awarded Barbara Jordan the Presidential Medal of Freedom, the country's highest civilian honor and The NAACP presented her with the Spingarn Medal. She was honored many times and was given over 20 honorary degrees from institutions across the country, including Harvard and Princeton. She was also elected to the Texas and National Women's Halls of Fame.

Barbara Jordan remained private about her illnesses, which finally included diabetes and cancer. She died of leukemia-related pneumonia on January 17, 1996. Breaking barriers even in death, Barbara Jordan became the first African American to be buried among the governors, senators and congressmen in the Texas State Cemetery.

Elijah Eugene Cummings (January 18, 1951 – October 17, 2019) was an American politician and civil rights advocate who served in the United States House of Representatives for Maryland's 7th congressional district from 1996 until his death in 2019.

The district includes just over half of the city of Baltimore, including most of the majority-black precincts of Baltimore County, as well as most of Howard County.

Cummings was born in Baltimore, Maryland, the son of Ruth Elma and Robert Cummings. His parents were sharecroppers. He was the third child of seven. When he was 11 years old, Cummings and some friends worked to integrate a segregated swimming pool in South Baltimore.

Cummings graduated with honors from the Baltimore City College high school in 1969. He then attended Howard University in Washington, D.C., where he served in the student government as sophomore class president, student government treasurer and later student government president. He became a member of the Phi Beta Kappa Society and graduated in 1973 with a Bachelor's degree in Political Science. *Cummings received 12 honorary doctoral degrees from universities across the United States, most recently an honorary doctorate of public service from the University of Maryland, College Park in 2017.*

Cummings graduated from law school at the University of Maryland School of Law, receiving his Juris Doctor in 1976, and was admitted to the bar in Maryland later that year. He practiced law for 19 years before first being elected to the House in the 1996 elections.

Five-term Congressman for Maryland's 7th congressional district, Kweisi Mfume resigned in February 1996 to take the presidency of the NAACP. Cummings won a crowded seven-way Democratic primary—with 37.5% of the vote. In the special election, he defeated Republican Kenneth Kondner with over 80 percent of the vote. He defeated Kondner again in November by a similar margin to win the seat in his own right. Congressman Cummings was reelected 11 more times in the contests which followed, never dropping below 69 percent of the vote. He ran unopposed in 2006.

Cummings lived in the Madison Park community in Baltimore and was an active member of the New Psalmist Baptist Church. He married Joyce Matthews, with whom he had a daughter, Jennifer J. Cummings. He had a son and a daughter, Adia Cummings, from other relationships. He married Maya Rockeymoore Cummings in 2009, who was elected chairwoman of the Maryland Democratic Party in December 2018.

For 14 years, Cummings served in the Maryland House of Delegates. In the Maryland General Assembly, he served as Chairman of the Legislative Black Caucus of Maryland and was the first African American in Maryland history to be named Speaker Pro Tempore, the second highest position in the House of Delegates.

Cummings also served on several boards and commissions, both in and out of Baltimore. He served on numerous Maryland boards and commissions including the Board of Visitors to the United States Naval Academy and the Elijah Cummings Youth Program in Israel. In his role as chair of the Oversight Committee, Cummings presided over the first public testimony by President Trump's former lawyer, Michael Cohen, and was a leading figure in the impeachment inquiry against Donald Trump.

Cummings introduced the Presidential and Federal Records Act Amendments of 2014, a bipartisan bill signed into law by then-President Barack Obama in December 2014.

Cummings underwent surgery to repair his aortic valve in May 2017 and was absent from Capitol Hill for two months. In July 2017, he developed a surgery-related infection but returned to work. Cummings was later hospitalized for a knee infection.

Cummings was diagnosed with rare form of cancer called thymic carcinoma in 1994 while serving as a member of the Maryland House of Delegates. It was revealed in November 2019 that Cummings had lived with the cancer for 25 years, though it was not stated as the cause of death.

Cummings died on October 17, 2019, at Johns Hopkins Hospital at the age of 68 from "complications concerning longstanding health challenges", his spokeswoman stated. Cummings is the first African American lawmaker to achieve the honor of lying in state at the nation's Capital.

On October 25, 2019, the official funeral for Cummings was held at the New Psalmist Baptist Church in Baltimore and was attended by members of his family and various political figures including former Presidents Barack Obama and Bill Clinton, former Secretary of State Hillary Clinton, former Vice President Joe Biden, along with Nancy Pelosi, John Lewis, Amy Klobuchar, Elizabeth Warren, and Alexandria Ocasio-Cortez.

Eric Leroy Adams (born September 1, 1960) is the Borough President of Brooklyn, New York City. He was the first African American to hold the position.

Adams was born in Brownsville, Brooklyn. He was raised in Bushwick, Brooklyn, and South Jamaica, Queens. He graduated from Bayside High School in Queens in 1978. He subsequently received an associate degree from the New York City College of Technology, a B.A. from the John Jay College of Criminal Justice, and an M.P.A. from Marist College. By his own admission, he was a D+ student.

Adams served as an officer in the New York City Transit Police and in the New York City Police Department (NYPD) for 22 years, after being asked to "infiltrate" the police at the behest of the Reverend Herbert Daughtry, of the House of the Lord's Church in Brooklyn. He graduated from the New York City Police Academy in 1984. He started in the New York City Transit Police, and continued with the NYPD when the transit police and the NYPD merged. He worked in the 6th Precinct in Greenwich Village, the 94th Precinct in Greenpoint, and the 88th Precinct covering Fort Greene and Clinton Hill. While serving, he co-founded 100 Blacks in Law Enforcement Who Care, an advocacy group for black police officers, and often spoke out against police brutality and racial profiling. During the 1990s Adams served as president of the Grand Council of Guardians, an organization of black officers.

In 1993, while President of the Ground Council of Guardians, Adams accused politician Herman Badillo of betraying his Hispanic heritage by having as his wife a white, Jewish woman, instead of a Latino.

In 1994, Adams, endorsed by the Nation of Islam, was defeated by Major Owens in the Democratic primary for the 11th Congressional seat in central Brooklyn. Adams was first elected to the New York State Senate in 2006, serving for four terms, until late 2013. He represented the 20th Senate District, which includes parts of the Brooklyn neighborhoods of Brownsville, Crown Heights, East Flatbush, Park Slope, Prospect Heights, and Sunset Park.

As a freshman state senator, in 2007 and 2008 he was among the legislators who suggested a pay raise for themselves, though they ranked third highest in pay among all state lawmakers in the United States. On December 2, 2009, Adams was one of the 24 state senators to vote in favor of marriage equality in New York State. He spoke in support of the freedom to marry during the debate before the vote.

Adams was a vocal opponent of the NYPD's "stop and frisk" policy, which predominantly affected young Black and Latino men, and which in 2000 the U.S. Commission on Civil Rights had said constituted racial profiling. In 2011 he supported calling for a federal investigation into stop-and-frisk practices. He sought to stop the NYPD from gathering data about individuals who had been stopped but not charged.

In 2012 Adams served as co-chair of New York's State Legislators Against Illegal Guns. Adams and five other mostly African-American state lawmakers wore hooded sweatshirts in the legislative chamber on March 12, 2012, in protest of the shooting of Trayvon Martin, a Florida teen who was killed by George Zimmerman.

On November 5, 2013, Eric Adams was elected Brooklyn borough president with 90.8 percent of the vote, more than any other candidate for borough president in New York City that year.

Adams, in his role as Brooklyn borough president, appoints the members of each of the 18 community boards in Brooklyn, half of which are nominated by local members of the City Council. Community boards members represent their neighbors in matters dealing with land use and other specific neighborhood needs.

In 2016, he launched a digital app process for board membership, which has increased applications by 10 percent, and he intends – under the authority granted by a 2015 state law – to appoint youth members to every community board. In 2016, Adams also invested $26 million and an additional $55 million in 2017—half of his allotted budget that year – to improve STEAM (Science, Technology, Engineering, Arts and Mathematics) education across Brooklyn schools.

In September 2017, Adams unveiled his recommendations for the future of the Bedford Union Armory in Crown Heights. His recommendation was to disapprove the application with conditions, while calling for the inclusion of a greater amount of affordable housing on site. The Bedford Union Armory proposals would contain recreational facilities, spaces for locally based non-profits, as well as two new residential buildings, including a condominium building along President Street in place of the Armory's stables. In November 2017 Eric Adams was reelected as Brooklyn borough president.

In January 2018, Adams announced a partnership between his administration, Brooklyn Community Services (BCS), and Turning Point Brooklyn to establish a first-of-its-kind a mobile shower service that will travel across the borough to serve homeless Brooklynites and other at-risk populations, such as day laborers, sex workers, and runaway LGBTQ+ youth.

In February 2018, Adams supported State Senator Hamilton and Assembly Member Richardson in calling for statewide K-12 instruction of Black history. In April 2018, Adams hailed a first-of-its-kind empowerment partnership with Kennedy Conglomerate Inc., a venture started by local entrepreneur Kareem Kennedy, for a mobile barber service to which he has allocated $3,000 in discretionary funding to provide free haircuts for the homeless. Borough President Adams has also advocated for making two-year CUNY colleges free.

Stacey Yvonne Abrams (born December 9, 1973) is an American politician, lawyer, and author who served in the Georgia House of Representatives from 2006 to 2017, and served as minority leader from 2011 to 2017. Abrams was the first African American female major-party gubernatorial nominee of the United States. In February

2019, she became the first African American woman to deliver a response to the State of the Union address.

Abrams, the second of six siblings, was born to Robert and Carolyn Abrams in Madison, Wisconsin, and raised in Gulfport, Mississippi. The family moved to Atlanta, Georgia, where her parents pursued graduate degrees and later became Methodist ministers. She attended Avondale High School, where she was selected for a Telluride Association Summer Program. While in high school, she was hired as a typist for a congressional campaign and at age 17 she was hired as a speechwriter based on the edits she made while typing.

As a college freshman in 1992, Abrams took part in a protest on the steps of the Georgia Capitol, in which she joined in burning the state flag. At the time Georgia's state flag incorporated the Confederate battle flag, which had been added to the state flag in 1956 as an anti-civil rights movement action. It was designed by Southern Democrat John Sammons Bell, an attorney who was an outspoken supporter of segregation.

In 1995 Abrams earned a Bachelor of Arts in interdisciplinary studies (political science, economics and sociology) from Spelman College, *magna cum laude*. While in college she worked in the youth services department in the office of Atlanta mayor Maynard Jackson. She later interned at the U.S. Environmental Protection Agency.

As a Harry S. Truman Scholar, Abrams studied public policy at the University of Texas at Austin's LBJ School of Public Affairs, where she earned a Master of Public Affairs degree in 1998. In 1999 she earned a J.D. degree from Yale Law School.

In 2002, at age 29, Abrams was appointed the deputy city attorney for the City of Atlanta. Abrams represented House District 89, which includes portions of the City of Atlanta and unincorporated DeKalb County, covering the communities of Candler Park, Cedar Grove, Columbia, Druid Hills, Edgewood, Highland Park, Kelley Lake, Kirkwood, Lake Claire, South DeKalb, Toney Valley, and Tilson. She served on the Appropriations, Ethics, Judiciary Non-Civil, Rules and Ways & Means committees.

Abrams's first major action as minority leader was to cooperate with Republican governor Nathan Deal's administration to reform the HOPE Scholarship program. She co-sponsored the 2011 legislation that preserved the HOPE program by decreasing the scholarship amount paid to Georgia students and funded a 1% low-interest loan program for students.

On August 25, 2017, Abrams resigned from the General Assembly to focus on her gubernatorial campaign. Abrams ran for governor of Georgia in 2018. In the Democratic primary she ran against Stacey Evans, another member of the Georgia House of Representatives, in what some called "the battle of the Staceys". Abrams was endorsed by Bernie Sanders and Our Revolution. On May 22, she won the Democratic nomination, making her the first black woman in the U.S. to be a major party's nominee for governor.

In her historic bid to become governor of Georgia, Stacey Yvonne Abrams electrified not only multitudes of voters of the Peach State but supporters nationwide.

As Georgia's tightest gubernatorial race in more than 50 years came to a close, Abrams confirmed that Georgia Secretary of State Brian Kemp had enough votes to be certified to occupy the statehouse but refused to concede the race. She asserted in her speech to supporters,

"Concession means to acknowledge an action is right, true or proper. As a woman of conscience and faith, I cannot concede that."

After winning the primary, Abrams secured a number of high-profile endorsements, including one from former President Barack Obama.

Almost a week before election day, the Republican nominee, Brian Kemp, cancelled a debate scheduled seven weeks earlier in order to attend a Trump rally in Georgia. Abrams lost the election by 50,000 votes and immediately sued the Georgia board of elections, citing allegations of voter suppression. Her position is that Kemp, who oversaw the election in his role as Secretary of State, had a conflict of interest and suppressed the election turnout by purging 670,000 voter registrations in 2017 and that about 53,000 voter registrations were pending a month before the election.

On January 29, 2019, Senate minority leader Chuck Schumer (D-NY) announced that Abrams would deliver the response to the State of the Union address on February 5. She was the first African American woman to give the rebuttal to the address, as well as the first and only non-office-holding person to do so since the SOTU responses began in 1966.

Abrams has completed seven international fellowships and traveled to "more than a dozen foreign countries" for policy work. She is a lifetime member of the Council on Foreign Relations and spoke at CFR's Conference on Diversity in International Affairs in 2019.

On April 30, 2019, Abrams announced that she would not run for the U.S. Senate in 2020. On August 17, 2019, Abrams announced the founding of Fair Fight 2020, an organization that will assist Democrats financially and technically to build voter protection teams in 20 states. Abrams is Fair Fight Action 2020's chair.

Ayanna Soyini Pressley (born February 3, 1974) is an American politician serving as the U.S. Representative for Massachusetts's 7th congressional district since 2019. Her district includes the northern three-fourths of Boston, most of Cambridge, parts of Milton, as well as all of Chelsea, Everett, Randolph, and Somerville.

A member of the Democratic Party, during the Democratic primary, Pressley defeated 10-term incumbent Michael Capuano, who gained backing from some of America's most celebrated black politicians, a group that included civil rights legend Rep. John Lewis (D-GA) and Massachusetts first African American governor, Deval Patrick.

Pressley ran unopposed in the general election and was previously elected as an at-large member of the Boston City Council in 2010. She was the first black woman elected to the Boston City Council.

Pressley was born in Cincinnati, Ohio, but raised in Chicago, Illinois, the only child of mother Sandra Pressley, who worked multiple jobs to support the family and also worked as a community organizer for the Chicago Urban League advocating for tenant's rights, and father Martin Terrell, who struggled with addiction and was incarcerated throughout Pressley's childhood, but eventually earned multiple degrees and taught at college level. Pressley's parents' marriage eventually ended in divorce.

Pressley grew up on the north side of Chicago and attended the Francis W. Parker School. While at the prestigious private school, she was a cheerleader, did modeling and voice-over work, appeared in Planned Parenthood bus advertisements, and was a competitive debater. During her senior year of high school, she was voted the "most likely to be mayor of Chicago" and was the commencement speaker for her class.

Her mother later moved to Brooklyn, New York where she worked as an executive assistant and later remarried. When Pressley was elected to the Boston City Council, her mother would often attend the public meetings, wearing a hat that said, "Mama Pressley."

From 1992 to 1994, Pressley attended the College of General Studies at Boston University, but she left school to take a full-time job at the Boston Marriott Copley Place to support her mother, who had lost her job. She took further courses at Boston University Metropolitan College, also known as MET.

After leaving Boston University, Pressley worked as a district representative for Representative Joseph P. Kennedy II (D–MA), for whom she had interned during college. The work included assisting constituents with Social Security claims and working with senior citizens, veterans, and people with disabilities. Pressley became Kennedy's scheduler, then worked as constituency director, before becoming the political director and senior aide for Senator Kerry. During 2009, Pressley served as United States Senator John Kerry's (D-Mass.) political director.

Pressley was first elected to the Boston City Council in November 2009. Upon being sworn in on January 4, 2010, she was the first woman of color to serve in the 100-year history of the Boston City Council. The only woman in a field of 15 candidates, Pressley earned one of four at-large spots on the city's 13-member council with nearly 42,000 votes.

In her first year as a City Councilor, Pressley formed the Committee on Healthy Women, Families, and Communities, which addresses issues such as domestic violence, child abuse, and human trafficking. She worked collaboratively with community members to develop a comprehensive sexual education and health curriculum and update the expectant and parenting student policy. Both were successfully implemented into Boston Public Schools.

Pressley topped the ticket again in November 2013 and November 2015, and placed second in November 2017.

In January 2018, Pressley announced her challenge to incumbent United States Representative Michael Capuano in the 2018 Democratic primary nomination for the Massachusetts's 7th congressional district. No Republican even filed, meaning that whoever won the primary would be all but assured of victory in November.

The 7th district is traditionally Democratic and is the state's only district where the majority of residents are not white. Capuano received endorsements from civil rights veteran and U.S. Representative John Lewis of Georgia as well as U.S. Representative Maxine Waters of California.

Pressley was endorsed by *The Boston Globe* and local chapter of the hotel and electrical worker union, Grassroots movements including Democracy for America, Brand New Congress and the Justice Democrats supported Pressley. She received the endorsements of former Massachusetts Democratic Party chair John E. Walsh, Massachusetts Attorney General Maura Healey, former Newton mayor Setti Warren and Boston city councilor Michelle Wu.

In the September 4, 2018, Democratic primary election, Pressley defeated Capuano by a margin of 59% to 41%.

Pressley is the first African American woman elected to represent Massachusetts in Congress. Pressley is a member of the informal group known as "The Squad", whose members form a unified front to push for progressive changes such as the Green New Deal and

Medicare-for-all. The other members of "The Squad" are Ilhan Omar (D-MN), Rashida Tlaib (D-MI), and Alexandria Ocasio-Cortez (D-NY) Pressley is the oldest and most politically experienced of the four, who asked her to act as spokesperson after Trump attacked them.

In an interview with The Boston Globe in July 2019, Pressley said her office has received death threats after president Trump's tweets of July 14, 2019 and in general since her election.

On September 17, 2019, Pressley filed a resolution that calls for the House Judiciary Committee to launch impeachment proceedings against Supreme Court Justice Brett Kavanaugh.

In November 2019, Pressley introduced a criminal justice reform resolution that calls for decriminalizing consensual sex work, abolishing cash bail, legalizing marijuana, abolishing capital punishment, and solitary confinement, and shrinking the U.S. prison population by greater than 80 percent. The house resolution is called The People's Justice Guarantee.

During her victory speech following the September primary election, Pressley called out President Donald Trump, claiming he is "a racist, misogynistic, truly empathy-bankrupt man. She supports the Impeachment of Donald Trump.

Pressley lives in Dorchester, Massachusetts with her husband, Conan Harris, and her stepdaughter. In January 2020, Pressley revealed that she had been diagnosed with alopecia areata, resulting in the loss of all of her hair, and saying in a public announcement "I want to be freed from the secret and the shame that that secret carries with it."

Former Boston City Council Member, Ayanna Pressley, became the first African American congresswoman from the state of

Massachusetts. The persistent Pressley set her path to victory by building grassroots support to beat the local and national political establishment.

The first Somali and one of two Muslim women elected to Congress, Omar, 37, now assumes the Minnesota congressional seat previously occupied by Rep. Keith Ellison, the former deputy Democratic National Committee Chair who is now the state's Attorney General. Already engaged in political battles over her tweets critical of Sen. Lindsey Graham and the nation of Israel, Omar has not received a unanimous welcome as the freshman legislator joins the highly-coveted House Foreign Affairs Committee.

Ilhan Abdullahi Omar (born October 4, 1982) is an American politician serving as the U.S. Representative for Minnesota's 5th congressional district since 2019. The district includes all of Minneapolis and some of its suburbs.

Omar was born in Mogadishu, Somalia on October 4, 1982, and spent her early years in Baidoa, Somalia. She was the youngest of seven siblings, including sister Sahra Noor. Her father, Nur Omar Mohamed, an ethnic Somali from the Majeerteen clan of Northeastern Somalia, worked as a teacher trainer. Her mother, Fadhuma Abukar Haji Hussein, a Benadiri (a community of partial Yemeni descent), died when Ilhan was two. She was raised by her father and grandfather thereafter. Her grandfather Abukar was the director of Somalia's National Marine Transport, and some of Omar's uncles and aunts also worked as civil servants and educators. She and her family fled Somalia to escape the war and spent four years in a Dadaab refugee camp in Garissa County, Kenya, near the Somali border.

After first arriving in New York in 1992, Omar's family secured asylum in the U.S. in 1995 and lived for a time in Arlington, Virginia, before moving to and settling in Minneapolis, where her father worked first as a taxi driver and later for the post office. Her father and grandfather emphasized the importance of democracy during her upbringing, and at age 14 she accompanied her grandfather to caucus meetings, serving as his interpreter. She has spoken about school bullying she endured during her time in Virginia, stimulated by her distinctive Somali appearance and wearing of the hijab. She recalls gum being pressed into her hijab, being pushed downstairs, and physical taunts while she was changing for gym class. Omar remembers her father's reaction to these incidents: "They are doing something to you because they feel threatened in some way by your existence." Omar became a U.S. citizen in 2000 when she was 17 years old.

Omar attended Edison High School and volunteered there as a student organizer. Omar began her professional career as a community nutrition educator at the University of Minnesota, working in that capacity from 2006 to 2009 in the Greater Minneapolis–Saint Paul area.

She graduated from North Dakota State University in 2011 with a bachelor's degree, majoring in political science and international studies. Omar was a Policy Fellow at the University of Minnesota's Humphrey School of Public Affairs.

In 2013, Omar managed Andrew Johnson's campaign for Minneapolis City Council. After Johnson was elected, she served as his Senior Policy Aide from 2013 to 2015. During a contentious precinct caucus that turned violent in February 2014, she was attacked by five people and was injured.

In 2016, Omar ran on the Democratic–Farmer–Labor (DFL) ticket for the Minnesota House of Representatives in District 60B, which includes part of northeast Minneapolis. On August 9, Omar defeated Mohamud Noor and incumbent Phyllis Kahn in the DFL primary. Her chief opponent in the general election was Republican nominee Abdimalik Askar In November Omar won the general election, becoming the first Somali American legislator in the United States

Omar was elected to the Minnesota House of Representatives in 2016 on the Democratic–Farmer–Labor Party line. Her term began on January 3, 2017.

In 2018, she was elected to the U.S. House of Representatives, marking a number of historic electoral firsts: she is the first Somali-American, the first naturalized citizen from Africa, and the first non-white woman elected from Minnesota. She is also one of the first two Muslim women (along with Rashida Tlaib of Michigan) to serve in Congress.

On June 5, 2018, Omar filed to run for the United States House of Representatives from Minnesota's 5th congressional district after six-term incumbent Keith Ellison announced he would not seek reelection to that office. Omar won the August 14 primary with 48.2% of the vote

Following Omar's election, the ban on head coverings in the U.S. House was modified, and Omar became the first woman to wear a hijab on the House floor.

Omar received the largest percentage of the vote of any female candidate for U.S. House in state history. She was sworn in on a copy of the Quran owned by her grandfather.

MILITARY NOTABLES WHO MAKE THE GRADE

Corporal Freddie Stowers (January 12, 1896 – September 28, 1918) was an African-American corporal in the United States Army who was killed in action during World War I while serving in an American unit under French command. Over 70 years later, he posthumously received the Medal of Honor and Purple Heart for his actions.

Stowers was born in Sandy Springs, South Carolina, the grandson of a slave. Before the war, he worked as a farmhand. He married a woman named Pearl, with whom he had one daughter, Minnie Lee.

Stowers was drafted into the Army in 1917, and assigned to Company C, 1st Battalion of the segregated U.S. 371st Infantry Regiment, originally part of the 93d Infantry Division (Colored).

Stowers was part of a new division that, by the end of the war, included a commissioned African American officer, and saw sustained combat. Due to compromises with the institutional racism of the day, this combat did not take place under American command: although his unit had arrived in France as part of the American Expeditionary Force, Stowers' regiment, like the others in the division, was seconded to the 157th French Army "Red Hand Division", badly in need of reinforcement, under the command of the General Mariano Goybet.

Early on the morning of September 28, 1918, while serving as squad leader of Company C, 371st Infantry Regiment, 93rd Division,

Stowers' company was ordered to assault *Côte* 188, a tall, heavily defended hill overlooking a farm near Ardeuil-et-Montfauxelles, in the Ardennes region of France. Stowers went above and beyond the call of duty when his company led the attack at Hill 188, Champagne Marne Sector, France.

At first, the German defenders offered stiff resistance, bombarding the Americans with mortars, raking them with machine guns and keeping up steady rifle fire. The advance was not halted, however; with the Americans steadily gaining ground, and the Germans communicated their surrender with verbal and hand signals. This however proved to be a ruse, and as Company C drew near the German trenches, the machine guns opened up again. Within minutes, the company's strength was reduced by half. The lieutenant commanding Stowers' platoon went down, followed by the more senior noncommissioned officers. Corporal Stowers, trained to lead a section of a rifle squad, was now in command of a battered and demoralized platoon.

Stowers began crawling toward a German machine gun nest and shouted for his men to follow. The platoon successfully reached the first German trench line and reduced the machine guns by enfilade fire. Stowers then reorganized his force and led a charge against the second German line of trenches. During this assault, Stowers was struck by an enemy machine gun, but kept going until he was struck a second time. He collapsed from loss of blood but ordered his men not to be discouraged and to keep going and take out the German guns. Inspired by Stowers' courage, the men forged ahead and successfully drove the Germans from the hill and into the plain below. Stowers, meanwhile, succumbed to his wounds on *Côte* 188. He is buried, along with 133 of his comrades, at the Meuse-Argonne American Cemetery and Memorial east of the village of Romagne-sous-Montfaucon.

Shortly after his death, Stowers was recommended for the Medal of Honor; however, this recommendation was never processed. In Stowers' case, the official position is that his recommendation was "misplaced," which is plausible given that three other MOH recommendations for black soldiers were at least processed, even if the decision to award the Distinguished Service Cross remains controversial and possibly racism-related.

In 1990, at the instigation of Congress, the Department of the Army conducted a review and the Stowers' recommendation was uncovered. Subsequently, a team was dispatched to France to investigate the circumstances of Stowers' death. Based on information collected by this team, the Army Decorations Board approved the award of the Medal of Honor. On April 24, 1991—seventy-three years after he was killed in action, Stowers' surviving sisters, Georgina and Mary, received the medal from President George H.W. Bush at the White House.

Stowers Elementary School on Fort Benning, Georgia, and the Corporal Freddie Stowers Single Soldier Billeting Complex on Fort Jackson, South Carolina, are both named in his honor.

Harriet M. Waddy (June 20, 1904 – 1999) was one of the two highest-ranking black officers in the women's Army Corps in World War II.

Born in Kansas, Harriet was brought up by her maternal grandmother. She went on to graduate from Kansas State College of Agriculture and Applied Science. Before entering the military, she was an aide to civil rights pioneer Mary McLeod Bethune. In the 1930s, when Waddy collaborated with Mary in the Bureau of Negro Affairs, her certainty about a singular point emerged: participation at every level of national affairs was the key to inclusion for African Americans.

More than 6,000 black women signed on with the Women's Army Auxiliary Corps during World War II. The war lasted only six years. In a span of time black women flooded the United States Army in legions to serve their country and find new opportunities for independence, stability, and education. But the cloud of discrimination hung in the air and black women were relegated mostly to positions that amounted to little more than glorified domestic staff.

Harriet West Waddy had no way of knowing, as one of those thousands of women, she would significantly change the face of America's armed forces for black women. Waddy's career spanned 25 years of America's segregation era. Her tenure started with the completion of her Women's Army Corps (WAC) training at Fort Des Moines, Iowa. Throughout World War II, only two black women received the rank of major during WAC training. Waddy was one of them. After her promotion, she served as an aide for WAC director Col. Oveta Culp Hobby. Here, she was ideally placed as an active agent to change inclusiveness for black women in the military.

She was known as First Officer Harriet M. West at the beginning of her enlistment. Harriet had a different destiny in mind, even though she was criticized for remaining in uniform while her military sisters suffered. She said that enlisting in a segregated military, which does not represent an ideal of democracy, did not mean a retreat from our fight, but the opposite. She felt that it was a step closer to vanquishing the barriers of discrimination.

Her position as an adviser to the Army on racial issues meant having an amplified voice for spotlighting inequality in the armed forces. To that end, Waddy recruited black women into the Army. Her assignment included gathering information from black women in WAC installations across America about their treatment. The recipient of this report was First lady Eleanor Roosevelt.

Although married four times, Waddy never had children. Four years after her promotion to lieutenant colonel, she retired from active duty in 1952 – but remained in the Organized Reserve until 1969. In 1999, Waddy died at the home of friends at age 94 in Las Vegas, Nevada.

Daniel "Chappie" James Jr. (February 11, 1920 – February 25, 1978) was an American fighter pilot in the U.S. Air Force, who in 1975 became the first African American to reach the rank of four-star general in the armed forces. Upon being promoted to general, the Tuskegee Airman was named commander of the North American Air Defense Command, which made him responsible for all aspects of defense for the United States and Canada.

Daniel James Jr. was born on February 11, 1920, to Daniel and Lillie Anna (Brown) James. Daniel James Sr. worked for the Pensacola city gas company, while his mother, Lillie Anna James, was a high school teacher who established a private school for her own and other black children in Pensacola, Florida. His mother would continue to run the "Lillie A James School" until her death at the age of 82. James graduated from the Tuskegee University in 1942, receiving a Bachelor of Science degree in physical education.

He attended the famous Tuskegee Institute and instructed African American pilots during World War II. He flew combat missions during the Korean War and Vietnam War, and received the Defense

Distinguished Service Medal, two Air Force Distinguished Service Medals, two Legion of Merits, three Distinguished Flying Crosses, Meritorious Service Medal and fourteen Air Medals.

James continued civilian pilot training under the government-sponsored Civilian Pilot Training Program. He then enlisted in the Aviation Cadet Program of the U.S. Army Air Forces on January 18, 1943, receiving his commission as a 2d Lt and pilot wings at Tuskegee Army Airfield, Alabama, on July 28, 1943. He remained at Tuskegee as a civilian instructor pilot in the Army Air Corps later that July. Throughout the remainder of the war James trained pilots for the all-black 99th Pursuit Squadron.

After completing P-40 Warhawk training and then B-25 Mitchell training, James served as a B-25 pilot with the 617th Bomb Squadron of the 477th Bomb Group at Godman Army Airfield and then at Lockbourne Army Airfield from January 1944 till the end of the war. He did not see combat himself until the Korean War.

While serving in Lockbourne, James next served as a P-47 Thunderbolt pilot with the 301st Fighter Squadron from July 1947 to October 1948, and then served as on the staff of the 332nd Air Base Group at Lockbourne from November 1948 to September 1949.

In September 1949, James went to the Philippines as flight leader for the 12th Fighter-Bomber Squadron, 18th Fighter Wing at Clark Field. In July 1950 he left for Korea, where he flew 101 combat missions in P-51 Mustang and F-80 aircraft. His combat missions were with the 67th Fighter Bomber Squadron, 12th Fighter Bomber Squadron, and 44th Fighter Bomber Squadron.

James returned to the United States, and in July 1951 went to Otis Air Force Base, Massachusetts, as an all-weather jet fighter pilot with the 58th Fighter-Interceptor Squadron, later becoming operations officer. In April 1953, he became commander of the 437th Fighter-Interceptor Squadron, and assumed command of the 60th Fighter-Interceptor Squadron in August 1955.

James next was assigned to Headquarters U.S. Air Force as a staff officer in the Air Defense Division of the Office of the Deputy Chief of Staff for Operations. In July 1960 he was transferred to RAF Bentwaters in England, where he served successively as assistant director of operations and then director of operations, 81st Tactical Fighter Wing; commander, 92nd Tactical Fighter Squadron; and deputy commander for operations for the 81st Wing. In September 1964, James was transferred to Davis-Monthan Air Force Base, Arizona, where he was director of operations training and later deputy commander for operations for the 4453rd Combat Crew Training Wing.

James went to Ubon Royal Thai Air Force Base, Thailand, in December 1966, as deputy commander for operations, 8th TFW. In June 1967, under Colonel Robin Olds, he was named wing vice commander when Col. Vermont Garrison completed his tour. Both in their mid-40s, they formed a legendary team nicknamed "Blackman and Robin". James flew 78 combat missions into North Vietnam, many in the Hanoi/Haiphong area, and led a flight in the "Operation Bolo" MiG sweep in which seven Communist MiG-21s were destroyed, the highest total kill of any mission during the Vietnam War.

He was named vice commander of the 33rd TFW at Eglin Air Force Base, Florida, in December 1967. He was awarded the George Washington Freedom Foundation Medal in both 1967 and 1968.

While stationed at Eglin, the Florida State Jaycees named James as Florida's "Outstanding American of the Year" for 1969, and he received the Jaycee Distinguished Service Award. He was transferred to Wheelus Air Base in the Libyan Arab Republic in August 1969 as Commander of the 7272nd Fighter Training Wing. He received the Arnold Air Society Eugene M. Zuckert Award in 1970 for outstanding contributions to Air Force professionalism.

James became Deputy Assistant Secretary of Defense (Public Affairs) in March 1970 and was designated principal Deputy Assistant Secretary of Defense (Public Affairs) in April 1973. On September 1, 1974, he assumed duty as vice commander of the Military Airlift Command (MAC), headquartered at Scott Air Force Base, Illinois.

On September 1, 1975, Daniel James was promoted to the four-star rank of general (O-10) and assigned as commander in chief of NORAD/ADCOM at Peterson Air Force Base, Colorado. On December 6, 1977, he assumed duty as special assistant to the Chief of Staff, U.S. Air Force.

James retired from the Air Force on January 31, 1978. Daniel James died of a heart attack on February 25, 1978, just two weeks after his 58th birthday and three weeks following his retirement from the Air Force. He was buried with full military honors at Arlington National Cemetery. He was survived by his wife, Dorothy Watkins James, their daughter, Danice Berry, and two sons, Daniel James III and Claude James.

MEDIA AND PUBLIC RELATIONS EXPERTS WHO MAKE THE GRADE
FEATURING WBLS-RADIO PERSONALITIES

World's Best-Looking Sound since 1972, **WBLS** has been America's most recognizable black radio station, laying the foundation for feel-good crossover tunes and a sincere dedication for community outreach. WBLS' unique attention to the community has made it a heritage staple, resting at 107.5FM. For decades, it has been and continues to be the #1 source for R&B music and lifestyle, reaching the tri-state area with a clear, crisp signal sharing music and information.

107.5 WBLS-FM is a New York Urban Adult Contemporary station with over 2 million listeners. About 60% of WBLS-FM's listeners are between the ages of 25-54. Broadcasting from its signal are award-winning and internationally known personalities like Doctor Bob Lee, Steve Harvey, Lenny Green, Anne Tripp, Donnie McClurkin, Dahved Levy, DJ Marley Marl, Bishop Hezekiah Walker, Neicy Tribbett, Déjà Vu, Shaila, Fred Buggs, Jeff Foxx, and many others.

"Doctor" Bob Lee is one of the most recognized entertainment personalities in New York. For more than 30 years, he's had a rewarding career as a Radio and TV personality, DJ, author, motivational speaker, consultant and entrepreneur. He hosts BLS – Bob Lee Show, a music-intensive radio series. For more than ten years, Lee has also hosted the weekly live television program "Open," which broadcasts on BronxNet, a world-wide cable television station. The program features news and topics affecting the community and also treats viewers to new and established musical guests. In addition to his on-air roles, Bob manages community affairs and government relations for WBLS.

Lee started out as a DJ for 88.7 WTNY Radio in 1978 while he attended the New York Institute of Technology, where he later received his BA and MA in Communications. He eventually went on to be music director, program director and general manager for WTNY. He also started Doctor Bob Lee & Company, a mobile-DJ business where he traveled to colleges and universities to play, cut and mix/blend recorded music for numerous celebrations. In 1980, Lee joined 107.5 WBLS as an intern. In 1981, he won the Top DJ Award for 98.7 KISS-FM.

Throughout my career on radio I have had the opportunity to work with countless colleagues who made great contributions to the broadcasting industry, either behind the scenes or on the air in front of a mic. I acknowledge and salute all those named here and the many that I have encountered who are not listed. Thank you all for your many years of mentoring, partnering and support.

Ann Tripp currently provides the twice-hourly "news and views" on nationally syndicated "Steve Harvey Morning Show" on WBLS. She is also the host of "Healthful Solutions" (on cable), a narrator of certain SHOWTIME television specials, and is the executive producer, researcher and "voice" of the nationally-syndicated Black History Minute (United Stations Radio Network), where she profiles the historic, cultural, political and social milestones of African-Americas. Ann is a member of the National Academy of Television

Arts and Sciences, the New York Press Club and the National Association of Negro Business and Professional Women Clubs, Inc.

NYC-native **B.K. Kirkland** replaced radio legend Frankie Crocker at WBLS in 1976, helping the station score its highest-ever afternoon numbers. He's been at the forefront of smooth jazz and classic R&B on a national scale and is a Gallery award recipient as one of the top 100 radio personalities in America.

Dahved Levy, with his trademark catch phrase, "Dahved Levy, rockin' you! Rockin' you!" is a benchmark in Caribbean radio, Dahved is a trailblazer and innovator in the field of broadcast media. He was the first person to host a Caribbean-focused show on mainstream radio in New York. In just four months, his show skyrocketed to the No. 1 program in its time slot. The show's success led to numerous other radio gigs and he soon became the first announcer/DJ to be on three separate radio stations simultaneously in the competitive New York market.

Possessing an easy charm, quick wit, distinctive voice, and an unabashed preference for the controversial, Dahved skillfully combines talk, humor, newsworthy events, celebrity interviews and music, without missing a beat.

During the course of his career, Dahved has interviewed numerous world leaders, business executives, sports figures and entertainers. Some key international figures include Winnie and Nelson Mandela, former chairman of Air Jamaica Gordon "Butch" Stewart, and numerous Caribbean leaders like P. J. Patterson (Jamaica's Prime Minister), Owen Arthur (Barbados' Prime Minister) and former Haitian President Jean Bertrand Aristide. He's also had the pleasure of having dialogues with the likes of Bill and Hillary Clinton, Bill Cosby, Donald Trump, Johnnie Cochran, O.J. Simpson, Minister

Louis Farrakhan, Rev. Al Sharpton, Dr. Betty Shabazz, Mike Tyson, Spike Lee, The Fugees, Sean Paul, Jay-Z, Janet Jackson, and Jennifer Lopez, among many others. Due to his groundbreaking interviews, Dahved has received numerous awards, including the Radio Award of Merit from the New York Association of Black Journalists (NYABJ).

A "radio personality without borders," Dahved frequently leaves the comforts of his New York studio to experience the different cultures of which he speaks. His travels have brought him to South Africa, Nigeria, Ghana, Senegal, Egypt, Brazil, and the Caribbean. With his new post at Tempo, Dahved expands his legacy even further and sets the litmus test for anyone wishing to embark on a career in broadcast media.

Deja Vu In the Afternoons: Balancing community issues and on-air responsibilities proved to be a challenge but maintaining spiritual balance has always been Deja's key to success. She's programmed radio stations across the country and is still heard on 107.5 WBLS and daily on Sirius/XM's The Heat.

"You never know what you can do until you try", a mantra repeated and believed by "Déjà Vu". This Life Coach & Media Personality has been trying and achieving goals in radio for years. The power of the microphone taught Deja that connecting with her audience was not just a byproduct of a cushy job, but a responsibility to inspire and motivate the people that listened to her daily program. She capitalized on this mission by launching her own teen non-profit organization called "The Flava Unit", whose members give back to society by performing service projects.

Calvin Douglas "Doug" Banks Jr. (June 9, 1958 – April 11, 2016) was an American radio personality and host of The Doug Banks Radio Show.

The Philadelphia-born, Detroit-raised Banks began his radio career broadcasting on his high school's radio station. Local station WDRQ took notice of his talent and offered him a spot as a temporary late-night weekend disc jockey for a country music station. After high school, Doug successfully turned his temporary trial into a permanent multi-year gig at KDAY in Los Angeles, California. Soon after, in April 1979 he started at KMJM-Majic 108, as "The Unknown DJ"

Banks then moved on to the LA station KFI, which helped to pave the way to a morning show slot in Las Vegas at KLAV. Doug's next two stops were KDIA in Oakland, California, and WBMX (now WVAZ) in Chicago, Illinois. From 1986 to 1995, Banks did nights, mornings, and afternoons for WGCI-FM in Chicago.

Next, the ABC Radio Network offered Banks the opportunity to do a nationally syndicated show. Originally, Banks started with an afternoon show from the same studio as the "Tom Joyner Morning Show." In 1997, Banks wanted to move to a morning show instead and the studio across the hall from Joyner's was made ready. The new show, hosted by Banks along with new sidekick **DeDe McGuire**, rose to become one of the top-rated syndicated urban programs in America. In January 2008, the show was cancelled, but Banks relaunched the show, this time in the afternoon drive under the new name, *The Ride with Doug and DeDe*.

Unlike his previous show where Mainstream Urban/Hip Hop/R&B music was played, Banks's new program was aimed at the Urban Adult Contemporary audience, similar to what is played on Joyner's and Steve Harvey's shows. In July 2010, Banks moved his show to American Urban Radio Networks and renamed it *The Doug Banks Show*. Banks died from complications of diabetes and kidney failure on April 11, 2016. Banks is survived by a wife, three daughters and a son.

Carlos DeJesus was one of the Earliest backers of Hip-Hop, and one of the first to play Hip-Hop music on the air in 1979 (Sugar Hill Gang;s "Rappers Delight" on WKTU). He grew up in lower Manhattan (Alphabet City). Carlos attended Valley Forge Military Academy in Wayne PA, and Columbia University BYC, where he was an On-Air Radio Personality for Alma Latina WKCR-89 FM in 1971. Carlos was also an On-Air Radio Personality for WBLS - 107.5 FM New York City 1977-78; an On-Air Radio Personality WGCI-107.5 FM Chicago (Gannet Co Inc) from 1978-79; and an On-Air Personality, then Program Director at WKTU-92.3 FM from 1979-1983; and later he hosted the TV show New York Hit Tracks- WABC-TV from 1983-1986. Carlos died February 13, 2013.

Clay Berry is a radio veteran with over 40 years in the communications industry. Mr. Berry began his illustrious radio career at age 13, in Virginia and Washington DC as a part-time-radio personality. His radio career then took him to Connecticut, White Plains and finally New York City where it encompassed the varied roles of Board Operator and Traffic Director, as well as Assistant Program Director. Clay Berry has been Producer and / or Senior Producer of several radio programs including The Doug Banks Morning Show, The Rick Party Morning Show, the Paul Mooney Morning show and the Steve Harvey Morning Show.

Mr. Berry's media and music expertise has been used in television and film while working with Spike Lee as music researcher on *Crooklyn, Get on the Bus* and *Girl 6*. Clay Berry's voice has been featured on advertisements in both commercial and public broadcasting.

Clay Berry was the Executive Producer and co-host of the Hal Jackson's Sunday Classics heard on 107.5 WBLS in New York City with Hal Jackson's wife and co-host, Debi B. Hal Jackson's Sunday Classics was New York's longest-running classic soul radio show (with the largest listening audience in radio history, every Sunday for well over 20 years).

Frankie "Hollywood" Crocker (December 18, 1937 – October 21, 2000) was a disc jockey who helped grow WBLS, the music radio station in New York. Crocker was the master of ceremonies of shows at the Apollo Theater in Harlem and was one of the first VJs on VH1, the cable music video channel, in addition to hosting the TV series Solid Gold and NBC's Friday Night Videos. As an actor, Crocker appeared in five films, including Cleopatra Jones (1973) and Five on the Black Hand Side (1973). He is credited with introducing as many as 30 new artists to the mainstream. When Studio 54 was at the height of its popularity, Crocker rode in through the front entrance on a white stallion. Crocker, a native of Buffalo, coined the phrase "urban contemporary" in the 1970s, a label for the eclectic mix of songs that he played.

Fred "Bugsy" Buggs is one of New York's most well-liked radio personalities reigns on 107.5 WBLS.... Bugsy started his media career in New York City almost 25 years ago and has graced radio stations in Florida, Washington, D.C., New Jersey, Philadelphia, and New York!

After hosting several radio shows across the east coast, he returned back home and became the Assistant Program Director and Music Director for KISS FM. Bugsy's expertise in production and artist development later landed him a job with Def Jam Records where he helped to develop some of the biggest names in the business including Redman, Biz Markie and Big Daddy Kane. After a year at Def Jam, his love for radio called him back to the airwaves. Bugsy is truly a legend and he has definitely made his presence known in both the world of radio and records.

Gladys Knight, known as the "Empress of Soul," is an American singer, songwriter, actress, businesswoman and author. A seven-time Grammy Award winner, Knight is best known for the hits she recorded during the 1960s, 1970s, and 1980s with her group Gladys Knight & the Pips, which included her brother Merald "Bubba" Knight and her cousins Edward Patten and William Guest. Knight has recorded two number one Billboard Hot 100 singles ("Midnight Train to Georgia" and "That's What Friends Are For"), eleven number-one R&B singles, and six number-one R&B albums. She has won seven Grammy Awards and is an inductee into the Rock and Roll Hall of Fame along with The Pips. She also recorded the theme song for the 1989 James Bond film License To Kill. Knight is also listed as one of Rolling Stone magazine's 100 Greatest Singers of All Time.

Hal Jackson was an American disc jockey, radio personality, a legendary broadcaster, radio station owner, and philanthropist who broke a number of color barriers in American radio broadcasting.

Throughout the 1960s Jackson continued to work in stations along the East Coast. Jackson continued to break down the racial barrier in entertainment. In 1971, Jackson and Percy Sutton, a former Manhattan borough president, co-founded the Inner-City Broadcasting

Corporation (ICBC), which acquired WLIB — becoming the first African-American owned-and-operated station in New York. The following year, ICBC acquired WLIB-FM, changing its call letters to WBLS ("the total Black experience in Sound").

In 1990, Hal Jackson was the first minority inducted into the National Association of Broadcaster's Hall of Fame. In 1995, he became the first African-American inducted into the National Radio Hall of Fame. In 2001 the Broadcast and Cable Hall of Fame inducted Mr. Jackson. For over 11 years he hosted a radio program rated #1 by Arbitron in its time slot on 107.5 WBLS in New York, the Hal Jackson Sunday Morning Classics.

In 1995 Jackson became the first African American to be inducted into the Radio Hall of Fame. He was given a Pioneer Award by the Rhythm and Blues Foundation in 2003. In October 2010 he was named a "Giant in Broadcasting" by the Library of American Broadcasting. Jackson was also inducted into the Guinness Book of World Records as being the oldest broadcaster, with a record 73 year-career.

Jackson continued to host Sunday Classics on WBLS every Sunday, with **Clay Berry** and **Deborah Bolling Jackson (Debi B.)**, his wife of 25 years. He passed away of natural causes on May 23, 2012 in New York City at the age of 96. Hal often signed off the air with the motto; reminding listeners, "It's nice to be important, but it's more important to be nice."

Imhotep Gary Byrd is the first radio personality since his mentor, Hal Jackson, to broadcast from three different New York City stations –WLIB-AM, WBLS-FM, and WBAI-FM.

He is the award-winning host, creator, and executive producer of The GBE, the longest running Black radio broadcast in the history of New York City. His career as a multi-media radio personality, spoken word-recording artist, songwriter, and motivational speaker has always focused on "raising human consciousness thru communications." In a career that spans over 40 years, Byrd, as a modern-day griot, is dedicated to "telling our story and lifting every voice."

Imhotep was invited to Inner City Broadcasting's WLIB-AM by the late Chairman Emeritus Percy Sutton. At WLIB-AM, Byrd transformed The GBE into The Global Black Experience. From there he broadcasted live from the Apollo Theatre and became even more respected in his field. The extent of his popularity was evidenced in the 1992 birthday tribute to Imhotep at The Apollo. It was standing-room-only.

Imhotep has received numerous awards and honors. Among them are the prestigious Hal Jackson Award from the International Association of African American Music and the Living Legend Award from the Living Legend Foundation. He has also been inducted into the National Black Sports and Entertainment Hall of Fame, along with the legendary Frankie "Hollywood" Crocker and Byrd's brilliant musical collaborator, Stevie Wonder. Imhotep was named as a Black Media Legend for McDonald's Faces of Black History 2011 Tribute.Imhotep was also honored at the New Federal Theatre's 40th Anniversary Gala, along with Mayor David Dinkins, Sidney Poitier, Ruby Dee,Amiri Baraka, Ntozake Shange, Alicia Keys, George Faison, Terrie Williams and others as "individuals who changed the cultural life of America".

Jeff Foxx is an institution. A popular force in New York City radio, Jeff has been "rockin' the box" for more than 20 years. And there is more to Jeff Foxx than just a smooth, friendly voice. He's also a gifted musician and composer and now he's taking the time to write songs that he hopes will one day soon receive the same exposure that he has doled out to artists since he began in radio in 1981.

From Cleveland to Chicago to New York, Jeff Foxx's personable and pleasing voice has made him a pioneer. He invaded NY airwaves in the late 1980s before there was a Hot97 or even formal rap radio, he introduced the world to De La Soul and Public Enemy while keeping Black music alive and expanding. He's done radio solo, as a duo, and as a part of the Sirius Satellite Network. Jeff currently holds down afternoon drive right here at 107.5 WBLS.

Ken 'Spider' Webb is one of New York's most popular morning radio personalities. Since the late 1960's native New Yorkers depended heavily on his voice to get them going early every morning with classic soul music, 'the color of the day', plenty of laughs and family humor. Ken has made radio his life-long profession, beginning his on-air career in amateur radio at the age of 13. After 6 years as a Television Broadcast Engineer/Instructor at Brooklyn College (CUNY), in July of 1971 Ken became the very first radio 'morning man' for Inner City Broadcasting's flagship station, WBLS-FM (NYC) where he raised WBLS-FM morning ratings to the #1 position.

In 1983, Ken moved to RKO Broadcasting's WRKS-FM and brought its morning ratings to the #1 position for the very first time in that station's history, where it remained until 1995 when he returned to WBLSWLIB-AM, WWRLAM and WQCD-NY (CD101.9).

In the area of community service, Ken founded the WBLS Sure Shots Benefit Basketball team in 1972 and the KISS Kards Benefit Basketball team in 1983. In 1985 Ken began syndicating his 2-hour weekly radio jazz show, "Jazz From the City" from his own studio in Long Island New York. The 2-hour weekly jazz show aired in Japan on the 40-station network, The Tokyo FM Network], the Philippines, the Caribbean and 150 stations in the US. He has also developed an internet radio marketing and advertising company, Webb Internet Radio Network and hosts his daily Sirius/XM Satellite Radio show, 'Soul Town."

The Quiet Storm Lenny Green: He has proven that his love for music has made him one of the best in the broadcast industry, receiving *Billboard Magazine's 1999 Air Personality of the Year Award*. Outside of radio, some other things that Lenny has a love for is acting, cross-country skiing, playing tennis and encouraging children to pursue their dreams.

Now you can hear our "Love Man" weeknights from 7PM to 12AM on 107.5 WBLS.

Leslie Calvin "Les" Brown (born February 17, 1945) is an American motivational speaker, author, former radio DJ, and former television host.

Brown was born with his twin brother, Wesley, in Liberty City, a low-income section of Miami, Florida. He was adopted by Mamie Brown, a 38-year-old single woman who worked as a cafeteria attendant and domestic assistant. Brown claims that he was declared "educable mentally retarded" while in grade school, damaging his self-esteem and confidence.

According to many of Brown's speeches, when he first decided to get into public radio he was repeatedly unsuccessful. It wasn't until the on-air failures of the previous afternoon DJ that he was hired full-time. Upon his termination from the radio station, he ran for election in the Ohio House of Representatives and won. He was a member of the Ohio House of Representatives from 1976 to 1981.

After leaving the Ohio state legislature, he shifted his career to television and became a host on PBS. Brown was a member of the Peabody Awards Board of Jurors from 1982 to 1988. In 1989, he was the recipient of the National Speakers Association's Council of Peers Award for Excellence.

As a motivational speaker, he uses the catch phrase "it's possible!" to encourage people to follow their dreams. In September 1993, he began hosting a new talk show, *The Les Brown Show*. After nearly four months, it went on hiatus on December 3, 1993, and on January 17, 1994, King World Productions replaced the show with *Rolonda*, hosted by Rolonda Watts. Later in 1994 he was a recipient of Toastmasters International's Golden Gavel.

He formed the company Les Brown Enterprises Inc. to support his career as a motivational speaker and was on KFWB in California for a daily syndicated radio program from 2011 to 2012.

Brown collaborated with John C. Maxwell for a candid look into the lives of professional speakers called "The Good, The Bad, and The Ugly".

Brown married Gladys Knight in 1995; they divorced in 1997. He has nine children: Calvin, Patrick, Ona, Ayanna, Tayloria, Thad, Sumaya, Serena and John-Leslie. He also has 15 grandchildren and two great grandchildren.

Shaila started out working part time as an announcer/hostess of a rhythm and blues program in Buffalo, where she was seasoned for four years. After 10 years in professional radio Shaila joined the KISS FM family in 1994 and is now adding a sincere sister-friendly flava to 107.5 WBLS.

Shaila's charm and strong belief in God has taken her through a long and prosperous road in radio. After graduating from Buffalo State College with a B.A. in radio and television, Shaila was talented enough to immediately begin her professional career in broadcasting.

Shaila is a woman of character and substance. One of her accomplishments that she is most proud of is when she became the first African American woman to win the New York City Teen Beauty Queen Pageant. In the summer of 2000, both WPIX television and the New York Post featured Shaila as one of the top five Radio Divas in New York.

Skip Dillard, Operations Manager for WBLS and WLIB has the ability to step outside the box of just urban radio and explore other formats and various aspects of the industry. He has consistently reinvented himself and he has a lot of experience, leverage, and value to fall back on because of it. He continues to educate himself and take on new challenges in order to KEEP growing.

Skip started his career in Norfolk, VA. After working at WBLK in Buffalo as a Program Director. He worked in several other markets before landing in New York at WBLS. In 2003, he took a break from the industry to work at Billboard writing for the Airplay Monitor.

When it comes to programming it helps Skip to get out and talk to people and get involved in the community. He is currently active on three non-profit boards including the Living Legends Foundation, the Greater Harlem Chamber of Commerce and the American Foundation for the University of the West Indies and he volunteers for other initiatives in the area. Circle of Sisters is WBLS' annual signature event, taking place at the Jacob Javits Convention Center in Manhattan. It is the largest expo for women of color outside of

Essence and Skip proudly enhances the event on both digital platforms and innovative concepts yearly.

Research helps you keep track of today's fast-changing audiences. From content that drives engagement to music, there's much to be learned from how your audience uses technology. As a programmer my greatest challenge is I'm never off the clock. I'm always working while finding time to learn, teach and help grow my business."

A great programmer must have strong management skills, a love for research and a willingness to get out into your marketplace, the ability to adapt to change and knowing you are always a 'student' of what you do. Effective time-management is also very important. As well as being a little nerdy, weird and an insomniac.

Steve Harvey is the host of the **Steve Harvey Morning Show** radio program, and the popular TV shows Family Feud and Celebrity Family Feud and The Steve Harvey Show. His popularity continues to grow to global proportions, bolstered by his new role as host of the Miss Universe Pageant. Harvey is currently one of the most powerful voices in media, touting a career spanning nearly 30 years as a top stand-up comedian, actor, award winning TV personality and talk show host, best-selling author, entrepreneur, and humanitarian.

Anthony "Tony" Brent Gray (born May 1, 1958) is an American radio broadcast executive. He is President of Gray Communications Inc., based in Chicago and established in 1990. Gray Communications is a programming consultancy that serves urban contemporary, Urban AC and hip hop stations in the United States.

On April 21, 2010, Gray was named one of *Radio Ink* magazine's "Most Influential African Americans in Radio." The annual list is compiled by broadcasting trade publication Radio Ink, which accepts nominations for outstanding contributions to the promotion of the African American radio industry. This marks the second consecutive year Mr. Gray has been recognized by Radio Ink.

Tony Gray previously served as Operations Manager in New York at WRKS (98.7 FM) and as programming executive in Philadelphia, Detroit, St. Louis and New Orleans.

Vy Higginsen is an American theater producer, playwright, former disc jockey, and radio and television personality. She is the founder and executive director of the Mama Foundation for the Arts, and the co-writer of the 1983 musical *Mama, I Want to Sing!*, the longest running black off-Broadway musical in American history.

Higginsen grew up in Harlem, New York City in a musical family; her parents, sister, and grandmother all sang. Her father was a Pentecostal minister. When her sister, singer Doris Troy, won Amateur Night at the Apollo Theater and began touring, Higginsen came along with her. Higginsen graduated from the Fashion Institute of Technology.

Higginsen became the first female advertising executive at *Ebony* magazine. She later worked as a contributing editor for *Essence*, then published and edited her own magazine, *Unique NY*.

Higginsen moved on to work in radio for ten years, hosting shows on WBLS and WWRL, and reporting for WNBC-TV and The Metro Channel.

In 1983, Higginsen co-wrote and co-produced the musical *Mama, I Want to Sing!* with her husband-to-be, Ken Wydro. The play was based on the life of her sister, Doris Troy. The show opened at the Heckscher Theater in Harlem in 1983 and ran there for eight years, becoming the longest-running off-Broadway black musical in history. Higginsen played the role of the narrator in the musical. Her brother, Randy, and sister Doris also appeared in *Mama*. The play was made into a film of the same name, in which Higginsen also appeared along with her daughter, Knoelle.

Higginsen and Wydro wrote and produced two sequels to the successful musical: *Sing, Mama 2* and *Born to Sing: Mama 3*. They also wrote and produced the musical *Alive: 55+ and Kickin'*, which was featured on the newsmagazine *60 Minutes* in 2015.

In 1999, Higginsen founded the Mama Foundation for the Arts, a non-profit arts organization in Harlem. In 2006, she created Gospel for Teens, offering free gospel music instruction to teenagers through the foundation. The program was featured on *60 Minutes*, in a show that won two Emmy Awards in 2012. In 2012, Higginsen also founded Harlem Records, an independent record label.

PEOPLE TO KNOW IN BLACK HISTORY & BEYOND

MORE WBLS PERSONALITIES AND COLLEAGUES WHO MAKE THE GRADE :

- Al Forsyth
- Al Roberts
- Anthony Richards
- Bat Johnson
- Billy Bredette
- Bob Frederick
- Carl Ferguson
- Champaign
- Charlie Burger
- Clarence Jones
- Cleo Rowe
- David Lampel
- Denise Colon
- Diana King
- Don Bob
- Don Early Allen
- Donnie Simpson
- Eddie O'Jay
- Fritz Marshall
- G. Keith Alexander
- Hank Span
- Janie Washington
- Jeff Troy
- Jim Snowden
- Johnny Allen
- Keisha Sutton
- Kirk Clemons
- Lawrence Gregory Jones
- Lamar Rene
- Lamonda
- Lisa Lopez
- Michelle Wright
- Mike Love
- Neville Bush
- Pat Prescott
- Percy Sutton
- Pepe Sutton
- Ricky Ricardo
- Ramond Anthony
- Rich Lamontte
- Reggie Rouse
- Ronnie Magnum
- Sergio Dean
- Stanley Barbo
- Susan Wong
- Vinny Brown

ABOUT THE AUTHOR
DOCTOR BOB LEE

Dr. Bob Lee, D.Cm. aka "Doctor Bob Lee" earned his B.A. and M.A. degrees in Communications from New York Institute of Technology.. He later earned his Doctorate of Community Ministries (D.Cm.) degree at the New Seminary for Interfaith Studies.

Dr. Lee is the President, Founder & CEO of the Make the Grade Foundation, a not-for-profit organization that provides mentoring and aid to school children. Make the Grade Foundation is a 501(c)(3) organization that facilitates and encourages academic achievement by implementing programs through the collaboration between parent, teacher, student, clergy and community by connecting and providing resources for today's youth.

Bob is a man who brings back the fruits of his success to the youth and disenfranchised of communities in need. His posture of humbleness and quiet attentiveness precedes the underlying wealth of knowledge, creativity and experience just below the surface waiting to spring forth.

Bob's impressive profile reads like that of an elder statesman who has reached the proverbial mountaintop. The rise above the pitfalls faced by an inner-city youth from an overcrowded, low-income household was all too common for the times. The struggle was not devoid of its share of bumps and bruises, encounters with law enforcement, drug-filled atmospheres and serious bodily injuries. But through it all, a small blessing of a childhood deal with an older sister would put the wheels of progress in motion. His sister offered him a job opportunity, which in reality was a well-devised plan to keep young Bob occupied, useful and monitored as she and her friends entertained themselves. Resolve came in a way that her young brother would become a 'junior partner' commissioned to be the disc jockey at neighborhood parties. The music was managed through a simple system. The 45s had color-coded spindle adapters to identify the fast from the slow songs. When the color Red or Yellow was called out, he knew when the crowd wanted to hear a fast or slow song. Bob viewed himself as the most important person in the room. The plan worked well for all and the seeds of a career had been planted.

Then there's the story of how Bob acquired the title "Doctor", at such a young age. He had accompanied his father to the doctor's office one day and was fascinated by the doctor's white coat hanging on the door and microscope on the desk. Doing what young boys do, Bob donned the oversized coat and peered through the lens of the microscope to see the unexpected microorganisms that actually had names and purposes in life. He was hooked to the extent that the encounter carried over to his curiosity about how life works. His knack for precision became a part of his personality. Hence, his friends dubbed him as the "Doctor."

The "Doctor" as a young man was no stranger to sports. He played football, baseball and basketball, but it was amateur boxing that showed him the importance of preparedness. Survival in the 'hood required the ability to talk the talk and walk the walk. At both, Bob was able to hold his own. But he quickly learned that resting on one's laurels is no substitute of preparation for a task. A bout with a formidable opponent tested the limits of his ability when he failed to properly get in shape. He paid for it dearly, but then came to know the value of being prepared when you walk in the door.

Music played an important role in the development of adolescents from the Queensbridge area of New York City in the early 1970's, and Bob Lee was no exception. He found that his creative mind was well-received by his peers when he manned the turntables as a DJ for house parties, festivals, schools, and charity work at hospitals under the mentorship of a neighborhood icon he looked up to Mr. Hank Carter. It was through this friendship and the linking of the two unlikely entities - music and community service - it all began to make sense to him. Both were satisfying and important parts of his life and would launch a journey that would benefit others as well as himself.

Doctor Bob Lee's popularity began to flourish on a grand scale as he reached a wider more diverse listening audience. By 1980 the momentum of his career was beginning to escalate. He was accepted as an intern at N.Y.'s hottest R&B radio station, WBLS, under legendary host Hal Jackson and Frankie Crocker. By 1986, he became a staple on the weekend addition of the "Quiet Storm" with the smooth baritone voicings of Vaughn Harper. Not long after, he became an integral part of the highly popular "Morning Show" with Ken Webb in which he developed the "On Time" program, encouraging students to stay in school, be on time and get a good education, while spotlighting positive outlooks in the community and highlighting healthy food programs. All these shows became models for urban listening programs in cities across the nation.

In the years to follow Bob's career continued to skyrocket. The doors began to open to his own creative juices. He hosts "The Bob Lee Show", a music-intensive radio series. For more than ten years,

Lee has hosted the weekly live television program "Open," which broadcasts on BronxNet, a world-wide cable television station. The program features news and topics affecting the Bronx community and also treats viewers to new and established musical guests. In addition to his on-air roles, Bob manages community affairs and government relations for WBLS.

Bob is also the President & CEO of Bob Lee Enterprises, an umbrella for his many talents, including: motivational speaking and coaching, performing in bands, deejaying and consulting for companies who want to do grassroots promotions.

The marriage of entertainment and community service provided a suitable foundation in the building of Doctor Bob Lee. It's earned him his own unique place amongst today's stars of Hip Hop, R&B and Soul. He maintains a rigorous schedule of Radio, TV, DJing, book signings, speaking engagements and appearances. Though he's come a long way, Doctor Bob Lee maintains his never-ending quest to build a better future for today's youth. Bob helps college students interested in radio careers by serving as a mentor.

People to Know in Black History - Honoring the Heroes and Sheroes Who Make the Grade – Volume 2 is Bob Lee's fifth published book. His previous books include: 7 Ways to Make the Grade: A Living Guide to Your Community's Success: Parents, Teachers, Students, Community, Clergy, Health & Financial Literacy; Your Daily Dose of Quotes and Anecdotes – Featuring Words of Wisdom to Help You Make the Grade and Your Daily Dose of Quotes and Anecdotes II – Featuring Words of Wisdom to Help You Make the Grade – With Bonus Section and People to Know in Black History - Honoring the Heroes and Sheroes Who Make the Grade.

Follow Doctor Bob Lee on Facebook, Twitter, and Instagram.

IN CONCLUSION

Our list is expansive, but not nearly complete. We are pleased to tell you that ***People to Know for Black History and Beyond 2 - Honoring the Heroes and Sheroes Who Make the Grade*** is second volume of a multi-volume set.

Now that you have finished reading this book, ask yourself, "What common characteristics do all these people have?"

They are people put just like us with the burning desire to discipline themselves and do the things necessary to become successful.

**WHO ARE SOME OF THE PEOPLE YOU
CAN THINK OF THAT OF THAT MAKE THE GRADE?**

Tell us their story, Email: Makethegrade4u@gmail.com

REFERENCES

www.wikipedia.org

www.legacy.com

www.history.com

www.brittanica.com

www.biography.com

www.myheritage.com

www.patents.justia.com

www.americanthinker.com

www.famousblackinventories.net

INDEX

Alexander Emmanuel Rodriguez, 399
Aliko Dangote, 297
Alphonso R. Bernard, Sr, 249
Amelia Isadora Platts, 166
Angela Evelyn Bassett, 414
Anna Julia Cooper, 64, 422
Annie J. Easley, 374
Anthony "Tony" Brent Gray, 507
Anthony Tyrone "Tony" Evans, 357
Archbishop Wilton D. Gregory, 240
August Wilson, 415, 421, 422, 453, 454
Ayanna Soyini Pressley, 478
Ayesha Curry, 20, 21, 24, 29, 30
B.K. Kirkland, 495
Barack Obama, 30, 81, 97, 103, 171, 191, 198, 206, 207, 209, 210, 245, 248, 259, 276, 337, 363, 383, 386, 387, 421, 452, 470, 471, 477
Barbara Jordan, 466, 467, 468
Bernice Albertine King, 253
Bessie Virginia Blount, 261, 272
Bill "Bojangles" Robinson, 425, 428
Bill Russell, 386, 387
Blair Erwin Underwood, 419
Bob Lee, 493, 494, 513
Boris Kodjoe, 37, 38, 40, 41, 42
Brian Keith Price, 320
Calvin Douglas "Doug" Banks Jr., 497

Capers C. Funnye Jr, 244
Catherine Liggins Hughes, 289
Cathy Hughes, 289, 290, 292
Chadwick Aaron Boseman, 422
Charles Lenox Remond, 121, 123, 127
Charles Luther Sifford, 382, 383
Chief Joseph, 329, 330, 331
Ciara Princess Harris, 44, 46
Clay Berry, 498, 499, 501
Clifton Powell, 413
Congressman James Clyburn, 220
Corporal Freddie Stowers, 487
Dahved Levy, 493, 495
Daniel "Chappie" James Jr, 489
Danny Joseph Bakewell, 460
David Richmond, 98, 100
Debi B, 499, 501
Deborah (Debbie) Kaye Allen, 433
Debra L. Lee, 293
DeDe McGuire, 497
Deja Vu, 496
Diahann Carroll, 410, 411
Diane Nash, 85, 92, 93, 94, 95, 96, 97, 168, 352
Dolores Clara Fernández Huerta, 348
Dudley Randall, 294
Dwayne Johnson, 398, 399
Edison Uno, 347, 348
Edward Alexander Bouchet, 66, 68
Elder Watson Diggs, 316
Elijah Eugene Cummings, 468

Elizabeth Freeman, 104, 106, 109
Elizabeth Jean Peratrovich, 333
Eric Leroy Adams, 471
Fannie Lou Hamer Townsend, 172
Florence Delorez Griffith Joyner, 393
Forest Steven Whitaker III, 416, 417
Franklin Eugene McCain, 100
Fred J. Luter Jr., 358
Frederick Carlton "Carl" Lewis, 393
Frederick Douglass "Fritz" Pollard, 130
Frederick K.C. Price, 237
Fredrick Allen Hampton, 354
Gabrielle "Gabby" Christina Victoria Douglas, 403
Geoffrey Lamont Holder, 430
George Edward Foreman, 31, 32
George Mason IV, 32, 33
Geronimo, 326, 327, 328
Gloria Marie Steinem, 349
Golden Asro Frinks, 340, 341
Gwendolyn Elizabeth Brooks, 450
Hallie Quinn Brown, 62
Harold Lee Washington, 462
Harriet M. Waddy, 487
Harriette Vyda Simms, 153
Harry Belafonte, 254, 408, 409
Harry Tyson Moore, 154
Hattie McDaniel, 406
Henry Highland Garnet, 126, 128
Henry Louis Gates, 78
Hosea Lorenzo Williams, 346
Howard "Sandman" Sims, 427
Humberto Noé "Bert" Corona, 337
Ida B. Robinson, 234
Ilhan Abdullahi Omar, 482
Imhotep Gary Byrd, 501
James "Jim" Nathaniel Brown, 387

James Charles Evers, 345
James Edward Bowman Jr., 276
James Leonard Farmer, Jr., 338, 340
Janice Bryant Howroyd, 363
Jeff Foxx, 493, 502, 503
Jeffrey Preston Bezos (Jorgensen), 307
Jennifer Lynn Lopez, 448
Jennifer Thomas, 459
Jerry Lee Rice Sr., 394
Jesse Ernest Wilkins Jr., 87, 88, 90
Jibreel Khazan, 100
Joe Biden, 208, 471
John Boyd, 357
John J. Jasper, 229
John Lewis, 93, 168, 206, 207, 339, 471, 478, 480
John Stauffer, 321
John Wesley Carlos, 390
Joseph McNeil, 98, 100
Kamala Harris, 211, 222
Kelly Miller, 72, 73, 74, 202
Kenneth R. Thomas, 458, 459
Kobe Bryant, 10, 11, 12, 13, 14, 15, 16, 17, 18, 19, 304
Kwame Ture, 352, 353, 354
Laura Cornelius Kellogg, 133
Lawrence D. Bobo, 320
Lenny Green, 493, 504
Leon H. Washington, 457, 458
Leroy Robert "Satchel" Paige, 380
Leslie Calvin "Les" Brown, 504
Lucretia Mott, 118, 119, 120, 121, 122
Lucy Diggs Slowe, 318
Lynn (Butler-Smith) Whitfield, 411
María Rebecca Latigo de Hernández, 150

Maria Tecla Artemisia Montessori, 69
Marie Frankie Muse Freeman, 335
Marie Maynard Daly, 372, 374
Marjorie Stewart Joyner, 371, 372
Martin Luther King Jr., 95, 180, 181, 189, 201, 253, 336, 341, 409, 464
Marvel Jackson Cooke, 158
Michael Bakari Jordan, 13, 17, 29, 284, 288, 301, 305
Michael Spinks, 392
Moziah Bridges, 101, 102
Natalie Maria Cole, 446
Neil deGrasse Tyson, 279
Nellie May Quander, 315
Nellie Stone Johnson, 331, 333
Nicholas "Nick" Scott Cannon, 365
Nicole Ari Parker, 37, 38, 40, 42
Patrick Lavon Mahomes II, 402
Paul Cuffe, 324, 325
Paul Lawrence Kennedy, 431, 433
Rebecca Lee Crumpler, 263, 264, 267
Richard Allen, 224, 225, 226, 227, 228
Rihanna Fenty, 366
Robert "Bob" Nesta Marley, 445
Robert Louis Johnson, 286
Robert Smalls, 167, 328
Roy Emile Alfredo Innis, 350
Ruth M. Batson, 341
Ruth Washington, 458
Saint Elmo Brady, 369, 370
Samuel "Sammy" George Davis Jr., 438
Shaila, 493, 505, 506
Skip Dillard, 506
Stacey Yvonne Abrams, 474, 476
Stephen Curry, 7, 20, 24, 26, 30
Stephen Laurel "Twitch" Boss, 436
Steve Harvey, 103, 493, 494, 498, 507
Steven Allan Spielberg, 360
Stokely Standiford Churchill Carmichael, 352
Ta-Nehisi Paul Coates, 454
Thaddeus Stevens, 110, 117
The Greensboro Four, 98, 99
the Los Angeles Sentinel, 457, 460, 461
Thomas Edward Patrick Brady Jr., 400
Toni Morrison, 78, 451
Vanessa Bryant, 9, 12, 18
Viola Davis, 421
Vy Higginsen, 508
Walter Lincoln Hawkins, 375
WBLS, 493, 494, 495, 496, 498, 499, 501, 503, 504, 505, 506, 508, 510, 513, 514
Whitney Moore Young Jr, 343
Willa Beatrice Brown, 161, 163, 165
William "Smokey" Robinson Jr., 439
William Augustus Hinton, 268, 271
William Bradley "Brad" Pitt, 418
William Felton Russell, 386
Willie Howard Mays, Jr., 383
Wilma Glodean Rudolph, 389
World's Best-Looking Sound, 493

NOTES:

www.ingramcontent.com/pod-product-compliance
Lightning Source LLC
Chambersburg PA
CBHW070519010526
44118CB00012B/1031